Dalits

and the

DEMOCRATIC

REVOLUTION

Dalits
and the
DEMOCRATIC
REVOLUTION

Dr. Ambedkar and the Dalit
Movement in Colonial India

GAIL OMVEDT

Sage Publications
New Delhi/Thousand Oaks/London

First published in 1994 by

Sage Publications India Pvt Ltd
M-32 Greater Kailash Market I
New Delhi 110 048

Sage Publications Inc
2455 Teller Road
Thousand Oaks, California 91320

Sage Publications Ltd
6 Bonhill Street
London EC2A 4PU

Published by Tejeshwar Singh for Sage Publications India Pvt Ltd, phototypeset by Pagewell Photosetters, Pondicherry, and printed at Chaman Enterprises, Delhi.
Second printing, 1996

Library of Congress Cataloging-in-Publication Data

Omvedt, Gail.
    Dalits and the democratic revolution: Dr. Ambedkar and the Dalit movement in colonial India / Gail Omvedt.
        p.   cm.
    Includes index.
    1. Untouchables—India—Political activity—History—20th century.
    2. Ambedkar, Bhimrao Ramji, 1892–   I. Title.
DS422.C3053   1994   954.03'5'08694—dc20   93–11778

ISBN: 0–8039–9139–8 (U.S.-cloth)
          0–8039–9140–1 (U.S.-paper)
          81–7036–367–5 (India-cloth)
          81–7036–368–3 (India-paper)

Now, Now

Turning their backs to the sun, they journeyed through centuries.
Now, now, we must refuse to be pilgrims of darkness.
That one, our father, carrying, carrying the darkness is now bent;
Now, now we must lift that burden from his back.
Our blood was spilled for this glorious city
And what we got was the right to eat stones.
Now, now, we must explode that building which kisses the sky!
After a thousand years we were blessed with a sunflower giving fakir;
Now, now we must, like sunflowers, turn our faces to the sun.

Namdev Dhasal
in Mulk Raj Anand and Eleanor Zelliot (eds), *An Anthology of Dalit Literature* (New Delhi: Gyan Publishing House, 1992), p. 53.

Contents

List of Tables

Introduction

Namdev Dhasal's poem expresses all the anguish and aspiration of being a Dalit in India today: the sense of having been the exploited and oppressed builders of the great Indian civilization and of emerging out of centuries of darkness to claim their heritage, 'now, now'. Not unusually, it centres around B.R. Ambedkar, the legendary leader of the Dalit movement and one of the greatest of modern Indians; it proclaims a life-giving hope, a 'new sun'; and it threatens to 'explode that building' if this is not satisfied.

Such images of oppression, of darkness and light, of revolt, of smashing structures of exploitation pervade the poetry of the anti-caste movement. The image of the sun is frequent. Shripal Sabnis, a non-Brahman poet, writes of caste that

> *The sun of self-respect has burst into flame,*
> *let it burn up caste . . . .*[2]

The title, *No Room for the New Sun*, used for a recent English translation of Dalit poems, as well as many of the poems published, express similar themes.[3]

This study, an outgrowth of an ICSSR project on 'History of Dalit Movements in Maharashtra, Andhra and Karnataka, 1850–1975', focuses on the Dalit movement in the colonial period.

It defines it as part, in many ways the leading part, of a broader *anti-caste movement* which has been a central democratic movement of Indian society. In the pre-independence period this anti-caste movement comprised strong non-Brahman movements in Maharashtra and Tamil Nadu as well as Dalit movements in Maharashtra, Punjab (the Ad-Dharm movement), western U.P. (the Adi-Hindu movement), Bengal (Namashudras), Kerala (Narayanswami Guru's movement), Tamil Nadu (Adi-Dravidas), coastal Andhra (Adi-Andhras), and Hyderabad (Adi-Hindus). In addition there were non-Brahman ideological trends elsewhere and weaker or unorganized Dalit assertions in such areas as Mysore and Bihar. Independent India saw two decades of quiescence for anti-caste struggles, then a renewed upsurge from the early 1970s, marked by the founding of the Dalit Panthers in 1972. This time the Dalits and their organizations were clearly in the vanguard, with the non-Brahman castes, now known as 'OBCs' 'other backward castes', following. An account of this phase of the movement is given in my recent study of new social movements.[4]

The Dalit and non-Brahman anti-caste movements can be classified as 'anti-systemic movements' in the framework of such Marxist theorists as Immanuel Wallerstein, or, in the language of functionalist sociological theory, as 'value-oriented movements' as opposed to 'norm-oriented movements'.[5] That is, they challenged and sought to transform the basic structure of the Indian social system, replacing caste and the accompanying social oppression, economic exploitation and political domination by an equalitarian society. There were of course reformist trends in the movement as in other social movements of Indian society. These were represented within the Dalit movement by leaders such as Jagjivan Ram of the Congress and the Hindu Mahasabhaite Dalits such as M.C. Rajah and G.A. Gavai and their organizations; within the non-Brahman movements the Justice Party and the Non-Brahman Party of the Bombay Presidency represented conservative trends in contrast to the more radical Satyashodhak Samaj and Self-Respect movements. Reformist (incorporative, 'norm-oriented') trends were also embodied in Gandhi's 'Harijan' movement, which stood in the tradition of the broad upper caste social reform tradition which sought to cleanse Hinduism of its impurities, to 'lop off the excrescences' in the words of M.G. Ranade, i.e., to chop off the diseased branches of the tree with the intention of fostering its growth.[6]

In contrast, the anti-caste movement aimed at felling the tree. In this it was akin to radical Marxism, especially the Dalit-based Naxalite movement in Bihar in the 1970s, described by a sympathetic journalist in terms of resurrection and revolution:

> This man has risen from the grave: he seems to have gone berserk and is frenzeidly chopping the branches of feudalism. His desire is to see the 2500-year old tree felled here and now. So far he has only been humiliated, whipped and slain, denied the status of a man; his wife treated as a prostitute. Then somebody brought him news of Naxalbari and things began to change. The Harijan died, the Koeri was burnt; the new man who rose from the flames felt that he was neither a Harijan nor a Koeri but a man.[7]

A revolutionary message, a will to act against exploitation, a rise from oppression, from death to life, from darkness to light: the process has been going on in sporadic ways all over India since the nineteenth century. While the Naxalite movement has done this for the low castes of Bihar in recent years, before Naxalism, before even Marxism entered India, a revolutionary anti-caste movement had begun. In ways that had many parallels with militant Marxism it described a society based on exploitation; and in ways similar to that described by the journalist Arun Sinha, it brought a revolutionary democratic message. Another journalist, a major figure of the Maharashtrian anti-caste Satyashodhak Samaj (still uninfluenced by Marxism), writes

> India is a strange place which collects all sorts of social groups, divided by different religions, thoughts, practices and understandings. But broadly speaking, they can be categorized into two—the majority low castes who have been devoid of humanity for centuries and a handful who take their pleasure, call themselves superior and live at the cost of the majority. One's welfare is another's misery; that is their connection.[8]

In this context,

> Such a revolutionary wave reached the lowest classes so that a power of thought was created among them . . . . Those who

kindled among the innumerable lower caste majority the light and experience of who and what is causing us injustice, what are our rights, how we must throw away the injustice-these were the Satyasamajists.[9]

The main figures of this larger anti-caste movement, Jotiba Phule, Babasaheb Ambedkar and E.V. Ramasami 'Periyar', with many others throughout India (Narayanswami Guru in Kerala, Acchutanand in U.P., Mangoo Ram in Punjab) all attacked the system of exploitation at all levels, culturally, economically and politically.

They challenged the 'Hindu-nationalism' which was emerging as a consequence of the elite organizing from the nineteenth century onward to define Indian society, and the majority of Indian people, as essentially 'Hindu': not only did they criticize distortions and 'excrescences'; they attacked Hinduism itself by arguing that it was in essence Brahmanical, caste-bound and irrational. They asserted that Hinduism had not been the religion and culture of the majority but rather was an imposed religion; and that escaping exploitation today required the low castes to reject this imposition, to define themselves as 'non-Hindu' and take a new religious identity. Phule tried to formulate a new, theistic religion; Periyar promoted atheism; Ambedkar turned to Buddhism; others in the Tamil Nadu non-Brahman movement tried to claim Saivism as an independent religion; Narayanswami Guru formulated 'one religion, one caste, one god' while his more radical follower Ayyapan proclaimed 'no religion, no caste, and no God for mankind'. Whatever the specificities, the rejection of Hinduism remained a feature differentiating the anti-caste radicals from the reformers.

They were also economic radicals, though from different points of view, identifying themselves not simply with low castes but with peasants and workers as such. Phule strongly attacked the exploitation of peasants by the bureaucracy; Ambedkar and Periyar both supported and helped organize movements of peasants against landlords and workers against capitalists; and Ambedkar unambiguously identified himself as a socialist.

Politically they opposed the Indian National Congress as controlled by upper castes and capitalists (as 'Brahman and bourgeois' in Ambedkar's terms; as that of the *Irani arya-bhats*' in Phule's terminology, as *shetji-bhatji* or 'Brahman-Bania' in the language of the later non-Brahman movement) and sought for an alternative political front that would represent a kind of left-Dalit unity with a core base of workers and peasants. They (particularly Ambedkar) also insisted that this had to lead to the empowerment of Dalits and other exploited sections. In the language of the Dalit Panther's manifesto, 'We don't want a little place in Brahman alley; we want the rule of the whole country.'

This anti-caste movement, with its Dalit leading section, was part of the broader revolutionary democratic movement in India, along with the national movement and communist- and socialist-led working class and peasant movements. Ideologically and organizationally, it both overlapped and contended with these movements. In particular, Gandhism, which was prominent if not hegemonic in the National Congress, and Marxism, exemplified both in the communists and in the Nehruvian left within the Congress, provided the important context of this movement and its developing ideology.

Strikingly, while the Dalit movement in India began concurrently with the upsurge of both nationalism and Marxism, it is experiencing a second upsurge today in an era of the crisis of nationalities and of socialism. Nationalism is in crisis, with both Third World societies and former socialist countries buffeted by divisive ethnic struggles and by internal groups claiming their own 'nationality'; socialism is in crisis after the fall of the regimes and the development model that claimed to be based on Marxism.

This process involves new dilemmas and possibilities for the Dalit/anti-caste movement itself—the necessity of formulating new ways forward in regard to economic strategy, political structures, cultural interpretation. It requires a rethinking of the way in which the movement has been understood.

We have argued that the Dalit movement in particular and anti-caste movements in general should be seen as 'value-oriented' or 'anti-systemic' movements. This, however, has not been generally accepted, for these movements have been seen as basically reformist by the dominant left intellectual trends in India, while academic social sciences in general have focused their efforts on understanding caste as structure without dealing with the movements against it. Therefore, to establish our point it is necessary to establish a framework for the analysis of all social movements in the colonial period and today.

The major framework within which these movements have been

interpreted, even by academics, has been highly influenced by the Marxism of the twentieth century. This has had two important assumptions, first that 'class' (defined in terms of holding or not holding the means of production, or private property) has been the most important factor determining exploitation and oppression, hence both social structures and the movements to transform these; and second, that beyond simply class itself the 'national movement', defined as the anti-imperialist movement against colonial rule and characterized in terms of its main organizations (such as the Indian National Congress) has been the overarching movement of the Third World countries in the era of imperialism.

Within this perspective, Dalit and anti-caste movements could only be seen as diversionary. Marxists in India have veered between a rather sectarian pure class perspective (represented for instance by B.T. Ranadive and the CPI in its 'class sectarianism' period) and a pro-Congress nationalism (represented by the CPI in other periods and by neo-Marxist academics such as Bipan Chandra). Analysis of the Dalit movement has suffered from both interpretations. It has been seen as diversionary either from the economic class struggle because of its argument for the necessity of struggling against social oppression, or in terms of the needs of a national struggle because of its insistence on putting the needs of the most oppressed/exploited group first and because of its willingness to treat the Indian elite, not foreign powers, as the 'main enemy'.

Interpreting the Dalit movement in 'class' terms, Marxists have been able to see it as basically progressive due to its working class and poor peasant–agricultural labourer base, but hampered by 'petty bourgeois' leadership. In the colonial period, however, all Marxists along with most nationalists saw it as basically 'divisive' and dangerously pro-British. This was due to the belief that the 'main contradiction' was that of the oppressed Indian nationality and imperialism; as the historian Bipan Chandra puts it, the nationalist movement stood at the centre of the broad democratic revolution in India, and the National Congress was the core of this, with other major movements including working class and peasant movements having a complex relation to the Congress and only 'communal and casteist movements' forming 'an alternative stream of politics . . . not nationalist or anti-imperialist but [with] loyalist pro-colonial tendencies'[10] This position rests on two assumptions, first that the dominant trend of the National Congress was not only anti-imperialist but democratic and secular, and second that the 'nation' was a reality that could be taken-for-granted. In the words of Shashi Joshi, 'Anti-imperialist nationalism is historically given. Nationalism as an emotive force is intrinsic to being a victim of national oppression'.[11]

Within the mind-set that takes an overriding 'national oppression' as self-evident, Ambedkar's justification for compromise with the British on the grounds that 'we cannot fight all enemies at once' could seem only a betrayal.

But what was the 'nation' and what was 'national oppression' and the way to overcome it?

In contrast stands Baburao Bagul's assessment,

> The national movement was turned into a form of historical, mythological movement and ancestor worship . . . . Those who propounded inequality and did not wish society to be democratic, started eulogizing history, mythology and ages gone by because, in those mythological and historical ages, they were the supreme victors and leaders. The intelligentsia now harked back to and worshipped the past because of this. People such as Phule, Agarkar, Gokhale and Ranade who talked about misery and servitude of the Shudras and Atishudras, who criticized the *varna* system, and demanded social, economic and political reconstruction, were declared enemies and attacked from all sides. The intelligentsia won; they succeeded in turning the Indian liberation struggle into a lop-sided fight, and in reducing the other movements to a secondary status.[12]

This question, of identity and existence of the 'nation', was precisely the point taken up by Phule in the nineteenth century in opposing the elite-led nationalist project at its very beginning. His argument was that a society divided by caste could not constitute a genuine nation and that those claiming to represent the nation were in fact its destroyers since they not only ignored these hierarchical divisions but actually sought to maintain them as a basis for their power. It is, in fact, in regard to what constitutes the 'Indian identity' that the anti-caste movement has its basic strength today, in contrast to the now barren record of Nehruvite secularism, as a counter to the communalization of Indian politics.

The anti-caste movement was in its own way nationalist and

anti-imperialist; it saw opposition to colonial power as fundamentally connected with the struggle against what Marxists and nationalists would call 'feudalism', or the caste system; both, to it, were parts of a fundamental *national* struggle. It seems necessary to move beyond the narrow 'class' approach as well as the understanding of 'nationalism' only in terms of political opposition to a foreign power.[13] This involves taking a 'revisionist Marxist' approach at two levels: in terms of the relationship between 'superstructure' and 'base' (the ideological and the economic) and in terms of a vastly expanded analysis of the economic structure itself.

In terms of ideological issues and their relationship with economic structures, particularly as regards the 'new social movements', the recent influential writings of neo-Gramscian theorists such as Laclau and Mouffe seem important. These emphasize the 'democratic revolution' as a major global revolutionary ideology. The 'discourse-analytical approach' of Laclau and Mouffe, for example, stresses the struggle for ideological hegemony, without privileging class actors or particular class positions, arguing that even working class struggles will not be revolutionary or progressive unless they are articulated in a context of general emancipation. This context of emancipation has to be provided by an ideological discourse; as they put it,

> Serf, slave and so on, do not designate in themselves antagonistic positions; it is only in the terms of a different discursive formation, such as the 'rights inherent to every human being,' that the differential positivity of these categories can be subverted and the subordination constructed as oppression.[14]

Arguing for the increase of both repressive and emancipatory forces with the spread of capitalism, they see the emancipatory project as connected to the spread of a broad democratic ideology with values of freedom, equality and autonomy; these are inherently subversive of all forms of subordination and inequality, though subversion may be a slow and protracted process. From this perspective, the Dalit movement and the overall radical anti-caste movements were a crucial expression of the democratic revolution in India, more consistently democratic—and in the end more consistently 'nationalistic'—than the elite-controlled Indian National Congress.

In drawing our attention to the importance of ideology and 'discursive formulations', Laclau and Mouffe stress the understanding of ideological struggles and the way in which 'democratic' ideologies undergo transformations and deepenings; in this study we shall focus primarily on the development of ideologies of Dalit liberation (particularly that of Ambedkar) and their relationship to Marxism, as understood in the Indian context, and Gandhism.

However, a revised 'historical materialism' cannot limit itself to discussing the relationship between economic structure and ideology; there also has to be a deepened understanding of economic structure itself, and of the way in which world capitalism (which after all has provided the overarching framework for anti-caste movements) has operated not only in terms of the dialectic and contradictions between capital and wage labour, but has also incorporated and adapted non-wage forms of production. Here the new discussions of the ideological characteristics of the 'new social movements' have failed to confront the inherent flaws of a 'class analysis' that remains caught in orthodox emphases on control of the means of production (private property). In contrast, from within the new movements, theorists have raised the issue of seeing women's unpaid domestic labour and even 'natural' provisions of the 'conditions of production' as crucial to the accumulation of capital,[15] while 'worlds systems theorists' like Immanuel Wallerstein have stressed the role of non-wage labour (in his analysis, in particular serf and slave labour, while we would add petty commodity production, and caste-mediated forms), in being central to capital accumulation from the beginning. In these models also, not simply 'economic subordination' to holders of property but cultural/ community forms and force and violence play a major role. On this basis we can construct at least the elements of a revised historical materialist understanding not only of the linkage between the 'economic base' and the 'superstructure', but of economic processes themselves.

Such a framework will form the basis for the discussion of the pre-independence Dalit movement in this book.

This study focuses on Dalit movements in three major linguistic regions of India—Maharashtra, Andhra and Karnataka—and on the interaction of these movements with the nationalist movement and the 'class' struggles of the workers and peasants, as well as with the major ideologies of Gandhism and Marxism which guided these. Chapter 1 gives a background analysis of the caste system in South Asia along with a discussion of the main points of a revised historical materialism in the context of Dalit and left movement analyses. Chapter 2 discusses the particular regional context as well as the role of colonialism in structuring the movements. It also deals with the major ideological–political founder of the anti-caste movement in India, Jotiba Phule.

Chapters 3 and 4 deal with the 1920s, the period of emergence of the Dalit movements as organizational forces in many regions of India, taking up the different situations in the five regions (Bombay Province, Andhra delta in Madras Province, the Nagpur–Vidarbha region of Central Provinces, Hyderabad state and Mysore state) that the Telugu, Kannada and Marathi-speaking areas were divided into during colonial rule. Chapter 5, focusing on the 1930–32 period as a 'turning point', describes the confrontation of Ambedkar and the issues of caste raised by the Dalit movement with Gandhi, on the one hand, and the ideology of the Indian Marxists on the other. Chapter 6 deals with the 'years of radicalism' in the Bombay Presidency, from 1936 to 1942, when Ambedkar's Independent Labour Party was standing forth as a party of workers and peasants in opposition to the 'bourgeois-Brahman' Congress, and was actively involved in leading struggles. The failure of this period to develop into a broad movement unifying economic and anti-caste struggles was perhaps decisive for the future of independent India.

Inevitably, a study of the 'Dalit movement', necessarily means a study of Dr. Bhimrao Ramji Ambedkar's role in it. Being its historic leader and the formulator of its enduring ideology, Babasaheb Ambedkar was the dominating figure and active organizer of the movement in the Marathi-speaking regions. By the 1930s and 1940s he came to dominate the all-India movement as well, though his organizations never attained as strong a hegemony outside of Maharashtra. In spite of the organizational weaknesses of the Scheduled Caste Federation and the successor Republican Party, it is still 'Ambedkarism' as a broad trend which dominates the movement, and it is beginning to have an impact within social movements and circles outside the anti-caste movement as such. For that reason Ambedkar's theoretical framework is treated in a separate chapter.

Chapter 8 focuses on developments in Mysore (the Kannada-speaking region) during the 1930s and 1940s, while chapter 9 deals with the part of India that had the greatest rural communist strength and a major peasant revolt at the time of independence, Andhra. Here again we see a strong, mass-based oppositional movement proclaiming socialist goals, this time one taking insurrectionist forms, but again, as in the case of the Dalit movement in Maharashtra, meeting with organizational failure and political incorporation. Finally, a conclusion evaluates the achievements of the movement in the pre-colonial period, suggests the background for its re-emergence in the 1970s, and poses the problems it confronts today.

I would like to thank those whose support, intellectual stimulation and research aid was crucial in completing this work. Surendra Jondhale, V. Laxminarayan, G. Gnaneshwar, Vasanti Rasam, Madhav Deshwal and Meena Seshu provided important research assistance. Activists connected with *Dalit Voice* provided important research material. Through the years, discussions and interactions with activists and intellectuals of the Dalit movement and other social movements have been essential in helping me sharpen and formulate my perspective: I owe thanks to A.R. Desai, Sharad Patil, Bojja Tharakam, Vasant Moon, Gangadhar Patavane, Bhaskarrao Jadhav, Sudhakar Gaikwad, Kancha Ilaiah, Narendra Jadhav, Namdev Dhasal, Arun Kamble, Eleanor Zelliot, S.K. Limaye, Sudhir Bedekar, Sharad Joshi, and many others. Innovators in Marxist theory the world over have been part of the developing perspective here, and their names are too numerous to mention. Most of all, the arguments and critiques of Bharat Patankar have helped to bring to some kind of fruition this perspective on 'class and caste'.

Finally, I would like to thank the Department of Politics and Public Administration of Poona University and the Society for People's Participation in Eco-system Management (SOPPECOM) for providing facilities for completion of this manuscript.

NOTES

1. Namdev Dhasal, 'Now,Now', translated by Jayant Karve and Eleanor Zelliot, in Mulk Raj Anand and Eleanor Zelliot (ed.), *An Anthology of Dalit Literature* (New Delhi: Gyan Publishing House, 1992), p. 53.
2. Shripal Sabnis, in Barbara Joshi, (ed.), *Untouchable Voices of the Dalit Liberation Movement* (London: Zed Books, 1986), my translation.

3. Arjun Dangle (ed.), *No Room for the New Sun* (New Delhi: Orient Longman, 1992); this is the separately published poetry section of *Poisoned Bread: Translations from Modern Marathi Dalit Literature.*

4. *Reinventing Revolution: India's New Social Movements* (New York: M.E. Sharpe, 1993).

5. See Immanuel Wallerstein's original paper, 'The Rise and Future Demise of the World Capitalist System: Concepts for Comparative Analysis.' *Comparative Studies in Society and History* 16, 4 (September 1974). More recent brief statement's of Wallerstein's view of anti-systemic social movements (which he defines broadly as 'class' movements and 'national' movements), see 'Anti-Systemic Movements and the Three Worlds', *Lanka Guardian*, 1 June 1985 and 'Patterns and Prospects of the Capitalist World Economy' *Contemporary Marxism* No. 9, Fall 1984. For more conventional sociological functionalist analysis, see the most well-known work by Neil Smelser, *A Theory of Collective Behavior* (New York: Free Press of Glencoe, 1963).

6. Cited by Kumari Jayawardena, *Feminism and Nationalism in the Third World* (London: Zed Books, 1986), p. 80.

7. Arun Sinha, 'Class War in Bhojpur', *Economic and Political Weekly*, 7 January 1978.

8. Mukundrao Patil, *Din Mitra*, June 1913; cited in Gail Omvedt, *Cultural Revolt in a Colonial Society: The Non-Brahman Movement in Western India 1873–1930*, (Pune: Scientific Socialist Education Trust, 1976), p. 157.

9. Referring to the cultural background of nationalist revolt in one of the strongest centres of the 1942 movement, this is from a Marathi booklet on Nana Patil, the leader of the 'parallel government' in Satara, cited in Omvedt, *Cultural Revolt*, p. 122. The term I have translated as 'lower caste majority', is *bahujan samaj*, literally 'majority community', but while the language of exploitation is Marxian the reference is to the Dalit and Shudra castes.

10. Bipan Chandra, 'Introduction' to Bipan Chandra, Mridula Mukherjee, Aditya Mukherjee, K.N. Panikkar and Sucheta Mahajan, *India's Struggle for Independence, 1857–1947* (New Delhi: Penguin Books India, 1989), p. 28.

11. Shashi Joshi, *Struggle for Hegemony in India, 1920–1947: The Colonial State, the Left and the National Movement, Volume I: 1920–1934* (New Delhi: Sage Publications, 1992),

12. Baburao Bagul, 'Dalit Literature is But Human Literature', in Arjun Dangle (ed.), *Poisoned Bread: Translations from Modern Marathi Dalit Literature* (New Delhi: Orient Longman, 1992), p. 24.

13. For a discussion of African democratic movements that stress the role of both political and 'social' organizations in the independence struggles and the consequences of narrowing down the definition to only the political, see Mamdani, 'Africa: Democratic Theory and Democratic Struggles', *Economic and Political Weekly*, 10 October 1992.

14. Ernesto Laclau and Chantal Mouffe, *Hegemony and Socialist Strategy* (London: Verso, 1989), p. 154.

15. See in particular Maria Mies, *Patriarchy and Accumulation on a World Scale* (London: Zed Books, 1985) and James O'Connor, introduction to *Capitalism, Nature, Socialism*, 1, 1, 1988.

CHAPTER 1

Towards a Historical Materialist Analysis of the Origins and Development of Caste

■ INTRODUCTION: THEORIZING CASTE IN INDIA

Theories of caste are developed by social scientists in the academy for various reasons ranging from the analysis of a village or local society to the project of developing a general social theory. They marshall empirical data in their support, frame hypotheses, elaborate conceptual frameworks, and in general seek to work within the framework of a scientific paradigm laying claim to testifiable validity.[1]

Theories of caste also exist within the societies characterized by caste. They exist at two levels, one in the fragmented, unarticulated normally unconscious rules of behaviour embodied in the social relations characteristic of caste societies, and second in the articulated and elaborated ideologies which are used by those seeking to maintain or contest hegemony within the society or to challenge that society in a basic way. These marshall arguments, sometimes with an empirical reference but just as often with moral and spiritual references, to maintain support for the dominant structures of that society or to mobilize support for its change. In this way theories of caste have been both part of the on-going processes of Indian society and part of the movements (national, social) seeking to change the society.

Dalit and non-Brahman movements developed their own theories of caste, drawing upon the debates and theories put forward by those around them (from those of scholars to the theories of caste dominance to the arguments of those in other major social movements of their time), but with the specific focus of using theory as a guide for achieving the abolition of caste and the exploitation and oppression it involved. In taking this as their goal they made certain assumptions, i.e., that caste had an origin in history, and just as it had an origin it could have an end; that action of the oppressed and exploited could be effective in aiding this process. These constitute quite 'modern' assumptions and place them at odds with any theories assuming that caste is not only unique to South Asian society but is effectively eternal and unshakeable or existing at a level which large-scale social action cannot affect. They are basically assumptions I agree with, and there is no harm in describing the framework of this study as drawing not only on Marx but upon what is increasingly being called (at least in western India) 'Phule–Ambedkar thought'.

These theories of the non-Brahman and Dalit movement confronted two types of ideologies used to legitimate caste society. First were the traditional religiously-based ideologies, developed primarily by Brahmans, harking back to the laws of Manu and the 'creation hymn' of the Rig Veda, expressed, elaborated and ideologically glossed in the Puranic myths and renditions of the Ramayana and Mahabharata. At this level they debated both the validity of the sacred texts (shastras, smritis, etc.) and what they really meant. Upper-caste social reformers (from nineteenth century activists like Rammohan Roy and Agarkar to Gandhi) tried to argue for scriptural justification for a change in or even abolition of the *jati* and *varna* systems, whereas social revolutionaries like Phule, Periyar and Ambedkar agreed with the conservatives that the Hindu scriptures necessarily implied observation of caste hierarchy and used this to denounce them as irrational and exploitative.

With colonial rule another important theoretical approach entered the ideological arena to serve first as an ideological legitimation of the system of caste hierarchy replacing or supplementing an increasingly questioned religious basis, and then, reversed and turned against its earlier proponents, as a theory to oppose caste domination. This was the 'Aryan theory of race', originated by European Orientalists, propagated by British administrators in their censuses and provincial studies of caste groups, picked up by early modernist Brahmans as a way of asserting their equivalence with the white-skinned conquerors and their superiority to the darker-skinned lower castes, and then taken up by Jotiba Phule and later radicals. These theorists agreed that the majority middle and low castes (Shudras and Atishudras or outcastes in the *varna* interpretation) were descendents of 'non-Aryan' original inhabitants while Brahmans, Ksatriyas and Vaishyas were descendents of their Indo-European (Aryan, Vedic) conquerors, but argued that this meant the opposite from what the Brahmans claimed: it was the Shudras and Atishudras who embodied the values and national integrity necessary for a new India, while the upper castes and their scriptures represented only a society of exploitation, superstition, irrationality and backwardness.

Phule's was the first historical materialist theory of caste,[2] and it heralded major themes of the Dalit and non-Brahman movements that were to develop in the twentieth century. In Phule's hands it was much more than a simple 'racial theory'; rather Phule used the dominant racial framework of the 'Aryan theory' to evolve a total depiction of the role of violence and community; it has even been argued, by the historian G.P. Deshpande, that

> Phule was the first Indian 'system builder' . . . [the] first to attempt at transforming plural categories of history into singular or universal . . . [he] talked about knowledge and power much before Foucault did. In fact Foucault's post-Modernist analysis came at a time when Europe has literally seen an 'end of history' whereas Phule's efforts were to change the world/society with the weapon of knowledge.[3]

Later movements, however, lost these nuances and tended to assert it as a simple racial ideology of superiority against the increasingly aggressive (and sophisticated) ideologies of caste legitimacy used by the growing Hindu revivalist movement. In effect, emphasizing racial/ethnic contradictions became a weapon against those who stressed racial/ethnic solidarity of 'Hindus'.

The 1920s saw the emergence of Marxism, asserting a new theory of exploitation and liberation, claiming to have a total analysis applicable to India as to any society. It was rapidly picked up by a group of young, educated and mostly upper-caste radical nationalists searching for a mass base of the movement and eventually founding new communist and socialist parties. It also began to assert a powerful influence on the thinking of left Congressmen such as Nehru and his colleagues.

'Marxism' as a theory and ideology came into India and existed for fifty years (with the solitary exception of D.D. Kosambi) in a fairly mechanical, vulgarized form; its contribution to all liberation movements was its firm assertion that social systems and relations are *historical* (they have come into existence, change and will come to an end), *material* (they have a solid base in production and collective, non-ideal social forces), and characterized by *conflict, contradiction* and *exploitation*. Its disadvantage was that it took the overriding reality of 'class' and 'class struggle' so strongly as to assert the fundamental irrelevance of every other sociological category. Indeed, at first the power of the 'class' metaphor seemed so strong both for analysis and as a guide to action that it was easy for the proponents of Marxism and socialism to treat family, kinship, the state, gender, and in India of course caste, as not only secondary but practically non-existent factors. Its influence lay in its seductive strength, and it was an influence exerted not only on Indian activists but also on academics, to the extent that a large number of the Marxist-influenced theoretical and empirical studies even during the 1970s and 1980s identified their radicalism with their assertion that behind the apparent reality of caste ultimately lay class and its dialectics, a 'class content to a caste form'.[4]

This Marxist mechanical materialism not only succeeded in becoming the primary ideology guiding or at least uniting the developing working class and peasant movements of the country at a national level; it also exerted a powerful influence over the anti-caste movement. For even when this movement challenged Marxist thinking to assert the centrality of caste, it tended to do so with an acceptance of the fundamental framework exerted by Marxism. For Phule, economic and social and political domination, and exploitation had been interwoven factors (which is one reason why it is inadequate to call his a 'racial' theory), but Marxism set up, for decades to come, the paradigmatic polarities of 'class and caste', 'base and superstructure', 'economic and social/cultural/ ideological'. For communist and socialist activists (and for Nehruvite progressives) this meant taking class/the base/economic as primary; and for the anti-caste radicals it meant simply turning the polarity around. In doing so, in asserting that superstructure/cultural/ideo- logical factors were primary they identified 'caste' with the cultural/ ideological sphere in contrast to the economic sphere, and argued for the secondary role, if not ultimate irrelevance of, 'economics' and 'class'. This happened in part with Ambedkar himself, as we shall see in chapter 7, and also with the Lohiaite socialists; though the socialists as much as communists seemed to assume the irrele- vance of caste in the pre-independence period, once they came to theorize it as important in Indian society they too analyzed it as a non-economic cultural category.

Paradoxically, the influence of Marxism on anti-caste trends was thus to widen divisions. Rather than lead to an integrated theory combining economic/political/cultural factors, these were separated; activists theorized only about 'caste' and took 'class' for granted. Phule himself had had no theory of economic development or changes in mode of production as part of his overall analysis; but Ambedkar (and his contemporaries) also developed little of an independent economic analysis; they took from Marxism a broad economic radicalism and Ambedkar himself wrote considerably on financial issues, but little of this was integrated into their social- historical interpretations of the caste system, which was treated as an altogether independent field of analysis.

The equation of class/caste-base/superstructure also held when new Marxist thinking on caste emerged in the 1970s in the face of a challenge from a renewed Dalit and anti-caste movement. This again took the form of reasserting the importance of caste as a cultural/ideological factor. If the Naxalite trend in India seemed the most ready (by the 1980s at least) to pay attention to the social reality of caste, this was in part because the Maoist framework of 'contradictions' could allow an understanding which saw cultural or political factors as at times playing the 'leading role' in a contradiction. Similarly, Althusserian influence on academic Marxists could stimulate a view of the superstructure (including caste in India) as 'dominant' if not determinant in a pre-capitalist society. This led to an analysis (for instance that of my earlier works) which argued that in pre-colonial Indian society there were unique features of the structuring of economic relations as a result of caste, with *jajmani* (*balutedari*) relations being a central feature; in 'caste-feudal society' thus castes and class were interwoven while in contrast in the capitalist mode of production economic classes and castes could be seen as separating themselves from each other.[5]

Generally these revisionist attempts took for granted the basic 'class' or economic theories of Marxism, including the analysis of the capitalist mode of production and the Stalinist 'five stage' theory of history (primitive communism, slavery, feudalism, capitalism and socialism), simply identifying caste as the superstructure of feudal society.[6] They accepted the identification of the proletariat as vanguard and the peasantry as basically a backward, feudal class designed to disintegrate (or 'differentiate') under capitalism into a basically proletarianized agricultural labourer/poor peasant class and a basically bourgeois rich peasant/capitalist farmer class. They accepted the notion that not only socialism but also capitalism laid a basis in the forces and relations of production for eradicating caste relations. Thus they tended to argue that while caste is an important superstructural feature of capitalist society (important in the sense of requiring specific struggles to abolish it (a position that differentiates them from more traditional Marxists) its main function is to exercise a retarding role on the development of class struggle (for instance, when rural rich farmer elites from 'dominant castes' use caste ties to split the rural poor).

Within the new Dalit and anti-caste movement itself attempts to present a combined 'class–caste' approach gained prominence after 1970. An important recent version is that of Sharad Patil, who has put forward a combined approach based on what he claims is a new methodology of 'Marxism-Phule-Ambedkarism', which focuses not on caste as an ideological system but on jatis as entities, arguing that in pre-capitalist societies jatis themselves were basic units of production and exploitation.[7] In this approach, 'caste conflict' or *jati sangarsh* is seen as being equivalent to 'class conflict', not simply a distraction or obstacle to the real struggle and progressive in the sense of a fight against the basic exploitation of the system. Patil also identifies caste with 'feudalism' and argues that following the British conquest class relations associated with capitalism came into existence, so that a compound class–caste struggle is necessary today.

A major problem with this approach is that even in pre-British society, castes (jatis) were only superficially more concrete than 'class'. It is true that 'classes' cannot be simply identified in pre-British India, but neither did (or do) jatis exist as solid and delimitable social units. Sub-castes, as many anthropologists have pointed out, were the real units of endogamy and interaction, while the broader jati was often a category or identity rather than an actually existing group. Thus there were many different kinds of Kunbi-Marathas, Jats, Okkaligas, etc., and they acted in different ways in different areas. Further, the notion of *jati sangarsh* does not answer the question: which were the jatis in struggle, which were the fundamental exploiters and which exploited? This is not so simple. Brahmans might easily be identified as exploiters, Dalits and *balutedars* (Shudra service castes) as exploited. But what about Kunbis, Kapus, Vokkaligas, etc? Were they exploited or exploiters? Were they, as a 'dominant caste' in the village, exploiting Dalits and artisans, or were they an exploited peasantry? Sharad Patil's methodology, however much it is elaborated into a compelling account of ancient Indian history, has not even attempted to pose this question, let alone answer it; nor has it provided an obvious logic for his historical periodicization.

■ THE PRINCIPLES OF A HISTORICAL MATERIALISTIC THEORY OF CASTE

The problem with attempts such as those of Sharad Patil to develop a 'class–caste' analysis, as well as the recent 'ecological' theories of caste such as those of Madhav Gadgil and Ramchandra Guha,[8] is that they take too much for granted, in simply adding 'caste' to accepted class categories of workers, peasants, capitalists and landlords, without questioning the traditional conceptualizations of stages of history or modes of production. 'Class–caste' analyses have proved rather sterile as indeed have all the 'additive' theories (class and race, class and patriarchy, etc.) put forward in reaction to the new social movements of today.

In spite of the many problems with existing Marxist theories of class and economic exploitation, the basic approach of Marxist methodology is useful for an adequate understanding of the structure and role of caste in South Asian society. *The basic guideline for any analysis in the interests of the oppressed people is to ask: who are the exploiters and who are the exploited? How can the exploited organize their struggle to move in the direction of liberation? And what is the relation of the structures of exploitation to the historical possibilities of moving in the direction of liberation from exploitation?*. In the words of Marx. 'Philosophers have only interpreted the world; the point is to change it.'[9] And to answer this question, he does not begin with 'class', which is really a derived and secondary concept in the total theory, but looks at how humans organize their production and how what they produce, the surplus product embodying their surplus labour, is extracted and appropriated by the non-producing sections of society. In his words,

> The specific economic form, in which unpaid surplus-labour is pumped out of direct producers, determines the relationship of rulers and ruled . . . . It is always the direct relationship of the owners of the conditions of production to the direct producers—a relation always naturally corresponding to a definite stage in the development of the methods of labour and thereby its social productivity—which reveals the inner-most secret, the hidden base of the entire social structure and with it . . . the corresponding specific form of the state.[10]

This methodology leads us to look at the concrete forms of production in any society, the concrete forms of the *production, expropriation and accumulation of surplus labour*. In pre-British Indian society, for example, we can answer the question of whether 'dominant caste' peasants were exploiters or not by this criterion. Dalits and *balutedars* or artisans apparently worked for the 'village community' or the 'dominant' peasants. They produced tools, ploughs, ropes, etc., for agricultural production; they often worked as labourers on the land. But if we analyze what happened to their surplus labour, we can see that it was embodied in the crops grown by the peasants and that the greatest share of these crops was taken by the representatives of the state (jagirdars, rajas, *deshmukhs*, *sardars*, zamindars) and of religion (Brahmans). These exploiters therefore appropriated the surplus labour not only of peasants but also of the craftsmen, field labourers, etc. Therefore we can identify *exploited* jatis as the peasant castes (Kunbis, Kapus, etc.) and the Dalits, *balutedars* and others. And in identifying the *exploiters*, we have to note that it is not so easy to identify them in terms of jati, except for Brahmans who almost never laboured and always claimed an important share of the surplus. Besides Brahmans, the major exploiters were the holders of state and political power, and these included households not only from the 'peasant' jatis but also many from 'lower' jatis as well. But they were exploiters not as members of such a jati, but as holders of state power.

In this methodological approach, we do not begin with 'class'; the more basic concept is that of exploitation and the 'specific economic form in which unpaid surplus labour is pumped out of direct producers.' In the strict sense, classes come into existence only with capitalism and then only in the capitalist 'core' areas of factory production; peasantries, tribal communities, etc., are 'class-like' but their relations of exploitation are interwoven with community/tribal/kinship features in pre-capitalist systems and even when these are linked to capital accumulation in a capitalist world-system; thus their fight against exploitation takes place through communities, tribes, castes and kinship groups. Sharad Patil objects to the application of 'class' to pre-British India; but in fact the same objection applies to any pre-capitalist society.

'Class' as defined solely in terms of the ownership of private property and the ownership or control of the means of production does not explain major aspects of exploitation and capital accumulation. A theory of historical materialism applicable in current circumstances will have to incorporate the elements of violence, force, domination, knowledge suggested by (among others) Jotiba Phule. Certainly the issues arising out of the 'fall of socialism' in Eastern Europe, the general crisis of statist societies, implies this need for broadening, as does increased thinking about the 'conditions of production' stimulated by ecological issues; the analysis of caste in India also does so. Rethinking the workings of the capitalist system as such, in relation not only to caste but also to patriarchy, environmental issues, the peasantry and other 'classes', is on the agenda for today.

In analyzing how the caste system or *jati vyavastha* works, we would argue that it should not be seen merely as ideological or superstructural; neither should it be identified simply as a cluster of concrete and interacting jatis. It is a 'system'. Of what? Of a set of basically kinship-like social practices and the rules that surround them. The former are 'material'; the latter are 'ideological' but in the sense of often 'unconscious' rules of behaviour as contrasted with a conscious system of ideology (a distinction used by many anthropologists). For instance, the conscious ideology of *varna-shrama dharma* constituted a religiously-authorited system used to interpret and support the caste system and the economic exploitation involved in it; but it is different from the actual rules of behaviour defining expected behaviour among and between members of different jatis.

Thus, the endogamous principles and practices that constitute the jatis, the purity–pollution behaviour rules and occupational tasks governing the relations of hierarchy and exploitation existing among them, are the practices and rules that constitute the caste system. This set of practices and rules has its own dynamics and has deeply shaped Indian society and the Indian economic system; but it has also been shaped by changing economic relations, by conquest and the changes in state formations, by involvement with the market and wage labour—to mention a few of the non-caste aspects interacting with caste.

A few comments can be made about this methodological approach and our conceptualizations of the Dalit movement.

First, this definition of case takes in both the jatis and the system of hierarchical relations (from exploitation to purity–pollution rules) among them. A definition of 'caste' focusing only on jatis, even seen as existing in a hierarchy, tends to imply that 'caste struggles' or 'caste movements' are movements of a jati or set of jatis for rising in the system; they are not necessarily against the system and may result in leaving it intact. In this sense it is quite natural that 'caste movements' would not be seen as progressive. The system is not conceptualized at all. On the other hand, looking at the system only ideologically (even when the ideology is one of inequality) does imply that the exploited classes have an interest in overthrowing the caste system—but it tends to imply that all the exploited sections (workers, agricultural labourers, peasants, middle and low castes) have an equal interest in doing so and in preventing caste-created divisions among themselves. It fails to identify those groups with the greatest interest in being anti-caste. And caste becomes apparent only in terms of a backward ideology having a retarding effect on class struggle.

However, if we realize that the caste system both constitutes units of struggle (castes or jatis or collections of them) and that rules of hierarchy and domination are essential to their constitution, then the lowest castes have an inherent interest not simply in rising in the system but in overthrowing it ('middle' castes also have an interest in overthrowing it, but not so great). Any real movement of the most oppressed section, the Dalits, will have to confront the entire system. This is not to say that all collective actions by Dalits will do so; their actual development depends on the possibilities of the situation, question of alliances, support of middle castes, etc. But Dalit movements will have an inherent interest in moving in a radical direction.

Further, to the extent that jatis and the caste hierarchy define/constitute the relations of surplus production and extraction (which they do in varying ways and degrees at different historical periods), the anti-caste struggle is inherently also a 'class struggle', that is a struggle against economic exploitation.

■ THE SPECIFICITY OF CASTE: WHY SOUTH ASIA?

The caste system exists in the South Asian subcontinent and there only. While Brahmanic Hinduism strengthened it, even gave it its full 'realization', caste exists also in Muslim Pakistan and Bangladesh and among the Buddhist Sinhalese, while on the other hand the long historical influence of 'Hinduism' (Vaishnavism, Saivism) on South-east Asian societies did nothing to create a caste system there. Thus, caste is a social system characteristic of the subcontinent.

This fact by itself refutes oversimplified interpretations of almost any type. The identification of caste, for instance, as caused by, in some sense, Hindu religious ideology, cannot explain the fact that the system appears to have its origins before the consolidated dominance of Hinduism as a religion in India. Similarly, 'racial theories' of Aryan conquest, or theories describing caste as a simple crystallization of what was originally an economic division of labour, fail to explain why this happened in South Asia and not in other regions of the world: conquest, the development of economic surplus and an increasing division of labour, etc., are characteristic of almost all regions, not only of South Asia. Further, the Vedic Aryans or Indo-Europeans were not uniquely insistent on divisions by birth or race. Why only here did a caste system emerge?

The situation suggests that there were certain social-cultural features of the subcontinent itself, existing prior to the development of a surplus and prior to conquest, that pushed social evolution in a particular direction. This is the position of one of the most stimulating recent discussions of caste origins by Morton Klass, who argues that a particular system of interacting tribal social groups ('equalitarian' enclosed tribal groups) existed throughout the subcontinent and as economic inequality increased with the development of an agricultural surplus, a process took place in which, rather than each tribe becoming internally stratified, different tribes entered into exchange processes for the surplus, transforming themselves into jatis, some becoming landholding cultivators, some offering various types of services or labour but remaining corporate groups. According to Klass,

> South Asia as a *whole* became characterized by spreading rice and hard-grain cultivation in certain ecological zones, while other zones (as today) were characterized by hunting and gathering, shifting agriculture, herding and so on. This *totality* is the arena for sociocultural change . . . . I propose that the caste system came into existence *not* in Bengal or the Malabar Coast or the Indus Valley but over the entire subcontinent. Different regions and peoples participated in different and unequal ways, sometimes making a contribution and at other times remaining peripheral to developments.[11]

This locates the most important causal feature (or more accurately, a necessary condition for the emergence of caste) in the specific characteristics of pre-state South Asian society, prior to the Indus civilization and prior to the Aryan conquest. There is some archeological evidence for this uniqueness. Archeologists stress that since ancient times the subcontinent has had groups inhabiting different ecological niches and carrying on varying practices of food production/extraction (hunters, fishers, collectors, later agriculturalists) with some form of inter-community relations involving exchange of products. Stone tools in the subcontinent are frequently found in 'large factory sites', indicating that they were made by one group for much wider use, with some form of exchange. According to the Allchins,

> One of the distinctive features of South Asian culture in historic and recent times is the way in which it has encapsulated communities at many different cultural and technological levels, allowing them, to a large extent, to retain their identity and establish intercommunity relationships. Early Indian literature makes it clear that this was a feature of northwest Indian society during the first millennium B.C. It seems highly probably that its roots, like those of the cultural regions, extend back much further . . . .[12]

Gregory Possehl, analyzing Lothal, a port town of the Harappan period, writes of an alliance of the settlers with nearby hunting and gathering peoples. This relationship

> suggests . . . that within the late third and early second millennia B.C. a complex interlocking cultural mosaic was developing in South Asia . . . which suggests a growth of interdependence between sociocultural groups with fundamentally different systems of settlement and subsistence, material culture and presumably diverse cultural traditions. This is a form of cultural integration still found in India . . . . This interlocking relationship is also generally applicable to one of the essential aspects of caste organization if viewed as a total system.[13]

These various groups may be seen as proto-castes, and it may well be that they had the corporate–equalitarian features hypothesized by Klass; once a surplus developed, processes of conquest took place and states and cities were established, these groups, tribes becoming jatis, were integrated gradually into a hierarchical order that included relations of exploitation, domination and ideological concepts and practices of purity and pollution. Certainly crucial 'tribal' features are retained in jatis, ranging from closed boundaries between tribes to the retainment of 'clan' sections within many jatis.

But if India (in the words of anthropologists) is a 'tribal society rearranged to fit a civilization', this was possible because of the unique features of its tribal (pre-class) society. In an important critique of the concept of 'tribe', Morton Fried has argued that in fact 'tribes' as such (bounded economic–political units) did not exist prior to the formation of states; pre-state societies were much more fluid and amorphous than the concept of 'tribe' allows for, and 'tribes' as units came into being primarily in defensive reactions to state encroachment.[14] 'Tribal closure' may be a specific South Asian feature, but it is not a necessary characteristic of 'tribal' societies.

Can we trace this tendency to any broader 'ethnic' stream in South Asia? South Asian society is constituted, ethnically, of diverse strands—Aryan, Mundari (Austro-Asiatic), Sino-Tibetan, Dravidian. Of these the Mundari groups appear to have had a more equalitarian and matrilineal culture from earlier times: the Khasis today show the remnants of this in India; the Hos, Santhals, etc., are patrilineal but this is very likely an adoption from the surrounding 'Hindu' society over the years. Aryans or Indo-Europeans, while patrilinear nomadic warriors in their first appearance on the historical scene, were not ridden with caste-like distinctions until after they made their entry into India. Sino-Tibetan groups to this day have less of caste distinction.

This leaves the Dravidians. Can it be said that a tendency to closed-group formation and purity–pollution hierarchies had their origin among these, perhaps the most ancient peoples of the subcontinent? Tamil Sangam period literature, as described by George Hart, while relatively recent in historical times, gives some interesting indications because of the relatively low 'Aryan' impact in this period.[15]

First, very much embedded in Tamil social conceptualization is the theory of the five *tinais*, different types of environment inhabited by people have different productive relations to the land. These were described in about the third century AD as follows:

1. . . . tribes of ploughmen (*uluvar*) inhabiting fertile, well-watered tracts and living in villages called *ur*;

2. hill people who are foresters, make charms and tell fortunes, and may come out of the forest to work in the *panai*;
3. pastoralists, also called *ayar* (cowmen), *kovalar* (shepherds) and *idaiyar* (cowhered or shepherd);
4. fishing people . . .;
5. People of the dry plains called *eyinar*, *maravar* and *vedar* who are hunters of both the dry plains and the forests.[16]

With this, the relationship between communities suggested in archeological writings became conceptualized in Dravidian culture.

Second, not only were there discrete groups practicing different occupations (proto-castes); boundaries between them seem to have been most striking among the groups lowest in the social scale. Many of these groups were seen as polluting, and Hart argues that in fact the Brahmans (seen as of Aryan/northern origin) picked up concepts of purity/pollution from the indigenous Dravidians and then exaggerated them to maintain their own superiority.[17] The origin of the purity/pollution hierarchy is seen in the notion of sacred power, which is potentially dangerous if it cannot be checked:

Among those called low in the example just given there is one factor that virtually all share: they are rendered dangerous by the sacred power with which they come into contact in their occupations. The leather worker is infected by the soul of the cow whose skin he works; the man at the funeral by the spirit of the dead man; the washerwoman by the dirt (and especially the menstrual discharge) on the clothes she cleans; and the pulsitti by the dangerous gods who possess her. The drummers and bards were rendered dangerous by the gods who were thought to reside in their drums and lutes, and by their occupations, which involved controlling dangerous forces by playing during battle.[18]

Women were especially liable to polluting contact, and Hart views most of the extreme Hindu oppression of women, including widow seclusion and sati, as deriving from Dravidian traditions that attributed a sacred power to women that was dangerous if uncontrolled by patriarchal bondage.[19]

A final element in Tamil Sangam society is important for the analysis of caste. The basic social division was three-fold. The anthropologist Tyler has called it a division into 'the dominant, the dependent and the degraded'—the *canror* or warrior elite, the *ilicinar* or toiling commoners, and the unclean *pulaiyar*.[20] A recent study of caste at the other end of the subcontinent, in Nepal, has noted a similar tripartite division into the 'thread-wearing castes', the 'alcohol-drinking castes' and the 'water-not-to-be-taken-from castes', linking this to the theory of the three *gunas*.[21] Whatever its mythical or scriptural justification, the division describes the actual social reality of the caste system more accurately than the 'four castes' of the *chaturvarnya* ideologization. The four-fold division of Brahman, Ksatriya, Vaishya, Shudra was developed to legitimate the way in which divisions among the Aryans were solidifying and indigenous groups were being absorbed into a new system, but it is misleading in suggesting a simple 'division of labour' which has no immediate reference to purity/pollution concepts, and does not include untouchables.

In contrast, the three-fold division, which was also used by the Dalit and non-Brahman movements, makes it clear that impurity and with it untouchability are inherent to the system. The division into 'dependent' and 'impure' suggests that both those who performed demeaning manual labour and those who carried on activities having to do with dangerous and/or polluting occupations were exploited, but that there was a hierarchy and division among them. It is out of this dualism that the later Dalit and non-Brahman movements grew: on the one hand, Dalits have an inherent interest shared with all exploited (specifically with those classed as Shudra, low, dependent toilers) in destroying the system; on the other, as those defined as 'impure' and relegated to quarters 'outside the village' they have a special oppression and a special interest in a movement against the entire hierarchy based on purity–pollution. Though 'untouchability' only really solidified after the fourth to sixth centuries AD, its roots can be traced almost as early as caste in general.

Thus the largest indigenous people of the subcontinent, the ancient Dravidians, began to culturally conceptualize the relationships between environmentally specialized and equalitarian groups forming a kind of proto-caste system. They had, similar to many tribal societies, a notion of sacred powers in nature which were potentially dangerous, and a conceptual linkage of these with certain occupations and activities and with women. Such factors may well have given an initial social superiority to women and to these groups in early agricultural and herding–hunting–fishing societies. But as surplus accumulation grew and men and warriors gained dominance, the link with sacred power was reversed; the 'dangerous' became the 'polluting' and eventually 'impure' and 'low'. This process clearly had its beginnings with the largely Dravidian-based Indus civilization, but it developed only with the impact of the invading Indo-Europeans on the indigenous culture and the gradual emergence of the Brahmans as a group systematizing the notions of purity and pollution and the developing caste hierarchy, with themselves at the top. It climaxed with the constitution of the caste system, or *varnashrama dharma* as the dominant social structure of feudal state societies during the sixth to ninth centuries after a complex fight with competing religious–ideological traditions. In other words, while the 'necessary conditions' lay in the characteristics of the indigenous (primarily Dravidian) inhabitants of the subcontinent, we also have to look to the role of conquest, force and violence in the process of the developing economic surplus to adequately explain the emergence of caste.

■ THE DEVELOPMENT OF CASTE SOCIETY: 'REVOLUTION AND COUNTER-REVOLUTION'

While we can identify 'proto-caste' features in the early Dravidian culture, the caste system itself emerged in a process linked with the consolidation of class (economic) divisions, patriarchy and the rise of the state. The development of Indian caste society is seen in different ways of different theories of caste. Generally the more conservative social science theories, like the legitimizing ideologizations of the system, have little to say about any processes or 'stages' of development but instead take the system as either essentially existing or evolving in a smooth, harmonious process. 'Racial' theories also have tended to take the system as a given; once Aryan conquest institutes it, the forms of oppression are fixed and remain more or less unchanged. Even the recent 'economic' and 'ecological' theories take it as relatively unchanging.

In contrast the main radical theories, including those influenced by Marxism, emphasize stages in the development of caste. For traditional Marxists this means simply seeing caste in terms of the 'superstructure' of the orthodox five stages (primitive communism, slavery, feudalism, capitalism, and socialism). Modern variations on this include Dipankar Gupta, seeing varna as the superstructure of Asiatic society and jati as the superstructure of feudal society. Sharad Patil similarly uses an adaption of the five stages, which he identifies as matriarchal society, das-slave society (characterized by varnas; this itself is broken up into various types and sub-stages), and jati-feudal society beginning with the rise of states. Strikingly, one of the most interesting adaptions, apparently independent of Marxism, is Ambedkar's 'Revolution and Counter-Revolution', which divides the pre-Muslim period as divided into stages of (a) 'Brahmanism' (the Vedic period), (b) 'Buddhism', connected with the rise of the first Magadha–Mauryan states and representing a revolutionary denial of caste inequalities; and (c) 'Hinduism', or the counter-revolution which consolidates Brahman dominance and the caste hierarchy. All of these approaches share a concern for looking at caste in terms of uneven development, contradiction and radical and violent changes.

Generally we can identify four main periods following pre-class (or 'proto-caste') society, marked by specific features of the development of Indian social structure (including specific economic structures or 'class' forms, caste, patriarchy and the state): (a) the nearly 500 years of the Indus civilization; (b) the millennia-long period from its fall and the ascendency of the Indo-Europeans to the Gangetic valley states; (c) a second millennium stretching up to the consolidation of caste-feudalism and characterized by conflict between major 'religious' traditions of Hinduism, Buddhism and Jainism; (d) the period of medieval caste-feudalism characterized by the dominance of Hinduism and the later entry of Islam, stretching from the sixth-tenth centuries AD to colonial rule. All of these saw important developments and changes in the caste system.

The Indus civilization—one of the oldest in the world with impressive achievements in two major cities and numerous towns scattered over a huge geographical region—was the starting point for what we know as 'Indian civilization'. Unfortunately, because its script is not yet deciphered, we have little direct evidence of its social structure and cultural practices. The main language was almost certainly Dravidian. It was clearly a stratified society, with large and small houses indicating a major division into rich and poor. Yet the relatively weak development of weapons and the absence of other evidences of state machinery suggest that the major integrating role was played by cultural–religious unity rather than state power.[22] A proto-Shiva god and a goddess appear on many of the famous seals, and the earlier numerical predominance of female figurines suggests a matrilineal–matricentric heritage. Money was absent, and some archeologists believe that trade was carried on by special groups of wandering nomads, a development of earlier socially-mediated exchange between different types of production groups. It has also been argued that the famous granaries of Mohenjodaro and Harappa were, in analogy to the village grain-heap, repositories of agricultural produce distributed under administrative control to different groups who claimed by social tradition a share of the produce, a kind of precursor of the *jajmani* system.[23]

Finally, the uniformity of artisan products over a wide geographical territory is noted, 'so marked that it is possible to typify each craft with a single set of examples drawn from one site alone . . . the uniformity of forms and painted decorations which they display cannot be accounted for by trade'.[24] This suggests the existence of caste-like groups of occupational specialists, maintaining endogamy and cultural traditions over a wide territory while producing locally.

Thus, while there is as yet no direct evidence regarding the social system of the Harappans, there is indirect evidence that the 'proto-caste' features of subcontinental and Dravidian culture were carried forward among them. However, the transformation of the 'sacred' and 'dangerous' into the 'impure', something that has to be dominated and bound, seems to require the solidification of dominance in state power and warrior control. And these state and military features were conspicuously minimal in the Indus civilization, in comparison with all other earlier city–state societies.

After the coming of the Aryans we have better linguistic and literary evidence, though it has to be cautiously analyzed.[25] The Aryan advent cannot be simply understood as a conquest over equalitarian indigenous peoples which gave rise to the caste system. Nevertheless, 'Aryans' and 'conquest' did play a role. The Indo-Europeans were a patrilineal people, in contrast to local matrilineal traditions, though their patriarchy, tribal and statist, gave certain freedom to women. Once, however, they absorbed the notions of 'sacred power' and 'danger' associated with women and low castes in the Dravidian tradition, the resulting patriarchal synthesis in the context of group conflict was far more complete and violent in its control of women. Similarly, the tribal or lineage inequalities that intensified among Vedic people as they spread throughout India were not really 'caste-like',[26] but once they absorbed the 'proto-caste' features among the indigenous culture and various groups fought for dominance of the system, a caste hierarchy developed. *Chaturvarnya* did not actually describe existing social groups, but was rather an ideology overlaying the very different processes of transformation of 'proto-caste' tribal groups into jatis. In this Brahmans played a key role—Brahmans who derived both ethnically and culturally from indigenous as well as Aryan priestly groups, but who identified with the Aryans as they sought to legitimize and extend the total system of dominance and exploitation associated with caste in a period of developing production, surpluses and economic inequalities.

There was neither exactly an 'Aryan invasion' or an 'Aryan conquest'; it would be wrong to see the Aryans as a consistent ethnic group throughout (many scholars in fact describe two waves of entry, the less patriarchal 'pre-Vedic' Aryans who gave rise to the 'outer ring' of Indo-European languages such as Marathi, Bengali, Oriya, etc., and the Vedic Aryans).[27] The Indus civilization did not fall as a result of Aryan raids, but rather, apparently, through environmental degradation associated with deforestation and changing river courses; the Aryans may have given the finishing touch. They appear on the Indian scene as fairly flexible groups ready to adapt to local customs. A horse-driving, cattle-herding people, they adopted not only wheat and rice cultivation from indigenous Dravidian and Mundari peoples, they also intermarried frequently. Not only do the Shudras derive mainly from absorbed and dominated indigenous groups, the major twice-born varnas also had mixed origins. Large numbers of Brahmans were absorbed from pre-Aryans; the common term for merchant, *vani*, apparently derives from a term *pani* used for the richer of the pre-Aryan enemies; even a number of Ksatriyas may have had pre-Aryan or mixed origins—and one linguist suggests that both the terms 'Bharat' and 'Satavahana' derive from symbols meaning 'office-bearer' used for a Harappan ruling clan.[28]

With the period of the rise of the state in the Gangetic valley in the middle of the first millennium BC caste inequalities appear as more crystallized and began to get the stamp of legitimacy with the development of Brahmanic Hinduism, symbolized finally in the laws of Manu. In these, extreme forms of the subordination of women and Shudras were sanctioned, and Brahmans claimed superiority at the top of a hierarchy of purity–pollution and occupational specialization.

However, this period of the rise of the Magadha–Mauryan states has been characterized by Ambedkar as that of the 'Buddhist revolution' which was revolutionary in transcending Vedic tribal particularism and in denying caste and gender inferiority;[29] and at least some evidence shows that it inaugurated a long period of contention for dominance. As Thapar, for instance, points out, the Magadha–Mauryan area was seen as anti-Brahman or *mleccha* territory,[30] while early Buddhist literature (argued by scholars such as Uma Chakravarty to give a more accurate depiction of the society) shows inequality neither in the form of *varna* or *jati* but rather in 'class-like' categories such as the *gahapati* and *daskammakara* groups.[31] The Mauryan state had large areas of statist administration, with state-controlled lands and factories intermixed with privately controlled production. There is no evidence of the *jajmani* system for a long period, rather guilds were predominant. Further, even when we see signs of caste consolidation in northern India, the Satavahana era in the Deccan indicates a much more open, flexible, less caste-ridden society, as we shall see in chapter 2.

It is really only during the sixth to tenth century AD period, which scholars such as R.S. Sharma and Kosambi identify as the development of 'feudalism', that we see the definitive consolidation of Hinduism as the dominant religion using state power to maintain itself, the *jajmani*-linked village economy, land grants to Brahmans (and to other intermediaries) as a major element in 'feudal' tendencies, and the marking out of untouchables as a separately defined excluded group 'outside the village'. One scholar argues, for the case of south India, that this was a violent process:

Tamil literature makes it painfully clear that the foundations of the medieval synthesis were soaked in blood from battles that established the temple-centered, devotional Brahmanical religious ceremonial practice at the centre of the agrarian order . . . . The Sanskritic and temple-centered character of Tamil verse during medieval times distinguishes it sharply from earlier epochs and nourishes a popular belief in Tamil Nadu today that medieval South India succumbed to an invasion of Brahmans from the north.[32]

The long interregnum of a thousand years between the emergence of the first states in the Gangetic valley and the consolidation of the Brahmanic–Hindu social order suggests that the identification of 'Indian' culture with 'Hinduism' is badly mistaken, that the dominance of Hinduism was not so easily achieved and perhaps not inevitable, and that elements of revolt and opposition remained strong from the beginning. In this sense, though he does not take into account changes in production systems and the exploitativeness of the non-Hindu early states, Ambedkar's metaphor of 'Revolution and Counter-Revolution' makes the crucial point: the caste system came to dominance in India in a process of turmoil, warfare, contradiction and conflict. In particular, we may see its consolidation as a result of the alliance of Brahmanism (including both ideological forces and the temple and other religious institutions) and state power, of the coming together of Brahmans and the amorphous set of powerholders, chieftains and rajas of various caste and tribal origins who had their power confirmed in the emerging medieval synthesis.

■ Caste-Feudal Society

What exactly was the nature of this medieval synthesis? While Marxist activists have had no doubt that it was 'feudal' and early Marxist historians such as D.D. Kosambi and R.S. Sharma supported this position, more recently the notion of feudalism has been attacked. Influential works have been Burton Stein's analysis of Chola rule in Tamil Nadu as a 'peasant state' and Harbans Mukhia's argument that a basically 'free peasantry' controlled their own production process and developed improved agricultural technology while the state appropriated a portion of the surplus through 'coercive noneconomic means', so that conflict between peasants and powerholders was outside the production process and over the amount of revenue.[33]

In the ensuing debate, a number of points have come forward which make it clear that the Indian agrarian structure has to be characterized as 'caste-feudal' to capture its specificity.

1 There seems to be a general agreement, including Kosambi, Sharma and others, that the caste-defined village economy was becoming consolidated by the late first millennium: that is, what is known as the *jajmani* system in northern India, *balutedari* in Maharashtra and *ayagar* in the Dravidian areas.[34] This apparently replaced neither a slave economy (as Mukhia tends to picture it) nor a more independent economy based on Vaishya and *gahapati* peasants (as Sharma depicts it), but a mixed and open economy with some areas of slave production and in other areas both peasants and large landowners using hired labour and linked with trade and artisan guilds. The 'feudal' caste-defined village was not really that of a 'free peasantry', though peasants and artisans can be said to have controlled their means of production; rather, there was a strong element of caste-bondage. Basic producers were split into jatis performing defined caste duties and having on that basis a presumed right both to shares in the harvest as well as various social-religious perquisites. It is important to stress that *corvee* labour in India, or what is known as *vethbegar* or *vethi* was normally heavily caste-linked and defined in terms of such traditional caste duties. The degree of actual unfreedom of course varied, by area and caste, with Dalits suffering the heaviest bondage.

2 The state did not simply appropriate revenue through 'coercive' means; legal-ideological formalities playing the same functional role as 'property rights' differentiated it from a pure bandit state. While it did not have 'ownership' rights in the land, it did have legitimized claims to a definite share of the produce and the labour (performed as a caste-duty) which went into this and which was at times directly given as labour-service. But the 'state' was no bureaucratic machine that simply appropriated its share, nor was it an amorphous collection of looters; instead its share of various portions of it were continually alienated to local power-holders; the claim to be able to alienate rights in this way was, in fact, as one historian has argued, part of the claim to be a ruler.[35] These claims to the surplus, identified as *watan* rights in Maharashtra, as *amara* in Vijayanagar, were the central feature underlying the 'legal' claims of the intermediaries (later to be identified

collectively as 'zamindars') in the Indian version of feudalism.[36] Thus coercion linked with its ideological justification as upholder of *varnashrama dharma*, the basic Brahmanic ideology, was central to the medieval Indian state. And the powerholders of this political system (equivalent to 'feudal lords') were, along with Brahmans, the crucial section of the exploiting class.

3 If we are to characterize the 'ruling castes' of the caste-feudal system as 'Brahman' and 'Ksatriya', it has to be noted that 'Brahman' denotes both status (varna) and jati (or a set of jatis), while 'Ksatriya' denotes only a status. In most parts of India and for most periods in history these powerholders were drawn not from recognized 'Ksatriya' jatis such as Rajputs but from Shudra jatis, mainly from the Shudra jatis who were otherwise peasant cultivators, and sometimes from Adivasi tribes; it was their holding of power that gave them Ksatriya status. In spite of Burton Stein, this did not make India a 'peasant state' any more than it made it a 'Shudra state'. These concepts rest on a caste/class confusion. Toiling members of jatis some of whose members held political power might claim from this a higher ('Ksatriya', 'sat-Shudra') status and have pretentions to share in dominance, but (while such status did make some difference in daily life relations) this did not make them any less exploited. The blanket application of such categories as 'dominant caste' or 'managerial castes' can only be made by avoiding any analysis of production relations and surplus extraction.

4 This caste-feudal society was not a society of 'self-sufficient villages' in which the main exploiters were the dominant elite at the village level. Such a view neglects the wider context of a complex, highly productive and politically and socially sophisticated feudal society. First, the material base, the varied ecological niches and their interrelationship has to be noted. India had tracts of very rich agricultural production, centred on the river valleys and deltas and producing a large surplus with a highly stratified social order as well as drier agricultural areas characterized by a more egalitarian peasantry; the geographically largest area was under grasslands, shrub or forests. All of these had not only their own specific forms of production/extraction, but also material as well as social interrelations. Caste relations in traditional India included not only the *jajmani* relations internal to the village, but also relations

of exchange between villagers, forest dwellers, herders of the grasslands, and various other types of producers or gatherers.[37] These relations of exchange and most intra-village *jajmani* relations, though involving aspects of dominance and hierarchy, can be distinguished from the relations of exploitation which involved the extraction of surplus from the land and forest for the appropriation of exploiting sections.

Where the lines of exploitation lay varied according to region. In the relatively drier villages the situation is clearest. Here hierarchy existed but inequalities were less; peasants laboured on their own land; even Dalit labourers generally had claims to land (usually as *watan* lands given in return for their caste-service), while it was only state officials—jagirdars, inamdars, talukdars, *deshmukhs*, *desais*—who could be called anything like non-labouring 'landlords' or 'feudal lords'. (Forest-settled tribal villages represented an extreme case of this type.) The village headmen and accountants (*patils* and *kulkarnis* in Maharashtra) occupied a dual position, functioning sometimes as the lowest linchpin of the state power and benefiting from this, sometimes acting as *primus inter pares* or representatives of a village peasant brotherhood. Within this 'formal' structure, as surplus production grew, individual families could accumulate wealth and power; Frank Perlin has shown how in seventeenth century Maharashtra big families of both Brahman and Kunbi-Maratha background could use the accumulation of such *watandari* rights to form large estates.[38] But these were clearly different from the majority peasant communities of the village. They became part of the exploitative feudal structures as individuals or families, not as members of particular castes (in contrast to Brahmans, who as a caste were a part of the exploitative sections). Caste inequality certainly lay in the fact that the so-called 'dominant peasants'—Kunbis, Jats, Kammas, Reddis—were more likely to produce families who attained such power; but the powerholders also came from lower castes, even on rare occasions from those classed as 'untouchables'.

In the richer, irrigated villages we do seem to have 'landlord elites', at least by the end of the medieval period, including non-Brahmans as well as Brahmans. The most notable case are the Rajputs of the Gangetic valley, the Nairs of Kerala, and the Vellalas of Tamil Nadu who were primarily non-labouring managers of land and irrigation works, dominating a complex society and with near slave-like castes of Dalit labourers doing the main work on the fields. Ludden writes of the latter,

> In stark contrast with the dry zone, the wet zone was not a land of rustic warrior-peasants, but of two distinct peasant strata: one owned land, but did not labour; the other laboured without owning even, in many cases, the rights to its own labour power . . . [But] farms were small, they were worked with premodern technology; they were worked as a way of life and not as a business for profit. Farmers were, moreover, subject to taxation by ruling elites. Many peasant attributes thus apply to farmers within wet communities, though they comprised two strata, indeed two classes, defined objectively by relative access to the means of production and subjectively by their caste identity.[39]

There was still a fundamental difference between 'Brahman' and 'non-Brahman' villages, seen if we look at how the surplus was claimed. The crop was divided first into the *melvaram* ('upper share') and *kilvaram* ('lower share'). The former was controlled by the ruling elite of the locality, the *nattar* and was frequently assigned to Brahmans; out of this in fact the Brahman-controlled villages came to exist. The *nattar* were derived from the local Vellala peasantry, but this did not mean that that peasantry as such shared in the rule; in fact the division suggests that Vellala landholders always had to give a share of the crop to the rulers, while Brahman landholders did not. Peasants who cultivated the land or those who managed and supervised cultivation got the lower share. It seems the Vellalas were originally cultivating peasants and only as production and surplus increased did their role change to managing and supervising dependent labourers and tenants. The fact that they continued to give a large 'upper share' to powerholders showed their on-going subordination; Brahmans almost always lived off the upper share and only rarely did the supervisory tasks associated with the lower share.[40]

Thus, even in the case of the highly stratified villages of the irrigated river valleys and plains a fundamental distinction can be drawn between those whose labour contributed to the production of wealth and those who—as religious functionaries, predators and state officials—lived off this wealth. Land and its products provided the main source of wealth, but those who worked and managed the land (even when this involved managing the labour of inferior workers on the land and taking the products of craftsmen for use on the land) also had to turn over a major share of this wealth.

It was state power which gave the ability to claim this surplus. Its linkage to irrigation systems and land management is still relatively unresearched; while traditional states clearly took a responsibility for the maintenance of water systems and forests, much of water management activity was carried on at the village level. Thus, relations of violence and domination embodied in the state, and secondarily the cultural relations embodied in religious institutions, played key roles in the extraction of surplus. And this is true whether we are talking of the extreme village hierarchies of the highly productive irrigated river valleys and deltas or the less differentiated rural communities of dry lands, grasslands, forests and hills. In caste terms it can be said that Brahmans benefited from and lived off this surplus as communities (jatis) whereas the non-Brahmans who became 'lords' and rulers or state officials in the system did so as powerful individual family-clans. In this limited sense it can be said that the distinction between 'Brahman–non-Brahman' was a fundamental one, and that peasants, even when they were a 'dominant caste', were basically a part of the exploited sections.

At the same time, wherever we look in the traditional Indian system, hierarchy and inequality among the exploited stands out clearly. Such inequality existed among all feudal societies (it has been estimated, for instance, that in medieval Europe nearly one-third of all peasant families were landless); but in India it was institutionalized in the caste system. Cultivating peasants with firm rights to the 'lower share' or to supervising the village distribution of the 'grainheap' were at the top of village hierarchies; artisans and subordinate tenants had rights that were both institutionalized and secondary; herders and forest-dwelling hunters and gatherers exchanged sometimes on a basis of inferiority, sometimes with more independence; but everywhere the lowest castes of Dalits/untouchables performed the most menial labour and were fundamentally differentiated from the others in being classed as 'impure'.

■ CONCLUSION: DALITS AND THE ANTI-CASTE STRUGGLE

The lines of exploitation in pre-British India, as defined in terms of the production, extraction and accumulation of surplus, were structured through the caste system or *jati vyavastha*. This identified a particular caste division of labour involving specific forms of hierarchy among the exploited, with at least three major groups identified in most villages: toiling peasant castes, most of whom were simply cultivators but with some 'village management' powers held by a dominant lineage (*biradari, bhauki*); artisans and service castes performing particular caste-duties within a *jajmani–balutedari* system; and (often lowest among those classed as *balutedars*) a large caste of general labourers working for the village and its dominant sections and classed as 'untouchable'. Tribals and pastoralists outside the villages were also among the exploited sections.

The unique position of 'untouchables' was not simply in living outside the village and performing the most 'polluted' occupations; it was also that their position within the caste division of labour made them the most exploited. This is not simply a matter of a traditional 'caste occupation'. Looking only at occupation, the Chamars of north India would have their analogue in the Chambhars of Maharashtra and the Madigas of Andhra in that all were traditionally leather workers. But more important was the *functional* position of Chamars in the caste division of labour, in being general village servitors, similar to the Mahars of Maharashtra. Nearly everywhere in India there was one large 'untouchable' caste which performed this role, working as field labourers (and in almost slave-like conditions in the hierarchical irrigated villages) and as general village servants working for the village headman as well as visiting 'state' officials. This gave them a key labouring role both in terms of agricultural production and as servants of the wider state machinery. They were the most clearly 'proletarianized' segment of the exploited within a wider system of exploitation.

The 'exploited' as a whole included a very wide range of castes, the broad 'toiling caste' majority. Clearly it was a system which had built-in contradictions among the exploited. Dalit labourers suffered from the domination of village peasants; they also faced exclusion and oppression from all caste Hindus, even from castes themselves ranked very low in the hierarchy. In addition there were often two major 'untouchable' castes in a single region (Mahars and Mangs in Maharashtra, Chamars and Chuhras in north India, Malas and Madigas in Andhra) who were traditionally competitors, opposed to each other and claiming a higher status in the hierarchy. These divisions and contradictions to some extent justify the characterization of caste as having a *retarding* effect on 'class struggle' in that it institutionalized divisions among the exploited.

However, the other side of the picture must not be forgotten. The existence of relatively large jatis at various levels among the exploited represented groups united by social ties who could play a leading role in revolt around which other groups, large and small, could rally. Both 'peasant' jatis (Jats, Kunbis, etc.) and the large Dalit jatis could play this kind of 'vanguard' role, with the difference that the greater proletarianization of the Dalits would tend to make their struggles more revolutionary. 'Peasant' jatis were also exploited, also had an interest in revolt; but this was often modified because of their relative privilege even as exploited toilers and because of the ease for their leaders to gain a share in dominance. 'Peasant–jati revolt', the crucial form of struggle in the pre-British period, could be a powerful force when directed against central state power (as in the case of the 1857 revolt, perhaps, or in the rising of Kunbi peasants under Shivaji), but it could also be directed into simply the establishment of a new level of feudal intermediaries (as in the thesis that the eighteenth century was one of a kind of 'rise of the gentry' in which Jats, Marathas under the Peshwas and others simply created new feudal states).[31] (This of course, can also be said of peasant revolt in societies like China.) Dalit revolt, in contrast, was more likely to be 'anti-systemic' and perhaps for this reason is hard to trace as a collective factor in the pre-British period.

'Caste struggle', like 'class struggle' could become revolutionary only when it could pose an alternative, a more advanced system, rather than being simply a negative protest or a competitive struggle for more economic or social–cultural rights within the framework of exploitation. But whether it could do so obviously depended upon the possibilities of the historical conjuncture. In the early era of transition when the caste system of exploitation was being constituted, the limitations of the anti-systemic role of religions like Buddhism and Jainism were that they could not be linked to a more productive historical system. (The Buddhist sangha, as many commentators have noted, embodied equalitarian and collective features from the tribal period, but only as a refuge from the world; Buddhism also tended to be linked with the more mercantile, open kingdoms of the period.) During the period of the medieval synthesis after the defeat of these 'heterodox' religions only a negative rebellion appears to have been possible, represented by the bhakti cults which embodied aspirations to equality but accepted a Hindu framework for this-worldly social interaction.

It was only from the time of British rule and the rise of a capitalist–industrial society that a more equalitarian and more productive society became a historical possibility and was posed as such in the ideologies of radical democracy and socialism. This period saw the rise of new working class struggles, the taking on of new forms in peasant struggles, but it also saw a new anti-caste revolt which was increasingly spearheaded by a Dalit liberation movement.

NOTES

1. For the most important classic studies of caste see Emile Senart, *Caste in India: The Facts and the System* (London: Macmillan, 1930; originally published 1896 in French); Celestin Bougle, *Essays on the Caste System*, translated by D.F. Pocock (Cambridge: Çambridge University Press, 1971, originally published 1908); Max Weber, *The Religion of India: The Sociology of Hinduism and Buddhism* (Glencoe: The Free Press, 1954); Arthur Hocart, *Caste: A Comparative Study* (New York: Russell and Russell, 1950); J.H. Hutton, *Caste in India: Its Nature, Function and Origin* (Bombay: Oxford University Press, 1969, first published 1946); Herbert Risley, *The People of India* (Calcutta: Thacker, Spink and Company, 1908); Nripendra Kumar Dutt, *Origin and Growth of Caste in India* (London: Kegan Paul, Trench and Trabner, 1931); Louis Dumont, *Homo Hierarchus* (Chicago: University of Chicago Press, 1971); McKim Marriot and Ronald Inden, 'Caste Systems', *Encyclopedia Britannica* (1974) and 'Towards an Ethnology of South Asian Caste Systems', in Ronald Inden, (ed.), *The New Wind* (Mouton: The Hague, 1977); M.N. Srinivas, 'The Dominant Caste in Rampura', *American Anthropologist* 61, 1959; 'The "Untouchables" of India', *Scientific American* December 1965; and 'A Note on Sanskritization and Westernization', *Far Eastern Quarterly*, 15, No. 4, August 1956; David Mandelbaum, *Society in India*, two volumes, (Berkeley: University of California Press, 1972); W.H. Wiser, *The Hindu*

Jajmani System (Lucknow: Lucknow Publishing House, 1936); Thomas Beidelman, *A Comparative Analysis of the Jajmani System* (Association for Asian Studies, Monographs, 1959); Pauline Kolenda, 'Toward a Model of the Hindu Jajmani System', *Human Organization*, 22, 1, 1963; and *Caste in Contemporary India; Beyond Organic Solidarity* (Menlo Park, California: Benjamin-Cummings, 1978).

2. Jotirao Phule, *Samagra Wangmay* (Bombay: Government of Maharashtra, 1991); for English translations see Jotirao Phule, *Selected Writings, Volume I: Slavery*, translated P.G. Patil (Bombay: Government of Maharashtra, 1991); for accounts of his work see Rosalind O'Hanlon, *Caste, Conflict and Ideology: Mahatma Jotirao Phule and Low Caste Social Protest in the Nineteenth Century* (Cambridge: Cambridge University Press, 1985). For an exposition of Phule's historical materialism see Gail Omvedt, 'Jotiba Phule and the Analysis of Peasant Exploitation', in *Jotiba Phule: An Incomplete Renaissance* (Surat: Centre for Social Studies, 1991).

3. See the introduction to Omvedt, p. vi.

4. Important recent Marxist arguments include Joan Mencher, 'The Caste System Upside Down, or the Not-So-Mysterious East', *Current Anthropology* 15, 1974, and Claude Meillasoux, 'Are There Castes in India?' *Economy and Society* 3, 1973; the title suggests the basic perspective, argued in part against the 'homo hierarchus' position of the uniqueness of India: India is like the rest of the world, class and exploitation are dominant, the oppressed don't necessarily accept the values of their exploiters and so on.

5. See for instance, Goran Djurfeldt and Staffan Lindberg, *Behind Poverty: The Social Formation in a Tamil Village* (London: Curzon Press, 1972); and Ashok Upadhyaya, 'Class Struggle in Rural Maharashtra (India): Towards a New Perspective', *Journal of Peasant Studies*, 2, 7, January 1980; Gail Omvedt, 'Caste, Class and Land in India: An Introductory Essay', in Omvedt, (ed.), *Land, Caste and Politics in Indian States* (Delhi: Authors Guild, 1982); Partha Chatterjee, 'Caste and Subaltern Consciousness', in Ranjit Guha (ed.), *Subaltern Studies 6* (Delhi: Oxford University Press, 1989).

6. In taking 'varna' as the superstructure of the Asiatic mode and 'jati' as superstructure of feudalism, Dipankar Gupta simply provided another variation of this basic model; see *From Varna to Jati: The Indian Caste System from the Asiatic to the Feudal Mode of Production* (Montreal: McGill University Working Paper 22, 1978).

7. Sharad Patil, *Das-Shudra Slavery, Volume I* (Delhi: Allied Publishers, 1980) and *Das-Shudra Slavery, Volume II* (Poona: Sugawa Publications, 1990); 'Caste and Class', *Economic and Political Weekly*, Special Number, February 1979). See also the writings of Kancha Ilaiah, especially 'wealth, Patriarchy and Culture', *Frontier*, 21 March 1987.

8. Madhav Gadgil and Ramchandra Guha. *This Fissured Land· An Ecological History of India* (Delhi: Oxford University Press, 1992). For an important new discussion of the relation of caste to India's economic structure, also essentially arguing for its function in maintaining a stagnant economy but extending this into a critique of India's post-colonial development policies, see Deepak Lal, *The Hindu Equilibrium Volume I: Cultural Stability and Economic Stagnation, India 1500 BC–AD 1980* (London: Oxford University Press, 1988.)

9. Bharat Patankar, *Mudda Ahe Jag Badalnyaca* ('The Point is to Change the World') (Bombay: Shalaka Prakashan 1989) gives a Marathi exposition of the general theoretical approach used here.

10. Karl Marx, *Capital*, Volume III (New York: International Publishers, 1967), pp. 791–92.

11. Morton Klass, *Caste: The Emergence of the South Asian Social System* (Philadelphia: Institute for the Study of Human Issues, 1980).

12. Bridget and Raymond Allchin, *The Rise of Civilization in India and Pakistan* (Cambridge: Cambridge World Archeology Publications, 1982), p. 11.

13. Gregory Possehl, 'Lothal: A Gateway Settlement of the Harappan Civilization', in Possehl (ed.), *Ancient Cities of the Indus* (New Delhi: Vikas, 1974), pp. 217–18.

14. Morton Fried, *The Notion of Tribe* (Berkeley: Cummings Publishing House, 1975).

15. George Hart, *The Poems of Ancient Tamil* (Berkeley: University of California Press, 1975).

16. Burton Stein, *Peasant State and Society in Medieval South India* (Delhi: Oxford University Press, 1980), p. 56.

17. Hart, *Poems of Ancient Tamil*, pp. 132–33.

18. *Ibid.*, p. 122.

19. *Ibid.*, pp. 93–119.

20. Stephen Tyler, *India: An Anthropological Perspective* (San Francisco: Goodyear Publishing Company, 1983).

21. G. Kondos, 'The Triple Goddess and the Processual Approach to the World', in Michael Allen and S.N. Mukherjee (ed.), *Women in India and Nepal* (Australia ANU Monographs on South Asia, 1982).

22. See Walter Fairservice, 'The Origin, Character and Decline of an Early Civilization', in Possehl, *Ancient Cities of the Indus*.

23. Tyler, *India: An Anthropological Perspective*, pp. 68ff.

24. Allchin and Allchin, *The Rise of Civilization*, pp. 193, 197.

25. Patil's use of this material ignores many methodological rules, but it brings out some important aspects of patriarchal and sexual (clan, family) relations that have to be analyzed in connection with caste. For an important combination of literary–mythological and archaeological evidence, see Romila Thapar, *Ancient Indian Social History* (Delhi: Orient Longman, 1978) and *From Lineage to State Social Formations of the Mid-First Millennium BC in the Ganges Valley* (Bombay: Oxford, 1984).

26. See R.S. Sharma, *Shudras in Ancient India* (Delhi: Motilal Banarsidass, 1980) and Thapar, *Lineage to State*.

27. See chapter 2, note 1.

28. See Thapar, *Lineage to State*; Kosambi, *An Introduction to the Study of Indian History* (Bombay: Popular Prakastan, 1975), and Iravathan Mahadevan, 'Study of the Indus Script through Bi-Lingual Parallels', in Possehl, *Ancient Cities of the Indus*.

29. B.R. Ambedkar, *Revolution and Counter-Revolution in Ancient India, Writings and Speeches Volume 4* (Bombay: Government of Maharashtra, 1989).

30. Thapar, 'Image of the Barbarian in Early India', in her *Ancient Indian Social History*.

31. Uma Chakravarti, 'Towards a Historical Sociology of Stratification in Ancient India: Evidence from Early Buddhist Sources'. *Economic and Political Weekly*, 2 March 1985 and 'The Social Philosophy of Buddhism and the Problem of Inequality', *Social Compass*, 2–3, 1986.

32. David Ludden, *Peasant History in South India* (Princeton: Princeton University Press, 1985), pp. 204–5.

33. Stein, *Peasant state and Society*; Harbans Mukhia. 'Was there Feudalism in Indian History?' *Journal of Peasant Studies*, 8, 3, April 1981 and the replies published in a second special issue of this journal 12, 2–3, 1985 on 'Feudalism and NonEuropean Societies', especially R.S. Sharma, 'How Feudal was Indian Feudalism?' T.J. Byres, 'Modes of Production and Non-European Colonial Societies'; Irfan Habib, 'Classifying Precolonial India'; Burton Stein, 'Politics, Peasants and the Deconstruction of Feudalism in Medieval India'; Frank Perlin, 'Concepts of Order and Comparisons with a Divergence on Counter-Ideologies and Corporate Institutes in Late Pre-Colonial India'; and Harbans Mukhia, 'Peasant Production and Medieval Indian Society' in that issue.

34. Sharma, 'How Feudal was Indian Feudalism', p. 36; Kosambi, *Introduction*, pp. 306–8; Kathleen Gough, 'Modes of Production in Southern India', *Economic and Political Weekly*, Annual Number, 1980, reporting a system of paying village servants and 'slaves' from the crop share from Chola times onwards (p. 343). Stein, in 'Vijayanagar', *Cambridge Economic History of India*, Volume I (Cambridge: Cambridge University Press, 1982), pp. 110–12, argues that the *ayagar* system was consolidated in the Vijayanagar state but had its roots in earlier Hoysala and Kakatiya kingdoms.

35. Andre Wink, *Land and Sovereignty in India: Agrarian Society Under the 18th Century Maratha Svarajya* (Cambridge: Cambridge Oriental Publications, 1986).

36. Perlin, 'Concepts of Order'; Kotani Kiroyuki, 'The Vatan System in the 16th–18th Century Deccan: Towards a New Concept of Indian Feudalism', *Acta Asiatica*, 48 (Tokyo: Toho Gakkai, 1985).

37. Along with Gadgil and Guha, *This Fissured Land*, see the section on 'Caste and Environment' in *The State of India's Environment 1984–85; The Second Citizen's Report* (Delhi: Centre for Science and Technology, 1985), pp. 162–67 and Madhav Gadgil and Kailash Malhotra, 'Adaptive Significance of the Indian Caste System: An Ecological Perspective', *Annals of Human Biology*, 10, 5, 1983, pp. 465–78.

38. Frank Perlin, 'Extended Class Relations, Rights and the Problems of Rural Autonomy in the Eighteenth Century Maratha Deccan', Journal of Peasant Studies, 5, 2, 1978.

39. Ludden, *Peasant History*, Princeton, pp. 93–94.

40. Stein, *Peasant State and Society*, pp. 167–69.

41. Wink, *Land and Sovereignty*.

Appendix: Redefining Class

The 'class–caste' question, which is a subject of much political and theoretical debate today in India, cannot be resolved simply by adding a conceptualization of 'caste' to a taken-for-granted 'class analysis'. It requires a rethinking of a total methodology, of class also.

'Class', as many have argued, is not a fundamental concept of Marxism; the analysis of exploitation, of surplus value, of forces and relations of production, are much more basic. Nevertheless 'class' has become, socially, almost an identifying concept of radical socialist movements and of Marxist analysis. Socialists are those who believe that 'all history is the history of class struggle'; Marxists are those who theorize by giving a 'class analysis' which deciphers the meaning of political and social events in terms of the interests of bourgeois, proletarian, petty bourgeois, etc., groups involved.

Nevertheless, Marxism is in a state of theoretical crisis today, and much of this is involved with the problem of 'class analysis' itself. 'Class' in fact is a term that is used by Marxists in rather different ways. At one level it has a broad, sometimes almost metaphorical or poetic, meaning referring to exploitation and the fight against exploitation, contradiction and conflict. In this broad sense, it indicates an identification with the oppressed and exploited and with their struggles, an affirmation that their struggles have a meaning and a reality; we might say that in the broad sense 'class' simply refers to exploitation, to the groups that are defined in the social processes of production, extraction and appropriation of surplus labour. Any fight against exploitation is thus a 'class struggle' and any movement for liberation, because it has to confront an exploitative system, must be a class struggle.

In the more strict sense, 'class' is defined in terms of ownership of the means of production and the argument for a 'class analysis' is that the most important contradiction and process of struggle is between those groups who toil and do not own the means of production, and those who are able to appropriate the fruits of toil without toiling themselves on the basis of their ownership and control.

The basic problem for Marxist analysis today is not so much that features other than 'class' (such as 'caste', 'gender', 'community' or 'race') are appearing as important social realities. If we limit ourselves to recognizing this we continue to fall into the trap of identifying these other realities as fundamentally 'non-economic'. Rather, it can be seen in the *non-coincidence of the narrow and the broad meanings of class*. That is, 'class' as defined in terms of private property (ownership versus non-ownership of the means of production) does not explain some very important processes of exploitation or the appropriation of surplus labour. Some owners are exploited (e.g., small peasants); some non-owners exploit (e.g., controllers of state property in societies described as 'socialist'; lords and upper castes in certain feudal societies). Proletarian husbands may benefit from the exploitation of their wives' unpaid labour. Moreover, many ecologists would even argue that nature itself can be 'exploited' in the double sense that resources from nature incorporated into the accumulation cycle increase the accumulation of capital, and that this has a destructive effect on the ecologies of regions that provide such resources.

Faced with this situation, two responses can be made. One is to try to extend the definition of 'class' to cover all cases of exploitation. There are various ways to do this. Using the concept of 'control' rather than 'ownership' the definition of capitalist can be broadened to cover the managers of state (and private) property who control production and accumulation and use these positions to enrich themselves. This is done by many Marxists who want to deal with the class nature of statist societies by describing them as 'state capitalist' or 'social imperialist'. Similarly, referring to 'conditions of production' rather than 'means of production' so as to broaden the definition of 'owners' to include those who possess or control all the various inputs and factors which make production possible. In relation to the peasantry this allows us to conceptualize the role of state officials, industrialists, etc., as capitalists in terms of capital accumulation.

An extensive description of such a way of extending the definition of both 'capitalist' and 'worker' particularly with regard to the peasantry, can be cited from Andrew Turton's analysis of class relations in rural Thailand in which great numbers of peasants

> who might *appear* to be possessors or owners of the means of production . . . should not be so regarded. For we need to consider what we understand by effective means and *conditions* of production in the new economic conjuncture, and what constitutes effective control over them . . . . Even when land is owned with full title . . . its use and value are often lost through neighboring mining or plantation activities, through the very crop imposed, through state forestry schemes, and the often illegal depredations of private capitalist timber companies, through the declaration of military training or war zones etc. Irrigation water is lost through deforestation, especially by capitalist enterprises, through hydro-electric schemes, preferential sale of water to factories, pollution by mines, factories and plantations, and even through tourist development. New inputs have become crucial new factors of production: new seeds, strains, breeds; fertilizers, pesticides, herbicides, machinery and petroleum products, mostly imported, and so on. These means are not owned, nor is their reproduction controlled, by the retail credit purchaser, any more than the crops themselves which are pre-contracted to the seller of inputs. There is also a whole cartel of

controlling factors, including technology, information and decision making, of which the inputs are the most visible products. The owners of *these* means of production are thus able to control the labour process, time, skill, health, even the family and community life, of the direct producers.[1]

In these ways, then, class is redefined so that the 'new class' controlling post-revolutionary societies are essentially capitalists; so are the bureaucrats and political leaders who control the inputs and access to land and other factors which make peasant production possible in many Third World societies; while the 'peasants' themselves are viewed as essentially labourers for capital. In a similar approach, Olle Tornquist's studies of communist failures in India and Indonesia, *What's Wrong with Marxism?* use an extended definition of 'rent capitalism' to look at state managers as accumulating capitalists.[2]

The problem with this form of broadening the definition of class is that it still accords a privilege to the 'core' definition (wage workers producing surplus value remain the defining centre of any class and accumulation processes); it is in a sense theoretically imperialist. We might compare it to the Vishwa Hindu Parishad definition of 'Hindu' which asserts that Sikhs, Jains, Buddhists, etc., are also Hindus but still manages to keep the 'sanatani Hindus' taking Rama as their god and following the authority of Brahmans as the defining centre of the religion. The problem with Marxists extending the definition of 'class' is that, in a similar vein, they are willing to accord exploited class status to peasants, women and other sections, but still give the 'privilege' in terms of exploitation to the factory proletariat.

There are other problems with the extended definitions. They still do not face the issue of incorporating 'nature' into the analysis of the process of capital accumulation: is nature exploited or not, in any meaningful sense?[3] Nor do they confront the major theoretical point coming out of the work of Maria Mies and others of the 'German school of ecofeminists', that the role of violence and force in exploitation and the primary accumulation being that of the forcible extraction of surplus from subsistence producers.[4] Even beyond this it can be argued that the primary 'relations of production' are those between producers and consumers; early non-exploitative societies are 'subsistence societies' in which production is for self-consumption, gradually extended through kin and other social networks to mediated exchange; and only with the breaking of these direct links and the establishment of an alienation between consumer and producer do exploitative 'relations of production' between owners/non-owners, producers/looters, etc., even begin. One of Marx's fundamental errors was, from this point of view, to treat consumption as simply passive, a reflection of production.

But even if we could extend the definition of class to cover all types of exploitative relations, there seems little point in doing so. What we are doing is redefining 'class' to be equivalent to exploitation, to positions in the process of producing, extracting and appropriating surplus (surplus labour, not surplus value). But if we do this, then it becomes clear that the concept of class becomes redundant. Using it may add rhetorical force; it may help us to claim all the emotional fervor that has historically been part of the conscious organization of 'class struggle', but it adds nothing to analysis. The basic issue is to analyze the processes of exploitation. Once this is done, the goal is achieved; we have helped define the struggle against exploitation. Calling the groups involved 'classes' and the struggle 'class struggle' adds only to our rhetoric, not to the analysis.

It seems better, therefore, to use 'class' in its narrow (and familiar) sense, and to make it clear that this does *not* define all forms of exploitation and that 'class struggles' are not the only forms of struggles against exploitation. Other struggles (of castes, women, communities of various types including oppressed nationalities) are also struggles against exploitation, they have inherently an economic aspect to them and cannot be defined as 'superstructural' and 'ideological' in contrast to a privileged class-economic form. The difference between these struggles and 'class' struggles is that they also are explicitly political, cultural, ethnic, etc., but their economic aspect cannot be sidelined.

'Class processes' and 'class struggles' then define those processes involved with the extraction of *surplus value*; this is certainly a crucial part of capital accumulation and with 'capitalism' as a world system it has moved to its centre. But being in the 'centre' does not mean it is the whole, and does not mean it can transform the whole. Capitalism as a system is not simply based upon the extraction of surplus value through wage labour; it rests fundamentally not so much on wage labour as on the commodity form, in which the direct links between producer and consumer are broken and the extraction of surplus from the direct producer in the form of the commodity (paid through wages or prices or not paid at all) forms and basis of capital accumulation.

Thus capital accumulation also includes processes of pure plunder, of extraction and underpricing, in underpricing, from nature, from peasants, from women involved in subsistence household production, even from entire communities. The sphere of surplus value and capitalist production in the narrow sense (manufacturing and processes of wage labour) rests on another, much larger sphere of exploitation in which natural products and surplus labour of those outside the spheres of capitalist production are brought into the cycle. Thus 'class struggle' in the narrow sense—of wage workers resisting extraction of surplus value and fighting to control the means of production at the centre—is not liberatory and will not break the system unless it is joined to the struggles of the communities, tribes, castes, women and others who are on its 'periphery'.

'Caste' refers to the crucial form in which community/ethnic-linked struggles take in the particular socio-historical context of South Asia; it has its material aspect in defining the processes of exploitation and appropriation of surplus labour, but these are also crucially linked to kinship and ideological factors. With the formation of caste society, direct subsistence production and equalitarian kinship-mediated exchanges of productions are replaced by exchange of (and claims to produce) produced by toilers who are considered duty-bound by birth to a particular function in the entire production system. Even when these exchanges may be relatively equal, or not highly unequal, in material terms, they involve oppression in the form of birth ascription; but they are also normally likely to become materially unequal, because they include ideological justifications for the accumulation of surplus by political powerholders who are assumed to play the role of upholders of the sacred *chaturvarnya* system and by Brahmans who are the symbols of purity in a presumed 'exchange' with the gods. Thus the caste system provides for the accumulation and consumption by non-producers who are the high castes in the system and the controllers of state power, and with the impact of colonialism these caste forms of production and accumulating surplus are partially maintained, partially transformed and utilized for channeling surpluses into the commodity chain and the centralized accumulation of the capitalist world system.

NOTES

1. Andrew Turton, 'Limits of Ideological Domination and the Formation of Social Consciousness', in Turton and Shigeharu Tanabe (ed.), *History and Peasant Consciousness in South East Asia* (Osaka, Japan, 1984), p. 34.
2. Olle Tornquist, *What's Wrong with Marxism? Volume 1: Capitalists and the State in India and Indonesia* (New Delhi: Manohar, 1989) and *Volume 2: Workers and Peasants in India and Indonesia* (New Delhi: Manohar, 1991).
3. James O'Connor, introduction to *Capitalism, Nature, Socialism*, 1,1, 1988.
4. Maria Mies, *Patriarchy and Accumulation*; Maria Mies, Claudia von Werlhoff and Veronica Bennholdt, *Women; The Last Colony* (New Delhi: Kali for Women Press, 1989).

CHAPTER 2

Caste, Region and Colonialism: The Context of Dalit Revolt

This study focuses on the Dalit movement in three specific states, Maharashtra, Andhra and Karnataka. In this chapter the specific context of the movement will be examined: first, its regional specificity, including geographical and social features and the most prominent castes among both Dalits and Shudras; and then the colonial transformation, which provided the immediate background to revolt.

■ THE DECCAN, GEOGRAPHICALLY AND HISTORICALLY

While we will look at similarities and differences among the three states studied here, it is also important to note what they have in common as a 'region' compared to other parts of India. Though one has an Indo-European language and the other two Dravidian, nevertheless Marathi is also considered to have a Dravidian 'substratum' and there are broad social structural features common to all three. These include what Iravati Karve has described as a 'southern' type of kinship system with preferential cross-cousin marriage among the main castes. In addition the 'three-way' caste division (Brahman, non-Brahman, Untouchable) seems particularly prominent here. There are no recognized 'Ksatriya' jatis anywhere in the south, and the three states (in contrast to the more inequalitarian hierarchies of Tamil Nadu and Kerala) are characterized by the dominance of large peasant jatis with landholding rights who historically supplied many of the zamindars and rulers but remained classed as 'Shudra' in the varna scheme. In addition, all three states have large and vigorous Dalit jatis.[1]

These three contiguous linguistic regions in many ways constitute a single larger geo-historical region, centred on the 'Deccan', the main part of penninsular India. In the north the Satpura and Vindhya mountains and the Narmada and Tapti rivers provided a relative barrier against influences from the mainly Hindi-speaking regions of north India; after Ashoka the penninsula was never really effectively ruled by northern-based kingdoms. From the major watershed of the Western Ghats (Sahyadris) the Deccan plateau slopes south-eastward, and the major rivers run from west to east. In the south, a broad dividing line marked by the watersheds of the Godavari and Krishna rivers (together with its tributary the Tungabhadra) separates the region from the southern-most Tamil and Malayalam-speaking regions; these, based on the more inequalitarian rice-growing coastal belts, with more prehistorical linkages to Sri Lanka and more isolated from the north, have had a somewhat separate historical development.[2]

The Deccan supra-region also has its irrigated rice-growing areas, the high-rainfall west coast (Konkan and Kanara) and the Godavari and Krishna deltas on the east coast. However, the Deccan plateau itself, with the Sahyadris blocking much of the monsoon rainfall, is hot and semi-arid. Maharashtra is marked by black lava soils especially in the west, Andhra and Karnataka by red soils; but the entire region has had as its primary economic base a herding economy linked to a dry-crop agriculture (millet—primarily jawar, bajra and ragi).

Historically and prehistorically, this region also has had a unique identity. The Allchins write that

it cannot be overemphasized that in Karnataka, Maharashtra and the Southern Nuclear Region the settlements of the third-second millennia appear to be ancestral to those which we encounter there from the beginnings of [written] history.[3]

They describe sites contemporaneous with the early Indus cultures of the north-west and centred on cattle-herding, or 'neolithic cattle pens' found in many forested areas. The latter have been located primarily in Kannada areas, but evidence for a cattle-centred herding economy is found throughout, and even after cultivation began (after about 2000 BC) herding still remained a crucial feature. The humped Indian cattle is believed to have been domesticated within this region, and, as Romila Thapar points out, 'Yadava' puranic traditions were associated with a western–southern India diffusion of cultures linked with a pastoral economy. Later ruling lineages (the Tulus, Rashtrakutas, Hoysalas, Yadavas of Devagiri and, it may be added, the later Mysore British-supported royal family, the Wodeyas) all claimed Yadava descent, and Thapar writes that 'the interest of this tradition lies in the coincidence of the diffusion of Black and Red Ware associated with the megalithic culture in the peninsula during the first millennium BC.'[4]

Prior to this period a 'chalcolithic' culture had developed mainly in the north Deccan (now Marathi-speaking), using copper and stone tools, growing various gains (rice, wheat, barley, etc.) and pulses, herding sheep and goats as well as cattle, using some cotton. Northern influences are visible in this and it is argued that Indo-European speakers may have arrived around this time (ca. 1500–1000 BC). However the important period of historical transition is what Thapar refers to as that of 'megalithic cultures' in the period 1000–500 BC, associated with the adoption of iron tools and weapons, a common pottery tradition, and the building of large megaliths or funerary monuments. Iron made possible the clearing of forests in the more fertile river valleys and thus a greater development of cultivation, and this laid the basis for a more settled village economy and the extraction of its surplus by a state-centred ruling class. Many archeologists believe that it was in this period of the spread of settled agriculture (rice in the coastal areas and millet and gram in others) that the major Dravidian languages stabilized in roughly their present area.[5]

This first Deccan civilization involved a mixture of northern influence and a Dravidian base. In this process the Dravidian element appears as dominant. Southworth has argued that even the term 'Yadava' is likely to have been Dravidian in origin, deriving from *yadu-van* or 'herding people'. Noting the contrast, established by linguists such as Grierson, between the 'outer group' of Indo-Aryan languages (Marathi, Bengali, Oriya, etc.) and 'inner group' languages such as Hindi, he describes the former as

> the earlier arrivals, who mixed more freely with the indigenous peoples, learned their language and adopted many of their customs (including cross-cousin marriage). The 'inner group', were the Vedic Aryans, the ones who from the beginning defended and propagated the ideas of caste, purity and hierarchy (as well as patriarchy).

These outer-ring languages, Southworth argues, embodied an amalgamation of cultures and ethnic streams from the time of the Indus Civilization. The 'pre-Vedic Aryans' were very likely present in the later phases of the Indus Civilization, among pastoralists who provided meat and milk to Harappan cities. After their fall, these mixed, outer group languages spread throughout much of India in the period 1700–500 BC 'as the most viable forms of intergroup and inter-regional communication'. With the rise to hegemony of the Vedic Aryans in north India in the same period,

> the stage was set for the consolidation of Aryan-speaking kingdoms throughout northern India, and the struggle between the orthodox Brahmanical Hinduism (propagated through Sanskrit) and the various dissident groups who used the more 'evolved' forms of Indo-Aryan.[6]

The greater equalitarianism and flexibility of southern society is also suggested in its first great state, that of the Satavahanas. While the Guptas may have represented (in Ambedkar's terms) a 'Hindu Counter-Revolution' in the north following the decline of the Mauryan empire, it was the Deccan that produced the largest empire in India for quite a long period:

> In 27 BC Magadha was conquered by the explosive power of the mighty Andhra (or Satavahana) dynasty of south India. Apparently originating somewhere between the penninsular rivers Godavari and Krishna, homeland of the Dravidian Telugu-speaking people . . . the great Andhra dynasty spread across

much of south and central India from the 2nd century BC to the 2nd century AD. Conquering the northwest Deccan region of Maharashtra, the Andhras later established their capital at Paithan on the Godavari . . . . The elder Pliny wrote of the 'andarae' as a 'powerful race' controlling numerous villages and at least thirty walled towns plus an army of 100,000 infantry, 2000 cavalry and 1000 elephants. For four and a half centuries after 200 BC, the mighty dynasty ruled India's midland, ranging north of the Vindhyas . . . and south to the Tungabhadra and Krishna rivers which divided them from Tamilnadu. Amravati on the banks of the Krishna, which was later the southeast capital of the Satavahanas, flourished in its trade with Rome, Ceylon and Southeast Asia, and may well have been the most prosperous city of India during the second century of the Christian era.[7]

Though they are called 'Andhras', the first known capital of the Satavahanas is Paithan in Maharashtra, and it is the Satavahana king Hala who is supposed to have been the author of the *Sattasai* or *Gatha Sapthasathi*, the first major work of Maharashtri Prakrit. This had important similarities in metre and theme with Tamil Sangam literature; indeed, according to Hart the main difference from early Tamil is in the lack of concern with chastity. The *Kamasutra*, that work of a luxuriant court life, was also composed under the Satavahanas, and Kosambi has argued that most of the Jatakas in fact come from this region and period. When it is added that the one Sanskrit play that depicts a peasant revolt against an unjust king (and centres around a courtesan, a woman depicted as leading a quite independent life), the *Mrchhakatika* or 'Little Clay Cart' also comes from this region, a general picture emerges of a less caste-ridden, more open and commercialized, relatively non-patriarchal, flexible society.[8] This may give some substance to Sharad Patil's argument that the Marathi region was characterized socially by matriarchy and matrilineal tribal social forms and religiously by the predominance of tantric cults.[9]

Along with this cosmopolitan orientation depicted in the literature, a religious pluralism seems evident. The patron deity of the Satavahanas was Khandaka (Khandoba), and while this fact seems sufficient for historians to describe them as 'Hindu' it is evident that Buddhism and Jainism flourished; the great caves of the

Western Ghats, primarily Buddhist and Jain throughout this period, were carved in this time.

As the location of the caves indicates, an important base for Satavahana prosperity was extensive trade with Rome, the Arab countries and South-east Asia, carried on through both west coast and east coast ports. The economy appears to have been highly commercialized, with craft production in guilds more than the *jajmani*-based production. Very likely it was based, agriculturally, on the type of *gahapati*-controlled production described by Chakravarti[10] in which substantial landholders quite often worked the land with *das-kammakara* hired labourers. But large areas were still under forest or grasslands covered by nomadic herdsmen; here tribal structures prevailed, though the tribes were in the process of being converted into jatis and subordinated in one way or another to state control. Buddhism and Jainism were associated with the commercialized agrarian economy, while it appears that 'hero cults' (or the *bhuta* cults as Da Silva describes them for Kanara) such as the gods Khandoba, Jotiba, etc., in Maharashtra were often associated with the transitional rural and forest-based or pastoral groups.[11]

The resurgence of Brahmanic Hinduism after the Satavahanas came in open and often violent combat with the 'heretical' religions of Jainism and Buddhism, which denied both god and the authority of the Vedas; but it could only compromise with and absorb the various indigenous hero cults and local gods and goddesses. In the far south the stabilization of Brahmanic Hinduism is linked to Pallava rule (sixth to ninth centuries), coming after the 'Kalabhra' interregnum, described in Brahmanic religious writings as a period of terror in which rulers were warrior-kings linked with Jainism from the semi-arid zones. Here we see violent and uncompromising confrontation linked to peoples of different areas as well as to religion and caste.[12] In the northern part of the penninsula, the kingdoms that succeeded the Satavahanas—the Chalukyas, the Rashtrakutas, etc.—also appear more clearly as 'Hindu'; the Rashtrakutas, who dominated the Deccan between the eighth and tenth centuries are renowned as builders of the great rock-hewn Kailasa temple of Siva at Ellora. However the Siva tradition with which they linked themselves could also express equalitarianism, as it did particularly with Basava of Karnataka (twelfth century) whose social radicalism involving the rejection of caste and Brahman dominance led to the formation of Veerashaivism, separating itself as a religion from Hinduism. The Mahanubhav cult in Maharashtra was similarly more radical than the later, and Vishnu-identified, Vithoba cult centred at Pandharpur.

In general, however, these equalitarian aspirations of the Saivite and Vaishnavite bhakti cults came later, after the absorbed popular cults were used to establish the hierarchical caste society. The dominance of Brahmanic Hinduism also meant feudalization, including the gradual emergence of a landlord 'gentry' (zamindars) through the land-grant process; the consolidation of the *jajmani/balutedari*-based village economy; the crystallization of untouchability with its definition of a most polluting and servile group; and the general use of the ideology of *varnashrama dharma* to legitimize the authority of Brahmans at the top and of the state which maintained dharma, and the performance of servile labour by the Shudras and Atishudras at the bottom. This dominance was crystallized with the rise of the regionally-based Hoysala, Yadava and Kakatiya kingdoms from the eleventh century.

Nevertheless, while these Marathi, Telugu and Kannada 'nationalities' were linked with an orthodox Hinduism caste-feudalism, there are powerful arguments (most recently brought forward for Maharashtra by Sharad Patil) that there were counter-posed equalitarian 'non-Brahman' trends in them, in Maharashtra marked by the tantric cult and sections of the bhakti movement, in Karnataka probably by Basava's Veerasaivism. The rise of Shivaji in the seventeenth century, in contrast to the Peshwa feudal restoration which followed him, has been described as a peasant-based revolt, fighting not only the Mughal overlords but Hindu–Maratha *watandari* feudalism, and with an intriguing tradition of anti-Brahmanism.[13]

■ THE JATIS: PEASANTS

One of the most striking common features throughout the three linguistic regions is, as noted, the nature of their major castes, in particular the most numerous 'peasant' and Dalit jatis.

The main peasant jatis, the Kunbi-Marathas of Maharashtra, the Vokkaligas in Karnataka (including many Lingayats who are in origin Vokkaligas) and the Kapus, Kammas, Velamas and Telaga of Andhra, are named from vernacular terms having to do with agriculture or simply denoting 'peasant': *kunbi, kapu, vokkaliga*. In all cases there were numerous internal differences of family, lineage, caste–sub-caste (or 'marriage circle', to use Klass' term), all in some sense and to some degree overridden by the common identity as land-controlling cultivators. In Andhra, for instance, there was by British times a crystallization into four separate castes of Kammas, Kapus, Velamas and Telagas; however

> all four of these large castes closely resemble one another in appearance and customs and seem to have branched off from one and the same Dravidian stock. Originally soldiers by profession, they are now mainly agriculturalists and traders, and some of them in the north are zamindars.[14]

The differences between peasant jatis included different origin legends, different linkages to traditional Andhra conditions, and a marked regional distribution: Kapus were found more in the Telengana and Rayalaseema region, Kammas only in coastal Andhra, Velamas primarily in Telengana.

In Karnataka, according to James Manor, there were an extremely wide variety of discrete castes/sub-castes, with little in common except a linkage with agriculture, who were nevertheless lumped together in the censuses as 'Vokkaligas' (from the word *vokku* meaning 'to thresh'). This segmentation leads him to describe them as 'not a single community but a number of quite different castes of cultivators.'[15] However, as many anthropologists (for instance, Klass) have pointed out, the jati itself never constituted the unit within which marriages took place but served as the unit of status-occupational identification; in this sense Vokkaligas had a common jati identity which gradually solidified with the economic and political developments of the colonial period.

In Maharashtra, the term 'Kunbi' came to name the broad cultivating group (similar to Kurmis of northern India), one that has been almost impossible to 'split up' into clearly defined sub-castes. There were major status gradations among Kunbis, linked to local landed position and to distinctions between the original 'shareholders' in a village and 'guest cultivators' of various types and articulated in claims to being among the higher lineages— *shahhanavkuli, packuli* (the '96 families' or 'five families'). The more aristocratic of these called themselves 'Marathas' and over a period of time, especially after the non-Brahman movement of the 1920s, this term became applicable to almost all sections of Kunbis in western Maharashtra. In Vidarbha and in the Konkan there were clear jati distinctions between 'Marathas' and 'Kunbis', but elsewhere it was practically impossible to distinguish, and it was always open for a powerful and rich but previously low-ranked 'kunbi' family to establish marriage relations with the more aristocratic *shahhanavkuli* Marathas. (This tradition has continued in Maharashtra up to the time of its most well-known example, Y.B. Chavan).

These peasant jatis provided most of the 'state overlords', variously known as *deshmukhs*, zamindar, *nayaka*, and these families holding power and land differentiated themselves from the common peasantry with various status titles (such as *dora* in the Telengana region). Yet they never managed to clearly constitute themselves as separate jatis or to successfully claim Ksatriya status. At the village level, the oldest and strongest among the main landholding lineage became the headman, the lowest linchpin in the state administration. Their title (*patil* among the Kunbis, *gauda* among the Vokkaligas, *reddi* among the Kapus, *chaudhuri* among the Kammas) very often came to be taken as a caste–family name for a much wider group. Yet this vast majority were exploited peasant cultivators, at best claiming status precedence and some privileges over the *balutedars* and Dalits of their villages, but classified still as Shudras and treated as rustic 'village idiots' in numerous popular proverbs and stories, as these examples regarding the Kunbis suggest:

The Kunbi caste is crooked as a sickle but by beating it becomes straight.
Kunbis and flour improve with pounding.
A Kunbi has no sense; he forgets whatever he learns.
The Kunbi died from seeing a ghost, the Brahman from the wind in the stomach, and the goldsmith from bile.
The Kunbi is always planting, whether his crop lives or dies.[16]

The Shudra–cultivator status was also linked with a relatively more liberal treatment of women. The 'aristocrats' and overlords among them picked up the purdah and *gosha* customs of secluding women, including the imposition of sati upon widows, but the majority of village cultivators had vigorous, independent women who worked in the fields and who played important economic and even managerial roles.

Finally it has to be added that, besides being invariably described (by early British census-writers) as 'skillful and industrious cultivators', these major *jatis* also had warrior traditions, which they shared with most of the low castes of the region.

■ THE JATIS: DALITS

While the major 'peasant' jatis made up 25–30 per cent of the population of their respective states (and often constituted 50 per cent or more in the individual villages where they were found), the two major Dalit jatis made up roughly 15 per cent. And it is striking that the region has almost everywhere two such relatively large Dalit castes, firmly marked off from one another and traditional rivals. These were the Mahars, Malas and Holeyas on one hand (about 10 per cent of the total population) and the Madigas and Mangs (about 5 per cent) on the other.

Mahars in Maharashtra, Malas in Andhra and Holeyas in Karnataka were linked together both by observers and in their own self-identification. They were the major field-labouring jati throughout the region, and specifically the jati responsible within the *jajmani* division of labour for general village service. As described by Zelliot for the Mahars, these quite extensive service duties included:

- acting as village watchmen, tracking thieves;
- arbitrating boundary disputes, e.g., over lands claimed by different peasant families;
- serving as guides and messengers for government officials; escorting the government treasury;
- calling landowners to pay revenue;
- sweeping village roads, repairing the *caudi* (village square) and village well;
- removing dead cattle;
- carrying messages to other villages or houses (especially regarding deaths).[17]

All of these duties were done by the Holeyas and Malas in their areas (with the exception of removing dead cattle, which was done in Andhra by the Madigas as a result of their connection with leather-work). It may be noted that they fall into two categories, some involving service to the 'village' or to its majority cultivating caste; while others involved service to higher-level state officials. It was this complex of labour-services that made the Mahar–Mala–Holeya group the major category of 'bonded labourers'. Besides these, of course, Dalits performed field labour, intermittent and often wage-paid in the drier and mixed regions, more permanent and slave-like in the wet coastal areas.

Some of these traditional services, in particular that of arbitrating boundary disputes, are linked with a long tradition of these castes as ancient 'sons of the soil', with a notion that they possess inherent traditional knowledge regarding the land. For instance one British official wrote in describing the Holeya *kulwadi* (it is intriguing that the term is used for Kunbis in Maharashtra),

All the thousand and one castes, whose members find a home in the village, unhesitatingly admit that the *kulwadi* is *de jure* the rightful owner of the village. He who was, is still, in a limited sense, 'lord of the village manor'. If there is a dispute as to the village boundary, the *Kulwadi* is the only one competent to take the oath as to how the village ought to run.[18]

These duties carried with them a relatively substantial *watan* right, or claim to some portion of the village land in return for their performance. This meant that in much of Maharashtra and Karnataka, at least, the Mahars and Holeyas had a foothold as small peasants. As the British and the Mysore raja recognized this right, by the early twentieth century it was reported that in Mysore state the Holeyas (and the Madigas in some areas) were at least sub-tenants everywhere while a few had risen to comparative prosperity and even affluence, with some involved in money-lending and coffee cultivation.[19]

Mahars in Maharashtra also retained this status. In Andhra these rights appear less in evidence; it may be the greater subordination of Malas in the coastal region and the greater 'feudal' nature of Hyderabad state had eroded these land rights by the twentieth century; but even so Thurston notes that Malas in the western regions (Telengana and Rayalaseema) had a better position, retaining their traditional lands, and were in some cases well-to-do cultivators.[20] It is also possible that the 'frontier' quality of Vidarbha and Telengana as forests were cleared for cultivation provided some minimal opportunities for Dalit poor peasants, as well as for the 'peasant' jatis.

Economically Malas in eastern Andhra and Mahars in Vidarbha were also weavers of coarse cloth; women did the spinning, men the weaving, with cotton often provided by a particular family of peasant cultivators they worked for. Finally, they shared with other peasant and low castes of the region something of a military tradition. The Mahars had been employed in Shivaji's army to watch the jungles, act as escorts and keep forts supplied with wood and fodder, while Mahar legends report a special duty of guarding the palace of Jijabai, Shivaji's mother. The British army recruited them while fighting their Indian foes, and in the final battle of 1818 against the Peshwa army, Mahars made up half the small Indian force killed at Koregaon, an event which later Dalit movement leaders pointed to with pride and as an illustration of their hatred for the Peshwas.[21] As for the Malas, Thurston describes them as originally a tribe of freelance warriors of the hills, 'who like the tiger, slept during the day and worked at night', who were paid mercenaries raiding and looting under the 'Poligars' of the Vijayangar regime. He argued that they 'belong to a subjugated race and have been made into the servants of the community.'[22]

In contrast to the Mahar–Holeya–Mala group (who can also be identified with the Paraiyas of Tamil Nadu, the Vankars of Gujarat and so on) stand the Madigas and Mangs (today referred to as Matangs) who were smaller jatis and somewhat less extensively spread out. These also inhabited settlements outside the village proper and provided general field labour, but lacked the traditional status of general village servant and the *watan/inam* lands and claims that went with this. As a result they were poorer and more of them were landless. These castes had specific jati duties, though different ones: rope-making in the case of the Mangs, leather work for the Madigas. It is striking that though the Madigas were leather workers and thus in terms of 'occupation' similar to the Chambhars of Maharashtra and Chamars of northern India, their structural position within the village caste system identified them with neither of these but rather with the Mangs (Maharashtrian Chambhars are a smaller caste, slightly higher in status; north Indian Chamars were, like Mahars and others, general village servants in addition to their leather working tasks). Their own traditions identified them with the Mangs and both claimed the heritage of an ancient 'Matangi' dynasty.

Differences between the two Dalit castes continued even when they took up 'newer' factory labour or such like under colonial rule. The Mahar–Mala group managed generally to claim the more skilled and slightly higher-paid work. Thus Mahars could get a foothold in the textile mills in both Nagpur and Bombay and in parts of dock jobs, whereas in Andhra Thurston notes that while both Malas and Madigas took up factory jobs, the Malas often held more skilled jobs (engine drivers, valve men, moulders, turners) whereas Madigas did unskilled work.[23]

Finally, the Mangs and Madigas provided the bulk of lower-caste converts to Christianity, whereas the Mahars, Malas and Holeyas made up the main social base for the Dalit movements of the twentieth century.

In spite of differences, the main Dalit castes shared some important religious customs. These show important aspects of the 'sexual dynamics' of the relations among castes. The fundamental aspects are that connection with mother goddesses is particularly strong; members of these Dalit castes often served as priests in popular cults and sacrifices; and there was a prevalence of a particular type of *devadasi* custom throughout the three states.

One particularly important sacrifice of buffalos and goats is described in detail by Thurston for the Telugu areas. This was carried out in the name of the goddess, particularly in times of famine or to ward off other evil fortune, and with the participation of all the non-Brahman castes of the village, with a Madiga serving as the main priest or 'Poturaza' but with Malas also linked with the sacrifices. A Brahmanized explanation of the custom refers to the legend of Sunkulammia, daughter of a Brahman pandit, tricked into marriage by a handsome Mala youth who had come to study, concealing his caste identity. Learning of it, she burnt herself to death:[24]

Before doing so she cursed the treacherous Mala who had polluted her that he might become a buffalo and his children turn into sheep, and vowed that she would revive as an evil spirit and have him and his children sacrificed to her, and get his leg put in her mouth and a light placed on his head fed with his own fat.[25]

These were the details of the sacrifice.

This depiction of the horrors of a relationship of a Dalit man with a high-caste woman contrasts with the legitimation of its reversal as seen in the *'devadasi'* tradition. In one sense the now popular term is misleading since there is a major contrast between the Dalit version of the custom and the *devadasis* who served as dancers and performers of many rituals in some major temples, whose rituals were connected primarily with stories of Krishna. Their life centred around the temple precincts and they formed relations mainly with Brahman priests and the kings.[26] In contrast, the Dalit girls were dedicated to the goddess Yellama/Renuka in a ceremony carried out on full moon nights in temples in Saundatti (Belgaum district in Karnataka) and in Kurnool district in Andhra and some other places. Following this 'marriage to the god' most of the girls remained in their own village; they were considered accessible to any man but at the same time not bound or polluted by sexual relations. They remained independent, given the status of a man in many family ceremonies; their children usually took their name; and they had some important ritual prerogatives in village ceremonies. These girls were known as 'Murali' among Mahars, 'Matangi' among the Madigas and 'Basavi' (said to be from a term *basava* applying to a bull roaming the village at will and which is said 'alludes to the footloose position of the women').[27] The spits and curses of the 'Matangi' at all castes during such village rituals (even to Reddis and Kammas, though few Brahmans were involved) were believed to purge them of uncleanliness.[28]

Whatever the 'matriarchal' or 'matrilinear' remnants that can be seen in the custom, by late feudal times it also helped to institutionalize the sexual accessibility of Dalit women for high caste men. The women who were classified as 'Matangi', 'Murali', etc., clearly had independence and some position in society, socially recognized and ritually affirmed; at the same time the element of sexual exploitation cannot be denied. The contrast between such an institutionalization of relationships between Dalit women and upper/middle caste men and the absolute banning of the reverse relationship is striking; it shows the 'dialectics of sex' that continued to exist in the relationships between jatis in the villages.

■ CASTE AND LAND: INTER-REGIONAL VARIATIONS

Many of the specific characteristics of agrarian class–caste relations can be linked, we have argued, to local characteristics of climate and land. A generally more equalitarian, small peasant or peasant-herding economy is fostered in the drier or 'mixed' eco-types, contrasted to the hierarchalized relations between land-managers and labourers in the irrigated wet-rice regions.

Broadly speaking, the available data on landholdings and caste patterns, while limited, back this up. First, we have data on the spread of land owned and operated by size category, by region within each state (Table 2.1). While these are from 1971, they undoubtedly indicate a long historical pattern. They show, first, a relatively smaller average size of landholding and a higher degree of landlessness in the coastal areas—the Andhra delta, coastal Karnataka (Kanara) and Konkan in Maharashtra. These were areas of wet-rice and garden (e.g., coconut, mango) cultivation where even relatively smaller holdings could provide substantial wealth, and where the condition of Dalits as field labourers was most oppressive. Extreme examples of this coastal eco-type are of course Thanjavur in Tamil Nadu and the Kerala coast; but in our states also Brahmans were the main landlords in the Konkan and Kanara regions, Brahmans and elite Kammas and some of the other 'shudra' castes in the Andhra delta.

It can also be noted that average land sizes are the smallest overall in Andhra, next in Karnataka and largest in Maharashtra, an indication partly of the relative poverty of agriculture in the dry Deccan plateau regions.[29] Finally, in all cases there is more land-lessness in terms of 'land operated' than in terms of 'land owned', while the opposite is true of the 0–1 acre category, indicating that these small fragments of land were simply not cultivated.

Data on agrarian structure (classes or occupational categories) by regions come from the British censuses of the early twentieth century (Table 2.2), and to some degree show degrees of landlord–tenant relations that were, after independence, overridden in the

TABLE 2.1
Land Distribution by Region, 1971

| | \multicolumn{6}{c}{*Percentage of Households in Each Acreage Category*} |
	None	*0–1.00*	*1.00–2.50*	*2.50–10.00*	*10.00–25.00*	*Over 25.00*
Land Owned						
Andhra						
Delta	11.89	49.21	18.42	15.84	3.87	0.78
Telengana	7.09	29.27	19.50	30.69	10.04	9.49
Rayalaseema	9.20	29.37	17.92	30.92	9.49	3.11
Karnataka						
Coastal	40.26	28.70	8.97	19.45	2.27	0.35
Inland (E)	23.57	13.57	16.76	35.03	8.56	2.50
Mysore	13.09	19.93	21.05	39.09	6.01	0.82
Bombay K.	8.32	19.88	11.50	32.99	20.84	6.47
Maharashtra						
Konkan	20.34	23.67	22.18	28.40	4.04	1.38
Deccan	18.09	16.32	14.74	31.91	14.54	4.39
Khandesh	27.58	10.81	8.94	31.89	16.18	4.62
Marathwada	8.31	25.61	4.63	28.05	22.96	10.43
Vidarbha	10.35	27.95	6.78	29.12	18.60	7.19
East	9.79	21.75	17.59	41.99	7.51	1.37
Land Operated						
Andhra						
Delta	49.31	12.81	17.84	15.67	3.68	0.68
Telengana	27.41	10.18	18.76	29.99	10.42	3.49
Rayalaseema	29.44	10.19	17.57	30.04	9.48	3.25
Karnataka						
Coastal	45.16	6.58	13.76	29.90	4.19	0.42
Inland (E)	36.31	2.93	16.25	33.08	8.93	2.49
Mysore	25.07	6.13	21.73	40.38	5.83	0.86
Bombay K.	31.45	1.65	8.96	28.94	21.57	7.42
Maharashtra						
Konkan	28.75	12.92	24.31	29.30	3.49	1.25
Deccan	26.19	8.13	14.40	32.06	14.57	4.79
Khandesh	36.25	0.60	7.54	35.52	15.44	4.61
Marathwada	34.94	1.00	4.10	25.57	23.30	11.11
Vidarbha	36.92	1.01	6.17	28.46	19.80	7.64
East	27.85	7.11	15.65	40.25	7.72	1.42

| | \multicolumn{2}{c}{*Average land per household*} | \multicolumn{2}{c}{*Gini Coefficient Ratio*} |
			1971	*1981*
Andhra	3.43		0.7030	
Delta		1.93		(0.6612)

Table 2.1 (Continued)

	Average land per household	Gini Coefficient Ratio 1971	1981
Telengana	4.83		
Rayalaseema	4.68		
Karnataka	5.43	0.6547	
Coastal	1.74		(0.6229)
Inland (E)	4.74		
Mysore	3.44		
Bombay Karnataka	8.00		
Maharashtra	6.51	0.6488	
Konkan	3.18		(0.6325)
Deccan	6.01		
Khandesh	6.24		
Marathwada	9.53		
Vidarbha	7.76		
East	4.11		

Source: All-India Debt and Investment Survey, 1971–72, *Assets and Liabilities of Rural Households, Statistical Tables, Volume II (Regions within the States)* (Bombay: Reserve Bank of India, 1972) *Assets and Liabilities of Households* as on 30 June 1981 (Bombay: RBI), Table 9.4.

direction of more capitalistic, wage-labour relations. All the censuses show the broad categories of *landlord* ('income from rent of land'), *cultivator* and *agricultural labourer*; but only for some regions do we have a break-up of these into 'cultivating owner/tenant' and 'farm servant/field labourer'. For assessment of the degree of landlordism, figures for tenancy are much more indicative than those of 'income from rent of land'; unfortunately the tenancy figures are not available for Hyderabad state. For the areas where they are available, however, there is clearly higher tenancy in the Delta region of Andhra and even more so in north and south Kanara and the Konkan. The distinction between 'farm servants' and 'field labourers' also indicates a greater degree of traditional bondage in agrarian relations where there are more 'farm servants', as was true in Telengana and the Delta districts (and in Nagpur–Wardha as contrasted to Berar, which may be linked to the *malguzari* settlement in the former region).

The data on caste and occupation (Table 2.3) are perhaps the most interesting. These show that while Dalits tended to be agricultural labourers, there were significant qualifications to this, with regional variations. The Holeyas (and even more the Madigas)

TABLE 2.2

Land and Occupation by Region, 1921

[Percentage of Male Workers in Each Occupational Category]

	Number of workers	Income from rent of land	Cultivators (total)	Cultivating owners	Cultivating tenants	Other cultivators	Agricultural labourers	Farm servants	Field labourers	Total % in agriculture
Mysore State	1,293,285	2.23	57.53	(52.74)	(4.79)		11.72	(1.75)	(10.47)	71.48
Hyderabad State										
Telengana	839,242	4.94	70.51				24.74	(11.53)	(13.22)	94.81
Marathwada	448,710	9.49	63.71				25.34	(1.44)	(25.35)	98.54
Karnataka dist.	553,921	23.74	55.12				18.58	(3.83)	(14.79)	97.44
Madras Presidency										
Delta	3,612,102	5.82	51.08	(28.03)	(23.05)		17.47	(8.46)	(9.01)	74.37
Rayalaseema	1,187,867	4.14	47.97	(42.13)	(5.84)		18.86	(3.34)	(15.51)	70.97
South Kanara	381,867	3.60	51.50	(12.84)	(38.66)		14.83	(1.68)	(13.14)	69.93
Central Provinces										
Nagpur-Wardha	1,038,449	1.05	36.57				26.11	(10.00)	(16.11)	63.73
Berar	1,013,110	1.86	32.36				37.56	(6.32)	(31.23)	71.78
Bombay Presidency										
Khandesh	472,586	1.79	62.83	(51.57)	(4.80)	(6.46)	31.80			96.42
Deccan	676,566	3.73	72.01	(43.13)	(7.18)	(21.70)	18.25			93.99
Konkan	360,773	4.39	77.90	(20.77)	(50.43)	(6.70)	6.65			88.94
Bombay Karnataka	630,400	4.30	62.46	(48.35)	(11.51)	(2.60)	24.66			91.42
N. Kanara	94,692	5.37	66.16	(16.76)	(43.22)	(6.18)	18.35			89.88
Madras (1911)										
Delta	2,648,335	3.44	65.85	(32.47)	(33.38)		30.24			99.53
Rayalaseema	885,339	4.35	61.05	(60.65)	(6.40)		28.63			94.03
S. Kanara	253,227	3.64	74.60	(19.72)	(54.88)		21.77			100.00

Calculated from the Census of India, 1911, 1921.

TABLE 2.3
Caste and Agrarian Occupation, 1921 (Male Workers)

	Actual workers (Numbers)	Recorded principal occupation (%)		
		Income from rent of land	Cultivators	Field labourers
Mysore State (1921)				
Brahman	51,221	17.13	21.79	0.35
Lingayat	142,366	3.15	79.43	2.62
Vokkaliga	246,329	0.44	89.83	2.08
Holeya	157,289	0.97	35.95	37.72
Madiga	63,363	1.58	45.13	26.17
Hyderabad State (1921)				
Brahman	79,345	7.37	17.52	0.32
Maratha	500,638	6.99	60.90	16.33
Lingayat (shopkeepers)	170,508	3.50	9.01	1.30
Kapu	291,130	1.60	51.56	26.15
Telaga	146,230	1.01	61.22	15.68
Mahar/Mala (menial service)	130.008	3.79	8.40	8.25 (65.33)*
Madiga (menial service)	203,492	0.65	10.28	10.16 (83.54)*
Chambhar	37,991	1.07	4.21	7.69
Madras State (1911)				
Brahman, Telugu	27,029	34.53	32.37	0.29
Brahman, Canarese	10,647	13.96	71.89	0.08
Holeya	29,696	—	3.29	75.46
Mala	196,259	0.18	14.78	71.89
Madiga	79,924	1.17	10.71	54.71
Central Provinces and Berar (1921)				
Brahman	149,193	3.22	36.67	6.22
Maratha	65,520	4.29	46.00	27.78
Kunbi	385,268	55.00		34.08
Mahar/Mehra (cotton weavers)	280,101	2.09	22.37	41.02 (11.33)*
Mang (native musicians)	26,007	1.25	3.42	47.73 (21.97)*
Bombay Presidency (1911)				
Brahman, Chitpavan	10,407	17.00	2.47	0.13
Brahman, Deshastha	14,494	18.68	64.55	2.69

Table 2.3 (Continued)

| | Actual workers (Numbers) | Recorded principal occupation (%) | | |
		Income from rent of land	Cultivators	Field labourers
Lingayat	205,813	3.24	83.54	22.39
Maratha	426,649	1.58	47.63	14.93
Kunbi	319,813	1.59	66.88	20.67
Mahar, Holeya, Dhed	69,542	0.75	48.79	22.63
Mang, Madiga	22,672	0.52	16.60	41.71

* Refers to traditional caste occupation.

in Mysore state, and the Mahars and Mangs–Madigas in Bombay Presidency and the Central Provinces–Berar were economically in a somewhat better position in the sense that a respectable proportion of them were 'cultivators'. Mahars in Bombay Presidency even came close to competing with Kunbis in this respect. The Malas and Madigas in Madras Presidency and Hyderabad state were much worse off in having a much higher proportion of workers as field labourers or in 'menial service' and only a small foothold as 'cultivators'. Similarly Holeyas in Madras Presidency (who were almost entirely of the south Kanara district) were, in contrast to those of Mysore state, overwhelmingly field labourers.

Finally, a specific look at the occupational pattern among women workers is suggestive (Table 2.4). Data indicate low work participation of women among the Brahman castes in all regions; contrastingly, among the 'peasant' jatis it is quite high (except for the Vokkaliga in Mysore state), while it is highest of all among the Dalits. And everywhere the incidence of female participation in agriculture is much higher than that of male workers and more so as 'field labourers' than 'cultivators'. It is clear that women were substantial 'economic producers' along with men and that they tended to be more proletarianized; though this meant primarily that their wage labour was mainly as agricultural labourers and as unskilled casual labourers, they also participated substantially as toiling peasant cultivators (and their labour on family farms was undoubtedly underestimated, in 1921 as in 1971–81!).

TABLE 2.4
Caste and Agrarian Occupation, 1921 (Female Workers)

	Percentage of female to male workers	Income from rent of land	Cultivators	Field labourers
Mysore State (1921)				
Brahman	10.58	37.38	25.61	2.62
Lingayat	20.34	13.25	49.47	17.80
Vokkaliga	18.71	2.09	72.13	7.57
Holeya	35.22	1.26	11.35	61.63
Madiga	31.51	1.96	13.12	56.36
Hyderabad State (1921)				
Brahman	18.12	15.68	33.97	—
Maratha	63.03	3.06	54.60	31.71
Lingayat	52.49	6.44	16.73	1.92
Kapu	50.95	1.21	70.07	19.75
Telaga	75.22	1.08	57.26	20.87
Mahar/Mala (menial service)	98.83	2.66	13.90	39.50 (37.24)*
Madiga (menial service)	84.63	1.00	7.86	38.94 (73.55)*
Chambhar	59.70	0.76	10.37	2.98
Madras State (1911)				
Brahman, Telugu	26.69	54.60	34.74	0.11
Brahman, Canarese	28.10	14.74	69.25	0.40
Holeya	37.73	—	2.45	84.43
Mala	85.53	0.16	8.48	87.55
Madiga	70.69	3.98	2.89	82.31
Central Provinces and Berar (1921)				
Brahman	34.58	2.71	45.61	15.40
Maratha	51.23	2.55	21.97	58.00
Kunbi	70.79	—	32.65	62.16
Mahar/Mehra (cotton weavers)	91.28	0.40	16.56	60.25 (9.76)*
Mang (native musicians)	99.42	0.20	1.29	66.04 (2.41)*
Bombay Presidency (1921)				
Brahman, Chitpavan	15.00	30.17	3.14	1.54
Brahman, Deshastha	11.09	40.08	22.77	2.43
Lingayat	56.45	3.49	25.41	46.24
Maratha	68.53	1.57	47.67	30.84

Table 2.4 (Continued)

	Percentage of female to male workers	Income from rent of land	Cultivators	Field labourers
Kunbi	71.63	1.07	54.23	41.33
Mahar, Holeya, Dhed	76.63	0.34	43.50	41.52
Mang, Madiga	79.13	0.55	6.33	66.79

Sources: Censuses of India, 1911, 1921.
* Refers to traditional caste occupation.

These are twentieth century data on caste and land and it is possible that some of the patterns they show have been influenced by social–economic developments beginning with colonial rule. For instance, the greater economic opportunities in Bombay and Nagpur (the textile industry and others) apparently helped Dalits even in the rural areas to improve their landholding positions;[30] the greater 'feudal' backwardness of Hyderabad state may have maintained or even worsened low-caste bondage. Still, many of the patterns are historically quite ancient, and indicate the relatively more equalitarian traditions of the northern Deccan and the economic assertiveness of Dalits which helped to lay a basis, in the twentieth century, for a powerful and revolutionary low-caste movement.

■ CASTE AND COLONIALISM

In the first quarter of the nineteenth century when British rule became a reality five famines occurred that took the life of about a million people. In the second twenty-five years there were two famines, and about four hundred thousand dead. In the third twenty-five years there were six famines and the toll of death became five million. And in the last twenty-five years of that century what do we see? Eighteen famines! And the estimated death toll of from 15 million to 20 million! . . . . Gentlemen, what must be the cause of this? To put the cause in plain words, it is the government policy the British have followed.

The aim has always remained to limit the growth of trade and industry in this country. This is not simply a logical fault; but the effort to rule India in such a way that it will always remain a customer of British goods. This is the recognized thread of the British state. It is due to this policy that India has been turned through ages into a poor country. In the process of establishing this poverty who have been the main victims? Those dalit peasants who still cannot fill their stomachs for six months have provided the majority of victims . . . . Gentlemen, you cannot sit singing the praises of the British bureaucracy for simply giving us improved roads, improved canals, railways, a stable administration and new ideals of geography or for stopping internal wars. There is scope for praising the maintenance of law and order. But, gentlemen, nobody including dalits can live by eating law and order; they live on bread and we cannot forget this . . . . I would be the first to agree that the praise given to the British would vanish once we turned our attention to the forcible extraction of profit by big capitalists and landlords from the poor working people of this country. However, I cannot understand how you can expect the British government to liberate people from the exploitation of the capitalists and landlords . . . .

Let us think about this from only your limited perspective. Before the British came your condition was extremely miserable due to untouchability. Has the British government done anything to remove your untouchability? Before the British came you could not take water from village wells. Has the British government made any effort to give you that right? Before the British came you could not enter temples. Can you do that today? Before the coming of the British you could not be employed in police service. Does the British government give you employment now? Before the British came you had no permission to be in the army. Is this opportunity open to you now? Gentlemen, you cannot give a positive answer to any of these questions. Those who have ruled this country for such a long period could have done many good things. But there has definitely not been a single fundamental change in your situation . . . . During the British period the faults of the social structure and the patches of the varna system have been kept as they were.[31]

With these powerful remarks, the rising leader of India's Dalit movement, Dr. B.R. Ambedkar, was giving his reply to those sections of Dalits and non-Brahmans who believed that colonial rule had been an unambiguous liberating force. In doing so, he drew on the broad Marxist critique of colonialism, which had by his day also become the nationalist critique.

British colonial rule was the force which incorporated India into world capitalism. What was its effect on caste? It is true that the general Marxist analysis of imperialism, which stresses the linkage of the exploitation of the Third World with the development of capitalism in Europe, provides the best beginning point for any understanding of the processes of caste–class development in India during British rule. However the standard interpretation of this focuses too much on the wage labour/capital relation as the driving force, and sees the main dynamic in the expansion of capital from the centre. Rather, taking off from Marx's brief comments on 'primitive accumulation' and the role of force and violence in history, we argue that non-wage forms of accumulation, including women's domestic labour; the extraction of cheap natural resources; the extraction of surplus (primarily from Third World peasants) through slave and serf relations and petty commodity production, have been equally crucial.[32] Within contemporary interpretations of Marxism, perhaps the most helpful analysis along these lines, less inherently 'Orientalist' in its assumptions about the stagnation of non-European relations and systems of production, has been the 'world capitalist systems' theory represented by Immanuel Wallerstein and others. This takes commodity production, not wage labour as such, as the defining feature of a 'world capitalist system'. It sees non-wage labour in the periphery (primarily serfdom and slavery, in Wallerstein's interpretation) as playing a major role in accumulation at a world scale. In doing so it treats the dynamics of the system as not simply deriving from the impetus of capital formation and the surplus value relation at the 'centre' but also from the dialectic between 'centre' and 'periphery', with dynamic also coming from the movements of the exploited in the Third World. As Wallerstein puts it,

A capitalist world-economy began to form centered on the European continent in the sixteenth century. From the beginning this involved the establishment of integrated production processes we may call commodity chains. These commodity chains almost all tended to traverse the existing political boundaries. The total surplus extracted in these commodity chains was at no point distributed evenly in terms of the geographical location of the creation of the surplus, but was always concentrated to a disproportionate degree in some zones rather than in others. We mean by 'peripheries' those zones that lost out in the distribution of surplus to the 'core' zones. Whereas at the beginning of the historical process, there seemed little difference in the economic wealth of the different geographical areas, a mere one century's flow of surplus was enough to create a visible distinction between core and periphery in terms of three criteria: *the accumulation of capital, the social organization of local production processes, the political organization of the state structures.*[33]

Thus, colonialism for India meant a political organization that shaped the traditional caste–feudal structures and Mughal bureaucracies to the needs of a new British–controlled colonial state; a restructuring of 'local production processes' that meant an increased 'peasanticization' as many traditional crafts were destroyed and peasants thrown back on the land, often to specialization in crops not for their own subsistence or local consumption but for the needs of Europe; and an accumulation process that directed surpluses to countries far from India itself but also helped to strengthen the political bureaucracy within India. In the process the traditional structures of caste were used, transformed and in some ways even strengthened.

India was integrated into the system, along with most of the rest of Asia and Africa, during the period 1750–1850.[34] In truth, it had been part of the 'events' of world capitalism from the beginning; but Vasco da Gama's landing could not produce the conquest and plunder of a subcontinent so easily as could that of Columbus. By the seventeenth century Europeans geared to establish foothold; by the eighteenth beginning their real conquest. The traditional marking dates for the incorporation of India into the world capitalist system can be said to be 1757 (the battle of Plassey) and 1857, the supercession of the East India Company by the British state and the 'first war of independence' (or the last major resistance war of the traditional society). Intermediary dates of central importance, particularly for the area of this study, are the defeat of Tipu Sultan in 1799 and of the Peshwas in 1818, marking the triumph over the strongest enemies of the British, and the treaty with the Nizam of Hyderabad in 1800.

On conquest, Bombay Province was formed consisting of western Maharashtra, Gujarat and northern Karnataka. After the defeat of Tipu, Mysore state was created and given back to a former Hindu ruling dynasty, but the rich coastal districts were taken away and north Kanara given to Bombay Presidency (south Kanara along with Malabar went to Madras Presidency). In 1766–67 the British had already gained control over the 'Northern Circars' (Andhra delta) by getting a firman from the Mughals and checking the Nizam's efforts at control; the 1800 treaty saw the cession of Rayalaseema or the 'ceded districts' also to Madras Presidency and the leasing of the relatively rich cotton-growing districts of Berar (Vidarbha) to the Central Provinces. Thus, though the Nizam was left with the biggest princely state in the subcontinent, its most prosperous regions were put under direct British rule.

Thus, the conquest and incorporation of India saw the reorganization of the Marathi, Telugu and Kannada-speaking regions to fall under three separate British provinces and two major princely states.

The restructuring of local production processes to allow for accumulation of capital towards the centre had several major aspects in India.

Politically it meant that the caste–feudal 'watan' states were restructured for surplus production geared to the cycles of a capitalist world economy. The British adapted Mughal–Maratha and other bureaucratic ruling structures, maintaining a good deal of feudal privilege. In the zamindari areas and the princely states they allowed the feudals to directly appropriate the surpluses and hand over only a portion to the British; while in the ryotwari areas the continued existence of 'inam' (revenue-free) holdings was allowed (for instance it is estimated that in the classic ryotwari area of Bombay Presidency at least one-third of the area was under various forms of non-ryotwari holdings during the mid-nineteenth century).[35] Nevertheless, the independent power of feudal rulers came to an end and the colonial bureaucracy, with the British in command, ruled India for purposes fundamentally different from those of previous caste–feudal administrations—as the brightest 'jewel in the crown' providing revenue to maintain a world-conquering army and navy and surpluses for European consumption and accumulation.

This shift in political power had a complex effect on caste relations. At the lowest level, in the villages, the traditional *jajmani* division of labour survived, and one scholar, Chris Fuller, has argued that the destruction of the previous feudal state strengthened the position of the village-based 'dominant caste':

> The granting of private property rights in land to those responsible for the revenue destroyed the structure of the distributive system. Where there had previously been a complex hierarchy with many levels, now only its bottom half, the part within the village (the *jajmani* system) remained. The top half vanished and was replaced by a single link between the owner and the government defined according to principles diverging fundamentally from those of the past.[36]

But this did not simply mean a strengthening of the 'dominant caste' within the village since in crucial ways the subordination of the village to the bureaucracy increased. It also meant a shift in power relations within the ruling bloc; the strengthening of Brahmans relative to 'Ksatriya' political powerholders.[37] The power of the state to extract surpluses grew though gradually, and entry to the state machinery was now via the British educational system. Former zamindars and maharajas retained a good deal of their pomp and influence; princely states continued to 'rule' over a full one-third of the country though always under the heavy hand of the British. But many of the former political powerholding groups and families were in a sense 'pensioned off'. As the British bureaucracy extended its hold, it was its 'servants' or 'employees' who extended their power, and it was largely the literate castes, primarily Brahmans, who managed to gain new monopolies of these bureaucratic positions.

The fact that the British-run courts continued to implement a religious 'private law' defining family/gender/caste relationships as interpreted by Brahman pandits and Muslim mullahs also helped to maintain a caste orthodoxy over significant spheres of life. Women, for example, could not open bank accounts and hold control of financial affairs until after independence; while courts enforced the control of girls by fathers and husbands.

Economically the commodification process of incorporation into a capitalist economy meant increased regional specialization and the fostering of cash-crop exports concurrent with the destruction of much of the previous regional and national-level self-sufficiency. Mainly this, at first, meant increased production of crops such as indigo, raw silk, opium and cotton. Land revenue was both a primary mode of extraction of the surplus and the financial basis of the colonial state (including the maintenance of that powerful weapon of empire, the British Indian army) until the 1930s when peasant struggles very nearly brought it to an end. A heavy revenue demand from the peasants also forced them into cash cropping to meet their needs for cash. Money-lenders, who advanced credit on the crop-lien system and took control of the marketing of the crop in ryotwari areas, were crucial intermediaries in this process; but its central significance was to subordinate the entire peasantry (rich, poor, wage labourer, *balutedar* and all) to production for the needs of a European market (raw materials for European industrialization, new 'luxury' consumption goods such as coffee, tea and cocoa for the European middle and working classes). It was a process of accumulation via the state for a world capitalist system.

The forced specialization in many raw materials, the destruction of many artisan industries through competition with cheap European manufactures, all led to what one historian has called the 'peasantization' of the economy.[38] Further, the exorbitant revenue demands and the increased cash-crop production took place in the context of local environmental destruction. Forests were degraded and occasionally devastated as trees were cut down to build railways, cultivation was extended into previously forested areas, and the state gradually brought all forest lands under direct control to develop a 'scientific forestry' aimed, once more, at catering for world market needs. As a result, forest areas and commons could no longer provide, to the same degree, 'inputs' for agriculture and various subsistence needs for villagers.[39]

One result was a significant decline in living standards to a point considerably below that existing during Mughal times.[40] Descriptions by British observers of the mid-nineteenth century indicate an almost uniform impoverishment even in regions like East Khandesh which were traditionally comparatively wealthy:

Beyond the precincts of the towns, and our military cantonments, and out of the line of high roads, the villages consist, for the most part, of miserable huts, inhabited by a squalid peasantry whose very appearance denotes a state of destitution. Even in villages which present a better aspect the enquirer soon finds that throughout the length and breadth of the land, the people are struggling against poverty and debt.[41]

The heavy incidence of famines during British rule, cited so force-fully by Ambedkar in his 1930 speech, was an indication of the way the entire peasantry had been forced to the margin of existence. And, as he pointed out, the heaviest burden of all of this continued to fall on the lowest castes and on women and children, those who lacked entitlements to the land and other sources of sustenance.[42]

Direct wage labour was also exploited. Late to develop, factory production increased very gradually; in data cited by Anupam Sen there were 815 factories with an average daily workforce of 350,000 in 1894; 3,400 factories with 1,171,000 workers in 1919, and 10,466 factories with 1,751,000 workers by 1939; not a very large number for the subcontinent.[43] But labour was also used in railways and docks and, of course, for all the construction and irrigation projects built. More significantly, it was used not only in India itself but throughout the empire, as low-caste, often Dalit labourers migrated to work in plantation economies, spanning from the West Indies to South Africa to South-east Asia and Fiji.

This worldwide movement of Indians has been cited by David Washbrook as a significant factor in the organization of the imperial system. Washbrook stresses the role of the 'scribal, military, and trading and banking groups' (i.e., the Brahman, Ksatriya and Vaishya varnas).[44] But, while these were junior partners in exploit-ation, at the bottom of the system, providing the most exploited producers of surplus, bonded and overworked to exhaustion and death, were huge numbers of India's Dalits and Adivasis who migrated to work in plantations from the West Indies to the Fiji islands.

Colonialism thus had a complex effect on the functioning of the caste system. It did not simply create 'classes' along with 'castes'. On the one hand new groups like a factory working class and plantation proletariat came into existence, and new professionals and some businessmen developed from high caste Brahmans and

Banias. A 'peasantry' also acquired an accentuated existence, increasingly linked to production for the world market. But while at one level formally non-scriptive openings (such as education and entry into factory occupations) could mean that a very few from the lower castes could win their way into non-traditional occupations, by and large caste channeled workers to segmented labour markets: Brahmans continued to have near-monopoly control over administrative positions and professions; merchant castes (Banias, Jains, Chettiars) became money-lenders, merchants and businessmen; middle Shudra castes dominated factory occupations, while miners and plantation workers were drawn from the lowest groups. Caste hierarchy thus remained, with Brahmans at the top and the most mobile; with the middle 'peasant' castes impoverished and in many ways more attached to villages (except for the very meagre openings in factories) than they had been before, and with the lowest castes, especially Dalits, also mobile but so greatly impoverished and exploited as to find it very hard to benefit from such mobility.

■ NATIONALISM AND ELITE RESISTANCE

The intelligentsia, that is the Indian national leadership, divided the national liberation movement . . . into two warring factions: a political movement and a social movement. They also declared those who organized social movements, those who theorized on agriculture and industry, to be stooges of the British and traitors. The national movement was turned into a form of mythological movement and ancestor worship . . . . Those who propounded inequality and did not wish society to be democratic, started eulogizing and sublimating history, mythology and ages gone by because, in those mythological and historical ages, they were the supreme victors and leaders . . . . The Indian intelligentsia do not wish to accept the present with its revolutionary potential.[45]

This harsh critique by the Dalit writer Baburao Bagul captures a major reality of the nationalist upsurge in India. As the 'English-educated elite', i.e., the politically dispossessed Brahman ruling class, began to mobilize, they had two goals or thrusts: first, to regain their rule in the state as against the British, and, second, to maintain their position against the masses within the Indian 'caste–class' hierarchy. They organized as 'nationalists' to demand first a greater share in rule of the empire and then aspiring to lead a movement for complete independence; and they also organized as 'social reformers' to challenge many aspects of tradition. However, their concern to maintain their own power vis-à-vis the castes and classes below them meant that nationalism was weakened and social reform primarily came to mean restructuring the relations of caste and patriarchy to make them compatible with 'modernization'. In the process the ideology of caste hegemony was incorporated within an emerging racially/ethnically based 'Hindu nationalism' or *hindutva* in which upper castes were identified as 'Aryans' (equivalent to Europeans) and the Vedas were identified as the core of Hindu religion.

The Indian National Congress, formed in 1885 after a series of provincial organizing attempts, was at first only a limited petition-making body whose perspective fell far short of self-government and democracy, focusing instead on administrative reforms that would give scope for elite participation. Its attacks on British racism and raising of the issues of economic exploitation as in the 'nationalist economic theory' evolved by Moderates which attempted to explain Indian poverty through the drain of wealth[46] did express broad national interests. Its resolutions included protests against the salt tax, the treatment of Indian labourers abroad, and the sufferings caused by forest administration, all issues of genuine mass concern. Yet the social base of the Congress is insufficiently understood by describing it as 'middle class' and implying that its members were detached from any major interest in the system of production and exploitation. Its members, whether lawyers, educationalists, journalists, etc., were also upper castes, overwhelmingly Brahmans, and they invariably had connection with the land through intermediate tenures and often as zamindars and moneylenders. Thus powerholders in the Congress up to the very end tended to oppose anti-landlord legislation and the efforts to protect peasants and tenants. For instance, though Lokmanya Tilak had sent his agents from the Poona Sarvajanik Sabha into the countryside in 1896–97 to popularize the legal rights of peasants affected by famine, both he and the moderate Gokhale bitterly opposed a

Bombay government move to restrict transfer of peasant lands to money-lenders in 1901. Defending landlordism, Tilak stated,

> Just as the government has no right to rob the sowcar and distribute his wealth among the poor, in the same way the government has no right to deprive the khot of his rightful income and distribute the money to the peasant. This is a question of rights and not of humanity.[47]

Thus it was the heirs of Tilak, defending the *khots*, that Ambedkar confronted in his leadership of the anti-landlord struggle in the Konkan during the 1930s; and in similar ways throughout the country both Dalits and non-Brahman peasants found their needs not only simply ignored, but at first also opposed, by the Congress nationalists. At the same time, the 'Brahmanic' interests of the elite, particularly as against 'Bania' traditions, were consistent with a certain degree of anti-capitalism, demands for nationalization and the fostering of a state-controlled economy.

Social reform efforts are usually considered more linked to the needs of the Shudra and Dalit castes. Yet in fact they functioned to provide an upgrading and 'modernization' of high-caste domination. The Prarthana Samaj in western India avoided such issues as caste and untouchability; women's education was taken up and there were hesitant steps forward on other issues of women's rights, but always argued for in terms of the needs of reformed men for a better family atmosphere; independent women activists such as Pandita Ramabai, Tarabai Shinde and Anandibai Joshi were nearly all marginalized.[48] The approach of the moderate Brahmans of Maharashtra was perhaps best expressed in the remark of M.G. Ranade that social reform was in 'the great Hindu tradition . . . of seeking out ancient principles in order to restate them'; instead of destroying the structure the reformer should 'lop off diseased overgrowth and excrescences and . . . restore vitality and energy to the social organism.'[49]

Bengal's Brahmo Samaj was comparatively more radical. It was thoroughgoing in its attacks on contemporary social customs of caste and on the subordination of women; it undertook major campaigns advocating widow remarriage, and it identified with a proclaimed monotheism rather than either the Vishnuite bhakti movement of Bengal or the Kali 'mother goddess' tradition. For these reasons, its members were segregated as an independent religious sect, with a separate law applied to them. Yet the Brahmo Samaj also essentially functioned as a 'modernizing' lifestyle for English-educated upper castes, and it continued to identify, if not with 'Hinduism' as such, with an Aryan 'Golden Age' in which the period of Muslim rule could be treated as medieval darkness and blamed for the degeneration of India.

The Arya Samaj, founded later than the other two, was the most aggressive in both its social reform and in identification with Vedic 'Aryanism'. It had its initial base among Punjabi trading castes in contrast to Maharashtrian Brahmans and Bengal *bhadralok*, and it sharply attacked some current Hindu practices including 'idolatry and polytheism, child marriage, the taboos on widow remarriage and foreign travel, and Brahman predominance.'[50] But to Arya Samajists the mitigation of casteism meant seeing all the main Hindu castes as descendants of Vedic Aryans, and absorbing untouchables within these by a *shuddhi* or 'mass purification' campaign. More than the other two organizations it attained a mass following, including some Dalits. The effect was both a process of 'sanskriticization' and a spectacular rise in membership from 40,000 in 1891 to half a million by 1921.[51] This also meant an increasingly militant confrontation with Muslims and an increasing identification of nationalism with Hinduism.

Thus, even before Veer Savarkar developed a thoroughgoing 'Hindutva' ideology during the 1920s equating 'Hinduism' and 'nationalism', the dominant elite ideological trend by the end of the nineteenth century was that of a revitalized Hinduism equated with nationalism. This was expressed in a range of ways. There was an organizational upsurge of orthodox forms of Hinduism, with Hari Sabhas and Sanatan Dharma Sabhas, Kumbha Melas and a big conference in Delhi in 1900 which started a Bharat Dharma Mahamandal.[52] At the same time 'moderate' social reformers were attacked as 'anti-nationalist'; the Social Conference was denied the use of the Congress pandal at the 1895 session by the Tilakites; a storm was raised to oppose the Age of Consent Bill in 1891 with arguments that foreign rulers had no right to interfere in social and religious customs.[53] Religious symbols (with implicit anti-Muslim interpretations) were used to popularize nationalism. Shivaji was depicted as founder of a 'Hindu raj', while the Ganapati festival in Maharashtra and the Kali cult in Bengal were linked to elite nationalism. Vivekananda, flashy and charismatic, exemplified the emotional appeal of this thrust: sharp words of criticism for existing 'degeneration' combined with passionate evocation of the glories of the past; emotional appeals for identification with the 'Daridra-narayana', the Shudra and untouchable, without any clear programme; a macho, almost martial image in which abstention from sexuality was linked to revolutionary dedication; and institutional efforts (the Ramakrishna mission) that focused on social welfare without any hint of social reform.[54]

There were contrapuntal elements in both nationalism and elite social reform: genuine concern of many of the early reformers to wipe out social evils; identification by young militants such as Bhagat Singh with revolutionary mass activity and the working classes. Yet the refusal or inability, even by the revolutionary militants, to confront Brahmanism and the reality of caste hegemony weakened their understanding of the masses they sought to 'liberate'. Linkages with the exploited low-caste peasants and workers were normally paternalistic and bureaucratic, while there was no resistance from the more left forces to the identification of the Indian majority as 'Hindu'. The ultimate result was that neither the Nehruvian 'secularism' nor Gandhian 'Ram-raj' could provide an Indian identity that was liberatory for Dalits and low castes; in Baburao Bagul's terms, they not only harked back to the past but accepted a high caste version of it.

■ STRUGGLES OF THE EXPLOITED

The toiling castes—Shudra peasants and artisans, Dalit village labourers, Adivasi forest-dwelling peasants—were subjected to new forms of exploitation by colonial rule, with their traditional 'caste duties' used for new forms of surplus production which aided centralized accumulation in nations far from their homes. Sometimes this meant they were bound to 'traditional' forms of village-based production and social relations even more than before, with an increased 'peasanticization' and solidification of *jajmani* relations. Sometimes it meant physical mobility as Dalits and Adivasis migrated thousands of miles to become plantation labourers; sometimes it involved recruitment into new factory and mining work with increased collective relations and the potential organizing power of the 'proletariat'. In most cases of this new labour recruitment, however, the terrible oppression of the labourers, high mortality rates, lack of education and maintenance of ties with home villages meant that mobility had few advantages for organization.

As a result, struggles of the most exploited sections were slow to develop; initial struggles were those of various types of peasantry, often under traditional leadership, and the slow organizing of the lowest castes under a few educated or semi-educated activists for new rights of access to economic opportunity. Because colonial exploitation involved the extraction of surpluses mediated through caste and community relations, very often caste and community became, in reaction, issues and weapons of resistance for the exploited.

The major form of resistance was through peasant revolts and movements; these took many and varied forms, ranging from seemingly traditional 'restorative' tribal uprisings to agitations against local exploiters (landlords and money-lenders) to both sporadic agitations and sustained campaigns against the British bureaucracy especially on forest issues and land revenue issues. In the early period these movements and agitations had only local, traditional leadership drawn from the peasant castes/communities themselves; later various types of nationalist and non-Brahman elites began to involve themselves in mass campaigns.

Dalits are not generally thought of as peasants; they were most often labourers, whether in plantations or (more rarely) factories or in the villages of their origin. Where they were peasants they were usually poor peasants. Thus, in left academic discussions of peasant organizing and 'class differentiation' among the peasantry, there is a tendency to consider that early peasant movements were often those of 'rich peasants' with poor peasants, and particularly Dalits, benefiting little from their agitations.[55] Yet Ambedkar had referred to 'Dalit peasants' being the primary victims of colonial exploitation, and made a major effort to identify his first political party, the Independent Labour Party, with 'workers and peasants'. It is worth, then, examining to what degree the traditional 'worker–peasant alliance' made sense in colonial India, in situations where there was often extreme hierarchy and fragmentation among the peasantry.

In fact, the formal categorical distinctions between 'cultivator' and 'agricultural labourers' masked a good deal of overlap, with the poorest villagers working both on their own land and on that of others and often migrating for wage-labour during part of the year. Nor were urban 'workers' themselves a solidly distinguished category; there was continual migration from the villages to specific jobs and maintenance of village links (often with the strong economic aspect that peasant members of the family in the villages bore the costs of reproduction of labour power). While the economic processes of production and accumulation of surplus defined degrees of exploitation and economic interests, it was traditional caste and community forms that determined the way in which individuals participated in these various processes.

The distinction between 'rich peasant' and the poor peasant-labourers is also unfruitful as a way of classifying rural struggles. Throughout the nineteenth century there were complex struggles and efforts of peasants to resist the worst of their exploitation, and gradually living standards did rise. But it cannot be proved that this was a 'rise of the rich peasants' in the sense that a polarization was occurring in village society in such a way that rich peasant gains were at the expense of greater exploitation and dominance over poor peasants and labourers. For instance, Sumit Guha's studies of the rise of the land market in western Maharashtra show that during the nineteenth century nearly all peasants were so crushed by the burden of high taxation and low prices that money-lenders were impelled to use the crop-lien system (i.e., taking control of the crop and selling it themselves); by the early twentieth century a moderate prosperity meant that a land market could emerge with some money-lenders gaining control of land and some peasants able to sell crops themselves, achieve some prosperity and engage in money-lending and labour-hiring on their own.[56] But to say that this 'rich peasantry' constituted a new exploiting section as part of a rising class of 'agricultural capitalists' aspiring to be part of the ruling class (which is the way many analyse such movements as the non-Brahman movements and the Satyashodhak Samaj) is entirely a matter of definition. Most studies, including Guha's, show that there was in fact a gradation more than a sharp break between 'classes of the peasantry' and that normally the prosperity of the 'rich peasant' was precarious and subject to the buffetings of famine and depression. Gradation in degree of wealth and access to resources does not itself constitute 'classes'.

The most detailed study of the Deccan region during the colonial period, by Neil Charlesworth on the Bombay Presidency, shows that as the peasantry gained access to economic benefits, the circle of beneficiaries began widening; while only a minority of peasants upgraded this standard of living during the late nineteenth century, by the 1900–1930 period wage labourers and tenants were also sharing in gains due to rising prices, while the depression, in contrast, tended to increase rural polarization and reverse 'centripetal tendencies'. Charlesworth concludes:

> In so far as the first stage of commercialization was pioneered by the minority with resources—carts, implements, and access to credit—to latch on to market opportunities, in many localities it developed as a stealthy process, peripheral to the central concerns of the village economy. After 1900 commercialization, in the more advanced regions and localities, had eaten into the heart of the village economy and its operations, but, coincidentally, the distribution of rewards from commercial agriculture and economic opportunities in general seem to have become more broadly based . . . . The rule may be, then, that more extensive commercialization tempers social stratification, and this may apply in other parts of Asia as well as India . . . . In this way the process of agrarian change in the Bombay Presidency differs radically from the classic Marxist 'agrarian transition' involving the complementary formation of a class of rising agricultural capitalists and a landless proletariat. Instead, it accords more closely with Goodman and Radcliffe's 'second formulation', drawn from Latin American cases, where 'peasant producers may be incorporated into commodity production and exchange but retain ownership of the means of production and control of the immediate production processes.'[58]

While incorporation and commercialization may have 'tempered social stratification' *within* the village; exploitation and social stratification on the societal level (between the villagers and the bureaucracy and national/international bourgeoisie) was in fact intensified.

An example of the broad process of exploitation through commercialization leading to a broad unity of resistance can be seen in the Bardoli anti-revenue struggle of 1928. For western India it was the climax of peasant resistance to expropriation of the surplus via land revenue. It was also an illustration of the complex hierarchies of caste and community linked to the struggle, and there has been a debate about its 'class' meaning. Charlesworth himself hesitates in describing Bardoli as a 'rich peasant' or 'middle peasant' struggle; he rules out the former on the argument that typical rich peasant politics cannot mobilize the masses of the peasantry, the latter because Bardoli had become a region of high differentiation and tenancy by the 1920s.[59]

The problem here lies partly in the definitions of 'rich' and 'middle' peasants in which the one is associated with commercialization, the other with an unreal image of a purely subsistence non-hiring cultivator. In fact the very complex population of Bardoli, ranging from the Dalit-tribal Raniparaj ('forest-dwellers', originally called more crudely 'Kaliparaj' or 'black people') to the Vanias, Anavil Brahmans, Parsis and peasant Kanbi-Patidars, had in common exploitation through commercialization in which low prices and high revenue demands combined to squeeze the entire rural sector. The ground for mobilization in Bardoli was prepared by Gandhian 'constructive work' centring among the Patidars and Kaliparaj tribals, and the struggle itself saw a wide mobilization of peasants, labourers and more elite commercial classes.[60] Charlesworth claims,

> Bardoli illustrates the alternative conditions for an assertive peasant politics. Where the commitment to commercial agriculture was socially extensive, then fluctuations in demand conditions could create grievances across different social groups. To be more specific, if the bulk of the Bombay peasants had been engaged in cash-crop production in the 1920s, then the price falls of the agricultural depression might have reaped a whirlwind of mass protest.[61]

Not only did the Bardoli Dalits participate in the struggle but, as we shall see, Ambedkar himself expressed his support for it. The fact is that the very unevenness and variabilities of the colonial exploitation processes imposed on a hierarchical traditional society meant a high degree of differentiation among the exploited. This did not necessarily mean polarization; instead it meant a differential impact of exploitation. Thus a broad unity of resistance could be created but only by linking the varying economic demands of variously exploited groups, and by articulating these with culture and community. The ability of any political movement among the exploited to create such a broad unity and to take up cultural along with economic issues was to be decisive; in the end it was the Gandhian-led Congress which succeeded in doing so, not the left aspirants to working class leadership.

■ JOTIBA PHULE AND SHUDRA–ATISHUDRA UNITY

Have the Brahman members of the Sarvajanik Sabha ever allowed the Mahars to sit along with them in the organization and have they ever cared to discuss sundry matters pertaining to their unfortunate practice of eating the flesh of dead animals? or have they ever cared to send a memorial to the Government about these matters? . . . . But you will surely find many petitions in the records of the Sarvajanik Sabha to the effect that the English government be pleased to appoint Hindus as collectors . . . .
There cannot be a 'nation' worth the name until and unless all the people of the land of King Bali, such as the Shudras and Ati-Shudras, Bhils and fishermen etc. become truly educated and are able to think independently for themselves and are uniformly unified and emotionally integrated.[62]

To Jotiba Phule (1826–1890), the nineteenth century social revolutionary and main founder of the anti-caste movement in India, the national unification of the masses of the people in India required an attack on Brahman domination and Hinduism itself. This attack he carried on at all levels, elaborating a theory of history along with a reinterpretation of Indian mythology, and communicating it to the masses with polemic tracts, songs, plays and organization-building.

The 'Aryan theory of race' constituted the most influential common discourse for discussing caste and society in Phule's time. European 'Orientalists' used it to assert an ethnic kinship between Europeans and ancient Vedic peoples; members of the Brahman elite such as Tilak used it to claim at once a 'European'-type superiority over the low castes of the subcontinent. At one level, Phule simply reversed it, arguing that the low castes, whom he sometimes called 'Shudras and Ati-Shudras' and sometimes simply listed as 'Kunbis, Malis, Dhangars . . . Bhils, Kolis, Mahars and Mangs', were the original inhabitants of the country, enslaved and exploited by conquering Aryans who had formulated a caste-based Hinduism as a means of deceiving the masses and legitimizing their power.

In his hands, though, it was more than a simple theory of racial oppression; an emphasis on the equalitarianism of the original peasant community, and on the role of force and violence along with ideology as factors in history, and a stress on the current exploitation of the peasantry by the British-headed but Brahman-dominated bureaucracy made it a holistic interpretation. Phule consciously sought to bring together the major peasant castes (these were, besides the Kunbis or cultivators, the Malis or 'garden' cultivators and Dhangars or sheepherders) along with the large untouchable castes of Mahars and Mangs in a common 'front' against Brahman domination. The aristocratic *sardars* among the Kunbis, or Marathas, were scorned but not directly attacked, while even the merchant castes were more or less ignored in an effort to focus on the Brahmans as the primary exploiting money-lenders. Phule was also highly critical of the British, but generally took the position of appealing to their goodwill, an early version of Ambedkar's later statement, 'we cannot fight all enemies at once.' Practically speaking, he succeeded in building a basis of support that ranged from relatively wealthy contractors to the poor Dalits who provided some 'street power', and made his Satyashodhak Samaj possibly the widest-ranging organization in India at the time in terms of caste membership.

The 'Aryan theory of race', interpreted in terms of a broader historical framework of a stress on force and violence in history, gave emphasis to a theory of exploitation that stressed the peasants as primary producers looted by the state. Here Phule's critique of the British colonial state was thoroughgoing, however much he stressed the domination in this of Brahmans in the bureaucracy. The state exploited the peasants through direct extraction in the form of taxes, cesses and 'funds' of various kinds, and indirectly through takeover of their lands; as a result 'the peasants are so looted that they have neither bread to fill their stomachs nor clothes to cover their bodies.' As his major work, *Shetkaryaca Asud* stresses, both the former regime of the 'Arya Brahmans' and 'the current government in its readiness to give its employees the pay and pensions they want levies all sorts of new taxes on the heads of the peasants and collects them so ruthlessly that the peasants have fallen under the burden of extreme debt.'[63] In addition, while previously poor peasants had scope for employment with feudatories as well as free use of forests and grazing land,

> now our *maibap* government officials, using their English wisdom, have at great expense raised up [*sic*] a huge new government forest department taking all mountains, forests, hills as well as wastelands and pasturelands under its control, so that the poor peasants have not a place left on the earth to feed their animals.[64]

Phule's descriptions of exploitation and his suggestions for economic development centre around the peasantry and agriculture, in contrast to the elite's fascination (even during the nineteenth century) for emphasizing industrial development. Here the focus is in fact very 'modern' in a green sense: it is on biotechnologies and watershed developments. He recommends the building of canals, bandhs, small and big dams to direct water to the fields, with soldiers and policemen providing the labour; returning to village control of all lands appropriated from them by the forest department; interbreeding with sheep and goats from other countries to increase production of organic manures as well as wool; sponsoring agricultural exhibits and holding training programmes and examinations, with awards for model farmers, to upgrade traditional skills; and reducing the pay of 'both white and black' government officials except for those in manual labour.[65]

Ideologically, the unity, rather the community of the exploited was sought to be built up first, by emphasizing the attack on Brahmanism and exploitation through religion, and second, by stressing the necessity of modern education and the acquisition of scientific knowledge, described as *vidya*, seen as in contrast to the Brahmanic and ritual-bound *shastra*. Phule's stress on education and knowledge showed a striking contrast with the upper-caste efforts to acquire technology while maintaining 'traditional' values (similar to the 'western science and eastern morals') of many cultures; he made it clear that education was a weapon to *change* 'eastern morals' and to bring about a kind of cultural revolution as well as a technological one. His defence of Pandita Ramabai

against the orthodox Brahmans who attacked her made that
clear, as he argued that while she had been a primary force in
encouraging education among girls, Brahmans had stopped send-
ing their daughters and daughters-in-law to schools since (they
were 'throwing away the scriptures' and revolting against family
authority)[66].

Phule both wrote new marriage ceremonies, following many
peasant traditions but without the use of Brahman priests, and
stressing equality between men and women, and in the end took
the radical step of proclaiming a new, theistic religion, the 'sarvajanik
satya dharma', with a strong, moralistic emphasis. But throughout
his stress on rationality and independent thinking remained, perhaps
best expressed in a very modern-sounding poem:

> All ideologies have decayed
> no one views comprehensively,
> what is trivial, what is great
> cannot be understood.
> Philosophies fill the bazar,
> gods have become a cacophony,
> to the enticements of desire
> people fall prey.
> All, everywhere it has decayed
> truth and untruth cannot be assayed
> this is how people have become one,
> everywhere.
> There is a cacophony of opinions.
> no one heeds another.
> Each thinks the opinion
> he has caught is great.
> Pride in untruth
> dooms them to destruction,
> so the wise people say,
> seek truth.[67]

And in fact, it was out of an expanding wave of consciousness
and quest, stimulated by the contradictions as well as the opportunities of the colonial period, that a new Dalit movement was to
grow.

NOTES

1. Frank Southworth has given many analyses of Dravidian influences on Sanskritic languages; see 'Lexical Evidence for Early Contacts between Indo-Aryan and Dravidian' and 'The Reconstruction of Prehistoric South Asian Language Contact' (manuscript); and 'Linguistic Stratigraphy of North India', *International Journal of Dravidian Linguistics*, III, 2 July 1974. The arrival of Indo-European speakers in the north Deccan is often linked with the 'Jorwe period' of about 1500–1050 BC; see Bridget and Raymond Allchin, *The Rise of Civilization in India and Pakistan* (Cambridge: Cambridge World Archeology Publications, 1982), chapter 10. Certainly a form of Dravidian appears to have been prevalent in much of the area before this, except for the east, including Nagpur where Gondi must have dominated and except perhaps for a possible original prevalence of Mundari languages in the tribal belt. See Iravati Karve, *Kinship Organization in India* (Bombay: Asia Publishing House, 1968) for a discussion of the kinship features.
2. See Clarence Maloney, *Peoples of South Asia* (New York: Holt, Rinehart and Winston, 1974), pp. 3–9, 8–10; David Ludden, *Peasant History in South India* (Princeton: Princeton University Press, 1985), pp. 18–19.
3. Allchin and Allchin, *The Rise of Civilization*, p. 353. See also Clarence Maloney, 'Archeology in South India', in Burton Stein, (ed.), *Essays on South India* (Honolulu: University of Hawaii Press, 1975), pp. 98–101.
4. Romila Thapar, 'Puranic Lineages and Archeological Cultures', in her *Ancient Indian Social History* (Delhi: Orient Longman, 1978), p. 253.
5. Maloney, 'Archeology in South India', pp. 9–11; along with many other archeologists and linguists Maloney also believes that Dravidian was a relatively recent historical import.
6. See Southworth, 'Prehistoric South Asian Language Contacts', pp. 11, 14, 19.
7. Stanley Wolpert, *A New History of India* (New York: Oxford University Press, 1977), pp. 75–76.
8. George Hart, 'Ancient Tamil Literature', in Stein, *Essays on South India*, pp. 55; D.D. Kosambi, *An Introduction to the Study of Indian History* (Bombay: Popular Prakashan, 1975), pp. 275–78, 280–81, 288.
9. See Sharad Patil, *Shivajicya Hindvi Swarajyace Khare Shatru Kon: Mahamadi ki Brahmani?* (Dhule: Satyashodhak Marxwadi Prakashan, 1992).
10. Uma Chakravarti, 'Towards a Historical Sociology of Stratification in Ancient India: Evidence from Early Buddhist Sources', *Economic and Political Weekly*, 2 March 1985.
11. Willie da Silva, *From Rta to Dharma* (Kanara: Pragati Publishers, 1985).
12. Burton Stein, *Peasant State and Society in Medieval South India* (New Delhi: Oxford University Press, 1980), pp. 63–80.
13. Recent Marathi books presenting this interpretation are Govind Pansare, *Shivaji Kon Hote?* ('Who was Shivaji') (Lok Wangmay, 1988) and Sharad Joshi et al. *Shetkaryanca Raja Shivaji* ('Shivaji the Peasants' King') (Shetkari Prakashan, 1988). Such an interpretation can be justified on the general evidence

of Shivaji's opposition to and ending of giving out rights in *watan*; see Andre Wink, *Land and Sovereignty in India: Agrarian Society under the 18th century Maratha Svarajya* (Cambridge: Cambridge Oriental Publication, 1986), pp. 269–70 and elsewhere. For a discussion of the social implications of various interpretations of Shivaji, see Rosalind O'Hanlon, *Caste, Conflict and Ideology: Mahatma Jotiba Phule and Low-Caste Social Protest in the Nineteenth Century* (Cambridge: Cambridge University Press, 1985).

14. Edgar Thurston, *Tribes and Castes of Southern India* (Madras Government Press, 1909), Volume III, pp. 94–98, 222–47, and R.E. Enthoven, *Tribes and Castes of Bombay* (Bombay: Government Press, 1905).

15. James Manor, *Political Change in an Indian State: Mysore, 1917–1955* (New Delhi: Manohar, 1977), pp. 34–36.

16. Cited in Gail Omvedt, *Cultural Revolt in a Colonial Society: The NonBrahman Movement in Western India 1873–1930* (Pune: Scientific Socialist Education Trust, 1976), pp. 71–72.

17. Eleanor Zelliot, *Dr. Ambedkar and the Mahar Movement* (University of Pennsylvania: Ph.D. dissertation, 1969).

18. Thurston, *Tribes and Castes*, Volume IV, p. 340.

19. *Ibid.*, p. 337.

20. *Ibid.*, p. 367.

21. See *Janata*, 20 August 1941.

22. Thurston, *Tribes and Castes*, Volume IV, p. 347.

23. *Ibid.*, p. 292.

24. *Ibid.*, pp. 337–42.

25. *Ibid.*, p. 342.

26. See Frederique Marglin, *Wives of the God-King: The Rituals of the Devadasis of Puri* (New Delhi: Oxford, 1985) for the Puri Jaganath temple *devadasis*. Amrit Srinivasan, 'Reform or Conformity? Temple "Prostitution" and the Community in the Madras Presidency', in Bina Agrawal (ed.), *Structures of Patriarchy: State, Community and Household in Modernising Asia* (New Delhi: Kali for Women Press, 1988) shows how the *devadasi*-originated dance was appropriated in the twentieth century by Brahmans and given the name of 'Bharatnatyam', with *devadasis* themselves stigmatized as prostitutes and barred thereafter from performing it. Girish Karnad's inaugural address to the second session of the Dalit–Adivasi Rural Literatures' Conference (Walwa, 29 October 1988) stresses this aspect of appropriation of low-caste and female-originated art forms by a bourgeois–Brahman elite and the need for Dalits and women to reclaim their heritage.

27. *Banhi*, August 1986.

28. Thurston, *Tribes and Castes*, Volume IV, pp. 293–95.

29. According to the All-India Debt and Investment Survey, *Assets of Rural Households* (Bombay: Reserve Bank of India, 1975), the average value of land per acre in Andhra was slightly higher than that in Maharashtra (though the value of land per cultivator was lower), but still much lower than that of other states in India, being about one-fourth that of Kerala and Punjab and one-third of Bihar.

30. Sumit Guha, 'The Land Market in Upland Maharashtra, c. 1820–1960', *Indian Economic and Social History Review*, 24, 2 and 3, 1987.

31. B.R. Ambedkar, Speech for the Depressed Classes Conference, Nagpur, 1930, in *M.P. Ganjare (ed.), Dr. Baḅasaheb Ambedkararchi hashane Khand 2* (Nagpur: Ashok Prakashan, 1974), pp. 78–80 (my translation).

32. See Gail Omvedt, in *Economic Review* (paper for Delhi seminar on 'The State, Social Movements and Democracy', New Delhi, 5–8 October 1992.

33. Immanuel Wallerstein, 'Development: Lodestar or Illusion', *Economic and Political Weekly*, 24 September 1988, p. 2018, emphasis mine.

34. Neil Charlesworth, *Peasants and Imperial Rule: Agriculture and Agrarian Society in the Bombay Presidency, 1850–1935* (Bombay: Orient Longman, 1985), pp. 67–68.

35. Immanuel Wallerstein, 'Incorporation of the Indian Subcontinent into Capitalist World-Economy', *Economic and. Political Weekly,* 25 January 1986.

36. Chris Fuller, 'British India or Traditional India: Land, Caste and Power', in Hamza Alavi and John Harriss (eds.), *Sociology of 'Developing Societies': South Asia* (London: Macmillan, 1989), pp. 34–38.

37. For a journalistic interpretation, but one not far from the point, see Girilal Jain, 'Ksatriya–Brahman Equation: Historic Shift Under the Raj', *Times of India*, 27 July 1988.

38. David Washbrook, 'South Asia, the World System, and World Capitalism', *Journal of Asian Studies*, 49(3), August 1990, p. 480.

39. For studies of forest policy and indigenous resistance to it see Ramchandra Guha, 'Forestry in British and Post-British India', *Economic and Political Weekly*, 29 October and 5 November 1983, and *The Unquiet Woods: Ecological Change and Peasant Resistance in the Himalaya* (Delhi: Oxford University Press, 1989); also J.F. Richards, 'Cotton Cultivation and Land Clearing in the Bombay Deccan and Karnatak, 1818–1920' (Mss. May 1981).

40. Wallerstein, 'incorporation', p. 32.

41. Cited in Sumit Guha, 'Commodity and Credit in Upland Maharashtra, 1800–1950', *Economic and Political Weekly*, 26 December 1987, A-133.

42. Amartya Sen, *Poverty and Famines: An Essay on Entitlement and Deprivation* (Oxford: Clarendon Press, 1981).

43. Anupam Sen, *The State, Industrialization and Class Formations in India* (London: Routledge and Kegan Paul, 1982), p. 78.

44. Washbrook, 'South Asia', pp. 488–90.

45. Baburao Bagul, 'Dalit Literature is But Human Literature', in Arjun Dangle (ed.), *Poisoned Bread: Translations from Modern Marathi Dalit Literature* (New Delhi: Orient Longman, 1992), pp. 282–83.

46. Sumit Sarkar, *Modern India, 1885–1947* (Delhi: Macmillan, 1983), pp. 86–95.

47. *Ibid.*, quoted on p. 69.

48. See Vidyut Bhagwat, 'A Review of the Women's Movement in Maharashtra', published in Marathi in *Paramarsh*, May 1989, pp. 40–42.

49. Quoted in Kumari Jayawardena, *Feminism and Nationalism in the Third World* (London: Zed Books, 1986), p. 80. See also Gail Omvedt, 'Feminism and the Women's Movement in India' (SNDT, 1983), Marathi summary in *Paramarsh*, May 1989.

50. Sarkar, *Modern India*, p. 74.

51. *Ibid.*

52. *Ibid.*, p. 75.

53. *Ibid.*, p. 73.
54. *Ibid.*, pp. 72–73.
55. The most extrème and clear-cut example is that of Jacques Pouchedass, 'Peasant Classes in Twentieth Century Agrarian Movements in India', in E.J. Hobsbawm (ed.), *Peasants in History: Essays in Honour of Daniel Thorner* (Delhi: Oxford University Press, 1980); but it pervades all Marxist writing.
56. Sumit Guha, 'Commodity and Credit:' see also Jairus Banaji, 'Capitalist Domination and the Small Peasantry: Deccan Districts in the Late Nineteenth Century,' *Economic and Political Weekly*, Special Issue, August 1977.
57. Charlesworth, *Peasants and Imperial Rule*, pp. 218, 223, 230.
58. *Ibid.*, p. 294.
59. *Ibid.*, pp. 282–89.
60. A factor stressed by Sarkar, *Modern India*, pp. 277–79 and analyzed by many studies of Bardoli, e.g., Anil Bhatt, 'Caste and Political Mobilisation in a Gujarat District', in Rajni Kothari (ed.), *Caste in Indian Politics* (New Delhi: Orient Longman, 1970), pp. 299–339. See also, Shirin Mehta, *The Peasantry and Nationalism: A Study of the Bardoli Satyagraha* (Delhi: Manohar, 1984).
61. Charlesworth, *Peasants and Imperial Rule*, p. 291.
62. See *Collected Works of Mahatma Jotirao Phule, Volume II: Selections*, translated by P.G. Patil (Bombay: Government of Maharashtra, 1991), pp. 25–26, 29.
63. Jotirao Phule, *Samagra Wangmay* (Bombay: Government of Maharashtra, 1991), p. 279.
64. *Ibid.*, p. 269.
65. *Ibid.*, pp. 329–33.
66. *Ibid.*, p. 372.
67. *Ibid.*, p. 440.

CHAPTER **3**

Emergence of the Dalit Movement, 1900–30: Nagpur, Hyderabad, Andhra, Mysore

■ INTRODUCTION: THE TUMULTUOUS TWENTIES

The decade of the 1920s saw the emergence of the Dalit movement as a conscious, organized force in the social and political life of Bombay Presidency, Nagpur (the Vidarbha area of the Central Provinces), Madras Presidency, and even to some extent in placid Mysore. Though much of the ground for Dalit advance had been laid earlier in terms of educational and social activities, the 1920s saw a qualitative leap forward.

At the global level turbulent post-war era was marked by the challenge of the Russian revolution, and in India by the British promise of new political powers to the Indians as set out in the Montagu–Chelmsford reforms. It was a period of advancing mass struggles and ideological upheavals. In India the working class began its major era of organization with the formation of the All

India Trade Union Congress (AITUC) in 1920. Peasant struggles arose, both against government rent levies and landlord oppression, and local organizations or kisan sabhas were founded in many areas, though it was not until the late 1930s that an all-India peasant organization was established. Along with peasant and worker struggles, nationalism itself was on a rising course: the Indian National Congress attained for the first time a mass membership and made rapid gains in new provinces and regions outside the established centres of Bengal, Madras and Maharashtra. Congress' new mass base was associated with the dominance of Gandhi and his particular combination of controlled, non-violent militancy, efforts to ally with Muslims in anti-British campaigns, and calls for social reform and 'constructive work'—all linked with the assertion of a Hindu identity, and a village-orientation justified in terms of an antagonism to 'industrial civilization' itself. But, while Gandhi represented in cultural terms a reformist Hinduism, rising non-Brahman movements in western and southern India and scattered Dalit movements throughout the country put forward a challenge to Hinduism itself with new, low caste, peasant and regional community identities.

In the context of a growing radical mass nationalism, this increasing activism of peasants, workers, Dalits and non-Brahmans could have provided a basis for a militant, combined struggle. But other, more ominous features existed during the twenties. Most important was the growing crystallization of Hindu–Muslim identities, increasingly seen as antagonistic, and the consequent development of religiously defined nationalism. In the case of Hindus this was marked by the formation of the Hindu Mahasabha in 1915 in north India and by the Rashtriya Swayamsevak Sangh (RSS or 'National Volunteers Organization'), a supposedly non-political Hindu cadre body in 1925. By and large it was these Hinduist elements in the Congress who allied with anti-Gandhian power-seekers in the 1926 elections to push for 'Responsive Cooperation' to run the new councils set up by the British government.[1]

Worker and peasant struggles, Gandhism, Hindu–Muslim tensions and the rise of Hindu nationalism, and non-Brahman political formations (the Justice Party in south India, the Non-Brahman Party in Bombay) all provided the ideological and organizational environment within which early Dalit organizing took place. At the same time, Dalit initiatives put pressures on these sections, making the issue of 'untouchability' a politically salient one. This process was at its most intense in Bombay Presidency, particularly the Marathi-speaking areas, where all elements—radical nationalism, Indian capitalism, a turbulent working class, assertive peasants, separatist non-Brahmans, orthodox Brahmans—seemed to be at their strongest. However, to some degree it occurred everywhere, in regions that remained to a significant extent independent of each other at least until the early 1930s when Ambedkar began to establish his position as an all-India leader. Thus we can get a better idea of the patterns involved by first analyzing organizing capacity of the Dalits in Nagpur, Hyderabad, Andhra and Mysore and then coming back to the awakening in western Maharashtra, the centre of the strongest Dalit movement, where B.R. Ambedkar rose to become its unchallenged leader.

■ NAGPUR (VIDARBHA)

Nagpur, almost in the exact geographical centre of India, was the city where some of the most momentous events of the Ambedkar-led Dalit movement took place: the 1930 Depressed Classes Conference which preceded his trip to London for the Round Table Conference and heralded the social radicalism of the 1930s; the 1942 Depressed Classes Political Conference in which the Independent Labour Party was wound up and the All-India Scheduled Caste Federation was established; and finally the 1956 *diksha* ceremony of mass conversion to Buddhism. Today the city remains an Ambedkarite stronghold with a conscious and militant Buddhist (ex-Mahar) community. Yet, paradoxically, while the Nagpur-Vidarbha region gave birth to a Dalit leadership of its own, this leadership tended to be pro-Congress and even pro-Hindu Mahasabha. Ambedkar had to clash with already established Dalit leaders in order to establish his own base in the area, which he had largely done by 1930. It is worth, therefore, examining early Dalit organizing in Vidarhba.

Nagpur, the 'city of snakes', was founded by the Gond raja of Deogarh during the seventeenth century. This raja was an opponent of the Mughal emperor; his rival, the Gond raja of Chandrapur a subordinate ally. In 1707, in a treaty with the Marathas, the

Mughal emperor returned lands which he had previously seized to Shahu Chhatrapati, the grandson of Shivaji, and gave him the right to collect revenue in both Gondwana and Berar. This right was in turn assigned to the feudatory Parsoji Bhonsla, whose descendents in 1743 established their capital at Nagpur aand brought in Brahman administrators, merchants and traders, and Maratha–Kunbi soldiers who took up the cultivation of land.[2] Thus the Gond tribals of the region began to be superceded, and it was in this period that Marathi replaced tribal languages around Nagpur itself, though it remained the language of the rest of the Vidarbha area for longer.

British conquest linked the Nagpur division (the present districts of Nagpur, Wardha, Bandhara and Chandrapur-Gadchiroli) with the Hindu-speaking districts of present-day Madhya Pradesh to form the Central Provinces. These had a form of zamindari settlement known in Nagpur as *malguzari*. In 1903, Berar, a rich cotton-growing tract capable of providing needed government revenue to an otherwise poor British province, was leased from the defeated Nizam of Hyderabad and annexed to the Central Provinces. Legally incorporated in 1935, it included the districts of Buldhana, Yeotmal, Amraoti and Akola, with a basically ryotwari settlement. The politics of Central Provinces– Berar were marked until 1935 with rivalries between Hindi-speaking and Marathi-speaking politicians and between Gandhians and Tilakites to gain control of the Congress, while in the Marathi-speaking areas both groups confronted a non-Congress challenge from non-Brahmans and a growing Dalit movement. Describing this political process, Baker argues that these greater 'internal' rivalries among Marathi speakers allowed Hindi politicians to gain control of provincial politics, though they came from a less-developed and less 'politicized' region.[3]

A relatively strong and independent Dalit movement grew in the Nagpur–Vidarbha region, linked to its social-economic characteristics. It was a relatively prosperous cotton-growing region from the nineteenth century, with accompanying trade and processing. The mills of Nagpur and some other major cities provided much needed employment with Mahars forming a larger section of the emerging industrial working class then in Bombay, comprising nearly 40 per cent of textile workers in Nagpur itself.[4] The commercialization of the agrarian economy laid the basis for undermining the traditional village *balutedari* system, and this, combined with the 'frontier' characteristics of eastern Maharashtra, aided the relative independence of Mahars. Many of the community were weavers, many more were small cultivators, and a few managed to become relatively affluent traders and bigger landholders, including four *malguzars*, two of whom later became followers of Ambedkar. With British rule and missionary activity a small but growing section gained access to education, and by the end of the nineteenth century began establishing their own schools. These educated and better-off Mahars generated a growing Mahar leadership, while the Mahar mill-workers,. weavers and poor peasants provided the community's militancy and the spread of the Satyashodhak movement among the region's non-Brahmans helped to give the militancy a radical ideological edge.

Among the early leaders, the most well-known even today is Kisan Faguji Bansode (1870–1946), of a rich peasant family of Mohapa (Nagpur district), who founded his first organization in his village in 1903 and many educational institutions after that, including a school for girls in 1907. He also started several papers, the *Nirikshak Hindu Nagarik* (1910), *Vithal Vidhvasak* (1913), *Mazur Patrika* (1918),and *Chokha Mela* (1931). *Mazur Patrika* was oriented to the increasingly active working class, but the names of others reflected his leanings towards the bhakti cult of Maharashtra; Bansode also wrote several books on the Mahar saint Chokhamela. Also important in this period was Vithoba Ravji Moonpandit (1860–1924) who concentrated on internal Mahar social reform. Of a slightly younger generation two men stand out: Ganesh Akkaji Gavai (1888–1974), from Amraoti district, who began by founding a 'Mahar Library' and 'Mahar Sudharak Mandal' in his home village, and Kalicharan Nandagawali (1886–1962), a less educated but wealthy *malguzar*, who is credited with founding the first girls' school and who became, with Gavai, the first Dalit member of the legislative council. Another important activist in the educational field was a woman, Jayabai Chaudhuri, a protege of Bansode.[5]

Even within the early group, important differences emerged that were to become clear by the 1920s. Bansode and Gavai, the most prominent leaders, educated and relatively articulate, were pulled into the orbit of the Tilakites and a pro-Hindu position, thus getting linked to nationalism; others remained aloof from what they saw as Brahman-dominated nationalism and joined Ambedkar along with most of the younger generation educated Mahars and the rural and urban masses in autonomous Dalit organizing. This process can be traced through several important conferences, a 1913 'Mahar Conference', the 1920 Akhil Bharatiya Bahishkrut Parishad ('All India Conference of the Boycotted'), and the 1930 Depressed Classes Conference, all held in Nagpur.

The organizers of the 1913 conference were the older Mahar elite, *malguzars*, contractors, *patils* and *patwaris*, foremen, clerks, teachers and railway employees; and it represented a coming together of all Mahar sub-castes with an emphasis on internal reform and educational advance. It stressed its support for the government, and the organization which was set up, with Vithoba Ravji Moonpandit as leader, called itself the 'Loyal Mahar Sabha'.[6]

In contrast was the Depressed Classes Association (DCA), organized in 1915 by Kisan Faguji Bansode and G.A. Gavai. This was influenced by Vitthal Ramji Shinde, a nationalist Maratha leader of western Maharashtra: the two had met him in 1910 and together joined the Prarthana Samaj; Gavai had also associated himself with Shinde's Depressed Classes Mission. Eventually these two and their younger followers (Raosaheb G.M. Thaware from Bandhara district, Hemachandra Khandekar from Nagpur district) joined either the Hindu Mahasabha or the Congress. This was correlated with the leaning to bhakti reformist Hinduism.

Anti-Hindu militancy had been frequently expressed in the region, with themes expressed by Bansode himself in a 1909 article:

The Aryans—your ancestors—conquered us and gave us unbearable harassment. At that time we were your conquest, you treated us even worse than slaves and subjected us to any torture you wanted. But now we are no longer your subjects, we have no service relationship with you, we are not your slaves or serfs . . . . We have had enough of the harassment and torture of the Hindus . . . . If you don't give us the rights of humanity and independence, then we will have to take our own rights on the basis of our own strength and courage, and that we will do.[7]

This linkage of the 'non-Aryan theme' and the declaration of autonomy used language that in this period was the common rhetoric of the non-Brahman Satyashodhak movement with its strong antagonisms to Brahmans (and Hinduism itself) and to the national movement. Yet Bansode's life-long attraction for Chokhamela and the bhakti cult, and his and Gavai's involvement in the Prarthana Samaj, seems to have pulled him away from cultural radicalism.

Politically many forces worked to absorb Dalit protest. The Tilakite tradition in Nagpur provided patronage links to Hindu nationalism, most importantly through B.S. Moonje, a Hindu Mahasabha leader, and Hegdewar, the founder of the Rashtriya Swayamsevak Sangh. Thus Gavai, who had been involved in many Dalit conferences (including north India 'adi-Hindu' conferences) during the 1920s, eventually supported a Hindu Mahasabha proposal for compromise during the 1932 clash between Ambedkar and Gandhi. He joined the Mahasabha in 1933 and harshly criticized Ambedkar's call for conversion in 1935. Thaware, who was involved with Gavai in the Depressed Classes Association, also joined the Hindu Mahasabha in 1941 and became a member of its executive, while Khandekar—a member of the earlier Mahanubhav bhakti sect—also became part of the DCA in 1930, opposed conversion, and finally joined Congress in 1942. Bansode never openly opposed Ambedkar, but after 1930 retreated to writing on Chokhamela and became increasingly irrelevant to Dalit social and political life.

This process slowly worked itself out during the 1920s. In 1920 itself, Bansode and Gavai called the Akhil Bharatiya Bahishkrut Parishad with Shahu Maharaj as president; due to Shahu's presence a large number of non-Brahman and Satyashodhak activists as well as Dalit leaders from western Maharashtra were present. The latter included Shivtarkar, Dr. Solanki and Shivram Janba Kamble of Poona, but most importantly of all, Dr. B.R. Ambedkar. But Ambedkar clashed bitterly with Gavai, using the occasion to denounce the Depressed Classes Mission and Shinde's hegemony in 'anti-untouchable' activity.[8]

Ambedkar's support began to grow in Nagpur. The rising generation of working class leaders, including Revaram Kavade and Dharmadas Nagarare (who were involved in a major 1919 strike and became part of the executive of the Nagpur Girni Mazur Sangh founded by Ruikar in 1923) joined him. So did most of the younger semi-educated generation who became involved in Nagpur organizations such as the Mahar Tarun Sangh. The group associated with Bansode and Gavai also wavered; for instance though Thaware joined the Hindu Mahasabha he continually expressed the fear that caste Hindus would not give up their injustice against Dalits and that independent electorates were probably necessary; in 1945 he joined the Scheduled Caste Federation but was later expelled. Nandagawali, an activist at points bracketed with the Bansode group, became an important supporter of Ambedkar, though he did not support the 1935 call for conversion.[9]

In spite of the prominence they gained as Dalit spokesmen, social reformers, members of the Legislative Council and many government committees and commissions, the Bansode–Gavai group could not maintain a Dalit mass base that was anti-Ambedkar and pro-Congress. Dalits as a whole remained aloof from the national movement, and rejected the support networks of both the 'Gandhian' and 'Tilakite' factions of nationalists, though they were heavily involved in working class militancy. Efforts to oppose Ambedkar's programme failed. Finally by the time of Ambedkar's visit of 1932, Gavai (who was by then working closely with Moonje) could not even make a nominal showing. According to a letter of Moonje,

> Mr. Gavai and his men could not muster strength and did not have the pluck or courage to create disturbances and show black flags as they had proposed to do . . . . The ignorant masses and mill hands who have been embittered and antagonized against the Brahmans and other high caste Hindus assembled in hundreds.[10]

'Hundreds' were to grow into thousands quite soon and into hundreds of thousands by the time of Ambedkar's final conversion ceremony in the 1950s as Nagpur, casting aside the reformist tendencies of its early Dalit leadership, became a stronghold of the militant Dalit movement.

This was really a clash between two models of advance for the Dalit movement. One, represented by the Bansode–Gavai generation of leaders, was basically a model of Hinduistic integration, which included Sanskritic reforms and an appeal to bhakti religious roots, and linked itself to support from nationalists and Hindu reformers, even conservatives. The other, represented by Ambedkar, with roots in the Satyashodhak movement and expressing an alliance with non-Brahman leaders, was basically an assertion of dalit **autonomy**, with an ideology that expressed contradiction and rejected Brahmanic and bhakti religious traditions.

Was Ambedkar's victory in Vidarbha so natural, so easily explainable by his status as the most articulate and powerful leader of the Mahar community? Localistic tendencies worked against him, and the local Mahar leaders had both an alliance with locally powerful politicians, and the weight of popular religious tradition on their side. Looked at in terms of problems and contradictions faced by Dalits, it could well be argued (as some do) that natural conflicts of interests between mainly middle-caste landed non-Brahman leaders and the mainly labourer and poor peasant Dalits could as easily lead Dalits to make an alliance with a reformist Brahman elite. But what we find in fact is that where non-Brahman hostility to a Brahman-dominated Congress nationalism was given up during the 1930s and where the Satyashodhak movement simply vanished as its activists were absorbed into Congress, the opposite process happened with the Dalit assertion of autonomy. Autonomy seems to have been the real issue here; autonomy and self-respect or *manuski* required a full rejection of Brahmanic ideology, and what the older leaders are castigated for with most bitterness is their degrading dependence on the Brahman politicians.

In Vidarbha, the basic **interests** of Dalits led them to such autonomy and rejection, while their relatively improved economic conditions built up their **capacities** to make this possible. Militancy met the needs of newly educated youth, an increasingly organized working class and the Dalit small peasants. And this meant militancy in both a social and economic sense, including an opposition to capitalism in the mills and landlordism in the rural areas. Here it was significant that where Punjabrao Deshmukh was voicing peasant demands and other Satyashodhak activists were involved in anti-landlord or anti-money-lender revolts at the time, it was the Tilakite Congress group which resisted any change in the *malguzari* system.[11] Caste and class radicalism were opposed by the Tilakite and Gandhian Congress leaders, expressed partly by non-Brahmans in the Satyashodhak movement and non-Brahman party—but carried on by Ambedkar into the 1930s and 1940s. It was not simply the fact that he was a Mahar leader, but that he was able to voice and organize the developing Dalit militancy, that made Nagpur a firm Ambedkarite centre.

■ ANDHRA (MADRAS PRESIDENCY)

Coastal Andhra shows another variation of the choices between autonomy and integration, as an independent Dalit movement began to emerge in the 1920s in a situation where agricultural commercialization laid the basis for a widespread rural movement but without the urban industrial centre found in Nagpur.

Seven districts of coastal Andhra (Srikakulam, Visakhapatnam, East and West Godavari, Ongole, Guntur and Nellore) and four districts of Rayalaseema (Kurnool, Chittor, Anantapur and Cuddapah) were included in Madras Presidency during colonial rule. These were disparate regions, the backwardness of dry and sometimes drought-stricken Rayalaseema contrasting with the economic energy that made the coastal region one of the most dynamic centres of development in the Presidency. It was primarily in the latter that a Dalit movement emerged.

Major irrigation schemes on the Krishna and Godavari rivers launched during the nineteenth century laid the basis for intensive cultivation of rice and other cash crops for a growing market; by the end of the 1920s, for example, over 42 per cent of the rice produced in Guntur district was marketed, generating fast-growing market towns such as Vijayawada, Guntur and Kakinadu.[12] The area, though formally under ryotwari tenure, had a considerable degree of zamindari holdings, and though the earliest industrial entrepreneurs were drawn primarily from large landlord families, merchants came from the traditional trading castes such as Komatis and Marwaris. At the same time, the development of agricultural enterprise provided the base for the assertion of a substantial peasant interest, mainly based among the Kammas. Commercialization meant unevenness, economic traumas and even a degree of polarization during economic crises.[13] It also eroded traditional caste and *jajmani* ties which had bound the Dalit labourers, and aided in the development of a mobile labour force with opportunities for some of the Malas and Madigas to move ahead. Mala migration to Burma from the late nineteenth century onwards was also a factor responsible for the slow advance.

In these economic circumstances a considerable amount of social change, cultural ferment and political turmoil occurred. Christian missionaries, concentrating in the coastal districts, converted a good many untouchables (mainly Madigas) and provided educational opportunities for many more. Hindu social reformers followed. Coastal Andhra was the site of one of the most radical elite-based reform movements outside of Bengal. Veerasalingam Pantalu was the nineteenth century pioneer, beginning with a bold widow remarriage movement and taking up issues such as dowry, prostitution, corruption of officials, and removal of untouchability.[14] He established the Brahmo Samaj in Andhra, and it was through this that the most important caste Hindu sponsorship of Dalit social advance took place. Early issues included not only education but acquisition of land; for instance, a Government of Madras bill on education 1895, called the 'Magna Carta of Panchama education', provided for schools, hostels and giving *poromboke* ('waste' lands) for institutional sites.[15] By the early twentieth century the Brahmo Samaj and other reformers were establishing ashrams for training untouchable cadre—including a Sevashram at Gudivada (Krishna district), started in 1912 by Sir Guduru Ramachandra Rao which called the most well-known ex-untouchable activists of the time to work in all Telugu-speaking districts. Among those many were to be active later during the 1920s, including Sundru Venkaiah, Kusuma Venkatramaiah, Kusuma Dharmanna and others.[16]

The Congress was dominated by a Brahman elite till the 1930s. However, beginning with 1917 an emerging non-Brahman movement in Madras Presidency challenged this dominance, putting forth a radical rejection of Brahman dominance, and laid the basis for many of the themes influencing Dalit movements, including a 'non- Aryan' or 'Dravidian' identity. But the Justice Party, the political wing of the movement, was in contrast to Maharashtra more elitist, with an Andhra leadership consisting primarily of zamindars and larger landholders, giving little scope for the participation of middle peasant Kammas and Kapus (beginning to identify themselves as 'Reddis' in caste associations). Though the Tamil non-Brahman movement became radicalized under the leadership of Periyar in the middle 1920s, taking up working class and anti-landlord issues and asserting both atheism and a radical perspective on women's oppression, this had little impact in the Telugu-speaking areas. Instead, in coastal Andhra the peasant Kammas and Kapu–Reddis asserted themselves organizationally in the 1920s through N.G. Ranga's peasant associations and the communist movement.[17]

Even before this, however, Dalits in coastal Andhra were asserting their organizational autonomy.

But, the context they were doing so had powerful, integrative-
Hinduistic pulls. Coastal Andhra also provided the base for an
emerging regional–nationalist consciousness. Demands for a
separate Andhra province began to be heard during the early
twentieth century after the Bengal agitation against Partition and
the Swadeshi movement. Many nationalists organized the Andhra
Mahasabha, which held annual conferences from 1913, and also
established a separate 'Andhra circle' within the Congress organization from 1918.[18] But this emerging Telugu consciousness
remained strikingly Hinduistic. It had a reformist tinge, with
Veerasalingam considered one of its forerunners as a founder of a
modern, mass-oriented literature, with the Andhra Mahasabha in
Hyderabad state associated with anti-untouchability efforts, widow
remarriage and opposition to *vethbegar*. Yet in spite of this linkage
to problems of the Dalits, Dalits themselves did not participate in
the formation of the 'Telugu consciousness', and it evolved first of
all as a Hindu consciousness. Partly this was due to the need to
reject the synthetic 'Deccani' Hindu–Muslim culture that many in
Hyderabad state were proclaiming. Nevertheless, it firmly identified early rulers such as the Satavahanas, Chalukyas and Kakatiyas
as Hindu, in spite of considerable Jain and Buddhist influences.
Indian unity also became symbolized as a Hindu unity, and as
Hargopal notes, an early twentieth century Telugu poem described India as a beautiful cow, the Hindus as its calves, and the
white man as the exploiter milking the cow by forcibly closing the
mouths of the calves.[19]

This Hinduistic and integrationist tendency can be seen clearly
in the two famous coastal Andhra caste Hindu novels written
about Dalits:[20]

Mallepalle ('Mala quarters' or 'Mala village'), by the famous
reformer Unnava Laxminarayan, describes the social and economic
effects of commercialization in the delta and the responses of
Dalits to this. Agricultural labourers are depicted as realizing the
manipulative potential of the new wage system in eroding real
wages; use of coercion, preventing cattle from grazing on private
lands, beating of Dalits and the eviction of poor peasants from
their lands are shown, along with a major crisis of traditional
cultural values. As Hargopal summarizes,

The main reason presented for the absence of class consciousness is the hegemony of the Hindu world-view conditioning the
consciousness of the Harijans. This prevents them from revolting. This theme is presented through one character who finds
several philosophical explanations for their degenerating living
conditions . . . . His elder son . . . opts for the Gandhian model
of resistance which broadly fits the Hindu philosophy of action.
He joins the 'panchama' movement launched by the scheduled
castes [and] attempts to organize his caste people. But the
landlord who smacks the potential of the movement violently
kills him. This act . . . gets absorbed by the peaceloving nature
of these groups coupled with the manipulations by the ruling
elite and the intervention of the state. This indicates not only
the structural constraints in which the poor Harijans were locked
but the cobweb of consciousness which permitted them little
concerted and organized action.[21]

Harijan Nayakudu ('Harijan Leader') written by N.G. Ranga
and published in 1933 reflected the ideological positions of this
peasant leader. The hero is a 'Harijan' social reformer who agitates
on various issues, opposing the violence against and abuse of
Dalits, organizing inter-caste marriages, establishing schools, fighting for entry into temples and use of public wells. Dalits are
depicted as allying with peasant Kammas in contrast with the
Kamma landlords who do not soil their hands.

Hargopal, as a Marxist, critiques the reformist (integrationist)
consciousness depicted in the Dalits' falling prey to themes of class
harmony and change of heart, in accepting their status as Hindus.
But what even the Marxist did not recognize (and it is striking that
even in the 1980s, and 1990s Marxists throughout India continued
to refer to Dalits as 'Harijans'), is that in the 1920s and 1930s
militant Dalits were thoroughly rejecting both the 'Panchama' and
the 'Harijan' identity and were organizing themselves as **Adi-
Andhras**.

The term 'Adi-Andhra' arose in the post-1917 period when
Dalits all over the south, influenced by the 'non-Aryan' themes of
the Dravidian movement, were identifying themselves as Adi-
Dravidians, Adi-Andhras and Adi-Karnatakas, original sons of the
soil. For coastal Andhra, the decisive year was 1917. At this time
the reformer Guduru Ramachandra Rao called a conference in

Vijayawada which was labelled a 'First Provincial Panchama Mahajana Sabha', with his protege Sundru Venkaiah as chairman of the reception committee. But on the evening of the first day, its president, a Dalit from Hyderabad named Bhagyareddy Varma, argued that the term 'Panchama' was nowhere found in the Puranas or other Hindu scriptures and that 'the so-called Panchamas were the original sons of the soil and they were the rulers of the country.' The delegates then rejected this term and constituted themselves as the 'First Adi-Andhra Mahajan Sabha'. Resolutions were relatively non-controversial, appealing to the government to nominate Adi-Andhras to the local bodies and the Legislative Council, and to establish separate schools and wells in Mala and Madiga areas. But caste tension showed up in the fact that delegates had trouble getting accommodation in the town, and for the three days of the conference the well-known Kanaka Durga temple was closed for fear of an attempted entry.[22]

After this Adi-Andhra conferences were held practically every year: at Gudivada in 1921 with Bhagyareddy Varma and Sundru Venkaiah again presiding; at Eluru in 1922 with Bhagyareddy Varma and Devendrudu; at Guntur in 1924 with Kusuma Venkatramaiah and Mutakki Venkateswarlu; at Anantapur in 1925 with Bhagyareddy Varma (this time a resolution asked for the rights of untouchables to use water from common wells); at Venkatagiri (in Nellore district) in 1926 with Devendrudu and Kamatam Shanmugan; at Narasapuram (West Godavari) with Bhagyareddy and Gottimukkala Venkanna; once more at Vijayawada in 1929 with Prattipati Audinarayana and Vemula Kurmayya; and at Anantapur again in early 1930 presided over by Devendrudu.[23] Except for Anantapur, all these were in the coastal Andhra region. After a brief hiatus around 1930, Adi-Andhra conferences were again held throughout the coastal region for a number of years in the 1930s.

The decade of the 1920s remains one in which the lack of historical and written documentation and efforts to uncover the history of the Dalit movement in coastal Andhra have left large vacuums in knowledge. But the very spread of the conferences throughout the districts indicates a broad rural base to the movement. So does the fact that by 1931 the Census indicated 838,000 people listing themselves as 'Malas', 665,000 as 'Adi-Andhras' and 612,000 as 'Madigas' in Madras Presidency.[24] The Adi-Andhra consciousness and the broad ideology of autonomy implied in it were becoming a significant social force in the Andhra coastal region, even while much of the mass-based Telugu consciousness was taking on a Hindu colouring and an acceptance of Brahmanism.

■ HYDERABAD

Another variation of the 'autonomy–integration' theme can be found in the specialized circumstances of Hyderabad state, where an active but factionalized Dalit leadership with almost no rural roots emerged during the 1920s.

The British had set up Hyderabad as the largest state in the Indian subcontinent, but left it with a backward economy. The richer agricultural regions which the Nizam had earlier controlled— Berar (Vidarbha) and coastal Andhra—were annexed to British territories. There was little development either of commercial agriculture or industry until after the first world war; education was limited, especially for Hindus; land relations were backward and it may not be inaccurate to call the state the most 'feudal' in the Indian subcontinent.

Hyderabad state consisted of nine districts of Telengana (Adilabad, Hyderabad, Karimnagar, Khamman, Nalgonda, Warangal, Mahbubnagar, Medak and Nizamabad), five of Marathwada (Bhir, Aurangabad, Parbhani, Nanded and Osmanabad) and three of the Hyderbad Karnatak (Gulbarga, Bidar, Bijapur: Of these the Telengana region made up 47 per cent of the population and represented the largest linguistic unit.

Based primarily on the Deccan plateau, between the Krishna and Godavari rivers, the state had mainly a dry economy cultivating jawar and bajra and limited rice, wheat and pulses as the main food crops. Through the 1920s the only cash crops were groundnut, tobacco and oil seeds (primarily in Nizamabad, Mahbubnagar, Karimnagar and Warangal districts). Irrigation and commercial agriculture did not really become significant until the 1930s when cotton and sugarcane cultivation began on a larger scale. Throughout the period, there was little growth of agriculturally-linked trade and business, and little development of roads and other infrastructure. Only minor industry developed in the towns of Hyderabad, Warangal and Aurangabad, with some coal mining in the Telengana region.

Thus it is not surprising that in spite of efforts to 'modernize' administration along supposed British lines by ministers such as Salar Jung in the mid-nineteenth century, the state remained backward. Nearly one-third of the entire area was under bigger jagirdars, of whom there were about 1,500 by 1949. In the state-controlled areas of ryotwari type land settlement, *deshmukhs* and *deshpandes* who had previously been revenue collectors were pensioned-off, but they retained large landholdings and continued to lord it over tenants and labourers. There was a limited growth of owner–peasant cultivation after 1930, which some analysts describe as a 'rich peasant economy' including immigrant peasants from coastal Andhra, but for much of the period actual tenancy remained high.[25] For the untouchable Malas and Madigas, this meant that traditional or caste–feudal forms of subordination retained their full force, and unlike the Mahars in Maharashtra or their castefellows in coastal Andhra, they had little opportunities to move into freer forms of either industrial or agricultural wage labour.

The autocratic Nizam regime also effectively repressed political developments. The Congress and communists alike hardly made a beginning, even through front organizations, until the late 1930s. Instead the Arya Samaj took on political importance, and fed into the Congress movement to give it a 'Hindu nationalist' tenor. Local Muslims and some Hindus (very often Kayasthas, a non-Brahman writer caste who had gained important bureaucratic posts in the Nizam regime) formulated an ideology of a multi-religious, pluralistic 'Deccani Hyderabad culture' form the nineteenth century, but this came under attack both form Hindus and those Muslims who sought to promote a more orthodox Islamic identity. Thus, even as the Dalit movement developed, it did so within a dangerously polarizing Hindu–Muslim tension.

Dalits faced pressures on both sides, to identify themselves as Hindus or with Muslims. In some ways there was a closeness in Dalit–Muslim relations in the Hyderabad area itself, yet it was a closeness characterized by ambiguity. The relationship was expressed in a saying quoted by one Dalit activist, 'The Dalit colony is the Muslim's in-laws' place', meaning that Muslims took wives/girls from among Dalits. But this was an unequal relationship. In the *devadasi* custom among Malas and Madigas, the *basavis* or *matangis* very often formed relations with affluent or noble Muslims in Hyderabad itself, and when the Dalit reformers moved to stop the custom in the 1920s, one result was to increase Muslim antagonism. Muslims were 'always after our girls', was a Dalit complaint. The 'closeness' thus had a clear element of sexual exploitation in it, though Muslims did not observe untouchability, and was symbolized in the naming of Hyderbad itself, after a Dalit girl (Bhagyamma or Hyder Ali) said to have been brought into the harem of the founding prince.[26] While other exploited sections identified both Hindus and Muslims as oppressors, and still others were led into the Hindu fold, there was some Dalit attraction to Muslim culture in Hyderabad. The period between 1920 and 1940 saw a clear split in the Hyderabad Dalit community on this issue.

In this narrow and communalized framework, a small but vigorous Dalit movement developed after 1910, based among Hyderabad Malas. This particular movement has the advantage of having its organizational history thoroughly documented by a later activist, P.R. Venkatswamy.[27] Two men stood at the centre of it in the early period, Bhagyareddy Varma and Arigay Ramaswamy. Bhagyareddy (1888–1939) was originally Madari Bhagaiah, a steward for a Catholic family who educated him, who became involved with, and later employed by, the Brahmo Samaj and took the name 'Bhagyareddy Varma' to emphasize the rights of Dalits to claim a high status, 'Varma" being Brahmanic and 'Reddy' indicating high status non-Brahman.[28] His organizing activity began in 1912 when he formed the Manya Sangam, with members including a building contractor, a confectioner-baker, the Superintendent of the Hyderabad public gardens and other employees, a disparate group which gives a sense of the emerging 'Dalit middle class', still without much education but, as a colleague described them, 'young and enlightened young men'.[29] At the same time Arigay Ramaswamy, who had been an office boy, carpenter and ticket collector on the railroads, began a social reform group in Secunderabad; and Madari Audia, the son of a butler, had started another Manya Sangam at Ghasmandy. All these organizations stressed internal social reform: attempting to ban drinking of alcohol and meat-eating at social functions, abolition of the *devadasi* custom. This group also found itself in conflict with the traditional 'caste *chaudhuris*' or headmen of the Malas, and worked throughout the 1920s to reform this system, settling up alternative 'courts' to handle disputes outside the state's courts and in the process to try to broaden caste customs.

As this emerging, partly-educated Dalit middle class began to enter social life, the radicalization among Dalits throughout south India brought with it an identification with the 'adi' ideology. It was Bhagyareddy Varma himself who presided over the momentous conference at Vijayawada in 1913 when the 'Panchama' identity was rejected, and over a number of conferences after that. Nevertheless, in Hyderabad itself organizing took up an 'Adi-Hindu' theme: four Adi-Hindu conferences were organized between 1912 and 1924, and gradually the main organizers began to use this terminology. In 1924 Arigay Ramaswamy formed the Adi-Hindu Jatiyonnati Sabha; not to be outdone, Bhagyareddy transformed his Manya Sangam into the Adi-Hindu Social Service League. This became the main organization of the Dalits of Hyderabad, a feat attributed to his energetic organizing and ability to gain support from liberal Hindu sympathizers. Along with the traditional aims of internal reform ('removing social evils, establishing schools, societies, reading rooms, bhajan *mandalis*'), the aims of the organization included 'removing ignoble appelations and spreading the identity of 'Adi-Hindu'.[30]

What exactly did the 'Adi-Hindu' identity connote? This term was spreading among sections of north Indian Chamars at this time claiming them to be exploited and conquered original inhabitants,[31] and Bhagyareddy himself travelled to north India for some of the conferences, notably two in 1927 and 1930, which described the 'depressed classes' or 'adi-Hindus' as 'descendents of the original inhabitants of this country who were rulers and owners of this land of their birth before, the advent of the Aryans to the country.'[32]

This was familiar anti-caste radicalism. But 'adi-Hindu' could also leave space for an identification as Hindus with simply the assertion added that Dalits could claim a high position within the total community, that they had been among the creators of the Hindu epics.[33] These were issues debated and discussed among Dalits, and the 1931 Hyderabad Census reported on the controversy:

A controversy recently raged in the press as to whether the Adi-Hindus are Hindus. While the caste Hindus maintained a discrete silence, two opposing sections of Adi-Hindus entered the arena. The Adi-Dravida Educational League argued that, judged by the history, philosophy and civilization of the Adi-Dravidas, the real aborigines of the Deccan, the Depressed Classes are, as a

community, entirely separate and distinct from the followers of
Vedic religion, called Hinduism. The League's contention was
that Hinduism is not the ancestral religion of the aborigines of
Hindusthan; that the non-Vedic communities of India object to
being called 'Hindu' because of their inherited abhorrence of
the doctrines of the Manusmruti and like scriptures, who have
distinguished themselves from caste Hindus for centuries past,
that the Vedic religion which the Aryans brought in the wake of
their invasion was actively practiced upon the non-Vedic aborigines, and that the aborigines, coming under the influence of
the Hindus, gradually and half-consciously adopted Hindu ideas
and prejudices. A section of Adi-Hindus emphatically repudi-
ated the above arguments in a statement in the press and
deplored the tendency of the Adi-Dravida Educational League
to seek to impose an invidious distinction. The concepts of God,
the mode of worship, the system of rituals and code of customs
and the manner of dress and way of life of the socially depressed
classes are identical with those of the caste Hindus, and therefore they maintain that religiously adi-Hindus are Hindus.[34]

This was a clear posing of the 'autonomy-integration' dichotomy in
terms of religious–cultural identities.

But who exactly was taking which side? The term 'Adi-Dravidian'
indicates a Tamil group; all the Telugu-speaking Dalits were describing themselves as 'Adi-Hindu', but there were differing trends
among them. Arigay Ramaswamy, according to Venkatswamy's
account, who was himself religiously inclined and adopted the
pose of a guru, seemed to have had tendencies towards an incorporative position:

'In our meetings he used to instill in us the sense of self-respect
and to feel proud of ourselves as we were the aboriginals and
masters of this land. The foreign invaders hostilely dubbed us as
'Rakshasas' in their Shastras and Puranas. At the same time he
insisted that we should give up the social evils which crept into
our society and due to which we were contemptuously treated
by the Hindus . . . . From Hindu platforms he talked of Vedanta,
defects in the social structure, criticized Brahmans and recited
atrocities against the Panchamas and the inhuman treatment
meted out to them in the abominable Manusmriti.[35]

This was by and large an integrationist position. In later times Ramaswamy opposed Ambedkar's 1935 call for conversion and joined the nationalist Andhra Mahasabha, staying with the 'right wing' of Gandhian Congressites when the split occurred between them and the communists. Later he followed his Congress connections to become part of the All-India Depressed Classes League (also called the 'Harijan League') led by Jagjivan Ram.[36]

Bhagyareddy's rejection of tradition was more radical. In treating untouchables as the original 'sons of the soil', in seeing Brahmans as outsiders pushing all the original Indians down to south India, he was said to have used the term 'Adi-Hindu' in a way in which 'Hindu' did not refer to religion but was given by foreigners to those living in India. He opposed temple entry movements generally, and at one of the important Adi-Andhra conference disputes in 1938 in East Godavari, refused to preside until all there agreed *not* to support a bill for temple entry then being introduced in the Madras provincial council by M.C. Rajah. He was also an ardent admirer of Buddha and celebrated Buddha *jayanti* for the first time in 1913 and again in 1937, two years before his death. While politically inactive during the 1930s, he gave his support mainly to the Ambedkarite group of Dalits in Hyderabad.[37]

The 'autonomy versus integration' dispute which we have seen in the Nagpur–Vidarbha region was playing itself out among the Dalits of Hyderabad in a context in which an appeal to identity as 'original inhabitants' dominated discourse. However, the limitations of the Hyderabad organizing efforts have to be noted. Almost all organizing contacts were limited to Hyderabad city, in contrast to Maharashtra and the Andhra areas. Although leaders like Bhagyareddy Varma made trips to north India and coastal Andhra, there is little evidence from accounts such as Venkatswamy's of vital rural contacts in Hyderabad state itself, though some village schools were said to have been founded. There was also clearly no working class of the type which lent such vitality in Nagpur and Bombay, and no sign of much thinking on economic issues during the 1920s.

Hyderabad Dalit politics was marked by intensive competitive struggles. During the 1920s these were primarily between Arigay Ramaswamy and Bhagyareddy Varma, founding rival 'Adi-Hindu' organizations, rival reformed caste panchayats, with occasional physical confrontation and fights between the factions. During the 1930s similar battles took place between B.S. Venkatrao and Arigay Ramaswamy, and later between Venkatrao and Subbiah. While there were ideological–political differences embodied in these disputes, the personal competition for leadership is striking.[38] In all of this none of the Hyderabad leaders seemed to be in a position to organize any mass movement. During the 1930s, Ambedkar's movement was to attain some significant mass base in the Marathi-speaking regions of the state, while the communists won a foothold in the rural Telugu districts using some of the same issues the Ambedkarites were using in other terminology—opposition to *vethbegar* and land for the landless. But the Telugu-speaking Hyderabad Dalit leadership appeared aloof from this; when they went as Dalits to the rural areas in the 1940s they most often went to Marathwada and there had to speak the language of Ambedkarism; they had little organic connection of their own. Perhaps because of this, for all the initial impulse towards an autonomous Dalit identity, in practical political terms the main Dalit organizations and leaders of Hyderabad were to be divided, in later years, between Hindu (Congressite) and Muslim (pro-Nizam) orbits.

■ MYSORE

In stark contrast to feudal, autocratic Hyderabad, Mysore state represented the epitome of reformism among the Indian princely states: reformism in taking up Gandhian 'constructive work', including untouchable-uplift programmes; reformism in providing for limited electoral participation; and reformism in its tradition of state-guided economic development. In spite of the very unGandhian implications of industrialization, Gandhi himself, who was a state guest several times, called it the nearest approximation to 'Ram-raj'.[39]

After the British victory over Tipu Sultan, the state had been restored to its earlier Hindu rulers, the Wodeyars, who had originated from a small low caste which claimed Yadava descent. In 1830 there was a revolt in the northern part of the state by its turbulent feudatories, the poligars. In suppressing it the British took over direct administration of the state. After 1861 a reformist governor used state funds for restoring irrigation works, repairing tanks, giving incentives to coffee production and building the beginnings of a railway system. Even so, the exploitation of the peasantry through commercial agriculture and high revenue demands in cash resulted in one million dead in a famine in 1876–78.[40] Shortly after this, in 1881, the state was restored to the Wodeyars and in spite of some tension over the amount of financial subsidy paid by the state to the British, the British alliance with Indian princes was little disturbed. While the Mysore maharaja became a hero to nationalists and contributed to Congress funds, its dewan Mirza Ismail, who represented it at the 1930 Round Table conference, was an important initiator of the 'federation' proposal for relations between the princely states and British India which became a centrepiece of the Government of India Act of 1935.

Common themes can be traced underlying all this British, princely and Gandhian paternalism. In Mysore the Hinduistic guiding spirit of this 'politics of petition and patronage' was given in a letter by Vivekananda written to the Maharaja on 23 June 1894:

The only service to be done for our lower classes is to give them education to develop their individuality. That is the great task between our people and princes . . . . Priest power and foreign conquest have trodden them down for centuries, and at last the poor in India have forgotten that they are human beings. They are to be given ideas, their eyes are to be opened to what is going on in the world around them, and then they will work out their own salvation . . . . My noble prince, this life is short, the vanities of the world are transient, but they alone live who live for others . . . . One such high noble-minded and royal son of India as your highness can do much towards raising India on her feet again and thus leave a name to posterity which should be worshipped.[4]

On the one hand a smothering paternalism while on the other was an economic development which managed to avoid major social turmoil. A certain amount of industrialization took place in Mysore, with some spectacular schemes after 1900, including electricity, the railway, textile mills, and a major iron and steel works. Most of this was centred in Bangalore, with only three other towns involved (Kolar with gold fields; Bhadravati with the iron works, and Mandya with a sugar factory). The overwhelming proportion of the working class was Tamil, and though many of these were Dalits and formed a base for a radical Dalit movement, there was a glaring social gap between them and the Kannada Dalits, little linkage with the Kannada rural areas.

In spite of major cash crops (oil seeds, coffee, sugarcane, mulberry, arecanut, cotton, tobacco), the rural economy was less differentiated, with a relatively small proportion of agricultural labourers, an insignificant proportion of tenants to owner–cultivators and of farm servants to field labourers. Both Holeyas and Madigas seem to have been well represented among 'Cultivators' (see Tables 2.2 and 2.3). The 1891 Census report indicated that although the Dalits were chiefly employed as labourers, still both Holeyas and Madigas held the status of landholders and 'as subtenants were found everywhere'; it also noted that many were revenue payers (that is, independent cultivators) and that they contributed a total Rs. 3 lakh towards land revenue, with Holeyas accounting for two-thirds and Madigas for one-third.[42] Dalits in Karnataka were relatively better off economically and freer socially compared to coastal Andhra and feudal Telengana, with more claim to the land, and less bondage to it.

The decade of the 1920s was dominated politically by the Brahman–non-Brahman conflict in Mysore state, but this was elite-based, with no rural connection, little articulation of a broad ideology and no effort at mass organizing. Caste associations formed after 1905 included the Veerashaiva Mahasabha, the Vokkaliga Association, the Adi-Dravida Abhi-Vruddhi Sangha, the Kuruba Association and the Central Muslim Association. These began to contest Brahman dominance in the Mysore administration. In 1918 they submitted a memorandum to the government, and the Miller Commission that year issued a report which was accepted by the government in 1919; this gave representation to the 'Backward Castes' but generally ignored the Dalits.[43] In a related development, a Praja Mitra Mandal, inspired by the Madras non-Brahman movement represented the interests of an alliance of non-Brahmans (primarily Lingayats and Vokkaligas) and Muslims, with some connection to the Muslim dewan Mirza Ismail; it remained pro-government and anti-nationalist. After the 1927–28 'Bangalore disturbances' among Hindus and Muslims, Brahmans used anti-Muslim communal sentiments to force Ismail to resign.[44] A more nationalist leadership emerged in 1930 to form the Praja Paksha; this merged with the Praja Mitra Mandal to form the People's Federation which ultimately merged with the Congress in 1937. A rural orientation began to be visible, with a linkage to district politics, the voicing of agrarian grievances, and a proposed programme of 'ryots conferences' in early 1935 which was abandoned after a government ban. But these broad linkages, mild even in the 1930s, were totally absent in the 1920s.

Thus, Mysore shows the same broad trends of political organization and development as other areas, but at a much lower level of turbulence, organizational and ideological activity. Above all, the 'non-Brahman movement' in the state was no movement at all, rather a lobbying effort of the non-Brahman castes which ignored Dalit interests and did not take up mass-based issues or provide any ideology or any broad-level sponsorship for Dalit organizational activity. The only non-Brahmans who played important roles in Dalit organizing—C. R. Reddy and Murugesh Pillai—were non-Kannadigas.

Nevertheless the Mysore case shows a particular aspect of responses to the issue of untouchability: Brahman sponsorship of Dalit organizations as a strategic reaction to the threat of non-Brahman political domination. From the 1920s 'Adi-Karnataka' movements (which we might distinguish from the 'Adi-Dravidian' tendencies among Tamil Dalit workers in Bangalore and Kolar) to the 'Harijan' activity of the 1930s, this role of Brahman patronage is clear. While Dalits got little from the limited Mysore type of non-Brahman organizing, Brahmans moved to fill the gap, offering a guided form of 'Harijan uplift' and an ideology of integration. Why did this happen? According to Manor, Brahmans could not hope for power in competition with the numerous non-Brahman castes, and so they contented themselves with 'the theatre of politics . . . in the satisfaction of being associated with a higher cause' of reformism. He also notes 'a tendency of some Congressmen to clothe Brahman communal sentiments in Gandhian wrappings.'[45] Another political scientist, Hettne, writes,

In terms of mobilization, the Harijans on the whole were as backward as in other respects. The Harijan movement had not been a movement of the Harijans, but a movement among caste Hindus, primarily Brahmans with Gandhian leanings, who devoted themselves to the 'uplift' of the depressed classes. The 'movement' had brought the Harijans within the Congress fold.[46]

However, there is no reason to assume that this Brahman activity had only symbolic political significance. A forward looking strategy could easily see that, against the Lingayats and Vokkaligas (who were to be 20 per cent and 13–14 per cent respectively in the unified Karnataka state), an alliance of some kind with the Dalits (who were 17–18 per cent) and other low castes was a natural strategic option.[47]

In this context, there was a fair amount of activity by the 1920s, though little of an independent Dalit movement.

Educationally some progress was made. By 1904–05 there were 76 schools for depressed classes, 37 government schools, 36 government-aided mission schools, and three unaided.[48] In 1915 there was a famous test case in which the government ordered a schoolmaster in the Sringeri jahagir to admit untouchables; there was protest from both caste Hindus and Muslims who withdrew students, but C.R. Reddy, then administrator of schools, prevailed upon the maharaja to declare that education was everyone's right. In 1919 the order was generalized to allow 'Panchamas' into all schools; again in spite of protest the maharaja stood firm.[49] By the 1920s a small educated section was making a limited entry into government employment: statistics showed there were 165 Dalits in 1918 of a total of 4,234; after the Miller Committee report they were only 13 of 1,051 new appointees up to 1924.[50]

Two Dalit organizations came into existence. The Adi-Dravida Abhivruddhi Sangam was led by Murugesh Pillai and apparently Tamil-based, though it sought to include Kannadigas; the Adi-Jambava Sangha was based on Madigas. Both organizations were limited to Bangalore and Mysore. Pillai, an assistant woolen master in Binny Mills, Bangalore, and apparently a Tamil non–Brahman who was active as a Dalit spokesman for three decades, was part of the Praja Mitra Mandal for a while and in 1917 supported the Miller commission, but later distanced himself from non-Brahman activities. Chikhahamanthaiah and Cheenigaramaiah were among the Kannada Dalits associated with the Adi Jambava Sangha. The former, with support from Murugesh Pillai and the

Tamil Brahman reformer Gopalswamy Aiyar (most prominent of the early Brahman patrons of Dalit causes) organized a 'political conference of Panchamas' in 1920. Ambedkar was invited for this but could not attend this due to a state ban on his entry. Other conferences were organized in 1923 and 1925 by the same group, with M.C. Rajah attending. These conferences passed resolutions on using the Adi-Karnataka and Adi-Dravida terminology. In 1921 an Adi-Karnataka Sangh (AKS) was registered with Gopalswamy Aiyar as president and the majority of other executive members being non-Dalits. The programme for the AKS included getting students admitted to educational institutions, access to tank water and temple entry.[51]

This activity functioned within the framework of 'the politics of petitions and patronage'. As shown in a statement presented to the maharaja in 1920 by 'Adi-Karnatakas and Adi-Dravidas of Mysore' (apparently Gopalaswamy Aiyar was a prominent figure behind this):

> On behalf of the 11 lakhs of the Panchama population of the state and in the name of the Adi-Dravida Abhivruddi Sangam, I beg to submit our deep spirit of devotion and loyalty . . . for the great act of emancipation graciously extended to our community . . . . we are an ancient community with a civilization, philosophy and history of which we reasonably feel proud. We are confident that our present unfavourable conditions are the outcome of our economic degradation. We are confident also that our social conditions will automatically improve with the improvement of our economic situation . . . . Our foremost need is education—more education, universal education . . . . Our next need is an opportunity to earn a decent living. We pray that at least one special agricultural settlement be organized in each district granting to each settler an extent of at least 5 acres dry and 1 acre wet garden land . . . advancing the necessary agricultural capital in some cases. As an additional safeguard we propose that such lands may be declared inalienable for two generations of holders in order to ensure the development of a prosperous agricultural community.[52]

The ideological themes here did not go beyond the 'Panchama' identity, the proclamation of an ancient greatness and an ancient community degraded only because it was poor; there was little mention of oppression and exploitation, no hint of any inevitable conflict due to caste, an avoidance of the issue of untouchability. This set the tone for most of the activity of the 1920s and after.

Dalits hardly spoke in their own voices in this process. When 'anti-untouchability' issues, defined as 'social issues', began to be taken up from the end of the 1920s, it was by caste Hindu organization, primarily Brahman-dominated like the Mysore League against Untouchability (a joint organization of the Praja Paksh and Congressmen which pressed for an anti-untouchability bill between 1930 and 1935) and the Harijan Sevak Sangh. These called for the right of Dalits to use all temples, roads, public places and tanks, joined with support for limited economic demands (getting government lands), and stressed internal reforms such as cleanliness, giving up meat-eating and drinking of alcohol, and the propagation of a Brahman Hinduism. All this was illustrated in a government statement in the Mysore assembly in June 1927 that

> The aim should be to 'Hinduize' them more and more, for they belong to the Hindu community really, and to offer them every facility to remain in the fold . . . . Alienated, they will introduce an additional element of heterogeneity which will in future complicate the already difficult problems of administration.[53]

In response a Dalit representative, Doddaiah, pleaded that 'with a view to promote the principles of Hindu Sanathana Dharma and Bhakti among the Adi-Karnatakas and Adi-Dravidas government should grant free sites and building materials for bhajan mandalis.'[54]

Still, within this integrationist model, some crucial economic issues were being taken up, and some assertion of Dalit *rights* was made, with hints of conflicts at the village level. Such conflicts, for instance, were rising over the traditional caste duties as Dalits refused work as *thotis* and *talaris*. In a 1925 assembly debate Murugesh Pillai claimed that Dalits were being asked to do all types of menial services, and were harassed and boycotted if they refused. He asked that they be relieved entirely of these duties or else paid directly by the government out of a special cess collected from peasants. The Revenue Commissioner (in a forecast of the Bombay government's response to Ambedkar's similar demands regarding the Mahar *watan*) replied that a salary could not be given, arguing that different forms of traditional remuneration existed, with Dalits given *inam* lands in some areas in return for their services, in others only traditional *miras* payments from the peasants. Some non-Brahman speakers in this debate accused Dalits of not working, remarking that if they were given lands they would not do the village work.[55] In placid Mysore, as everywhere, the caste form of *vethbegar* and the participation of the state in the exploitation of this labour was clearly emerging as an issue.

From the 1920s onwards Dalits were also asking for government wastelands and other lands for cultivation. They asked for land at concessional rates in the newly irrigated tracts of the Irwin Canal, but this was refused.[56] In October 1931 the Dewan made a major speech claiming that the government's programme of settling Adi-Karnatakas on land and giving them a proprietary interest 'is making very satisfactory progress', with 9,763 acres given that year.[57] In this case Murugesh Pillai also appears as a spokesman for getting such benefits as *rights* and not 'grants' for 'uplift', remarking that 'A large proportion of the land revenue . . . is on account of the labourers who are all Panchamas, and it is but right that the government give them all the required facilities.'[58]

But such language of 'rights' was rare. Even in the assembly debates, Dalits spoke out very little themselves on social issues; they were more vocal on economic issues such as land, education, traditional caste duties, while the 'social' issues were presented in a conservative, Hinduizing fashion with Brahmans dominant as spokesmen and non-Brahmans (with the exception of a few individual reformers) silent or opposing. There was no organizing of any campaigns, though some local clashes had been reported over the issue of tank water by the late 1920s in the various villages.[59]

A capacity for struggle clearly existed among the rural Dalit masses, but there were no leaders to organize it. The Kannada educated Dalits remained powerless and relatively voiceless. Without an industrial base or a vigorous political life, they had no access to an independent political organization. The limitations of the non-Brahman movement in princely Mysore deepened this weakness of the Dalit movement; the gap between the Tamil working class and the Kannada-speaking rural areas and educated middle class also exemplified an important absence. The 'Ram-raj' that was Mysore finally meant a stilling of Dalit advance—perhaps a symbolic killing of Shambuk. The Mysore maharaja's ban on

Ambedkar's entry into the state, in contrast to the honoured guest treatment given to Gandhi, shows the nature of reformism and the constraints on politics in the state. Dalits were unable, in the entire period before independence, to break through this, to achieve autonomy.

■ SUMMARY: POLITICAL CHOICES BEFORE DALITS

The preceding sections have surveyed the growth of the Dalit movement up to 1930 in regions mainly outside the scope of Ambedkar's early influence. The overview makes it clear that organizations, struggles and activists were emerging out of very different political and socio-economic conditions, from the largely backward political autocracy of Hyderabad state to the agriculturally-based commercial development of coastal Andhra to the industrial–agricultural centre of Nagpur–Vidarbha. These movements shared several features in common: they were nearly all based (and often limited to) on the largest 'untouchable' caste of the region, the caste which was traditionally assigned to 'general village service'; they emerged at first with sponsorship from caste Hindu social reformers; and they all had an inclination to the adoption of a 'non-Aryan' ideology, the claim to being 'the original inhabitants—sons of the soil' which was at that time sweeping the lower castes of south India.

Within this broad framework two distinct trends can be traced, representing the first and most basic choice for any Dalit in the twentieth century India. The first was a trend towards a radical assertion of autonomy from 'Hinduism' and from the social and political organizations of caste Hindus; the second was a trend towards integration. The first choice was represented by leaders like Bhagyareddy Varma of Hyderabad and by much of the 'Adi-Andhra' organizing of the 1920s; the second by Arigay Ramaswamy in Hyderabad, by Kisan Faguji Bansode and G.A. Gavai in Nagpur, and by most of the Mysore leaders. To some degree the 'adi' identity could lead back into an integration into Hinduism, exemplified for instance in claims by the Telugu poet Boyi Bhimanna that Dalits were the writers of 'Hindu' scriptures such as the Ramayana or Mahabharata: 'These are our literature; you have taken them

from us; Vyas is one of us, Valmiki is one of us.' These were claims
that were often coupled with a 'non-dualistic' spiritualism and
some very strong anti-Muslim attitudes.[60] The trend towards reabsorption into Hinduism often led via identification with the
bhakti movement, with saints such as Chokamela, as well as with
linkages to one or more Hinduistic social reform organizations, the
Prarthana Samaj or Arya Samaj in contrast to the Satyashodhak
Samaj or Brahmo Samaj.

It can be argued that both paths were open to Dalits; there was
no foregone conclusion that they would form an enduring autonomous movement that self-consciously defined itself as 'non-
Hindu' any more than non-Brahmans in Madras and Bombay
presidencies were able to do. There were in fact two paths, and
while the basic social oppression and economic exploitation of the
Dalits pushed them to a radical autonomy, at the same time there
were powerful pressures for absorption: the sheer social and political power of caste Hindus and their organizations, the readiness
of reformers to make some concessions, the Hinduistic tendencies
that came to dominate even movements opposing class exploitation.

Two choices existed, two paths. They led in fundamentally
different directions. The second path forced Dalits to confront
further choices in a way that the first path did not. Reabsorption
into Hinduism after all included the acceptance of Hindu leadership; and there were many around to make the claims of leading
the ex-untouchables and providing an ideology for their advance,
whether it was Gandhi's idealized village-centred 'Ram-raj' or the
communists' interpretation of class exploitation and an industrialized
classless socialism. In contrast, a radical assertion of autonomy not
only impelled Dalits to form their own organizations; it also forced
them to deal independently with some basic issues. Radical
autonomy after all did not mean a separation from the rest of
Indian society; it meant that Dalits themselves would have to
redefine and *reconstitute* their relations with the whole of Indian
society, with its various social groups, its historical and cultural
traditions. As untouchables, who were they historically? The question cried for both a religious answer and a social-historical interpretation. If they were not 'Hindus', then what? In fact a 'non-
Hindu' choice seems to have led naturally towards identification
with a religion such as Buddhism, which had a historical reality in
the Indian context; various other answers to the religious question—

Phule's *sarvajanik satya dharma*, Periyar's atheism—did not seem to have a mass appeal, while religions like Islam and Christianity had no link with ancient Indian tradition.

Historically, what was the explanation for caste and the exploitation and degradation of untouchables? Here the 'non-Aryan theory' held the field in the 1920s: they were original inhabitants enslaved by conquering Aryans. This had the advantage of being a historical and apparently scientific theory which dealt directly with caste in contrast to Marxism; but it was racial in its implications and left troubling questions.

An impulse to radical autonomy left important political choices unresolved. Forming their own organizations and leading a movement of their own meant that Dalits had to confront, on their own, all the questions that lay before any politically conscious Indian. It was not enough to simply characterize the Congress or the Hindu Mahasabha as being in the hands of Brahmans; they had to have a stand about British imperialism, including some kind of concrete response to the various proposals and reforms put before the people. They had to have some kind of analysis of economic exploitation and a policy of relating to the kisan sabhas and unions through which people were organizing economically, both because these included significant numbers of Dalits and because they represented new political forces impregnated with a new analysis of exploitation.

Finally, they had to confront political choices about who were their allies—which parties, which social groups. At times, as reflected in Ambedkar's remark that 'we cannot fight all our enemies at once', this meant making difficult choices about the 'lesser evil', for instance as between Muslims, the Congress, British imperialism. At other times it meant seeing forces or political parties as positive allies (the communists? the non-Brahman parties? the Muslims?). In terms of the traditional caste structure even once Dalits had defined themselves as separate and taken an 'untouchable/touchable' distinction as providing the first ground for action, they still had to look at the rest of the caste structure in a sharper sense: were all 'touchables' equally enemies or should one make distinctions, taking 'Brahmans' as the 'main enemy' while 'non-Brahmans' or 'Shudras' were potential allies even if they currently accepted Hindu ideology, even if they were at times the most direct exploiters of Dalits. Dalits faced such choices much as—to make a crucial comparison—communists faced choices of defining their relation with the national movement. And for Dalits, like communists, action in the face of such choices had to be based on some theoretical understanding of the total situation in which they found themselves, some *ideology*.

It was Bhimrao Ramji Ambedkar who was to provide this ideology and the leadership of the emerging autonomous Dalit movement and for this reason much of this analysis centres on his thought and work. Nevertheless the choices were faced by all activists and movements in India, and Ambedkar had to exert his leadership in the context of a varied pattern of responses, given by a vigorous mass-based movement.

NOTES

1. Sumit Sarkar, *Modern India: 1885–1947* (Delhi: Macmillan, 1983), pp. 233–37.
2. See D.E.U. Baker, *Changing Political Leadership in an Indian Province: The Central Provinces and Berar, 1919–1939* (Delhi: Oxford University Press, 1979), pp. 12–13.
3. *Ibid.*, pp. 3–7, 190–93.
4. Interview, Vasant Moon, 9 October 1989.
5. The most important sources for the early movement and the situation of Mahars in Vidarbha-Nagpur are Vasant Moon, *Dr. Ambedkarpurva Dalit Calval* ('Dalit Movement Before Dr. Ambedkar') (Pune: Sugawa Prakashan, 1987); Eleanor Zelliot, *Dr. Ambedkar and the Mahar Movement* (University of Pennsylvania: Ph.D. dissertation, 1969). See also M.E. Bhagwat, 'Vidarbhatil Dalit Vicharanci Netrutva', in P.L. Joshi (ed.), *Political Ideas and Leadership in Vidarbha Publisher* (Nagpur, 1980); Suganda Shende, 'Guruvarya Kisan Faguji Bansode', *Bahumat*, 18 February 1979, and Baker, *Changing Political Leadership*, pp. 115–17.
6. Moon, *Ambedkarpurva . . . Calval*, pp. 20ff.
7. Quoted Bhagwat, 'Vidharbhatil Dalit . . .', p. 297.
8. Moon, *Ambedkarpurva . . . Calval*, p. 47.
9. *Ibid.*, pp. 11, 47; Bhagwat, 'Vidarbhatil Dalit . . .', p. 305.
10. Quoted in Baker, *Changing Political Leadership*, p. 47.
11. See Gail Omvedt, *Cultural Revolt in a Colonial Society: The Non Brahman Movement in Western India, 1850–1935* (Poona: Scientific Socialist Education Trust, 1976), Chapter 11, esp. pp. 220–21; and Bhagwat, 'Vidarbhatil Dalit . . .' pp. 302–4.
12. For background on Andhra see Carol Upadhyaya, 'The Farmer-Capitalists of Coastal Andhra Pradesh', *Economic and Political Weekly*, 2 July 1988; Nata Duvvury, 'Commercial Capital and Agrarian Relations: A Study of Guntur Tobacco Economy', *Economic and Political Weekly*, 26 July 1986; G.N. Rao,

'Canal Irrigation and Agrarian Change in Coastal Andhra: A Study of Godavari District c. 1850–1890', *Indian Social and Economic History Review*, 25, 1988; N.G. Ranga, *Economic Organization of Indian Villages* (Bombay: Tarapoorewala Sons, 1924); G. Hargopal, 'Class–Caste Dimensions of Dalit Consciousness: The Case of Delta Andhra', Paper prepared for Class–Caste Seminar, Lonavala, December 1987) and 'Dimensions of Regionalism: Nationality Question in Andhra', in *Nationality Question in India* (Pune: TDDS, 1987).

13. This is stressed by Hargopal in 'Class–Caste Dimensions'.
14. Hargopal, 'Dimensions of Regionalism', pp. 373–74; John Leonard, 'Symbolic Conflict: Social Reform and Local Politics in South India, 1874–1892' (unpublished manuscript, University of California, Berkeley, 1970).
15. Uma Ramaswamy, 'Self-Identity Among Scheduled Castes: A Study of Andhra', *Economic and Political Weekly*, 23 November 1974, p. 1963; see also Ramaswamy, 'Scheduled Castes in Andhra: Some Aspects of Social Change', *Economic and Political Weekly*, 20 July 1974, and 'Protection and Inequality among Backward Groups', *Economic and Political Weekly*, 1 March 1986.
16. M.B. Gautam, 'The Untouchables' Movement in Andhra Pradesh', in *Andhra Pradesh State Harijan Conference Souvenir* (Hyderabad, 10–12 April 1976). While this is the most detailed, other useful articles in the same volume are those of N.G. Ranga, 'Reminiscences of Harijan Welfare'; J.R. Raju, 'The Champions of the Downtrodden in Andhra Pradesh'; and Y.B. Abbayasulu, 'Harijan Uplift in Andhra Pradesh: Yesterday and Today'. See also Abbayasulu, *Scheduled Caste Elite* (Hyderabad, 1976).
17. Carolyn Elliot, 'Caste and Faction among the Dominant Caste: The Reddis and Kammas of Andhra', in Rajni Kothari (ed.), *Caste in Indian Politics* (New Delhi: Orient Longman, 1970).
18. Sarkar, *Modern India*, pp. 129–30.
19. Hargopal, 'Dimensions of Regionalism', p. 375.
20. Both are summarized in Hargopal, 'Class–Caste Dimensions'.
21. *Ibid.*, pp. 2–3.
22. Gautam, 'The Untouchables' Movement', pp. 67–68.
23. *Ibid.*, and Abbayasulu, *Scheduled Caste Elite*, pp. 25–27.
24. *Census in India, 1931, Vol. XIV, Madras, Part I: Report* (Madras: Superintendent of Government Press, 1933).
25. On Hyderabad and especially the Telengana land system see Akhil Gupta, 'Revolution in Telengana, 1946–51 (Part One)', *South Asia Bulletin*, 4, 1 Spring 1984; D.N. Dhanagare, 'Social Origins of the Peasant Insurrection in Telengana (1946–1951)', *Contributions to Indian Sociology*, 8, 1974; and Barry Pavier, *The Telengana Movement, 1944–51* (Delhi: Vikas, 1981) and the review by Dhanagare, 'Telengana Movement Revisited', *Economic and Political Weekly*, 18 December 1982.
26. Interview, Jagamba Jaganathan, Hyderabad, 24 June 1987.
27. P.R. Venkatswamy, *Our Struggle for Emancipation*, 2 volumes (Secunderabad: University Art Printers, 1955).
28. Interview, Gautam, 20 June 1987.
29. Venkatswamy, *Our Struggle*, Volume I, p. 10.
30. *Ibid.*, pp. 13–40.

31. On North India see Owen Lynch, *The Politics of Untouchability* (New York. Columbia University Press, 1969); Mark Juergensmeier, *Religion as Social Vision: The Movement Against Untouchability in Twentieth Century Punjab* (Berkeley: University of California Press, 1978) and R.S. Khare, *The Untouchable as Himself: Ideology, Identity and Pragmatism among the Lucknow Chamars* (Cambridge: Cambridge University Press, 1984).
32. Resolution No. 6 of the All-India Adi-Hindu (Depressed Classes) Conference, Allahabad, 16 November 1930; from the collection of M.B. Gautam.
33. An approach expressed by Boyi Bhimanna, interview, 21 June 1987.
34. *Census of India, 1931, Volume XXIII, Hyderabad State, Part I: Report* (Hyderabad-Deccan: Government Central Press, 1933), p. 258.
35. Venkatswamy, *Our Struggle*, Volume, I, p. 20.
36. *Ibid.*, Volume I, pp. 75–78.
37. Interview, Gautam, 20 June 1987.
38. Venkatswamy's account makes this clear, and he ends with a bitter comment about the factionalism caused by the 'narrow and selfish interests' of the leaders; *Our Struggle*, Volume II, pp. 662–63.
39. James Manor, *Political Change in an Indian State: Mysore, 1917–1935* (Delhi: Manohar, 1977), p. 13.
40. Bjorn Hettne, *The Political Economy of Indirect Rule: Mysore 1881–1947* (New Delhi: Ambika Publications, 1978), pp. 30–55.
41. *Complete Works of Swami Vivekananda* (New Delhi 1950, Volume IV, p. 363.
42. *Census of India, 1981, Volume XV, Mysore, Part I, Report* (Bangalore: Government Central Press, 1893), pp. 250–53.
43. D.S. Chandrasekhar, *Social Background of Mysore Politics: Some Insights* (Kannada) (Bangalore: Ankara, 1983), cited by V. Lakshminarayana, report.
44. Manor, *Political Change*, pp. 63–65.
45. *Ibid.*, pp. 92–93.
46. Hettne, *Political Economy*, p. 341.
47. *Ibid.*, p. 336.
48. Chitra Shivkumar, *Education, Social Inequality and Social Change in Karnataka* (Delhi: Hindustan Publishing Company, 1982).
49. Chandrasekhar, *Social Background*.
50. *Proceedings of the Mysore Representative Assembly*, October 1924, p. 289.
51. Chandrasekhar, *Social Background*, p. 67.
52. Speeches of R.S. Dhurina, M. Kantahanage, *Proceedings*, p. 275.
53. *Ibid.*, June 1927, p. 5.
54. *Ibid.*, October 1927, p. 239.
55. *Ibid.*, September 1925, p. 158.
56. *Ibid.*, October 1930, October 1931, June 1932, p. 88, and June 1933, p. 181.
57. *Ibid.*, October 1931.
58. Chandrasekhar, *Social Background*.
59. Chandrasekhar, *Social Background*, pp. 8–10.
60. Boyi Bhimanna, interview, 21 June 1987.

CHAPTER 4

Emergence of the Dalit Movement, 1910–30: Bombay Presidency

If it is impossible to conceptualize the Dalit movement in India in the absence of Ambedkar, it is equally difficult to imagine, sociologically, Ambedkar coming out of any other region than the Marathi-speaking areas of Bombay Presidency.

These included three districts in the Konkan (Thana, Kolaba and Ratnagiri), five in western Maharashtra (Poona, Satara, Ahmednagar, Sholapur and Nasik) and East and West Khandesh (present-day Jalgaon and Dhule). Along with the Gujarati and Kannada-speaking districts, they comprised both the most industrialized and the most politically and sociologically vigorous of the provinces of British India. Bombay was the site of the first session of the Indian National Congress in 1885 and provided some of its leading politicians in both 'moderate' and 'extremist' factions. It was the site of the most radical and mass-based of the social movements, Phule's Satyashodhak Samaj, though its Brahman elite was more wavering in its social reformism than the Bengali *bhadralok* and, from the time of Tilak, had also provided a strong base for Hindu revivalism in the form of the Hindu Mahasabha and the Rashtriya Swayamsevak Sangh. Bombay also nurtured both early Indian capitalism and the militant working class which gave the Indian communist movement its first mass base. And finally, in the decade of the 1920s, in the context of rising working class and peasant organizing and the growth not only of nationalism but of a non-Brahman political party, Bombay Presidency saw the most vigorous Dalit movement in India emerge under the leadership of B. R. Ambedkar.

The reason for this social and political vitality of the Presidency and particularly its Marathi-speaking districts can be linked both to its relatively late conquest by the British and to the particular nature of its rural–urban linkages. The Marathi-speaking hinterland provided the army of industrial labour working in Bombay, in contrast to Calcutta where till independence the working class largely comprised of Hindi-speaking immigrants from north India while it was the dominant *bhadralok* (basically the three upper castes) with their landlord base who spanned rural and urban areas in Bengal. The Marathi Deccan had, as shown, a relatively equalitarian and less caste-stratified village economy; this had underlain the outburst under Shivaji during the seventeenth century and continued in spite of later Peshwa feudalization.

On top of this, the ryotwari settlement laid a basis for a vigorous peasant assertion under the strains of commercial exploitation, bursting out in various ways throughout the nineteenth century. Landlordism, of course, continued to exist, but it was relatively less dominant than in the other major area of commercialized agriculture dealt with in this study, the Andhra delta. And with a large percentage of the landlords being Brahmans they were socially more vulnerable in contrast to the non-Brahman (Kamma, Velama, etc.) zamindars dominant in Andhra. This relatively equalitarian village economy (suggested in Tables 2.2 and 2.3) provided a material base for a more vigorous unity of non-Brahman Kunbis and *balutedar* castes with the Mahars against the dominant Brahman landlords and Marwari and Vani money-lenders. It also gave the Dalits themselves, in particular the Mahars, the strongest rural base of any untouchable section in India. The peasant assertion of the Kunbis and related castes together with their access to industrial employment in Bombay provided a basis for a relatively 'proletarianized' militant ideology and organizational forms, while the position of the Mahars (of whom nearly 49 per cent were listed as 'cultivators' compared to 23 per cent 'field labourers' in the 1911 Census) gave them some strength to deal with the Kunbis (often their immediate foe if strategic ally) and organize for a more long-term radical struggle. This vigorous village economy linked to a turbulent industrial metropolis was a unique configuration. In contrast to the view of on-going peasant linkages as 'holding back' a true proletarian radicalism, in this case such linkages provided the main social foundation for the broad democratic movements of Maharashtra.

At the heart of the Bombay industrial centre was the textile mill area, which provided the most organized and politically conscious working class vanguard in Bombay, including not only economic struggles but social and political struggles such as the historic 1908 strike at the time of Tilak's sentencing. In 1918, according to Richard Newman, the average daily workforce in the Bombay mills was 121,129, made up of 94,601 men, 24,108 women and 2,510 children; this number rose to over 150,000 in 1922 and then declined to 138,000 in 1928 (of course including *badli* or temporary and other workers, the total number of those who were 'textile workers' was greater than this). Mahars made up slightly under 10 per cent of this workforce, mainly from the districts of Satara, Ratnagiri and Ahmednagar.[1] They were concentrated in the spinning department and menial forms of work, since the more highly paid weaving department barred them from entry due to pollution prejudices (the practice of holding a broken thread in the mouth while repairing it) that in the end were broken by automation rather than any struggle. Since weavers were the most solidly organized in the Girni Kamagar Union and other working class organizations, Mahars, along with Muslims and north Indians, tended to be relatively less involved in working class organizing.[2]

Similarly, Mahars were probably over-represented among the casual and unorganized sections of labour in the city as a whole. They were prominent, according to Zelliot, in construction, sanitary forces and the docks. Here a 1941 study revealed that recruitment was linked not only to caste but also to region: for dock workers, Satara Mahars dominated in shore labour; Sholapur, Poona and Satara Mahars in coal labour; Nasik and Ratnagiri Mahars in the dock railways. Mahars as a whole were 12 per cent of shore labour on the docks but 98 per cent of the lower-paid, more menial coal labourers.[3] This type of caste/village/region-linked recruitment also applied in the mills and continues to operate to the present day. In the city as a whole, by 1921, according to Zelliot, Mahars were 12 per cent of the workforce.[4]

This emerging Mahar working class, however exploited and discriminated against, nevertheless had enough collective concentration to constitute a relatively strong base for a social movement, one with on-going links to villages near and far. If the textile workers were the centre of Bombay working class life, it was Byculla and Kamathipura just south of the textile area that were the city centres of the Dalit movement.[5] Ambedkar's home through much of his life was located here, and even when he built a house of his own, 'Rajgraha', it was in Dadar at the northern side of the textile area. Even for poor workers Bombay provided a significant resource base, and as Ambedkar's biographer Khairmode notes, as Dalit consciousness and the movement grew, people stopped spending on Ganapati and other religious festivals and began to support a different kind of cultural assertion. And these resources and this assertion were transferred back and forth from city to villages, back and forth from an emerging educated section to the worker and poor peasant masses. In contrast to Hyderabad, where in spite of desires for autonomy Dalit leaders remained isolated from any rural base, the Dalit leadership in Bombay Presidency continually grew under pressure of the increasing demands of their people.

■ MAHARS BEFORE 1917: THE DOWNFALL OF 'UNTOUCHABILITY RELIEF'

There was some limited independent Dalit organizing before the 1920s. This took two forms. First, there was an agitation, of the usual petition-oriented type of the period, for continuing the recruitment of Mahars into the army and lower grades of government service. Gopal Baba Walangkar, speaking in the name of a Ratnagiri-based group, sent a petition as early as 1894, while two later ones sent on behalf of the Mahars of the Konkan and Deccan in 1904 and 1910 were organized by Shivram Janba Kamble, a retired Ratnagiri army man living in Poona. The first petition

claimed untouchables were former Ksatriyas but was sent in the
name of the Anarya Doshpariharakham of Dapoli, thus making a
'non-Aryan' claim; the second mentioned only the recent service
of the Mahars as justifying their equal rights.[6]

A second trend was the organization in several areas of Mahar
caste associations under the name of 'Somvanshiya', a sub-caste of
Mahars, which took up limited issues of internal reform and education. Shivram Kamble was involved with a Somvanshiya Sabha
in Poona, while a Somawanshiya Hitachintak Mandal was recorded
in Ahmednagar, which V.R. Shinde visited in the process of
forming his own mission for the untouchables.[7]

Caste Hindu reform efforts, however, held the stage before
1917, though they were to a large extent inspired and provoked by
the independent Mahar efforts. Among these, of course, the Satyashodhak movement provided important sponsorship for Dalit
organizing and did so with a perspective of alliance and autonomy
much more than the patronage-control of the more conservative
upper-caste elite.[8] Nevertheless the organizational base of the
conservatives was strongest, and their most important effort in the
period before 1920 was the Depressed Classes Mission of Vitthal
Ramji Shinde. Shinde was a member of the Prarthana Samaj and
the most prominent of the 'nationalist Marathas' who opposed the
non-Brahman party and attempted to draw the Maratha community
into the Congress movement.[9] His Depressed Classes Mission
performed the same function for the Dalit community, and drew
them not only into the Congress but into Hindu revivalist associations such as the Hindu Mahasabha.

The Mission was founded in 1906, after Shinde had returned (in
1903) from an abortive educational trip to England and had toured
India surveying other efforts at untouchability reform. Shinde was
the secretary and Narayanrao Chandavarkar, a prominent Brahman
reformer, the president. It focused on education and on propagation
of a reformed Hinduism. By 1908 it was reported to have 15 day
schools, 6 Sunday schools, 5 bhajan societies, 4 industrial schools
and seven 'missionary' propagandists in Bombay presidency.[10] In
October 1912 an Asprushata Nivaran Parishad ('Untouchability
Relief Conference') was organized by Shinde in Poona under the
presidentship of Dr Ramakrishna Bhandarkar; the Shankaracharya
of the Kolhapur *math*, Dr Kurtkoti, took part, and for three days
there was interdining among the untouchables and caste Hindus

who attended.[11] Shinde made energetic efforts to secure support for his work, from various maharajas, from even the Tuskegee Institute of Booker T. Washington in the United States, and by 1917 it had won recognition both among the mainly Brahman social-political elite and the British government as the leading organization working among untouchables.

However, 1917 saw the beginning of the downfall of such caste Hindu patronage and the rise of a new self-directed Dalit movement. The context was the political turmoil of the 1917–20 period, when almost all communities were being mobilized around the issues raised by the Montague–Chelmsford reforms; the immediate issues were those of who would represent untouchables, but the implications were to be much more profound.

The main agent of the new movement was the young Mahar graduate, Bhimrao Ramji Ambedkar. Ambedkar had graduated from Elphinstone College and spent three years at Columbia University and one at the London School of Economics with financial support from the Gaikwad of Baroda. He had worked for a brief period at Baroda on his return, but then left in anger at the treatment he received as an untouchable and became a professor at Syndenham College. Highly educated and articulate, from the very moment of his return in 1917 he was looked to as a leader of the community.

The stimulus of the reforms provoked the Maharashtrian elite into mobilizing untouchable support. But a series of 'untouchability relief' conferences called in 1917 were conspicuous by their *lack* of success in involving untouchables. The first meeting was called in December 1917 by Chandavarkar and Shinde, with Chandavarkar presiding and with the proclaimed purpose of honouring Ambedkar as a returned Mahar graduate as well as demanding political rights for untouchables. But Ambedkar disassociated himself from the meeting and refused to accept the honour. The meeting passed a resolution supporting the Congress and Muslim League (their Lucknow Pact being a current focus for nationalist expressions), but not before even so pro-Hindu an untouchable as G.A. Gavai had caused some turmoil by expressing doubts about what the Congress was actually doing for untouchables.[12]

The second was a major conference with Sayajirao Gaikwad, the ruler of Baroda, presiding and involving many well-known nationalist leaders, including Bipin Chandra Pal, Vitthalbhai Patel and Lokmanya Tilak, and with telegrams from the Shankaracharya and from Gandhi. Again demands were raised for the removal of untouchability and resolutions expressed support for the Congress. The meeting became well-known for Tilak's speech expressing his opposition to untouchability (he put it in terms of caste distinctions being disregarded in 'wartime') and his claims that he ignored it personally. But Tilak was afterwards harshly criticized, charged with avoiding the publication of his speech in *Kesari* and not being able to document any claims of his own disregard of pollution; and it was noted that he subsequently refused to sign a petition brought by Shinde. The Shankaracharya was criticized for avoiding attending the conference. And at the meeting itself, a Maratha reformer, Krishnarao Arjun Keluskar, raised a fuss by charging the delegates with only staying in the cities and ignoring the real problems of untouchability in the rural areas, citing as one example Ambedkar's experiences in Baroda.

The final blow to the 'untouchability relief' campaign of the elite came when such a conference was held as a part of a general Congress social and political conference during 5–8 May 1918 at Bijapur. This time Gandhi was in attendance. Asked to move the resolution expressing untouchable support for the Congress, he asked untouchables who were present to raise their hands. When no one did, he inquired how this could be called 'a conference of depressed classes' and refused to move the resolution.[13]

■ Ambedkar Emerges: Autonomy and Alliances

Given these events, it is not surprising that politically conscious untouchables should feel they were being used by caste Hindu leaders. It was now that Ambedkar made his claim to an alternative leadership, in three steps: submitting testimony to the Southborough Committee on Reforms, appearing at two major conferences of untouchables during 1920, and initiating a journal, *Mooknayak* ('Voice of the Mute'). The testimonial involved a conscious attack on Shinde; as Khairmode writes, 'untouchables were tired of Shinde's effort to hold a dictatorial monopoly over the movement.' He added that neither the government nor the Chandavarkar–Shinde group felt the need for the untouchables themselves to testify, and whereas Shinde was invited to testify, Ambedkar himself had to write to the government volunteering his submission.[14]

Ambedkar's written statement, as was to be true of all his political expressions, was argued at length and with force and eloquence. In contrast to Shinde, who had asked for reserved seats for untouchables in general constituencies, he asserted categorically that 'Untouchable Hindus' and 'Touchable Hindus' represented social groups as completely different as Hindus and members of other religions. In an eloquent assertion of identity and claim to autonomy,

> The right of representation and the right to hold office under the state are the two most important rights that make up citizenship. But the untouchability of the untouchables puts these rights far beyond their reach. In a few places they do not even possess such insignificant rights as personal liberty and personal security. These are the interests of the untouchables. And as can be easily seen, they can be represented by the untouchables alone.[15]

In arguing for more than a token representation, he stated,

> The Sultan will not, though he can, change the religion of Mahomad just as the Pope will not, though he can, overthrow the religion of Christ. In the same way a legislature composed of high caste men will not pass a law removing untouchability, sanctioning intermarriages, removing a ban on the use of public streets, public temples, public schools . . . . This is not because they cannot, but chiefly because they will not.[16]

And he was bitterly scornful of caste Hindu reformism, referring to the 'farce of a conference for the removal of untouchability', describing the rejection of a resolution by Dadabhoy Naoroji in the Imperial Legislative Assembly, and condemning Shinde's Depressed Class Mission in scathing language:

> The mission it must be said was started with intention of improving the condition of the Depressed Classes by emancipating them from the social tyranny of their high caste masters. But the mission has fallen on such bad times that it is forced to advocate

a scheme by which its wards or their representatives will be bounded slaves of their past masters.[17]

The British met none of the demands of the various claimants to grant representation to untouchables, and the Montague–Chelmsford reforms provided for only one nominated member in the Bombay Legislative Council. But the political assertion of Dalits had begun. Ambedkar and his colleagues decided that a public challenge to Shinde's leadership should be put forward in an independent conference of untouchables. The result was the Akhil Bharatiya Bahishkrut Parishad (also known as the All-India Depressed Classes Conference) held at Nagpur on 30–31 May 1920 with Shahu Chhatrapati of Kolhapur as president. The famous anti-Brahman maharaja had already helped launch Ambedkar's political career with a conference held at the Kolhapur state village of Mangaon on 20 March 1920.[18]

The Nagpur conference condemned the Depressed Classes Mission and its resolutions of support for the Congress, and, according to Ambedkar's longtime co-worker S.N. Shivtarkar, so great was Ambedkar's power of persuasion that even Shinde's disciple in Nagpur, G.S. Gavai, was forced into seconding it and expressing his own unhappiness with the Mission. The argument used was that no untouchable representative chosen by a caste Hindu majority could ever move against *chaturvarnya*; with this it was clear that to Dalits the assertion of autonomy distinguished a programme for the 'removal of untouchability' from the destruction of caste itself.[19] Shinde's political career as a representative of the Dalits was finished with this conference, though the final blow came only later (which was after Ambedkar returned from London a second time) when Dalit students in his hostel revolted at his autocratic ways. He died, reportedly, disillusioned and embittered, unable to sustain a position as a pro–Hindu nationalist Maratha caught between the cultural arrogance of the Brahman elite and a Dalit movement determined to fashion its own path.[20]

As noted, a choice by Dalits for a radical assertion of autonomy led to the necessity of making further choices. In Ambedkar's case, in the context of Maharashtrian politics, this clearly involved one major political choice: a rejection of the existing nationalist politics and an alliance with the non-Brahman movement. Ambedkar sought help from the most controversial figure of Bombay

Presidency, the maharaja of Kolhapur. And he maintained this stance throughout, seeking allies among the various leaders of the non-Brahman movement (often while being scathingly critical of them), working with them on various campaigns (as he did with S.K. Bole on the issue of *khoti* in the 1920s), unequivocally identifying with the Satyshodhak Samaj,[21] and writing in his introduction to *Who Were the Shudras*? that 'it is well known that there has been a nonBrahman movement in this country which is a political movement of the Shudras. It is also well known that I have been connected with it.'[22]

Behind this identification with the non-Brahman movement lay the logic of a movement that was essentially anti-caste and not simply a movement for 'untouchability removal'. Even assuming a radical assertion of the existence of 'untouchables' as a separate social group, it was not accurate to view other Hindus as an undifferentiated mass, all equally opposed to the Dalits due to their 'Hindu-ness'. An analysis of the caste system led to a focus on the hierarchy in it, with Brahmans at the top as the 'main enemy'. And if Brahmans (or the twice-born) were the main enemy, then the masses of non-Brahmans were potential allies, even if they presently accepted a Hindu identity, even if they too practiced untouchability.

The question was a poignant one, since non-Brahmans, especially the main peasant castes like the Kunbi–Marathas, often appeared as direct exploiters, the main perpetrators of atrocities on the Dalits. In Ambedkar's time as today, many put forward the thesis that 'dominant caste' groups such as the Marathas were the main enemy, and that an alliance with them was harmful if not impossible. As Eleanor Zelliot has written,

the caste difference between the two groups and their social situation—the Marathas were a landowning dominant caste, the Mahars a nearly landless minority—worked against any real cooperative effort between them. Although the Mahar grievances were voiced chiefly against the Brahmans, as it was the Marathas who dominated at the village level, the village protests in the form of quitting *balutedar* duties or claiming some form of social equality in fact got directed against the latter . . . . Just as the Justice Party in Madras failed to include significant numbers of

Untouchables, the non-Brahman movement in Maharashtra could not make common cause with Untouchables.[23]

But this analysis, which has become popular today as opponents of caste reservations for the 'backward castes' argue that they are the greatest perpetrators of atrocities against the Dalits, is directly contrary to that of Ambedkar. Although Ambedkar and his co-workers at times spoke of 'all caste Hindus' or all 'villagers' as the enemy, and while they frequently and scornfully criticized the hypocrisy of non-Brahman leaders, they never gave up attempts at alliance. If Marathas and similar groups were the 'dominant caste' at the village level, Ambedkar and others never had any doubt that Brahmans were the 'dominant caste' in the system as a whole. Thus he constantly attempted to make distinctions, to direct the thrust of organizing and rhetoric against the Brahmans (or big landlords and capitalists), to rally support from the Shudra castes. In this the non-Brahman movement, in particular its radical core, the Satyashodhak Samaj, had a crucial role to play because its ideology sought to arouse the Shudras or *bahujan samaj* not only against the Brahmans but against caste itself. Just as non-Brahman social radicals from Phule onwards had a qualitatively different approach to untouchables from the patronizing, incorporative attitude of the Brahmans (or Brahmanized reformers such as Shinde), so Ambedkar had a different attitude towards them. In a real sense he was the heir of Phule's call for a movement of Shudras and Atishudras.

The refusal of patronage and the assertion of independence in this has to be stressed, however, and the spirit of 'Ambedkarism' is perhaps best illustrated in a speech he gave on a celebration of the Mahad campaign held in March 1940. Addressing the Kunbis present, Ambedkar said, 'If we want to speak only of Maharashtra, then the time has come to say that only Mahars and Brahmans really understand politics.' Asking how many Kunbis were in positions of authority in government service, he went on,

The Mahar community has become resolute; it will not be suppressed and will no longer remain beneath your feet. This you must keep in mind. Now you yourselves at least should become conscious. In spite of being 70–80 per cent of the population, should you go on spending all your lives simply doing coolie work? Even if you go into Congress, Congress will not let you behave independently; you will have to toil as slaves of the Congress.[24]

■ THE MAHAD SATYAGRAHA: DALIT LIBERATION BEGINS

While the events of 1920 represented the beginning of the Dalit movement in Maharashtra, the decisive step that made it a liberation struggle was the 1927 Mahad satyagraha. This established Ambedkar as a leader of a growing movement; but at the same time illustrates a certain holding back with regard to crucial religious–cultural choices.

Ambedkar did not immediately begin organizing. He returned to England at the end of 1920 to complete his law degree, coming back to India only in 1923. Much of his time was taken up with personal life (including its tragedies, the death of four children), and the problems of survival. He worked as a lawyer and continued to teach at Sydenham College. He founded the Bahishkrut Hitakarini Sabha in 1924 as a forum for gathering people and organizing occasional forays into the countryside for conferences and meetings; and he was one of two new untouchable representatives nominated to the Legislative Council in 1926. But the main activity through much of this time seemed to be that of reading voluminously and thinking through the problems of untouchability and Indian/Hindu society—and of gathering people around him (students, workers, the newly educated elite) and putting forward the message of self-respect. He was rapidly becoming the focal point for the surging aspirations of the Dalits, as untouchables throughout western Maharashtra wrote to him, seeking to find an outlet to publish the struggles they were waging, the atrocities they faced. Like all 'charismatic leaders', Ambedkar was the creation of the movement he led as much as its creator.

The Mahad tank satyagraha illustrates both the role of mass readiness for action and the genuis of Ambedkar in giving leadership to it. The occasion was a 'Kolaba Zilha Bahishkrut Parishad' (Kolaba district conference of the boycotted) on 19–20 March

1927. This was the first mass rally of the Bahishkrut Hitakarini Sabha (BHS), and Mahad, a taluk town in the Konkan, had been carefully selected as a place where Mahar migrants to Bombay had strong connections and where there was nucleus of solid caste Hindu support. These included A.V. Chitre, a CKP (Kayastha) activist of the BHS, G.N. Sahasrabudhe, a Brahman of the Social Service Legue, and Surendranath Tipnis, another CKP who was president of the Mahad municipality; Chitre and Tipnis were later to be elected as MLAs in Ambedkar's Independent Labour Party, while Sahasrabudhe went on to become the editor of Ambedkar's weekly *Janata*.

The 1920s saw a sustained agitation for the opening of public places, particularly wells and tanks, to untouchables. It seems that Ambedkar had some kind of direct action in his mind from the beginning; Mahad municipality itself had already passed a resolution to open the Chawdar tank, though it had not been implemented. However, the actual resolutions passed at the conference were very general, and it was only after seeing the mood of the crowd of about 1,500 and after a good deal of discussion among the organizers on the morning of the second day that direct action was proposed. This was done suddenly: at the end of the meeting, rising to 'give thanks' to the organizers of the conference, Anantrao Chitre ('as decided beforehand I threw a bombshell') proposed to move to the tank and drink the water. The crowd surged forward and drank; after they had returned they were attacked by aroused caste Hindus fearing a further 'onslaught', this time on the temple. Drinking of the tank water, the rioting, the police complaints afterwards, and the subsequent 'cleansing' of the tank by horrified Brahmans all caused the event to resound throughout Maharashtra.

Ambedkar seized the opportunity to establish *Bahishkrut Bharat*, his second weekly, and rally sympathy and mass support. A further 'satyagraha conference' was planned in December to re-establish the right to drink water. This brought a vastly increased mass of Dalits—between 10,000 and 15,000—and featured the famous burning of the *Manusmriti*, a dramatic symbolic act that took away the sting from the fact that Ambedkar honoured the injunction of the district magistrate not to take water from the tank by calling off the 'satyagraha'. Later both events were known as the 'Mahad satyagraha', but it was the first day, 20 March, that was celebrated for a long time as Asprushya Swatantra Din or 'Untouchable

Independence Day', the day of the mass struggle of Dalits to assert their human rights.[25]

The Mahad satyagraha was thus the foundation for the liberation struggle of Maharashtra Dalits. Nevertheless, for some time even after this, Ambedkar was in some ways marking time, though he was involved in a tremendous amount of activity (including submitting a book-length testimonial to the Simon Commission in 1928 and writing a critique of linguistic provinces in response to the Nehru report in 1929) and was becoming more and more visible as a public leader. He continued reading voraciously, including social and religious literature on Hinduism. Closely following the fast-moving developments, he watched the temple entry movements go on and took cognisance of the various new reform efforts by caste Hindus as also of the Gandhian trend within the nationalist movement, the new communist movement and worker and peasant organizing.[26] He was still in the process of defining his attitude towards Hinduism and the Congress. While critical of Gandhi for not giving as much weight to untouchability removal as to Hindu–Muslim unity, he nevertheless had a soft spot for him: the tent for the December 'satyagraha conference' at Mahad featured Gandhi's photo, and as Ambedkar put it in a 1925 'Bahishkrut Parishad' in Belgaum, 'where no one else comes close, the sympathy shown by Mahatma Gandhi is by no means a small thing.'[27] Perhaps he saw in Gandhi and other new (and non-Brahman) leaders in the Congress the potentiality of a qualitatively differnt force.

The wait-and-see element of his attitude towards Hinduism was put in so many words when he explained why he refused to advise Dalits not to convert to Islam after a minor fracas over the conversion of four Mahars in Jalgaon: 'even if Ambedkar feels that it may be possible for untouchability to be removed while remaining in Hinduism, and is ready to wait and see for some time, this doesn't mean everyone can be convinced of this.'[28] It is also noteworthy that the resolutions at the second Mahad conference spoke in the name of *parmeshwar* and of the rights of Hindus, and put the stress on Hindu society purifying itself by removing untouchability.[29]

It is still true that from the very beginning Ambedkar was highly critical of Hinduism as a fundamentally inequalitarian religion, and was considering conversion as perhaps the only way out, as illustrated in an early speech at a 'Bahishkrut Parishad' at Barsi in May 1924 which Moon views as a predecessor of Ambedkar's

1936 speech on conversion.[30] And his absolute indifference to temple entry movements is clear. This contrasts with the incorpor-ativist attitude of Dalit leaders such as Kisan Faguji Bansode. Zelliot cites the 'militant' attitude of a 1934 poem.

> Why do you endure curses?
> Choka went into the temple resolutely,
> Why do you, ashamed, stay far off?
> You are the descendents of Choka.
> Why do you fear to enter the temple?
> Brace yourself like a wrestler, come,
> Together let us conquer pollution.[31]

The point is not that Bansode's interests were 'religious' or that those desiring temple entry were 'militant' or 'passive' (there were both among Dalits in the 1920s and 1930s); the point was that temple-entry was the symbolic high point of 'incorporation' into Hindu society, and even before they came to denounce it, leaders striving for an autonomous movement like Ambedkar or Bhagya-reddy Varma of Hyderabad were almost always uninterested in it and perhaps emotionally resistant to it.

Nevertheless, in many respects Ambedkar seemed ready to a certain degree in the 1920s to give Hindu society the benefit of the doubt. Perhaps this has something to do with the fact that he did not ask for separate electorates before the Simon Commission at a time when almost all other untouchable organizations were doing so (16 out of 18 who testified apparently demanded separate electorates, including G.A. Gavai) but for an increased number of reserved seats and adult suffrage.[32] And, he kept silent on the cultural–historical issue of Dalit identity, particularly regarding its most popular theme, the 'non-Aryan' identity in which Dalits claimed to be original inhabitants.

■ CLASS STRUGGLE: WORKERS, PEASANTS AND DALITS

While in some ways the late 1920s was a period of indecisiveness on cultural and religious issues, Ambedkar's basic outlook on economic and class issues appears more or less formed. This was clearest in regard to peasant and working class struggles. There is a kind of parallelism in the issues as they confronted Ambedkar and other leaders, and he approached them with the basic viewpoint of autonomy–plus–alliance. In both cases Dalits *were* workers and they *were* peasants; but as workers they were invariably in the lowest paid and most unskilled industrial jobs and as peasants they were likely to be landless or poor peasants who spent most of the time working as wage labourers as well as toiling on the caste-imposed tasks of untouchables. In both cases the 'problem of entry'—of getting jobs and getting land—could sometimes over-ride the question of organizing as workers and as peasants. In both cases they faced problems of caste discrimination, unwillingness of caste Hindu workers and peasants to accept Dalit leadership; the differences were a greater severity in village customs on the one hand, and the emerging role of communists on the other.

Ambedkar lived among industrial workers for most of his life. He was not so directly involved with the textile mill workers as the Nagpur leaders, perhaps because, in comparison, the proportion of Mahars was lower in Bombay. But he was taking note of communist and other organizing efforts, as well as the basic prob-lems of untouchables being excluded from the higher paid weaving jobs and being therefore less represented in organizing efforts. As he said in connection with the historic 1928 textile strike,

> In the recent Bombay strike this matter was brought up pro-minently by me. I said to the members of the union that if they did not recognize the right of the depressed classes to work in all the departments, I would rather dissuade the depressed classes from taking part in the strike. They afterwards consented, most reluctantly, to include this as one of their demands, and when they presented this to the millowners, the millowners very rightly snubbed them and said that if this was an injustice, they certainly were not responsible for it.[33]

Ambedkar here is critiquing an Indian communist tendency to 'demand' of the state something the organized class could and should do on its own.

In the second strike (1929), which resulted in a massive defeat of the Girni Kamgar Union, Ambedkar did in fact ask the untouch-able workers to go back. This was done, as a 2 May 1929 article in *Bahishkrut Bharat* pointed out, with a stress on the discriminated-against position of the untouchable workers and their sufferings at the hands of the money-lenders as a result of the strike; the union was condemned for calling it. It concluded cautiously, 'because so many untouchable workers have given pleas about this situation, Dr. Ambedkar has been forced to take the question in hand and protect the untouchable workers from a misdirected movement.'[34] In other words, in so far as the working class movement was concerned, the 'problem of entry' was taking precedence over organizing itself in the last part of the 1920s. This was a natural reaction for a leader of a community systematically excluded from employment (one could compare Blacks moving into working class jobs in Detroit and taking advantage of white workers' strikes to gain entry), and as in all cases, once entry was gained the Dalits tended to be among the most militant unionists. Nevertheless, Ambedkar was quite irritated at the communists for ignoring this issue, and he began to formulate his position against them. Articles following this in *Bahishkrut Bharat* argued that the trade union movement (which had to be supported) must be distinguished from the communist movement (a political movement aimed at revolution), and that he disagreed with the communists not about their aim of creating a socialist society but about the use of violent means to do so.[35]

On peasant issues and the problems of rural Mahars, Ambedkar's position was a presage of his 1930s radical organizing. His stand was pro-peasant and anti-landlord; he supported the actual movements of the decade. The first example of this was his opposition to the land revenue tax. In his first speech as a Legislative Council member in 1927 on the budget, he criticized the land tax for being imposed even in years when the peasants could earn no profit, and asked why a progressive income tax was not imposed which would hit hardest at jagirdars and *inamdars*.[36] This general position was repeated in the programmes of his later political parties, the Independent Labour Party and the Scheduled Caste Federation. He also upheld a small peasant economy. In 1928 when non-Brahmans united to organize the peasantry in opposition to a proposed 'small Holdings Relief Bill' designed to consolidate holdings, Ambedkar supported them. He argued that consolidation of holdings would only force the majority of small peasants into landlessness and lead to a concentration of holdings which had not previously taking place, adding economic power to the already existing social power in the hands of a 'Hindu oligarchy'. Further, he stated, given India's lack of capital in agriculture, holdings were not really 'too small' in terms of existing technology; if larger holdings had to be created it should be done through cooperatives of small farms 'without destroying private ownership'.[37] A longer related article on the issue saw the basic solution to a backward agriculture in transferring population from agriculture through industrial development.[38]

It is worth noting that these 'pro-peasant' policies were held even while recognizing that non-Brahman peasants were often oppressors of Dalit labourers. This comes out in the position of Ambedkar regarding the Bardoli struggle. Following the campaign, Vallabhbhai Patel had come to Maharashtra to attempt to generalize it with the formation of a Land League. Non-Brahman leaders called this a 'landlords' league' and accused the Patidars of exploiting their Duble ('Raniparaj') labourers. Ambedkar cited this as an obvious fact, but went on to remark that the Maharashtrian Brahmans had not up to that point shown the daring to lead any anti-revenue movement, and that the non-Brahmans were hypocritical because the Marathas among them had refused to support the fight of Kunbi and Mahar tenants against *khoti* landlords. Ambedkar then expressed his support for the Bardoli campaign in the following words:

> If all other remedies fail and the government refuses to take account of peasants' grievances, then are the non-Brahmans saying that the peasants should not do a peaceful movement against payment of revenue? Would the Bardoli peasants have been taken note of if they had not had the support of the no-revenue campaign in the Bardoli struggle?[39]

Aside from this general support for peasant movements, there were two important ways in which Ambedkar began, in the 1920s, to take up special problems of the Dalits. One was in fighting the specific caste-exploitation that was called in many areas *vethbegar* or *vethi*: Ambedkar initiated his campaign against the 'Mahar *watan*', through which Dalit labour was exploited as the general servant of the 'village', of its headman and the state bureaucracy. His detailed writings on this are a scathing indictment and revelation of the degree to which the British colonial state confirmed the existing caste–feudalism and utilised it for capitalist exploitation of the lowest section of rural toilers. Ambedkar notes that the

British had pensioned-off the inamdars and other feudal landlord sections, giving them access to rent without claiming any returns from them; that village-level *balutedars* such as the *patil* were simply given their former *watan* lands as private ownership and released from duties; but the Mahars and a few others (Mangs, Ramoshis) were forced to continue their labour with only the nominal reward of being given land at a lower rate of assessment.

Ambedkar took his first action on the issue when he brought the 'Hereditary Offices Act Amendment Bill' before the Legislative Council in March 1928, which would have turned the Mahars (along with the Ramoshis, Holeyas in karnataka and Vethias in Gujarat) into paid government servants, doing away with their various village honorariums and commuting their *watan* lands into ordinary private holdings. He warned the government that if nothing was done there would be 'a war between the Revenue Department and the Mahars', that if the bill did not pass he would spend the rest of his life organizing a general strike. 'I have definitely come to know that the *watan* is probably the greatest difficulty I have to face in carrying the Mahar population further', he said on 3 August 1928.[40] In fact he saw the Mahar *watan* as a major aspect of Dalit exploitation, and the false security it provided as a major socio-psychological barrier keeping the Mahars integrated into an exploitative village community. The Mahar *watan* struggle would go on throughout the 1930s and 1940s; it was the concrete form of the fight against 'feudalism' which Marxists in many parts of India have struggled against with the general term *vethbegar*.

The other question with which he was concerned was the 'problem of entry'; from the point of view of Dalit agricultural labourers it might be called a 'problem of exit'. It is noteworthy that throughout his career Ambedkar adopted almost no programme or campaign for agricultural labourers *as such*; his main concern was that the Dalits should cease being agricultural labourers, that they should escape from their landlessness either by securing industrial or white-collar employment, or by obtaining land for cultivation. Here the main type of land he became interested in was government 'forest land' or 'wasteland' (much of which had originally belonged to the village communities). In the late 1920s we can see him asking questions about this in the Council, in July and again in September–October 1927. Answers revealed, interestingly enough, that in the period 1923–26, of a total of 62,038 acres of land given for cultivation in the 'Northern Circle', 60,038 was given to 'Depressed Classes' (Dalits and Adivasis combined), in the 'Central Circle' of 19,168 acres 5,614 were given to Depressed Classes, while no applications were received for forest lands in the Kannada-speaking tracts and of the nearly 8,000 acres given in Pune, Ahmednagar and Satara almost all went to caste Hindus. Thus the Depressed Classes as a whole got 65,652 acres of land, but it is impossible to know how much of this went to the Dalits as such; very likely Adivasis in the Northern Circle got the most.[41] In any case, the statistics reveal a struggle from below going on for land, and again it was to be taken up later as a more thorough action campaign.

▪ CONCLUSION

The decade of the 1920s in Bombay Presidency saw the emergence of a vigorous Dalit movement under the leadership of Ambedkar, almost totally based on the Mahar caste. This movement decisively rejected the pro-Hindu 'integrationist' option represented by the Maratha leader V.R. Shinde and some of the Nagpur Dalit leaders; it chose instead a position of Dalit autonomy linked with a policy of general alliance with the non-Brahman movement, and of support for working class and peasant struggles qualified with concern to assure Dalits 'entry' as workers and peasants by gaining jobs and land. It also saw, with the Mahad satyagraha, the declaration in the struggle of the untouchables' right to live as full human beings.

At the same time, Ambedkar remained aloof from the interpretation of the Dalits as 'non-Aryan' original inhabitants, though this theme was associated in other regions with a stand for autonomy, annd though it had been pioneered in Maharashtra itself with the work of Jotirao Phule and was being expressed by non-Brahman ideologists in Ambedkar's own time. He also drew back from a decisive rejection of Hinduism and of the Gandhian trend within the Congress. This was consistent with the position he was to take at the 1930s Depressed Classes Political Conference in Nagpur. It was only later that he made a decision to take a fully anti-Congress stand to build an independent political party in the context of an anti-Gandhism that was to remain with him throughout his life. The decisive period, then, was the second Round Table Conference, the confrontation with Gandhi and the Poona Pact—the 'turning point' of 1932.

NOTES

1. Richard Newman, *Workers and Unions in Bombay, 1918–1929: A Study of Organization in the Cotton Mills* (Australian National University Monographs on South Asia 6, 1981), p. 51.
2. *Ibid.,* p. 219.
3. Eleanor Zelliot, *Dr. Ambedkar and the Mahar Movement* (University of Pennsylvania: Ph.D. dissertation, 1969), pp. 34–36.
4. *Ibid.,* pp. 35–36.
5. D.B. Khairmode, *Dr. Bhimrao Ramji Ambedkar* (Bombay: Pratap Prakashan, 1955), Volume II, p. 46.
6. Zelliot, *Dr. Ambedkar,* pp. 50–53.
7. *Ibid.,* pp. 44–49.
8. For details see Omvedt, *Cultural Revolt in a Colonial Society: The Non-Brahman Movement in Western India, 1850–1935* (Poona: Scientific Socialist Education Trust, 1976), pp. 151–52.
9. *Ibid.,* pp. 184–89.
10. Khairmode, *Ambedkar,* Volume II, pp. 226–27.
11. *Ibid.,* p. 229.
12. *Ibid.,* pp. 225–60 gives a detailed documentation of these conferences.
13. *Ibid.,* p. 257.
14. *Ibid.,* p. 277.
15. *Ibid.,* Appendix, p. 111.
16. *Ibid.,* p. 222.
17. *Ibid.,* p. 224.
18. A full account is provided in a memorial book, *Mangaon Parishad: Smruti Mahotsav Vishesh Ank* (Kolhapur, 1982, edited by Ramesh Dhavare).
19. Khairmode, *Ambedkar,* Volume I, pp. 280–81.
20. *Ibid.,* p. 237; Moon, *Dr. Ambedkarpurva Dalit Calval* (Pune: Sugawa Prakashan, 1987), pp. 100–1, gives an account of a united meeting of Dalits held in 1923 that condemned Shinde and his mission.
21. Ratnakar Ganvir (ed.), '*Bahishkrut Bharatatil' Dr. Ambedkarance Sphut Lekh* ('Dr. Ambedkar's articles in Bahishkrut Bharat') (Nagpur: Ratnamitra Prakashan, 1981), pp. 136–37. The Government of Maharashtra has recently published the full volumes of the newspaper.
22. Dr. B.R. Ambedkar, *Who Were the Shudras?* (Bombay, 1970), p. xxi.
23. Eleanor Zelliot, 'Learning the Use of Political Means: The Mahars of Maharashtra', in Rajni Kothari (ed.), *Caste in Indian Politics,* New Delhi (Poona: Orient Longman, 1970), pp. 44–45.

24. *Janata*, 7 April 1940.

25. The most authoritative account of the Mahad satyagraha and of some of the varying interpretations of it (with a strong attack on some caste Hindu distortions) is given by Ratnakar Ganvir, *Mahad Samta Sangar* (Jalgaon: Ratnamitra Prakashan, 1981), pp. 1–65. See also the newspaper and Bombay police accounts cited in *Source Material on Dr. Babasaheb Ambedkar and the Movement of Untouchables*, Volume I (Bombay: Government of Maharashtra, 1982), pp. 13–33, which give a sense of the degree to which the campaign became a major event.

26. Articles in *Bahishkrut Bharat* show this process; they are very wide-ranging in their scope of coverage, perhaps even more so than later articles in *Janata*, which perhaps more clearly focus on promoting the Swatantra Mazur Paksh.

27. M.P. Ganjare (ed.), *Dr. Babasaheb Ambedkaranci Bhashane*, Volume II (Nagpur: Ashok Prakashan, 1974), p. 2.

28. *Bahishkrut Bharat*, 12 July 1919; in Ganvir, '*Bahishkrut Bharatatil*', p. 206.

29. Ganjare, *Bhashane*, Volume II, pp. 21–37.

30. Moon, *Ambedkarpurva*, p. 121.

31. Cited in Zelliot, 'Learning the Use of political means', p. 39.

32. *Ibid.*, p. 45. The full text of Ambedkar's submission and his testimony before the Commission is given in *Dr. Babasaheb Ambedkar Writings and Speeches*, Volume II, edited by Vasant Moon (Bombay: Government of Maharashtra Education Department, 1982), pp. 315–500.

33. *Ibid,*, p. 474 (Ambedkar's testimony before the Simon Commission on 23 October 1928).

34. *Bahishkrut Bharat*, 3 May 1929.

35. *Ibid.*, 31 May 1929.

36. *Writings and Speeches*, Volume II, p. 2.

37. *Ibid.*, p. 129–37.

38. *Dr. Babasaheb Ambedkar Writings and Speeches*, Volume I, edited by Vasant Moon (Bombay: Government of Maharashtra Education Department, 1979), pp. 453–79.

39. See 'Communism paije tar karbandi ka nako?' ('If Communism is needed than why not an end to land revenue?') in *Bahishkrut Bharat*, 16 August 1929.

40. Speaking on the 'Hereditary Offices Act Amendment Bill' in the Bombay Legislative Council; in *Writings and Speeches*, Volume II, p. 87.

41. See Appendices to article on 'Small Holdings in India' in *Writings and Speeches*, Volume I, pp. 284–88.

CHAPTER 5

The Turning Point, 1930–36: Ambedkar, Gandhi, the Marxists

■ INTRODUCTION

The years between 1930 and 1936 were a 'turning point' in the
history of the Dalit movement in India. These years saw the All-
India Depressed Classes Conference at Nagpur in 1930; Ambedkar's attendance at the First Round Table Conference; his clash
with Gandhi before and at the Second Round Table Conference,
culminating in the Poona Pact of 1932; and the famous conversion
announcement in 1935, 'I have been born a Hindu but I will not
die a Hindu'. The events of 1930–32 led to Ambedkar's final
disillusionment with Hinduism, with even the best and most 'reformist' of the Congress leadership. At the same time these events
revealed the power represented by Ambedkar and by the Dalit
movement which had risen with him and confirmed him as the
unparalleled leader of the Dalits, forcing the Congress leadership
to deal with his demands.

Finally the events made it clear that in the search for autonomy, in the face of the fundamentally exploitative nature of class–caste society in India (which Ambedkar by 1930 named 'Brahmanism' and 'capitalism'), it was necessary to find ideological and organizational alternatives for the Dalits: a theory of exploitation and a path to liberation were needed. Having rejected the 'non-Aryan' theory, having forsaken liberalism and religious reformism, having accepted the exploitation of workers and peasants, with a rational and secular outlook, the natural direction for Ambedkar to move should have been left-ward: Marxism, which put forward a coherent theory of exploitation and the path to liberation, was already becoming a force in India. But, though it provided many themes against which Ambedkar reacted and some which he accepted, Marxism in its embodiment in the Indian communist movement failed to offer a real alternative. This failure also was clear by the 1930–35 period.

This chapter will examine the process of disillusionment with Hindu as well as Congress reformism; the power of the Dalit movement; and the failure of the communist alternative as seen in the events of 1930–35. In a sense we may look at it as an examination of the interaction of 'Ambedkarism', 'Gandhism' and 'Marxism'. However, none of these should be looked at as fully formed or developed ideologies: Ambedkarism, in particular, was incomplete, perhaps necessarily so as the ideology of an individual; and Indian Marxism was badly truncated, and, given the difficult objective conditions under which Indian communists worked during the 1920s and 1930s, could hardly hope to represent the full possibilities of the historical materialism which Marx and Engels had originated.

■ PATTERNS OF DALIT MOBILIZATION AND AMBEDKAR

Even the limited scope of this study, looking at only three linguistic regions of India and ignoring important Dalit organizing in Tamil Nadu, Kerala, West Bengal and north-west India, makes it clear that the Dalit movement was a widespread *social movement* aiming at fundamental change of a system seen as exploitative and oppressive, part of a broader anti-caste movement, with growing ideology and organization of its own.

The following generalizations can be made about these movements:

1. The Dalit movement did not emerge only in Maharashtra as a result of Ambedkar's leadership; there were similar trends, though of varying degrees of strength, in all regions.

2. The movement was genuinely anti-caste, not merely a caste-reform movement. Internal reforms (giving up drinking and meat-eating, rejecting customs which marked the caste as 'low' in a Brahmanic hierarchy, establishment of marriage relations among sub-castes) were themes everywhere, along with demands for education and entry into employment and political representative institutions. But beyond this, *some element of cultural radicalism and the assertion of autonomy from 'caste Hindus' can be seen everywhere.* In coastal Andhra, Hyderabad and Mysore this was associated with the 'non-Aryan' ideology which characterized Dalits as original inhabitants enslaved by oppressive Brahman–Aryan invaders. The theme, originating with Jotiba Phule, was taken up by the non-Brahman movements; among the Dalits it was expressed in the southern states with claims to 'Adi-Andhra', 'Adi-Dravida', 'Adi-Karnataka' and 'Adi-Hindu' status. The same theme can be traced in the writings of early Dalit leaders such as Kisan Faguji Bansode and Gopal Baba Walangkar, and had a common currency in the Maharashtrian non-Brahman movement. But because Ambedkar refused to accept it, it was not articulated in the main writings of the movement in Maharashtra. Ambedkar's own cultural radicalism took other forms.

3. Dalits as exploited workers, peasants and agricultural labourers were involved with economic or 'class' issues everywhere, and these were expressed in demands made in all the regions. The theme of *land* came up through the demand for wasteland/forest land for cultivation, made in coastal Andhra, Maharashtra and Mysore where Dalit peasants themselves were often cultivating such lands and their movement spokesmen were attempting to secure their rights. Similar attempts may have existed in Telengana and Marathwada, but the Hyderabad Dalit leadership was too isolated and the political process too aborted by the Nizam's autocracy to allow

organized expression of these issues during the 1920s and 1930s. *Opposition to vethbegar*, that is, to the feudal form of exploitation of Dalit labour, was also taken up in the campaign against the Mahar *watan* in Maharashtra and the opposition to the *thoti-talari* system expressed in Mysore. *Involvement in working class struggles* by Dalit activists is clear in Bangalore and Nagpur and in the attention to problems of textile workers shown by Ambedkar in Bombay.

While these themes were common, important *regional differences* also emerge. It is clear, for example, that an autocratic princely state (whether more heavy-handed and 'feudal' as in Hyderabad or reformist as in Mysore) helped to smother and delay the emergence of an independent Dalit movement. In particular, connection with rural areas and involvement with mass movements was more difficult and slow in both Hyderabad and Mysore. Second, the existence of an industrial working class was an important factor aiding the emergence of Dalit movements. Dalit presence in the working classes of Nagpur and Bombay stimulated radicalism and gave organizational experience in the Central Provinces and the Bombay Presidency. Radicalism and organization also existed among the Dalits working in the Bangalore and Kolar gold fields, but these were predominantly Tamil and the Tamil–Kannada linguistic–cultural gap prevented the transmission of this to the rural areas of Mysore. In contrast, Kannada-speaking Mysore, Hyderabad state, and coastal Andhra had no major industrial area to help provide a mass base and resources for a Dalit movement.

The difference made by regional variations in the position of Dalits as peasants and agricultural labourers is harder to assess. On the one hand it seems that a comparatively strong position (as existed in both Bombay Presidency and the Central Provinces) helped the Dalits to organize a movement. But if we look at Tables 2.2 and 2.3, Dalits in coastal Andhra were badly off by many counts compared to both the Dalits in Mysore and the Marathi-speaking areas: almost all were 'agricultural labourers' rather than 'cultivators' and there was a high percentage of 'farm servants', presumably those more subordinated to a traditional relationship, as opposed to free labourers. Coastal Andhra also had, historically, a more hierarchical agrarian society. Yet it gave birth to a vigorous 'Adi-Andhra' movement during the 1920s. This was undoubtedly stimulated by the possibilities opened up by commercialization and mobility. It is noteworthy that Dalits in the rural areas of Telengana did not mobilize in a similar way, though they existed in similar circumstances as found in coastal Andhra, while dalits in the rural areas of Mysore did not organize in spite of their much 'stronger' position (comparable to that of the Marathi-speaking areas) as independent small cultivators. More research is needed to clarify the various positions of Dalits at the village level, a comparison which cannot be easily assessed from crude regional-level statistics given by the censuses or recent sample surveys.

It is clear, however, that both western Maharashtra and the Nagpur-Vidarbha region had all the necessary ingredients for a strong and radical movement: a relatively free political life, with British reforms granting more and more legislative representation at district and regional levels; a vigorous industrial working class; a peasantry which was both predominantly one of small cultivators and one in which the Dalits (in this case Mahars) had a relatively strong position within the generally hierarchical and exploitative village framework; and intimate linkages between workers and peasants. It was these which lay the basis for Ambedkar's emergence into prominence as the major Dalit leader of the country.

Four things stand out about this Dalit movement as a whole:

First, though much weaker in organizational strength and financial resources, *the Dalit movement emerged as a political force at the same time as the non-Brahman movement and about the same time as the working class and peasantry were creating their organizational forms*. To put it another way, Dalits as a mass and the middle castes as a mass (*as* 'non-Brahmans', *as* 'workers' or *as* 'peasants') were entering politics at roughly the same time and making their presence felt as factors to be contended with by the leadership of the Indian National Congress and Hindu organizations such as the Hindu Mahasabha.

Second, the major force of the non-Brahman movement and the peasant and working class movements were to be politically absorbed into the Congress in the 1930s, so that the Congress came to be (by the 1940s) an 'anti-imperialist united front' in reality and not only in rhetoric. This process happened with the non-Brahman movement in spite of the historic opposition to and distrust of the Congress by Phule, in spite of efforts of Periyar to prevent it; it happened with the working class and peasantry in spite of continual tensions and betrayals of their interest by the bourgeois-dominated Congress, and largely because of the political decision of the communists to work within the Congress as an 'anti-imperialist united front'. *That this did not happen with the Dalit movement is almost solely due to Ambedkar.* Here we can see the role of the individual in history. If his leadership was on the one hand the creation of the particularly favourable conditions facilitating the rise of the Dalit movement in Bombay Presidency, on the other hand, his genius, his fight for autonomy and a political–ideological alternative also helped to create history. The trends for absorption of the Dalit movement did certainly exist during the 1920s: the appeal of the possibilities of reform; the courting of Dalits by various Congress factions from the Tilakites to Gandhians through various 'anti-untouchability' programmes; the cultural residues among Dalits themselves of bhakti and other forms of popular Hinduism. Many other Dalit leaders followed a path of integration, from M.C. Rajah of Madras and Arigay Ramaswamy of Hyderabad to the early generation of Mahar leaders in Nagpur, as well as many western Maharashtrian non-Mahar leaders (Rajbhoj, Shivtarkar) who were continually swayed towards the Congress and towards seeing themselves as Hindus. Ambedkar fought this tendency tooth and nail and maintained the independence of the Dalit movement. In doing so he was moving towards a total theory of exploitation and to the practice of building a liberation movement for the oppressed and exploited in the Indian context; that this was not fully successful is a separate question.

Third, *in taking the stand of building a political alternative to the Congress, in seeking an alliance with non-Brahmans (a Dalit-bahu-jan or Shudra-Atishudra alliance), in seeking to organize peasants and workers, and in fight for the destruction of the caste system and not just the 'abolition of untouchability', Ambedkar was maintaining and carrying forward a tradition begun by Jotiba Phule.* By the end of the 1930s it is true that his major political thrust was defeated; however this was due to the decisions and actions of forces beyond Ambedkar's control, not simply because of the inherent antagonism between 'Dalits and dominant caste peasants' or the fact that the formation of a new, independent anti-imperialist worker–peasant party was impossible.

Fourth, *Ambedkar's rejection of the non–Aryan theme, the ideology of Dalits being 'original inhabitants', was an important rejection* of a racial version of a historical–materialist explanation. This rejection is also not an 'obvious' thing to happen because the theme was very pervasive among Dalits and non-Brahmans of the time as an explanation of caste; it has currency today among all those who go on thinking of Brahmans as being descendents of Aryan invaders of 3500 years ago and Dalits as descendants of their conquered Dravidian foes. Ambedkar's rejection removed the element of racism from the Dalit movement under his leadership. But it left a gap, a need for a theory that could explain the historical character of caste exploitation. Much of Ambedkar's own historical writings constituted a search for this. This rejection also obviously gave scope for a different historical materialism— Marxism—to have an influence on Ambedkar's thinking about caste and society in general. What *failed* to happen in this regard during the 1930s is as important, finally, as the confrontation with Gandhism and Hindu revivalism.

■ FROM THE DEPRESSED CLASSES CONFERENCE TO THE POONA PACT

On 8 August 1930, in preparation for the First Round Table Conference in London, Ambedkar called an All-India Depressed Classes Conference in Nagpur. His presidential speech gives the themes central to the struggles of the coming decade.[1] He began with a discussion of the necessity for national independence, arguing that the multiplicity of castes, races, religions and languages did not make India unfit for independence. An eloquent and scathing indictment of imperialism attacked Britain's responsibility for the impoverishment of India, adding that it had done nothing to lighten either the burdens of untouchability or the exploitation of peasants and workers. At the same time Ambedkar argued that safeguards, especially for untouchables, were necessary for self-rule in the case of caste-divided India. Repeating his position of the Simon Commission testimony, he did not view separate electorates as necessary but only if adult suffrage was granted, and reserved seats, employment and strong legal measures against untouchability and social boycott were provided. Finally, Ambedkar's language of 'capitalists' and 'landlords', his continual reference to the Congress Brahman leadership as 'feudalists' indicates the strong note of class conflict and struggle.

These were the themes of an emerging 'Ambedkarite' politics, and they were expressed in his testimony at the conference itself. Attending along with M.N. Srinivasan of Madras to represent India's untouchables, he was unequivocable that untouchables needed political power and equally definite that this could only be gained within the framework of an independent India. In his opening speech on 20 November 'to put the point of view of the depressed classes', he stated,

> The point of view I will try to put as briefly as I can. It is this, that the bureaucratic form of Government in India should be replaced by a Government which will be a Government of the people, by the people and for the people. This statement of the view of the depressed people I am sure will be received with surprise in some quarters . . . . We have not taken this decision because we wish to throw in our lot with the majority. Indeed, as you know, there is not much love lost between the majority and the minority I represent. Ours is an independent decision. We have judged the existing administration solely in the light of our own circumstances and we have found it wanting.

Arguing that the goodwill of the British is irrelevant, he went on,

> The Government of India does realise the necessity of removing the social evils which are eating into the vitals of Indian society and which have blighted the lives of the downtrodden classes for years. The Government of India does realise that the landlords are squeezing the masses dry and that the capitalists are not giving the labourers a living wage and decent conditions of work. Yet it is a most painful thing that it has not dared to touch any of these evils. Why? . . . These are some of the questions raised by the Depressed Classes . . . . We feel that nobody can remove our grievances as well as we can, and we cannot remove them unless we get political power in our own hands. No share of this political power can evidently come to us so long as the British government remains as it is. It is only in a Swaraj constitution that we stand any chance of getting the political power in our own hands, without which we cannot bring salvation to our people . . . . We know that political power is passing

from the British into the hands of those who wield such tremendous economic, social and religious sway over our existence.
We are willing that it may happen, though the idea of Swaraj
recalls to the mind of many the tyrannies, oppressions and
injustices practiced upon us in the past . . . .[2]

Ambedkar spoke at the conference for a unitary state and adult
suffrage with reserved seats and safeguards for untouchables. It
was a minority position. With the Congress absent, the assembled
delegates consisted mainly of representatives of princely states and
various minority interests pushing for separate electorates, plus a
few representatives of India's 'liberals' and women's groups. Yet it
was this conference that shaped the 1935 Government of India
Act: a federal constitution in which the princely states could enter
as autonomous units; a slightly expanded (from 6.5 million to
about 30 million) electorate but hardly adult suffrage; and responsible government at the provincial level highly qualified by residual
powers given to British-appointed governors.[3]

The first conference was followed by the calling off of the Civil
Disobedience movement and the Gandhi-Irwin pact leading to the
appearance of M.K. Gandhi at the Second Round Table Conference, with all the prestige of the national movement behind him
and a claim to be the sole real representative of the Indian people.
Yet what followed was in a sense remarkable, or at least ironic.
The second conference and the Ramsey MacDonald Award (for
separate electorates) developed into, of all things, a confrontation
between Gandhi and Ambedkar. Why should this have happened?
From the nationalist point of view two things were objectionable
about the shape being given to the constitution in the first conference: the powers left to the princely states (i.e., its 'federal'
structure) and the separate electorates for minorities. Of all the
participants in the first conference, Ambedkar's position (adult
suffrage and reserved seats) was actually the closest to the nationalist one—and had there been any hope of giving a different shape to
the future constitution, some beginnings might have been made
here, in an alliance of nationalists with Ambedkar and liberal
representatives. Yet there was no real resistance from nationalist
forces (as represented by Gandhi, or from organized pressure
outside) to either the 'federal' structure or to separate electorates
for other minorities, only in the case of untouchables. Why?
Perhaps the simplest reason was that the nationalists had already

conceded the need for separate electorates to the powerful Muslim minority and had no strong interest in fighting for democracy in the princely states or opposing the federalism which institutionalized princely autocracy. When Ambedkar changed his position to support separate electorates (which he did when it was obvious there would be no universal suffrage) he came to represent, very simply, the most vulnerable force among all those claiming special protection.

However, along with these purely tactical considerations was the attitude of Hindu Congressmen, and Gandhi in particular, towards the Dalits and the issues of untouchability and caste.

In between the two conferences, Ambedkar had his first meeting with Gandhi in London in August 1931, and it took place in a turbulent atmosphere. According to B.C. Kamble's description, Gandhi treated Ambedkar with a lack of even normal politeness, while Ambedkar responded with a condemnation of the Congress, walking out after a scathing speech ending with the famous statement, 'Mahatmaji, I have no country.'[4] This was not dialogue, but confrontation. They confronted each other again at the conference, each speaking with emotion and eloquence, with the self-assurance of leaders who can gather masses behind them. Each claimed to speak on behalf of untouchables. There was a vast difference in points of view, with Ambedkar stressing the need for political power for the Dalits, and with Gandhi arguing for reform and protection from above: 'What these people need more than election to the legislatures is protection from social and religious persecution.'[5] But the emotional quality of the debate indicates an even deeper clash.

This began with the failure of consensus in the Minorities Committee and Gandhi's suggestion on 8 October that it be adjourned. Ambedkar took Gandhi's remarks as denying this representative status, and replied,

We cannot deny the allegation that we are the nominees of the Government, but speaking for myself I have not the slightest doubt that even if the Depressed Classes of India were given the chance of electing their representative to this Conference, I would all the same find a place here . . . . The Mahatma has always been claiming that the Congress stands for the Depressed Classes, and that the Congress represents the Depressed Classes more than I or my colleagues can do. To that claim I can only say that it is one of the many false claims which irresponsible people keep on making, although the persons concerned with regard to these claims have invariably been denying them . . . the Depressed Classes are not in the Congress.

Gandhi responded,

The claims advanced on behalf of the Untouchables, that to me is the unkindest cut of all. It means the perpetual bar-sinister. I would not sell the vital interests of the Untouchables even for the sake of winning the freedom of India. I claim myself in my own person to represent the vast mass of the Untouchables. Here I speak not merely on behalf of the Congress, but I speak on my own behalf, and I claim that I would get, if there was a referendum of the Untouchables, their vote, and that I would top the poll . . . I would rather that Hinduism died than that Untouchability lived. Therefore, with all my due regard for Dr. Ambedkar and for his desire to see the Untouchables uplifted, with all my regard for his ability, I must say in all humility that here the great wrong under which he has laboured, and perhaps the bitter experiences that he has undergone have for the moment warped his judgment. It hurts me to have to say this, but I would be untrue to the cause of the Untouchables, which is as dear to me as life itself, if I did not say it. I will not bargain away their rights for the kingdom of the whole world. I am speaking with a due sense of responsibility, and I say that it is not a proper claim by Dr. Ambedkar when he seeks to speak for the whole of the Untouchables of India. It will create a division in Hinduism which I cannot possibly look forward to with any satisfaction whatsoever. I do not mind Untouchables, if they so desire, being converted to Islam or Christianity, I should tolerate that, but I cannot possibly tolerate what is in store for Hinduism if there are two divisions set forth in the villages. Those who speak of the political rights of Untouchables do not know their India, do not know how Indian society is today constructed, and therefore I want to say with all the emphasis that I can command that if I was the only person to resist this thing I would resist it with my life.[6]

What was Ambedkar to think of all this? It must have appeared to him as unbearable arrogance, even as foolish arrogance—for behind Gandhi in the Congress stood not a band of sincere social reformers but (Ambedkar was convinced) a class of Brahman and other high-caste Indians concerned to maintain their monopoly of economic and social power within any 'swaraj'. Would separate electorates have been so harmful to the Dalits? Dalits themselves still debate the issue.[7] The point is that Gandhi, who feared a 'political division . . . in the villages' ignored the division that already existed; in his warning against the spread of violence, he ignored the violence already existing in the lives of the Dalits. Claiming to speak in the name of untouchables, claiming to represent their 'cause' and their 'vital interests', Gandhi was *not* speaking from their perspective; he was not even speaking as a *national* leader; he was speaking as a *Hindu* in his appearance at this Second Round Table conference.

Behind the moralism stood a direct political challenge: Gandhi was refusing to admit Ambedkar's representative status, claiming that the Dalits supported him and the Congress. From the time of this confrontation in London a political battle ensued in which all the entire Congress elite (as well as the pro-Congress sections of the press) sought to organize meetings of the untouchables, manoeuvre or produce Dalit spokesmen (for instance, a Dalit cricketeer, P. Balu) who took a line opposing Ambedkar, and do whatever they could to show that 'untouchables are denouncing Ambedkar' and that there was a 'wave of support for joint electorates'.[8] Ambedkar and militant Dalits responded with demonstrations (in which the newly formed Samta Sainik Dal played an important role) and seeking the support of various Dalit organizations.[9]

As far as Maharashtra was concerned, Ambedkar, clearly won the battle of mobilization; for instance, we can compare Gavai's failed effort to organize a demonstration in Nagpur in 1932[10] with the fact that 8,000 demonstrators who had turned up with black flags on Gandhi's return from the second conference could hold their own in a 'free-for-all'[11]—not a bad showing for an exploited section poorer than the majority of caste Hindus. It was primarily among non-Mahar Dalits that the Congress could make any impact at all. Outside of Maharashtra, it seems that Ambedkar won the support of the majority of existing organizations, though the generally low level of Dalit mobilization meant that neither

Gandhians nor Ambedkarites had much mass base or linkages at the time. An anonymous letter to the *Times of India* in January 1933, though exaggerated, put the point:

> Hindu politicians now embrace the depressed classes partly because of the latter's meteoric emergence into the political life of the country, and partly because of the apprehension of their own position in the future. They would now be ready to include the untouchables among Brahmans, not merely among Hindus, if Dr. Ambedkar wants it. This is the real condition today.[12]

In the political process that occurred with the confrontation with Gandhi in London, the Ramsey MacDonald Award on 16 August 1932, Gandhi's fast (begun 20 September) and the final Poona Pact (24 September), one event that stands out is the 'Rajah-Moonje Pact'. This represented an agreement between the Madras Dalit leader M.C. Rajah and B.S. Moonje of the Hindu Mahasabha, and it was worked out some time in January 1932.[13] With Rajah stood G.A. Gavai of Nagpur, and Ambedkar expressed to him his bitterness at the intervention. Rajah and Gavai had earlier called for separate electorates; now they were prevailed upon to support the idea of joint electorates, with Hindu spokesmen claiming that the Depressed Classes Association, with a supposed membership of 40,000, was the real all-India organization and Rajah, its long-time leader, the true Dalit spokesman.[14] To Ambedkar, Rajah and Gavai were simply acting as upper-caste agents in this matter, and he had already condemned the association in his Nagpur speech of 1930 as a nominal organization existing mainly on paper. In this he was undoubtedly right, but the DCA intervention illustrates more than this, and that is the degree to which not only Gandhians but also the Hindu nationalists were wooing untouchables.

Gandhi's threat of a fast hastened efforts to reach a compromise, and on 19 September a large conference of 'Hindu and Untouchable leaders' was held in Bombay that included Ambedkar, M.C. Rajah, P. Baloo, Madan Mohan Malaviya, Sir Tej Bahadur Sapru, M.R. Jayakar, Sir Chimanlal Setalvad, C. Rajagopalacharia, B.S. Moonje and A.V. Thakkar (in other words, primarily Hindu nationalists and Gandhians). It was at this meeting that the final agreement was hammered out by Sapru and Ambedkar in which a two-tier system of voting would allow untouchables first to select a panel of four Dalit candidates and then the general constituency (including caste Hindus) would decide among them.[15] This provided the basis of the Poona Pact once it was accepted by Gandhi; the result was finally that Dalits gained nearly double the number of seats given to them in the MacDonald Award.

Ambedkar had some reason to be satisfied with the final outcome; the seats reserved for the Dalits were nearly equivalent to their proportion in the population. Beyond this, however, the whole process brought out another reality. While the compromise agreement was hammered out with Ambedkar, the final agreement, the 'Poona Pact', was between Ambedkar and Gandhi. Gandhi as representative of caste Hindus; Ambedkar as representative of the Dalits. What Gandhi had sought to deny at the Round Table conference and what the Congress and Hinduist leaders were continually denying in their propaganda—*Ambedkar's position as the unchallenged* Dalit leader—was in practice confirmed.

It is also important to note the varied reactions to the fast and the Poona Pact itself. This is not just a matter of different 'interpretations', but of the fundamentally different perspectives of high-caste Hindus and Dalits (perhaps with other low castes with Dalits on this). For Gandhi the fast was one of 'purification', of seeking to 'purge Hinduism' of the 'blight of untouchability' and thus of motivating caste Hindus to take up the campaign against untouchability.[16] Almost all upper caste Hindus have also seen it in these terms. The result is that among the upper caste political trends it has been praised by Gandhians and by those who see it as an important step in maintaining the integrationist nature of Hindu society. It was condemned by Hindu revivalists as selling out the interests of Hindus (many upper castes, especially Bengalis, protested at the time over the overriding of their interests),[17] and criticized by leftists for leading people into a distraction from 'real' anti-imperialist work. For Ambedkar, of course, the whole issue was very different: the fast was directed against untouchables, that is, against the separate electorates given to them and in the interests of keeping them in the Hindu fold, and it was 'moral blackmail' since Gandhi's death would have provoked a violent backlash against Dalits throughout the villages. In fact rather than a moral dialogue, hard power politics was at play in the process of negotiation that settled the fast (Ambedkar noted that at the beginning

Gandhi was not even ready to concede reserved seats for untouchables).[18] It is hard to avoid the conclusion that this was a far more realistic assessment.

In the final meeting that occurred after the Poona Pact, Ambedkar is quoted as praising Gandhi's generosity, saying 'I am very grateful to the Mahatma . . . I must confess that I was immensely surprised when I met him that there was so much in common between him and me'. At the same time, he went on to express reservat᾿ ns, including the fear of 'whether the Hindu community will abide by it'.[19] These few words of Ambedkar have been taken as showing much more than they really represented. At the same meeting Rajagopalacharia said, he had

> told Mahatmaji that the greatest experiment in Satyagraha in which he ever succeeded was the conversion of Dr. Ambedkar. He had not converted Dr. Ambedkar by the coercive element in the fast but by the 'Satyagrahic' element in the fast.[20]

And this interpretation is today given by Ravinder Kumar:

> Gandhi had thus achieved what was a true Satyagrahi he always strove for: he had won his opponent's heart! . . . The differences between the two leaders, one an untouchable by birth, the other an untouchable by volition, were thus healed . . . . The agreement between the Mahatma and Ambedkar saved a society from turning into itself and committing collective suicide. Indeed, the Poona Pact was a victory won by Gandhi in the course of a struggle seeking to liberate Hindu society from a dangerous malformation lodged in the very core of its social being. It was, perhaps, the Mahatma's finest hour.[21]

This 'Gandhian' interpretation, however, is built on sand. A few words, uttered in the socially obligatory atmosphere of reconciliation that occurs after any negotiation, do not indicate a 'change of heart'. Ambedkar was burningly aware of the real issues of power politics in the process, and continued to view the fundamental difference as that between Gandhi's claim to represent the interests of untouchables by reforming Hindu society and the need of the Dalits to liberate themselves through political power. Gandhi's sincerity may have genuinely touched him, but the moral grandeur of an individual was never the point.

The differences between the two surfaced as soon as Gandhi started his League Against Untouchability (which was to become the Harijan Sevak Sangh) and Ambedkar attempted to intervene. There were two issues: whether the League/Sangh would be controlled by caste Hindus or whether the Dalits would have at least a share in control; and whether it would seek only to 'abolish untouchability' or aim at the abolition of *chaturvarnya* itself. Gandhi firmly held out for caste Hindu control on the grounds that since untouchability was an 'evil' of Hinduism that had to be purged, Hindus themselves must do this; he also stressed that he was not against *chaturvarnya* as a system.[22] It was simply impossible for Gandhi and Ambedkar to work together on this basis.

The events of 1930–32 were momentous. They showed the strength that the Dalit movement had achieved during the 1920s, catapaulting Ambedkar and the issue of untouchability into the centre of the political arena. At the same time they brought to Ambedkar the final disillusionment with Hinduism and leading the voice of Dalit militancy, he became convinced that autonomy would never be achieved within even a reformed Hinduism. The events made it clear that (*a*) Gandhi, who represented the best of Hinduism, would not budge from paternalism and acceptance of *chaturvarnya*; (*b*) in spite of the moralistic atmosphere that surrounded the fast and Pact it was hard bargaining and power (mobilizing strength) that counted; (*c*) large sections of caste Hindus did not support Gandhi in giving even limited rights and representation to the untouchables, as illustrated by the storm of opposition to the Poona Pact; and (*d*) other Dalit leaders could be used by the upper castes as long as they identified with Hinduism.

Following the Poona Pact, Gandhians began an anti-untouchability drive that included temple entry and bills in legislatures throughout the country as well as the longer-term 'Harijan campaign'. Ambedkar and his followers, in contrast, turned to a clear rejection of Hinduism and to economic and political radicalism, expressed in the conversion announcement of 1935 and the founding of the Independent Labour Party in 1936.

Ambedkar was confirmed in his belief that the caste system was exploitative and that autonomy was necessary. 'Untouchability' was not just a peripheral evil that could be removed without basic changes in the system; the system was inherently exploitative. Since only the exploited can remove exploitation by destroying a system and fighting their exploiters, autonomy was necessary; 'the emancipation of Dalits had to be the act of Dalits themselves'. This gave Ambedkar a natural tendency to look to Marxism, the theory and practice of historical materialism which was reaching India at the time and which also stressed exploitation, contradiction and the self-emancipation of the exploited. What then did the Indian Marxists have to offer?

■ MARXISM AND THE INDIAN COMMUNISTS

There was a striking absence of any section of left Congressmen in the negotiating process and no visible involvement of any kind (even in regard to commentary) by Indian Marxists in the events of the Poona Pact and the Gandhi–Ambedkar confrontation. This absence of the left contrasts to the active role of Hindu fundamentalists. This, in itself, is an important historical fact. It was not because leftists (communists or socialist-minded Congressmen) were too weak in influence to be involved in such a crucial political process; it was because they were uninterested in it. Marxists did not take part because they were unable to, but because they did not see the issue of caste and untouchability as important. Over 50 years later, E.M.S. Namboodiripad's comment in his *History of the Indian Freedom Struggle* makes this clear:

> However, this was a great blow to the freedom movement. For this led to the diversion of the people's attention from the objective of full independence to the mundane cause of the upliftment of Harijans.[23]

This indifference to caste becomes a central lacunae, at a time when Marxism was penetrating India as a powerful ideology. Though it sometimes seems that the British feared it to a degree far beyond its actual strength, there is no doubt that communism entered with something of an explosive force in the 1920s. However inadequately understood and formulated, numerous radical intellectuals throughout the 1920s and 1930s were convinced that something decisive and liberatory had happened in Russia, and they thrilled to 'Bolshevism', 'communism' and 'Marxism'. Innumerable activists appear to have gained a new dedication from the ideology, a readiness to work with fervor and self-sacrifice among the exploited masses of workers and peasants, a dedication to militant and disciplined organization. 'Let go of today, tomorrow will be ours; let go of individualism, organization is our law; let go of death, wealth will be found in life—the song of revolution is on our lips', as a Marathi song put it.[24] The condemnation of superstition and proclamation of a bold atheism and secularism which was capable of moving men and women to withstand suffering and death; the characterization of Indian society in terms of the exploitation of 'capitalism' and 'landlordism' and the claim that it was the toiling workers and peasants who had the true power to overthrow imperialism—all these were part of the Marxist appeal and corresponded to many realities of the society and needs felt by an emerging generation of young, middle class activists.

At the same time, worker and peasant struggles were not only on the rise in India, they were also posing before their leadership the question of the interweaving of caste with economic exploitation. Among the working class, the problem of the Dalits being excluded from the weaving jobs of the textile mills in Bombay was only the most stark example of a general phenomenon of 'segmentation' of the labour force. The same was true of the peasantry, with caste often forming the basis of organizing. The split between the middle castes (the 'dominant caste' peasants such as Kammas, Kapu–Reddis, Kunbi–Marathas, Kanbi–Patidars, Jats, etc.) and Dalits varied in nature from area to area, so that in some regions (Punjab and western UP and perhaps in coastal Andhra) the split between 'agricultural labourers' as a category and 'cultivators' as a category often coincided with that between Dalits and caste Hindus, while in other areas (Maharashtra, Bihar) there was a mixture of castes among agricultural labourers and to some extent among cultivators. This fact conditioned the formation of agricultural labourer unions, which emerged more spontaneously where a strong Dalit or Adivasi caste-community provided their base. In other areas there was a fairly large 'backward caste' section between the peasant–cultivator dominant caste and the Dalits which had contradictions with both and was beginning to organize separately by the 1930s. This produced the Backward Caste League in Madras Presidency which was formed in 1935 and based among Vanniyars, Kallars and Nadards;[25] the Ksatriya Association formed by Baraiyas and Patanvadias in Gujarat in 1937;[26] and the Triveni Sangh formed in 1934 by the Ahirs, Kurmis and Koeris of Shahabad district of Bihar.[27] All of these had some programmes concerned with peasant struggle and were involved with or fed into the Kisan Sabhas in Bihar and Gujarat.

Similarly, while the non-Brahman parties of the 1920s had by the last period of the decade begun to associate themselves with peasant issues, often in contradiction with the landlord element in the parties, new and often major regional political parties were formed during the 1930s combining peasant opposition to landlord or money-lender exploitation with expressions of anti-Brahmanism. These included not only Ambedkar's Independent Labour Party and Periyar's effort to transform the Justice Party to an anti-landlord, anti-imperialist association, it also included the Unionist Party in the Punjab and the Krishak Praja Party in Bengal, both of which won the 1936 elections in their respective provinces. The Unionist Party not only represented the combined cultivator interests (even though sometimes characterized as 'rich peasant') of Hindu and Muslim Jats, it also articulated these frequently in anti-Brahman language as being against 'Brahmans and banias' and it won the support of Mangoo Ram of the Ad-Dharm Dalit movement.[28] The Krishak Praja Party, based among Muslim peasants in opposition to a Hindu *bhadralok* landlord class, had a similar (if tension-filled) alliance with Dalit Namashudras.[29]

There were also some activists concerned with creating worker and peasant organizations and directly challenging the communists to take up caste issues. An early example is Dinkarrao Javalkar, the Maharashtrian non-Brahman who had worked with Jedhe during the early 1920s to form the nucleus of a nationalist non-Brahman group; it was he who during the period argued for transforming the Maharashtrian non-Brahman party into a workers' and peasants' party.[30] In 1929 Javalkar wrote,

It is the non-Brahmans who need Communism; even Brahmans have only adopted it as a deception and in the end they will have to sacrifice all their brahmanism for this. When the revolt was raised against Tsarism in Russia it was raised also against the bhikshukshahi (priesthood) there. But since the Communists here are bhikshuks, they are trying to establish the dominance of bhikshuks.[31]

In the face of this, the lack of attention to caste by the communist movement, and by Congress socialists before the Lohiaite intervention after independence, is striking. This can be seen in three ways: as a failure to press the issue in the workers' and peasants' organizations within which they worked; as a failure to form any separate organization or front to represent Dalits or take up struggles on caste issues; and as a failure to mention programmes for untouchability and caste issues in the political programmes of the Communist Party or other front parties.

In mass organizations the situation is fairly clear. The All-India Kisan Sabha, formed in 1936, made *no* mention of caste or untouchability in any of its programmes until 1945 when a September meeting of the Central Kisan Council worked out a 'Charter of Demands' that included as one clause, 'penalization for enforcing social disabilities on the "untouchables"'[32]. Doubtless Dalit issues were taken up (or were considered to be taken up) in condemnation of 'pre-capitalist forms of exploitation' and 'feudal bondage', and of course the campaign against *vethbegar* was there from the beginning. But the Marxist language of 'pre-capitalist' and 'feudal' did *not* automatically include caste; while the Kisan leaders never analyzed the specificity of Indian *vethbegar* which was so very often articulated in terms of caste duties.

Similarly, the All-India Trade Union Congress (AITUC) had brief resolutions against untouchability in the 4th, 5th and 6th sessions (1924–26), but then the subject was dropped and not until a unification of forces occurred in which the AITUC, the Red Trade Union Congress (RTUC) formed by the communists in their sectarian phase, and the more rightiest–liberal National Trade Union Federation came together did a large and comprehensive 'charter of working class demands' include 'abolition of all discrimination of caste, colour, creed, race and sex' and 'equal wages for equal work without any discrimination of caste, creed, race and colour.'[33] In 1942 an amended version of the AITUC included among its objects '(h) to abolish political or economic advantage based on caste, creed, community, race or religion'; this had not been mentioned in the earlier 1927 Constitution.[34] But these references to caste did not constitute an anti-caste or even an anti-untouchability programme.

The lack of attention paid to caste issues by these two important 'mass fronts' shows that it was not only members of the Communist Party but other leftists at the time (Congress socialists, Royists and the independents who later either joined the Communist Party or left the AIKS/AITUC) who failed to theorize the specificity of caste and see the importance of giving a programme of struggle for workers and peasants on caste issues.

Further, neither the communists or other leftists considered having a 'front' of their own on caste issues, or felt the need to establish relations with any existing Dalit organizations. This might be considered out of the question, but it should be remembered that the other two major political trends (Gandhian and Hindu fundamentalist) *did* have these. By the 1930s in fact three 'all-India' Dalit organizations had emerged. These were the Depressed Classes Association, which was the earliest; the Depressed Classes Federation, which was established by Ambedkar as a nominal organization in 1930 and build up as the Scheduled Caste Federation from 1942 onwards (in Marathi it was simply known as 'Dalit Federation'); and the Depressed Classes League (also known as the 'Harijan League') which was established by Jagjivan Ram in 1936. While none of these functioned at a vigorous all-India level, at least until the Scheduled Caste Federation, still the 'Association', the 'Federation', and the 'League' represented clearly different trends on the all-India level, the one with Hindu Mahasabha links, the second 'Ambedkarite', the third 'Gandhian'. They provided networks which locally-based Dalit organizations could associate with. Further, Gandhian–Congress ties worked at two levels, through the Harijan Sevak Sangh which was a caste Hindu organization and of course had the greatest funding and organizational network, but also through the 'League' which sought to mobilize pro-Congress Dalits.

The communists (and other leftists within the Congress) had nothing like this, nor did they seek to relate to any of the existing organizations by having cadres work within them (as for instance Communist women worked within the All-India Women's Congress). At local levels many communist cadres were of course involved in anti-untouchability campaigns, the most famous example being the Kerala communists, and many communists in their personal lives transcended and ignored caste distinctions. But there was never a programmatic involvement in 'social struggles'; rather, joining the party lessened whatever involvement had previously existed.

Finally, what did communist political organizations have to say on caste? 'Protection of Untouchables by legislation' found a mention in Singaravelu's proposed action programme for the 1923 Labour Kisan Party (notably, he was a non-Brahman) but was not included in the programmes of the Labour Swaraj Party or the Workers' and Peasants' parties formed after this.[35] Not until the second congress of the CPI in 1948 was the issue taken up in any kind of detail. Then the 'Political Thesis' included a 'Programme of the Democratic Revolution' of which point (5) was as follows:

> Just and democratic rights of minorities to be embodied in the constitution: Equality and protection to the language and culture of minorities; all liabilities, privileges and discriminations based on caste, race and community to be abolished by law and their infringement to be punishable by law.[36]

The 'Political Thesis' also contained five paragraphs on 'The Untouchables', the high points of which claimed:

> Forming the most exploited and oppressed section of our people, the six crores of untouchables are a powerful reserve in the struggle for democratic revolution. The Congress, led mainly by bourgeois leaders belonging to the upper castes, has consistently refused to champion the cause of the untouchable masses and to integrate the struggle for social and economic emancipation of the untouchables with the general struggle for national freedom. This has enabled reformist and separatist leaders like Dr. Ambedkar to keep the untouchable masses away from the general democratic movement and to foster the illusion that the lot of untouchables could be improved by reliance on imperialism . . . . To draw the untouchable masses into the democratic front, to break down the caste prejudice of the upper caste workers and peasants, to unite the common people of all castes against their common enemy—such are the tasks faced by the party. This task will have to be carried out by a relentless

struggle against the bourgeoisie of the upper castes as well as against the opportunist and separatist leaders of the untouchables themselves. We have to expose these leaders, tear away the untouchable masses from their influence, and convince them that their interest lies in joining hands with the other exploited sections and that only the victory of the democratic revolution will emancipate them from social degradation and slavery. Every discrimination against the untouchables must be denounced as a bourgeois attempt to keep the masses disunited, and every just demand of theirs must be fought for as a part of the common struggle for people's rights.[37]

The communists' fight for untouchable rights thus proposed a confrontation with Ambedkar, denouncing him as 'separatists', 'opportunistic' and pro-British. It also treated 'caste prejudice' as only bourgeois divisiveness, made no effort to go into the specificity of caste exploitation, and asked untouchables to join the 'democratic revolution' (of which they were a 'reserve' force, i.e., not the main one) without giving a single concrete programme for fighting caste or untouchability.

Why did all this happen? Two factors are generally pointed to by Dalits and others who have been burningly aware of this neglect: one, that the upper-caste origins of the Indian communists (a 'bunch of Brahman boys', in the words of Ambedkar[38]) made them unwilling to look at forms of exploitation which questioned their male, upper caste interests; and two, that Marxism itself was and is incapable of handling caste or other 'non-class' contradictions.

Both factors have an element of truth in them; yet both are historically contingent. The fact that communists were mainly upper caste certainly did influence their interpretations of Marxism and inclined them to ignore caste issues (just as the fact that they were male inclined them to ignore gender issues and the fact that they came out of urban petty bourgeois families inclined them to ignore specific problems of the peasantry). Yet individual members of 'oppressor' groups have always broken away ideologically and organizationally, depending very much on circumstances and organizational pressures. Had some initiative been taken by the communists, for instance, it would have led to more non-Brahman and Dalit recruitment into the party and this in turn would have led to some transformation of Indian Marxism. (This process happened with the South African Communist Party, originally based on white workers and taking a racist stance against the Blacks but later turning to them, incorporating their problems within the framework of understanding the issue as a 'national question' and recruiting many African leaders). The failure to recruit Dalit petty bourgeois activists is striking (for instance, in coastal Andhra where a generation of educated Dalit youth grew up in the 1920s and 1930s, we can find some being drawn to the Congress via the N.T. Ranga group, but almost none in the communist movement, in spite of the fact that communists more than the Rangaites had vigorous organizing among Dalit labourers). Even non-Brahmans were few in number. In other words, the problem is not simply that the communist movement originated as Brahman-dominated (in caste terms), but that it remained Brahman-dominated, that a process of transformation did not take place. And to explain this, we need to look beyond simply the numerical dominance of Brahmans in the party at the beginning and examine how either Leninist party practices and/or the pressures of British repression prevented transformation and broadening of membership.

In regard to the second point, a science of historical materialism, which Marx had initiated, is not incapable of handling 'non-class' factors such as caste and patriarchy. We find, to make a comparison, that Marx and Engels themselves did make some crucial theoretical points in the discussion of patriarchy and the role of reproduction, though these were not brought forward within the Marxist movement until women independently took up the issue nearly a century later. Existing writings on women's oppression and the 'origin of the family' did provide a base for some communist action on women's issues in the meantime. That even this much did not happen in regard to caste, in spite of the tremendous potentialities for an anti-caste movement in India, was at least partly a result of Marx and Engels' own lack of familiarity with India, not a flaw of historical materialism as such.

But there is no question that 'Marxism' as it came to exist in the Indian communist tradition led to a narrowing of vision, not only for members of communist and socialist parties, but also justified the ignorance of caste issues by other 'progressives' and 'leftists' in the Congress. The 'class' category provided a marvellous tool for Indian Marxists to interpret what they saw around them within one grand framework of a theory of exploitation and liberation, but at the same time blinding them to other factors in their environment, so that instead of being inspired by the multifaceted struggles of low-caste peasants and workers to develop their own theory and practice, they instead sought to narrow these struggles and confine them within a 'class' framework. In one form or another they said, seize state power, redistribute land and your problems will be solved. 'Marxism' was taken in practice as a closed theory, not a developing science. As a result there could be no dialogue with leaders like Ambedkar. Thus, when Ambedkar reacted to Marxism, he reacted to it only as a closed system which was at crucial points not simply indifferent but in opposition to struggles of the Dalits. He borrowed themes from Marxism, as we shall see later, but he never took it as a resource for analysis and action.

■ Communists, Nationalists and 'Worker–Peasant Parties'

The other crucial aspect in the relations of Ambedkar, the Dalit movement and the communists has to do with their attitude towards nationalism and political organization. Ambedkar's primary stress was the necessity for an independent party of workers and peasants which would also take up anti-imperialist programmes; the Independent Labour Party was his main effort in this direction.

For the communists, in contrast, it was difficult to visualize the role of an independent political organization of the exploited that would be between the vanguard proletarian political party and the 'all class' united front. During the 1920s, 'worker and peasant parties' were projected not simply as class parties of workers, peasants and petty bourgeois intellectuals, but as a revolutionary–nationalist alternative to the Congress. M.N. Roy spoke in somewhat different language of a 'revolutionary people's party'.[39] As the introduction to the Communist Party documents puts it,

> In the period 1925–30, when these parties were formed, they functioned both inside the National Congress, fighting for a revolutionary programme for the national independence movement, and independently, organizing class struggles and the trade union and kisan movement.[40]

By the 1930s, largely as a result of changes in international communist policy culminating in the 1937 Comintern Congress call for a broad 'anti-imperialist united front', this effort was dropped. Up to 1930 communists like Rajni Palme Dutt had continued to urge Indian communists to form a 'national revolutionary bloc', but till 1932 with the 'Open Letter to Indian Communists' there was no mention of this, and the stress was simply on the formation of an illegal Communist Party; communists were urged to be militant in anti-imperialist struggles but without any separate open organizational platform.[41] Communists worked inside the Congress, and they used the Congress Socialist Party (CSP, formed in 1934) as a vehicle for organizing the masses; the CSP of course was entirely internal to the Congress. During the 1937–40 period the communists drew all their activists into the Congress politically, and withdrew them from anti-Congress political forces such as Ambedkar's Independent Labour Party and Periyar's Self-Respect movement. The result was that while the Communist Party did exist as an underground party, the communists at the same time gave considerable support to building up the Congress as a political force. As a result other parties with peasant support base were deprived of the dedicated radicalism that communist cadres offered.

There is considerable debate about the viability of worker–peasant parties or whether it was necessary and correct for communists to work within the Indian National Congress. But the whole debate is vitiated by the tendency to see the issue as one of class (or caste or gender) oppression *versus* national oppression, and to then put it in terms of whether 'class' or 'anti-imperialism' constituted the 'main contradiction'. A policy of working within the Congress is attacked or justified on this basis; for instance, Liddle and Joshi have argued that 'Gandhi recognized the power of the women and low castes and contained it for the cause of independence, uniting the nation behind the freedom struggle at the expense of injustice within class, caste and gender relations.'[42] This formulation then leads to the reply that such a subordination was necessary because the interests of Dalits, women, etc., required first strengthening the national struggle. But that is not the main point. The charge against Gandhi, for instance, is not that he subordinated the interests of Dalits and women in nationalism, but that he subordinated them to bourgeois, male and Brahman interests. Such subordination not only weakened class and caste struggles but also weakened the anti-imperialist movement; a more revolutionary anti-imperialist movement could have been formed with the promotion of low-caste, women, worker and peasant interests playing a crucial role. The charge against the communists is not that they subordinated national to class interests, or (in a different period) class to national interests, but that they could not maintain a political organization to project a more revolutionary unity of all these interests.

The Indian communists did not see it this way; they did not see their role as communists as being radical anti-imperialists as well as organizers of the working class. The worker–peasant parties were viewed as simply a legal, open 'front' for the 'real' party, the proletarian Communist Party. In this sense the 'multi-class' nature of these parties was to be allowed no real autonomy and their 'national revolutionary' character was thus empty. In fact, just as a mechanical understanding of 'class' blinded the Indian Marxists to the independent role of 'caste' or 'gender', so it blinded them, in a different way, and in spite of their natural inclination to revolutionary nationalist struggle, to the really independent role of nationality and national exploitation. Thus while they veered away from working independently to working entirely within the Congress, at no point was this guided by the necessity to establish an independent national–revolutionary political platform. In any case, the fact that by the 1930s they were directing all their political efforts into the Congress meant a further rejection of dialogue with Ambedkar and other spokesmen for an independent anti-caste movement.

NOTES

1. M.P. Ganjare (ed.), *Dr Babasaheb Ambedkaranchi Bhashane*, Volume 2 (Nagpur: Ashok Prakashan, 1974), pp. 57–90.
2. *Dr. Babasaheb Ambedkbar, Writings and Speeches*, Volume II, edited by Vasant Moon (Bombay: Government of Maharashtra Education Department, 1982), pp. 503–6.
3. Sumit Sarkar, *Modern India, 1885–1947* (Delhi: MacMillan, 1983) , pp. 336–37.
4. B.C. Kamble, *Samagra Ambedkar Charitra, Part 7* (Bombay: Author, 1987), pp. 82–93; see also *Times of India*, 18 August 1931, reprinted in *Source, Material on Dr. Babasaheb Ambedkar and the Movement of Untouchables*, Volume I (Bombay, Government of Maharashtra, 1982), p. 52.
5. *Writings and Speeches*, Volume II, p. 661.

6. *Ibid.*, pp. 661–63.
7. See for example, Raosaheb Kasbe, *Ambedkar and Marx* (Poona: Sugawa Prakashan, 1985), and Kanshi Ram, *The Chamcha Age: An Era of the Stooges* (New Delhi: Author, 1982).
8. *Sources*, Volume I, pp. 53–83.
9. Almost all newspaper reporting, especially that of the nationalist *Bombay Chronicle*, indicates a hostility to Ambedkar; see *Sources*, Volume I, pp. 74–75.
10. See chapter 3; also reported in *Bombay Chronicle*, 7 May 1932 and 23 May 1932; cited in *Sources*, Volume I, pp. 78–79.
11. Zelliot, 'Learning the Use of Political Means: The Mahars of Maharashtra', in Rajni Kothari (ed.), *Caste in Modern Indian Politics* (Poona: Orient Longman, 1970), p. 48.
12. *Times of India*, 2 January 1932, in *Sources*, Volume I, p. 104.
13. See *Sources*, Volume I, pp. 72–83 for reports, including Ambedkar's letters to Gavai.
14. *Bombay Chronicle*, 2 April 1932 in *Sources*, Volume I, p. 76.
15. Ravinder Kumar, 'Gandhi, Ambedkar and the Poona Pact, 1932', in Jim Masselos (ed.), *Struggling and Ruling: The Indian National Congress, 1885–1985* (New Delhi: Sterling Publishers Pvt. Ltd., 1987), pp. 96–97.
16. *Ibid.*, p. 97.
17. See *Writings and Speeches*, Volume II, pp. 707–29, for details regarding objections, especially from Bengali Hindus.
18. *Times of India*, 19 September 1932, in *Sources*, Volume I, p. 87.
19. Cited in *Bombay Chronicle*, 26 September 1932, in *Sources*, Volume I, pp. 93, 98–99.
20. *Ibid.*, p. 100.
21. Kumar, 'The Poona Pact', pp. 98–99.
22. See the reports in *Sources*, Volume I, pp. 101–11.
23. E.M.S. Namboodiripad, *A History of the Indian Freedom Movement* (Trivandrum: Social Scientist Press, sd 1986), p. 492.
24. Song by G. Adhikari.
25. See Eugene Irschick, 'The Right to Be Backward' (manuscript 1971).
26. See David Hardiman, 'The Quit India Movement in Gujarat', in Gyanendra Pandey (ed.), *The Indian Nation in 1942* (Calcutta: Centre for Studies in Social Sciences, 1988), pp. 99–101. Hardiman stresses the conflicts between the Patidars and the Baraiya–Patanvadia group as the reason for the latter not supporting the 1942 movement in Kheda; however they did so in Broach, in spite of similar tensions, where the Kisan Sabha had mobilized them.
27. See Kalyan Mukherjee, 'Bhojpur: Dimensions of Caste–Class Conflict', Paper for Workshop on Caste and Class in Contemporary India (Bombay, ISRE, April 1979); Manju Kala, B.N. Maharaj and Kalyan Mukherjee, Peasant Unrest in Bhojpur', in A.R. Desai (ed.), *Agrarian Struggles in India after Independence* (Bombay: Oxford University Press, 1986). The role of the Triveni Sangh in opposition to the Bihar Kisan Sabha still has to be assessed, though at least one Marxist evaluates it positively; see D.N., 'Problem of Unity in the Bihar Struggle' *Economic and Political Weekly*, 7 May 1988. The Kurmis/Koeris/Ahirs (Yadavas) were the 'upper' backward castes, equivalent to Kunbis/Malis/Dhangars in Maharashtra, but they constituted about 20 per cent of the population compared to 13 per cent for the Bhumihar/Rajput/

Brahman groups; see Harry Blair, 'Rising Kulaks and Backward Classes in Bihar', *Economic and Political Weekly*, 12 January 1980.

28. Prem Chowdhry, 'Triumph of the Congress in South-East Punjab: Elections of 1946', Paper for Seminar on Economy, Society and Politics in Modern India, New Delhi: Nehru Memorial Museum, 15–18 December; Harkishen Singh Surjeet, 'Lessons of Punjab', *Nationality Question in India* (Poona: TDDS, 1987), pp. 312–14. It is difficult to find a detailed scholarly treatment of either the Triveni Sangh or the Unionist Party; see Mark Juergensmeier, *Religion as Social Vision: The Movement Against Untouchability in Twentieth Century Punjab* (Berkeley: University of California Press, 1978), for the Ad-Dharm alliance with the Unionist Party, where Mangoo Ram was an MLA on its ticket until the Unionist defeat in 1946. H.F. Owen in The Non-Brahman Movements and the Transformation of Congress 1912–22', in Masselos, *Struggling and Ruling*, p. 55, mentions both the Punjab and Bengal's Krishak Praja Party as representing non-Brahman interests, analyzing it (like most Marxists) as a result of a 'rising rural bourgeoisie'.

29. Sekhar Bandhopadhyaya, 'Caste and Politics in Colonial Bengal: A Case Study', in *In the Wake of Marx*, 4:1, 1988; J.H. Broomfield, *Elite Conflict in a Plural Society* (Berkeley: University of California Press, 1968), pp. 287–97; and Sarkar, *Modern India*, pp. 354–55.

30. Gail Omvedt, *Cultural Revolt in a Colonial Society: The Non-Brahman Movement in Western India, 1850–1935* (Poona: Scientific Socialist Education Trust, 1976), pp. 263–67. .

31. *Kaivari*, 29 January 1929, in Y.D. Padke (ed.), *Dinkarrao Javalkar Samagra Wangmay* (Poona: Sri Vidya Prakash, 1984), p. 243.

32. See M.A. Rasul, *A History of the All-India Kisan Sabha* (Calcutta: National Book Agency, 1974), p. 123. If there were any earlier resolutions on this they were not seen as important enough to be included in Rasul's summary of early AIKS meetings, conferences and struggles.

33. See Prem Sagar Gupta, *A Short History of the All-India Trade Union Congress (1920–1947)* (New Delhi: AITUC Publications, sd 1980), pp. 302–3.

34. *Ibid.*, pp. 95–96, 368.

35. See G. Adhikari (ed.), *Documents of the History of the Communist Party of India*, Volume 2 (Delhi: People's Publishing House, 1974), pp. 97–166, 591, 689; Volume 3A (New Delhi: People's Publishing House, 1978), pp. 155–83; Volume 3B (New Delhi: People's Publishing House, 1979), pp. 31–44, 165–80.

36. M.B. Rao (ed.), *Documents of the History of the Communist Party of India* (New Delhi: People's Publishing House, 1976), p. 85.

37. *Ibid.*, pp. 111–12.

38. Quoted in Omvedt, *Cultural Revolt*, p. 296.

39. Adhikari, *Communist Party*, Volume 2, p. 98.

40. *Ibid.*, p. 100.

41. See R. Palme Dutt, The Road to Proletarian Hegemony in the Indian Revolution', *The Communist International*, 16:13, 1 December 1930 and 14, 15 December 1930; and 'An Open Letter to Indian Communists', in *The Communist International*, Series II, 9: 10, 1 June 1932.

42. Joanne Liddle and Rama Joshi, *Daughters of Independence: Gender, Caste and Class in India* (New Delhi: Kali for Women Press, 1986), p. 35.

CHAPTER 6

The Years of Radicalism: Bombay Presidency, 1936–42

From Now On

Freedom loving youth, give up your laziness, from now on;
Breaking the noose of slavery, toil day and night,
The torch of noble self-respect has lit up the battlefield.
Become proud heros, manly lords, with scimitar in hand;
Do you bury your life in dust? from now on . . .
Cry out freedom's fight, take on whatever comes,
If all fight with one mind revolution will come to the world.
Then who will have the nerve to stand in your path?
Our ancestors were valorous, they triumphed in the war of Bharat—
For what do you tell these stories of the past?
Gandhi's superstitiousness will not be allowed;
Why do you ignore the staunch patriots of the nation?
Throw this accursed inequality into the flame of equality,
The powerful wind of inspiration has filled our bodies,
We'll fight at any time . . . from now on . . .
Remain the slaves of no one, take the pride of freedom,
Give your years as sacrifice for this work of truth.
Expell this dirt of inequality from the nation,
Give your ears to hear the sorrows of caste-brothers,
Do you remain bound? from now on . . .

> *Feed the future generations with education's nectar,*
> *Take this resolve within you, 'Freedom is my birthright.'*
> *In a united Indian nation, 'Jay Bhim, the Raja of dalits,'*
> *We are his servants; one leader, fresh proof,*
> *The devotees come, from now on . . .*
> *Lift to the skies the flag of the Independent Labour Party,*
> *Its symbol the blood of workers, the red flag remains;*
> *Keep its prestige aloft, a garland beyond price,*
> *This is the unity of the nation, immortal welfare, this demand,*
> *Go singing the song of victory, from now on . . .*

(Song by K.A. Dhegade, in *Janata*, 3 February 1940).

■ FORMATION OF THE INDEPENDENT LABOUR PARTY

On 15 August 1936 the formation of the Independent Labour Party (ILP, in Marathi the Swatantra Mazur Paksh) was announced. The four momentous years between the Poona Pact and this event had seen action primarily on socio-religious issues. These included the final failure of the Nasik temple-entry satyagraha led by Ambedkar's lieutenants, Ambedkar's dramatic announcement at a meeting in Yeola (Nasik district) that he would give up Hinduism, and the subsequent tornado of response by caste Hindus throughout the country. Ambedkar's speech, 'Annihilation of Caste', for a group of caste Hindu reformers in north India, the Jat-Pat Todak Mandal of Lahore, was cancelled because it centred on the argument that it was necessary to destroy *chaturvarnya*, and that the strangle-hold of the *shastras* must be broken in order to achieve this; the argument over this was the major debate between Gandhi and Ambedkar on the meaning of Hinduism.[1] The debates on religion, the search for an alternative faith, and the delving into Indian cultural–historical tradition would continue unabated, but in the years from 1936 through 1942 Ambedkar and the Dalits were caught up in waves of economic and political radicalism.

Political organization had become a burning necessity for the movement. The core of the confrontation with Gandhi had been the question of who represented the Dalits, and by 1936, with general elections declared at the provincial level, the Dalit movement had to prove its autonomy and power in practice. Further, in the context of disillusionment with incorporation into Hinduism, power became even more necessary. At a rally of 15,000 Dalits in Nasik in 1934 he made the point that:

the temple entry movement . . . was started because . . . that
was the best way of energizing the depressed classes and making
them conscious of their position. [Ambedkar] believed that he
had achieved that purpose and therefore had no more use for
temple entry. Instead he strongly advised the depressed classes
to concentrate their energy and resources on politics.[2]

Now, with the reforms and the elections, the time had come.

It is significant that the political thrust was made through a party
that projected itself mainly as a party of workers and peasants, not
simply of Dalits. To see the ILP as being simply modeled after the
British Labour Party neglects the Indian context.[3] The 1930s was a
period of mass radicalism. Though the Congress socialists and
later the communists decided to organize within the Congress as
an anti-imperialist united front, mass base of the Congress remained
volatile. Gandhian satyagraha techniques seem to have failed and
there was a resulting polarization. On one hand many Congressmen who had established mass appeal, Vallabhbhai Patel, Rajendra
Prasad, Rajagopalachari, swung to the right; it was this conservative
group, rapidly identifying with the Indian bourgeoisie, that was
consolidating its hold over the Congress machinery.[4] As a result,
disillusionment with the Congress was increasing among the radicalized youth, peasants and workers and continued to increase after
the Congress came to power in many provinces and failed to fulfil
radical-reformist promises. In the Indian princely states, also, a
new wave of militancy began in 1937–38, revitalizing a small state
people's movement and practically going beyond the ability of the
Congress to control it.[5]

It was also a period of alternative political projects, although the
'worker–peasant' parties of the communists had been given up.
Although the traditional non-Brahman parties of Madras and
Bombay Presidencies were in disarray, new parties which were
established (such as the Unionist Party in the Punjab and the
Krishak Praja Party in Bengal) can be called peasant-based 'non-
Brahman' parties. The Unionists organized Muslim, Sikh and
Hindu peasants against the 'Banias and mahajans' of the Congress'
while the KPP organized other Muslims and Namashudras against
the Bengali *bhadralok*. In this sense the ILP was part of a trend,
and its electoral success (it put up 17 candidates, 13 for Scheduled
Caste reserved seats and four for general seats; of these 11 reserved

and three general seats were won, plus four of 19 reserved seats in Central Provinces Berar)[6] was not so different from the gains scored by the better financed and broadly based Unionist and Krishak Praja parties.

The Congress did win the 1937 elections on a large scale, with 711 of the 1,585 provincial assembly seats and absolute majorities in five provinces,[7] but this was done with the support of the left (communists, socialists, Royists). In fact the Congress was being challenged both from within and without during the 1937–40 period, as newly asserting political forces emphasized the needs of peasants, workers and low castes (minorities and Dalits) as central to any real anti-imperialist struggle. The ILP was a part of this process and can only be understood in this context.

The programme of the ILP, published in 1937, described it as a 'labour organization in the sense that its programme was mainly to advance the welfare of the labouring classes.'[8] It supported state ownership and management where necessary, but even for workers its stress was on what is called today the 'unorganized sector', offering land resettlement and public works to aid the unemployed and landless. It promised measures to save peasants from the clutches of money-lenders, put up a strong opposition to land revenue, and campaigned for legislation for a more equitable system of tax as well as the establishment of land mortgage banks and agricultural producers' cooperatives and marketing societies. It also promised protection to tenants of *khot* landlords.[9] The radicalizing process of the time is seen in the fact that within two years the ILP went beyond this limited anti-landlordism to *lead* the struggles of tenants of abolish *khoti*.

Janata, Ambedkar's weekly, which had been founded in 1930, gives a living picture of how the party was projected. Bold headlines condemning capitalist and landlord injustices, reports of atrocities on untouchables, elaborately written and studious editorials presenting a generally socialist outlook, songs hailing worker and peasant struggles and the freedom struggles of the Dalits, as well as considerable reporting of meetings and events were featured on its pages. On 1 May 1937 a first page article on why a new party was needed after fifty years of the Indian National Congress put the basic case for the ILP: the Congress itself had decided it was necessary to build a movement of workers and peasants, but this was not consistent with its leaders self-interest; only the ILP had the true, militant and constructive programme for workers.[10] Just prior to this, under the heading 'Can Workers Cooperate with Congress' an article had condemned the argument of Roy and Ruikar that workers should join the Congress in order to work with other classes in the struggle against imperialism; this ignored the existence of other imperialisms and the class which was rejecting imperialism only to gain the right to exploit its own people.[11]

An important editorial written at the time of the Manmad Railway Workers' Conference in May, titled 'The Struggle of Workers and Peasants', claimed that the Congress was controlled by capitalist powers and that since it contained mutually opposing interests of capitalists, landlords, *sawkars* and peasants and workers, leaders like Nehru could only claim to praise socialism but do nothing to gain it. The role of caste was also pointed out:

> The Panditji's claim is that 'there is no other way than socialism for the Indian people to become free of their poverty, excessive unemployment, degradation and slavery'. You can take from any principle of socialism that a nation cannot really be free without destroying economic inequality—but is this possible for the Congress of which Pandit Jawaharlal is president? The Indian working class is completely blinded by social and religious inequality, and without removing these the class will never be organized.[12]

More concretely, editorials condemned Gandhian attempts to organize an alternative trade union centre based on the Ahmedabad Mazdur Mahajan and following the 'trusteeship' principle; this would cause a 'Split in the Working Class Movement'.[13] *Janata* also began, in the early months of 1937, a series of reports on the emerging anti-landlord movement in the Konkan, and this was stressed in the founding of the Ratnagiri branch of the ILP: since the interests of the class of capitalists, landlords, *khots* and *sawkars* were opposed to those of workers, peasants and tenants, a machinery was needed to enable peasants to give voice to their complaints, and with this aim party branches were being formed.[14]

Thus, the ILP was projected boldly as a party of workers and peasants; the fight against casteism was taken as a necessity for creating worker–peasant unity; and the Congress was condemned as a party controlled by exploiting classes which would neither end exploitation nor fight vigorously against British imperialism.

■ MASS STRUGGLES: WORKERS AND PEASANTS

The ILP soon became involved in mass struggles of workers and peasants, in particular the fight for the abolition of *khoti* landlordism, climaxing in early 1938, and a one-day general strike of textile workers on 15 November 1938 which saw the united action of Ambedkar, moderate labour leaders and the communists.

Discontent against the *khoti* system had been simmering for long in the Konkan. Along with the *malguzar* system in Nagpur, it provided the main exception in the Marathi-speaking areas to a general pattern of ryotwari settlement. The landlords were Chitpavan Brahmans and high-caste Marathas, the tenants were Kunbis, Mahars and other Shudra castes such as the Agris. The caste connections of the landlords with the Maharashtrian political elite made it difficult for any leadership of the struggle to emerge, as Tilak's earlier defense of landlordism had indicated and as Ambedkar stressed in earlier *Bahishkrut Bharat* articles.[15] Thus, though one British official had believed in 1890 that Ratnagiri district was 'ripe for a serious agitation, which may need the employment of troops if it breaks out',[16] nothing of the sort happened. A tenant strike was reported in salt-rice villages in Pen taluka in 1920–22, and some agitations in Chiplun in 1925.[17] But, though S.K. Bole (an Agri leader of the Non-Brahman Party in the Bombay Legislative Council) attempted to bring anti-*khot* legislation in the 1920s, and Ambedkar supported him in this, nothing came of it.[18]

Struggles began to erupt during the 1930s, centred on Chari in Alibag taluk. A.V. Chitre, a CKP activist then connected with N.M. Joshi's Social Service League, and N.N. Patil, a local Kunbi leader, had taken the lead in organizing a 'peasants' union' which was declared illegal in 1932. After the ban was lifted in 1934 the third session of the Kolaba Zilha Shetkari Parishad was held on 16 December with Ambedkar presiding. This time Ambedkar expressed an opposition to the strike method and promised to push for a fair 'arbitration board', but he also took note of the injustices suffered by the tenants.[19] Murders of *khots* by their tenants were also reported,[20] and it seems from Ambedkar's references that Bombay workers, both caste Hindus and Dalits, who had connections with Konkan tenants were involved from the 1920s in a

transmission of militancy.[21] The election campaign of 1937 sparked
a renewal of struggle. Three general candidates (Anandrao Chitre
from Ratnagiri West, Surendranath Govind Chitnis from Kolaba,
and Shamrao Parulekar for Ratnagiri East) and two Dalit candidates
(Visharam Gangadhar Savadkar for Kolaba and Gangadhar
Ragharam Ghatge for Ratanagiri) won for the ILP in the region,[22]
indicating that its victories in general constituencies had behind it
the anti-landlord struggles of peasants, as well as organizing on
caste issues.

In September 1937, Ambedkar introduced a bill in the Legislative
Council for abolition of the *khoti* system, a position more radical
than his party's programme. This was accompanied by the first
ever reported march of peasants to Bombay, numbering about
500, with working class support. Parulekar and Chitre, the main
organizers of the Konkan struggle, as well as Gujarati peasant
leader Indulal Yagnik and communist organizer S.A. Dange were
the main speakers at the rally.[23] An editorial in *Janata* noted that a
delegation of peasants had come to Ambedkar pleading for abolition of the system; it stated that while Ambedkar would make all
legal efforts, the peasants themselves had to fight: 'The Konkan
peasant class must not beg from khots and tyrants but come
forward in militant struggle'. Along with this they should broaden
their campaign to counteract the false propaganda of *khots* and the
Congress that landlords were '*avatars*' protecting peasant welfare.
It was becoming clear to the peasants, the editorial stressed, that
the ILP was their true protector, while the Congress was the
support of *shetjis, bhatjis, sawkars* and zamindars.[24]

Following the introduction of the 'Khoti Abolition Act, 1937' an
intensive campaign was carried out by the ILP. This included
public meetings of Konkan workers in Bombay, tours by activists
such as Chitre in the taluks of Khed and Chiplun where the
struggle was strongest, and a large public meeting held at Chari on
17 October 1937 which featured a big procession of 3,000 peasants
waving the red flag and included communist activists such as
B.T. Ranadive and G.S. Sardesai as well as Parulekar and Surendranath Chitnis of the ILP.[25]

With Dalits, radical caste Hindu activists in the ILP, communists and the support of Bombay workers, the anti-*khot* struggle was
picking up. A crucial condition for its success was the unity of
Dalit and caste Hindu tenants, specifically Mahars and Kunbis;

dedicated upper caste activists would not fully substitute for local peasant leaders. And it was after a Kunbi leader, Raghunath Dhondiba Khambe, joined the movement at the end of 1937 that the struggle surged forward. Khambe used the slogan *adhi potoba mag Vithoba* ('first fill our stomachs, then worry about the gods') to counteract, with economism, traditionalist religious objections to working with Dalits. Meetings of village representatives were held for Chiplun taluk (8 October 1937) and Mangaon taluk (18 December), involving 100 villages.[26] Then from December, Khambe and his 'Tillori Kunbi Shetkari Parishad' joined and began to tour Mahad, where 5,000 peasants were reported in a huge procession on 30 December; Khed in Ratnagiri; Chiplun, where a 10,000-strong crowd gave slogans of 'Ambedkar and Dadasaheb Khambe *ki jai*' and Dopoli, where a united meeting of 15,000 Tillori Kunbis, Mahars and Muslims was held.[27]

The climax was a march of 20,000 peasants to the Bombay council hall on 12 January 1938, the biggest pre-independence mobilization of peasants in Maharashtra.[28] (It can be compared with the figure of 15,000 claimed for 'All India Kisan Congress' rally in December 1936 at Faizpur, also in Maharashtra, held concurrently with the National Congress session).[29] With slogans of 'destroy the *khot* system', 'crush *sowkar* rule', 'victory to peasants' and 'long live Dr. Ambedkar' the peasants and workers heard speeches by Chitre, Yagnik, D.V. Pradhan (another important CKP associate of Ambedkar who was organizing municipal workers) and CPI members Lalji Pendse and S.S. Mirazkar. Finally Ambedkar spoke, calling for a united struggle in a speech which exemplified his left thrust of the period: 'Really seen, there are only two castes in the world—the first that of the rich, and the second that of the poor. Besides that there is a middle class. This class is responsible for the destruction of all movements!'

He went on to claim that while the toiling poor formed 80 per cent of the population, ignorance kept them from power:

If we understand the power of organization and self-reliance, we can take all authority in our hands. If we look at the last Civil Disobedience movement, we can see how the Congress made itself strong with the toilers' support. Congress made many promises for the welfare of the poor. But what do you see today? . . . Don't give your votes to Congress capitalists . . . .

> Just as we have organized and come here today, so we must
> forget caste differences and religious differences to make our
> organization strong. Khots are only one to two thousand in the
> Konkan; you toilers are about 13 lakhs. You are exploited by
> this handful. Take it into mind that Congress is supporting those
> wealthy. Due to casteism, toilers could not build a single strong
> organization—but now we see such an organization growing
> and this is a very happy thing.

Noting the support of communists, he concluded with 'a few words
to my communist friends':

> I have definitely read studiously more books on the Communist
> philosophy than all the Communist leaders here. However
> beautiful the Communist philosophy is in those books, still it
> has to be seen how useful it can be made in practice. The test of
> this philosophy has to be given in practice. And if work is done
> from that perspective, I feel that the labour and length of time
> needed to win success in Russia will not be so much in India.
> And so in regard to the toilers' class struggle, I feel the Com-
> munist philosophy to be closer to us.[30]

The peasant march was the climax of the anti-*khot* struggle of
the 1930s. Though agitation continued after this, including the
arrest of an ILP activist in 1940 for an inflammatory speech,[31]
Ambedkar's bill failed and a subsequent act passed by the Congress
gave only minor relief while maintaining the system.[32] Nevertheless, the struggle inaugurated a period of ILP interest in and effort
at dialogue with peasant struggles in other regions.

Before these began, the dramatic 1938 anti-landlord agitation
was followed by another equally dramatic event: a massive one-
day textile workers' strike under the leadership of Ambedkar and
the ILP in alliance with the communists.[33]

In contrast to the comparatively unorganized state of the peasantry, the Bombay working class scene was crowded with political
trends—communist, Royist, Congress socialists, moderate (N.M.
Joshi, etc.) Their conflicts had split the first workers' federation,
the All India Trade Union Congress (AITUC), and after 1929–30
three sections existed, the AITUC, the National Trade Union
Federation of the moderates, and the Red Trade Union Federation

of the communists in their sectarian 'class against class' phase. The Bombay textile workers and their Girni Kamgar Union were at the centre of both of these splits and of the process of coming together which culminated in the unity of the AITUC and NTUF at the April 1938 session of the AITUC in Nagpur.[34] Shamrao Parulekar, still with the ILP at the time but on his way into the CPI, attended this conference, which set the tone for a new wave of working class struggles.

Unity made it difficult for the Congress to simply repress the working class in the face of a rising crescendo of strikes from 1937 onwards. Against all their campaign promises and efforts to maintain a pro-poor image, Congress ministers were considering using Emergency powers to check the growing influence of communists and other radicals,[35] but this proved impossible. Instead, the ministry introduced an Industrial Disputes Bill in the Bombay Legislative Assembly on 2 September 1938. The bill, known as the first of the 'black acts' against Bombay workers, made conciliation compulsory and, under certain very ill-defined conditions, made strikes illegal.

Ambedkar took the lead in condemning the bill in the assembly. Describing it as the 'Workers' Civil Liberties Suspension Act', he made an eloquent defence of the right to strike as 'simply another name for the right to freedom', argued that 'under the conditions prescribed by this Bill there is no possibility of any free union growing up in the country', and made it clear that he would oppose the 'bad, bloody and brutal Bill'.[36]

Parulekar, who had attended an ILO conference at Geneva and returned to India on 8 September was apparently the first to suggest a one-day protest strike in an interview to the communist weekly *kranti*; Ambedkar quickly seized on this to announce that the executive committee of the ILP would organize a one-day general strike.[37] The Council of Action formed for the strike included the ILP, the communists and the moderates, while the socialists and Royists disassociated themselves on the grounds that it was an anti-Congress political strike.

The strike, held on 7 November was a historic event for the Bombay working class, with joint tours of leaders symbolizing trade union unity and with the Samta Sainik Dal (by then reported to be 2,000 strong, made up of Dalit youth and commanded by a former Mahar army officer) playing a major role. Its culmination was a public meeting of over 100,000 addressed by Dange and

Ambedkar. Clashes with the police left 633 workers injured and two dead, an event memoralized in later times by the Ambedkar movement as *jalsas* told the story of the strike.[38] There was total participation by Dalit workers as exemplified by the supporting strike of the Dalit municipal workers.[39]

This was the climax of Dalit–left unity, the coming together in action of Ambedkar's followers with the Indian communists who were then asserting leadership of the working class movement. But it proved to be only a temporary ad-hoc event that did not lead to further dialogue. An assessment by S.S. Mirajkar suggests why. Though this non-Brahman movement of the CPI had earlier been more sensitive than other communists to anti-caste issues,[40] he could only describe the significance of the strike as being that

> Some 15,000 untouchables workers who for years stood aloof from the workers and anti-imperialist struggle were for the first time listening to the inspiring message of the joint national struggle against imperialism.[41]

This suggested that it was simply assumed that the Congress must be the leader of the 'joint national struggle against imperialism', and that the communists were strongly putting forward such a political line during the strike. More important, there is nothing in Mirajkar's response to indicate that the untouchable workers had not simply 'stood aloof' from united struggles; they had been *kept* aloof by their segregation in the workplace and by casteist oppression. There was nothing to indicate that caste Hindu workers and the communists themselves might have something to learn from the ILP message of an all-round liberation struggle, against caste as well as class and national exploitation. Political–theoretical perspectives continued to be starkly different.

■ ORGANIZATION AND MOVEMENT

Before dealing with the complex dynamic of class/caste/national struggles in the remainder of the 'radical 1930s' it is important to examine the actual social forces behind the Independent Labour Party. There was a 'Mahar upsurge' arising out of the specific conditions of western India. Within this context there was an interactive process in which Ambedkar's leadership provided ideology and an organizational framework, while the driving force was that of the continuing assertions and agitations of the Mahar community (and to some extent other Dalits). The prototype of this can be seen in the Mahad satyagraha: a period (1920s) of constant proclamation by non-Brahmans and Dalits of the right to public places and success in passing many official resolutions to this effect, a near-spontaneous upsurge by Dalits at the Mahad conference to drink the water of the tank, and then the ability of Ambedkar to seize the occasion to make it a milestone event, founding *Bahishkrut Bharat* for propagating his message in detail and dramatically burning the *Manusmriti* to transform the failure to actually get access to the water into 'untouchable liberation day'.

Ambedkar has been criticized by some of his biographers for his neglect of organization-building. In Keer's colourful analysis,

> Ambedkar did not try to organize his political party on modern lines . . . . There were no regular annual conferences or general meetings . . . . When he wanted his people to assemble under his banner, he simply gave a clarion call and the organization sprang up like a crop in the rainy season. In the summer there would be nothing in the field, the banner resting in his study corner, and the people at home.[42]

This was clearly not true of the ILP phase of Ambedkar's political career. Keer's agricultural analogy could in fact be used to point out that crops, in spite of being seasonal and dependent on environmental factors, do not come up without human effort but require the toil and skill of the peasant. It is necessary to take into account the difficulties in organization-building in India at the time: the problem of transportation, the language barrier, the lack of educated activists to handle 'modern' details such as reports, accounts, correspondence. Ambedkar, like many movement leaders, was trying to do many things at once: work on an all-India as well as Maharashtra levels; build up basic theory; comment on current political events and issues; engage in day-to-day polemic and propaganda; arouse the masses and build an organizational machinery of activists. The problem can be seen even today in India in movements of mainly illiterate groups such as the Dalits, peasants and women; it was compounded in Ambedkar's time by the nature of his caste constituency. He simply towered so far above the rest of the activists working with him that it was difficult to do anything collectively. The Mahar working class community could provide good manpower and financial support, but only gradually was an educated section of Dalits coming up. The fact that a good section of the immediate co-workers of Ambedkar were drawn from caste Hindus, especially the 'writer' caste of CKPs (Kayasthas) showed this.

The seriousness about organizing can be seen in the pages of *Janata*. There were organizing tours and formation of taluk branches; While few of these branches give any idea of membership, the Bombay branch claimed 4,000 members in April 1929 and leaders asserted that this could be multiplied tenfold.[43] Elections to the executive committee were held, at least in Bombay, in May 1938, with five area offices opened for voting.[44] Tours in the Vidarbha–Nagpur area were regularly reported. There were recurring appeals for a 'building fund' and members were constantly urged to build up *Janata* as the mouthpiece of the movement. A significant event was the formation of the Samta Sainik Dal (SSD) as a volunteer squad; it was active in the textile strike and lead a successful fight against Congress volunteers in a black flag demonstration against Gandhi in 1932. Indeed in 1932 itself a letter from Ambedkar on his way to the Round Table Conference noted that all were praising the SSD, including Dr. Moonje who saw it as the only 'Hindu' force which could match the Muslim's 'Khilaf Pathak'.[45] Here at least Ambedkar was out-organizing both the Congress and the communists.

Mahar youth organizations were also started in many areas, and a 'woman's wing' came into existence in the sense that women's conferences were held concurrently with general Dalit conferences. All of this is what any 'modern' political party in India does. The fact that the Independent Labour Party had no formal 'conference' or 'congress' can be compared with the lack of any by the Communist Party between one of somewhat questionable status in 1928 and then 1948; the later Scheduled Caste Federation did have several formal sessions, while Ambedkar's other major political moves were legitimized by the All-India Depressed Classes conferences which were usually held in Nagpur.

There was also considerable cultural movement activity. Ambedkar and the ILP leaders were concerned with giving symbols to the movement. A flag was created, strikingly a red flag: as described in 1940 it had eleven stars in the upper left corner representing the provinces of British India; this claimed both an all-India status and a radical identity.[46] At the mass level there were festival occasions. There was a spontaneous tendency to take 'Ambedkar jayanti', his birthday (14 April), as a focus for celebration and assertion of collective identities from 1930 onwards. Ambedkar himself stayed away from these until his fiftieth birthday in 1941,[47] but could not or would not prevent them. He made an effort instead to establish the memorial day of the Mahad satyagraha, 30 March, as 'untouchable liberation day',[48] but the yearly meetings were outshadowed by the spontaneous 'jayanti'.

Today's powerful Dalit literature proclaims its founding from the mass cultural activities of the 1930s. Ambedkari *jalsas* began to be formed in 1938, building on the traditional *tamasha* from just as the Satyashodhak movement had done and anticipating communist efforts of the 1940s.[49] Poems published from time to time in *Janata* were another part of this popular literature. One, *Ya Pudhe* ('From Now On') published in 1940 expressed the Dalit struggle as a liberation struggle (see beginning of chapter). A 'Song of Peasants and Workers' in 1938 depicted the exploitation of peasants who sow the grain and till the field only to have the crop taken by the landlord; of workers who make clothes that only the rich can wear; of miners who dig gold and silver out of the earth to fill the pockets of the rich; and of armament workers who make weapons to give in the hands of the powerful. It concluded,

> *Reap the crops—but don't give*
> *one grain to the parasite!*
> *Mine the wealth—but don't give*
> *one particle to the thieves!*
> *Make clothing—but don't give*
> *even a rag to the idle,*
> *Make weapons—to take in your hands*
> *for your own self-defense!*
> *Victory to peasants, victory to workers,*
> *Long live the red flag!*[50]

Another song, this one in Hindi, titled 'Our Right' (paraphrasing Tilak's famous saying, 'freedom is our birthright'), took up 'non-Aryan' themes to describe the transformation of *varna* into class exploitation:

> *Bhils, Gonds, Dravids, their Bharat was beautiful,*
> *They were the people, the culture was theirs, the rule was theirs;*
> *The Aryas infiltrated all this, they brought their power to Bharat*
> *and Dravidians were suppressed . . .*
> *Brahmans, Ksatriyas, Vaishyas, all became owners*
> *Drinking the blood of slaves, making the Shudras into machines.*
> *The Brahmans, Ksatriyas and Banias got all the ownership rights.*
> *All these three call themselves brothers, they come together in times of crisis*
> *And work to split the Shudras who have become workers.*
> *'Congress', 'Hindu Mahasabha', 'Muslim League' are all agents of the rich,*
> *The 'Independent Labour Party' is our true house . . . .*
> *Take up the weapon of Janata*
> *Throw off the bloody magic of the owners' atrocities,*
> *Rise workers! Rise peasants! Hindustan is ours,*
> *Humanity will be built on labour,*
> *This is our birthright!*[51]

This popular culture of the movement expressed an all-around fight against exploitation which included not only the working class and peasant struggles described above but rejections of *veth-begar* and rejections of traditionally accepted religious rituals as superstitions. The many reports of atrocities in this period often reflected caste Hindu resistance to such Dalit effort to reject traditional caste duties; they were beaten and harassed for refusing to carry away dead cattle, for refusing to take part in village religious ceremonies. In one case it was reported that when a cholera wave in a Nasik village spared the Maharwada, people were beaten on the suspicion of witchcraft; the reporter argued that in fact the Maharwada was cleaner than the rest of the village and noted that most of its people were away in Bombay.[52] It seems that Dalits were moving up and out, and this was resented.

A report of a conflict in a Kolaba village during this period shows the remarkable self-assertion of the Mahars and the interweaving of social and economic issues—along with their own astute analysis of the contractions involved. In this village, Mauj Tarode, tensions had grown after the Mahars' refusal to participate in various 'Hindu' festivals; both the caste Hindus (Marathas and Kunbis) and the Mahars went to the police. The Maratha–Kunbi tenants allied with the village *khot* landlord and threatened the Mahars with retaliation if they did not participate in the Ganapati festival. The Mahars then made an idol out of flour and filled it with jaggery; they went to the sea but instead of submerging it as was the custom, they cut off its head and ate it, challenging the god to produce a miracle! This sparkling defiance infuriated the Marathas and Kunbis, but they could do little beyond petty harassment. The letter from the village inhabitants stressed that a prominent factor in the whole situation was the anger of the landlord due to the bills for abolishing *khoti* and the Mahar *watan* which Ambedkar had brought up in the assembly, and that he was using his influence over the Kunbi and Maratha tenants to instigate them against the Mahars; the Mahars in turn could be relatively free from the *khot's* tyranny since they held their lands directly from the government.[53] This 'people's analysis' took both economic and social factors into account and outlined a 'main contradiction' as being with the landlord. Numerous such struggles were going on throughout the period, but very rarely does such self-analysis make it into the printed record.

It is clear that while the mass force behind Ambedkar expressed economic as well as social contradictions, it was articulated along caste lines. Ambedkar made serious efforts to break out of the limitations of a movement mainly of the Mahar community; the Dalit movement after all projected itself as the movement of all 'Untouchables'. There were direct appeals to Chamar and Matangs in their own meetings and efforts to bring together Mangs and Ramoshis in the campaign against the *watan* system. ILP activists in the Khandesh area also attempted to join with Adivasis in land struggles. For instance Daulatrao Jadhav, the MLC from Dhule, fought for forest land for cultivation for Adivasis as well as Dalits, and 10,000 Bhils were reported to be attending the second session of the 'West Khandesh Dalit Conference' held at Taloda on 10 November 1954.[54]

The results of these efforts were that several prominent non-Mahars, including S.N. Shivtarkar and P.N. Rajbhoj, were associated with Ambedkar. The difference, however was that with the mass of their communities either inactive or stuck in village tradition, it was much easier for the few educated members to get co-opted by the Congress or the Hindu Mahasabha or to react individually against Ambedkar's overwhelming dominance in the movement. Nevertheless, the Mahar-based Dalit movement had its liberatory implications for other Dalit castes as well, and one of the most popular musical tributes to Ambedkar is a 1950s song of the Matang communist worker, Annabhau Sathe. While his party leaders of the time were finding it difficult to combine themes of 'caste' and 'class' struggles, this first great Dalit novelist, a people's poet who died penniless, whose family remains landless, could do so:

> *Take a hammer to change the world*
> *Bhimrao went saying!*
> *Why is the elephant sitting*
> *in the mud of slavery?*
> *Shake your body and come out,*
> *take a leap to the forefront!*
> *The rich have exploited us,*
> *the priests have tortured us,*
> *As if stones had eaten jewels*
> *and thieves had become great.*
> *They decided we were low and impure*
> *and kept us slaves for thousands of years,*
> *They heaped insults on our lives,*
> *they created these walls.*
> *Sitting on the chariot of unity*
> *let us go forward*
> *To win a united Maharashtra*
> *and hold to the name of Bhim!*

■ Class/Caste Contradictions and the Search for Alliance

By 1937–38 a combined struggle against class (economic) and caste (social) exploitation was being organized under Ambedkar's leadership. At a 'Railway Untouchable Workers' Conference' of the ILP on 12–13 February he articulated this as the necessity of fighting 'the two enemies of *Brahmanism* and *Capitalism*'. Noting that this was the first time untouchable workers were meeting as workers and not simply as untouchables, he justified the earlier stress on social grievances by noting, 'Whatever other people may say, they are grievances under the load of which our very manhood is crushed out.' He then went on to describe graphically the specific economic grievances, the relegation of untouchable workers to lower and more exploitative jobs. The necessity of an anti-Congress political stance was stressed and the ILP was presented as the party to fight on all these contradictions.[55]

Still, combining the fight against caste and economic exploitation was more difficult for Kunbi and other Shudra caste workers and peasants than for Dalits. While they were also exploited (even as a 'caste' or jati) and socially denigrated, their middle position in the system weakened their opposition to hierarchy; the fact that a few of them were landlords or rich farmers made it possible to appeal to caste sentiment against Dalits, to identify the whole group as sharing dominance. Ambedkar himself was primarily a leader of Dalits, however much he may have aspired to be something more; social prejudice, the reluctance of caste Hindus to accept someone lower in the hierarchy than themselves in a leadership position, made it very difficult, if not impossible, for Ambedkar to be a 'national leader' or 'class leader'.[56]

Uniting caste Hindus and Dalit workers and peasants thus required a search for allies. The period of the late 1930s and early 1940s was marked by such a search, in which Ambedkar focused on two categories of people: radical independent peasant activists and non-Brahman leaders. He made temporary alliances with the communists (and later was to see socialists as more solid allies, once they had left the Congress) and was ready to make such alliances in the future. But he disagreed on some basic issues of communist theory and strategy, and he never saw the Brahman-dominated main political trends (including communism) as more than temporary, 'tactical allies'. His 'strategic allies' he sought in the peasant movement and the non-Brahman movement.

Ambedkar's general tendency to identify with the non-Brahman movement has already been noted in chapter 5. There was never a real possibility of his joining the Bombay Presidency Non-Brahman Party (though he worked with leaders like S.K. Bole), but once the party was formally dissolved in the 1930s he lamented its loss. An article in *Janata*, on 'some non-Brahman leaders' joining the Congress, began with the praise of Phule and Shahu Maharaj, and went on,

> The movement of the non-Brahmans brought a great whirlwind to this country. This non-Brahman movement threw light on how the ignorant and suppressed majority of non-Brahmans were rendered helpless through the repression of the so-called 'pandarpesha' high-caste community in the social, economic, religious and political arenas. As long as these two great charismatic leaders were alive this movement did invaluable work for the awakening of the bahujan samaj. As a result the pandarpesha class began to stamp this awakened community as casteist. This self-interested class which gets its own bread buttered by singing the hymns of nationalism began to call others selfish and anti-nationalist.

The article went on to stress the mass upsurge of the period and argued that 'these staunch leaders of peasants and workers [the non-Brahmans] have made themselves available to the bourgeois Congress at a time of the full crisis of this toiling class.'[57]

Ambedkar noted later that he had tried constantly to dissuade non-Brahmans from entering the Congress, but 'they wouldn't listen'.[58] In 1942, just before he himself wound up the ILP he commented in a meeting of Konkan Dalits and caste Hindu peasants living in Bombay,

> I am anxious that the Depressed Class movement should make a common front with the working classes of other communities. With that object in view I clung to the Non-Brahman Party for ten full years in the hope that sooner or later it would rise to the

full height of its great mission of struggling for the freedom of the toiling masses of the great non-Brahman community. That party had in it the germ of the great principle of democracy. Its leaders unfortunately did not realize their duties and responsibilities and allowed the party to be smashed to bits under the double influence of Government and Congress patronage. Even now I would welcome if they did something in the matter. I do not at all insist that the non-Brahman labouring masses should join our party. Let them have their own party if they so desire; but we can certainly make a common front against the Brahmans, the capitalists, the landlords and other exploiting classes. By breaking up the party the non-Brahmans have committed a political suicide.[59]

Thus, after the mid-1930s there were no independent non-Brahman leaders in Maharashtra with whom Ambedkar could form an alliance. He attempted to do so with Periyar; when the great Tamil non-Brahman leader came to Bombay in January 1940, a discussion was reported in which an 'anti-Congress united front' to also include the Muslims was projected.[60] This had little outcome; the Tamil movement by itself was too far away and too weak at that time to provide a concrete base for a strong alliance.

Along with the crisis-ridden non-Brahman movement, Ambedkar showed interest (during the 1937–40 period) in the rising peasant movement in India. Following the organizing of the anti-*khot* struggle, *Janata* began carrying reports of the activities of the Kisan Sabha. These included accounts of the 'All-India Debt Release Day' to be celebrated on 27 March, and of the AIKS conference at Comilla in May 1938. The reports praised the militant and independent tendencies shown by the Kisan Sabha and its leader Swami Sahajanand, congratulating it for 'leaving the path of Gandhism'. They argued for an independent organization, refuting the claims that the Kisan Sabha should be based on non-violence and justifying its adoption of the red flag as the symbol of the unity of all the oppressed and exploited classes in the world. An editorial on this issue concluded that the differences between the ILP and Swamiji were only on the point of his illusions about the Congress: Swamiji was calling for an independent organization of the peasants for an economic fight against the landlords, but 'we see as equally necessary the peasants' independent political power'.[61]

Janata also carried reports on Kisan Sabha organizing in Gujarat by Indulal Yagnik and Pangarkar,[62] and a front page article on a satyagraha of 3,000 tenants in UP claiming their right to cut down trees on 'forest lands'.[63] But the focus of attention was the powerful Bihar peasant movement. There was, strikingly, no information on the equally active coastal Andhra movement (though, ironically, this was led by the non-Brahman Ranga while the Bihar leader was a Brahman)! Perhaps the Bombay-based Ambedkarites lacked information about Andhra, but perhaps also the reason was that Ranga and his followers at this time were solidly aligned with the Congress, while Swami Sahajanand and his Bihar associates were both militant and independent.

It is also significant that Ambedkar chose to attempt a dialogue with the Swami in spite of the fact that just prior to this Jagjivan Ram had formed a 'Bihar State Agricultural Labourers' League', charging that the Bihar Kisan Sabha was representing the interests of upper caste tenants who oppressed Dalit labourers. There is no direct evidence that Ambedkar knew about this attempt of Jagjivan Ram, but he did know of Ram's activities in organizing the 'All-India Depressed Classes League' ('Harijan League') which was also formed in 1936 as a means of drawing Dalits into the Congress.[64] He ignored Ram's letters on this issue, as he ignored the Andhra peasant leader who had written a book entitled 'Harijan Nayak'.

At the end of December 1938 a dramatic personal encounter of Ambedkar and Swami Sahajanand finally took place. It focused on just one issue: attitudes towards the Congress. Ambedkar did not raise at this time the question of how the Bihar Kisan Sabha was talking of caste, whether or not it was dealing with *vethbegar*, whether the upper caste Bhumihars and the 'backward caste' Kurmis and Yadavas were oppressing Dalit labourers, though he was obviously quite aware of these issues. Nor did he bother to ask what a Brahman like Swamiji was doing leading non-Brahman peasants. Instead, he focused on the political issue.

In response to Ambedkar's call for political independence, the Swami argued that while peasants needed their independent class organization, they should join the Congress as a 'broad anti-imperialist organizations' with 'traditions of struggle against Imperialism which could be claimed by no other political party'; further, no other political organization was known all over the country. This was the line of the entire left at the time. Ambedkar rejected it:

> The Congress is not engaged in an anti-imperialist struggle. It is using the constitutional machinery to advance the interests of the capitalists and other vested interests; it is engaged in bolstering them up by sacrificing the interests of workers and peasants.

Swamiji's response was that the leadership could be changed; Ambedkar retorted that this was impossible. He concluded by declaring his readiness to join the Congress if it led any really anti-imperialist struggle, challenging it to launch a struggle against the 'Federation' proposal of the Government of India Act of 1935, and saying that he would give in writing 'that the Independent Labour Party and I as its spokesman will join the Indian National Congress in any struggle that it may start to fight the Federation.'[65]

On this the dialogue broke down, as, in contrast to Ambedkar, Swami Sahajanand continued to have faith in the usefulness of working with the Congress; indeed it was the line pushed by the entire Marxist left. But the attempt revealed the core of Ambedkar's politics. While he was at this time rejecting the ideology of 'Hinduism' as a whole, he was clearly not rejecting 'Hindus' as a whole; he was identifying the ideological and political enemy as 'Brahmanism' and was striving to bring non-Brahmans, peasants and workers as social groups into a united political front that could maintain its independence from the Indian National Congress. The failure of such a front to emerge in the radical 1930s was the main cause for the inability of the ILP itself to continue as a militant party representing the interests of workers and peasants against both economic and caste oppression. And this failure was due in no small part to the policy of the Marxist left, socialists and communists alike, of working within the Congress.

■ CONTRADICTIONS: CLASS/CASTE AND IMPERIALISM

To all the upper caste left nationalists of the pre-independence period the 'main enemy' was imperialism. Ambedkar did not agree. Though he asserted his anti-imperialism again and again, and though he consistently argued that Dalits needed national independence in order to have a chance at political power, for him the main enemy was not the British but the internal class/caste exploiter. He was very frank about this position and its strategic requirements. In his speech at the Sinnar (Nasik district) conference of *watandar* Mahars in 1941, he declared that he had never organized an anti-British struggle because

> The Depressed Classes, surrounded by enemies on all sides, could not afford to fight on all fronts at once. I therefore decided to fight the two thousand year-old tyranny and oppression of the caste Hindus and secure social equality of the Depressed Classes before everything else.[66]

Ambedkar went on to say with pride that it was in fact the Mahar regiments who had brought British rule into India; by defeating the Peshwas, 'the Mahars won Maharashtra for the British'. Throughout the 1920s and 1930s the Dalit movement had held public meetings at the memorial in Koregaon in Poona district memorializing the British army soldiers killed in defeating the last Peshwa army in 1818: they included some 22 Mahars, about 10 Kunbis and a few Muslims; even today this memorial can be seen in calender art.

The implications are clear. For dalits and other low castes, and for large sections of toiling peasants and workers, the 'main enemy' was not imperialism but rather (in the language of the communists) 'feudalism' or (in the language of the non-Brahman movement) the 'Peshwai'. But 'imperialism' and 'feudalism' are indissolubly connected: the dominance of upper caste and landlord/capitalist interests in the Congress led to a slowdown in a decisive fight against British imperialism. This was shown time and again during the colonial period, and by the end of 1938 Ambedkar himself began to point this out. In his debate with Swami Sahajanand he had accused the Congress not only of representing capitalist and landlord interests, but also of not leading any true anti-imperialist struggle, and he had cited the example of 'Federation', that is the compromise of the Congress with princely states. This was a new note in Ambedkar's public stance, and from 1939–41 the anti-imperialist aspect of ILP ideology came to be stressed more and more.

This was first expressed in the opposition to Federation. Six months after his discussion with Swami Sahajanand, he addressed the annual function of the Gokhale Institute for Politics and Economics on 29 June 1939. Published in full form as 'Federation versus Freedom', this long and studied tract gave an exhaustive account of the proposed constitutional structure, concluding that it would be disastrous for the people of India because it accepted the permanent sovereignty of princes who entered the proposed Federation. It described the new constitution as the result of popular struggles, but argued that it left 'British India' helpless before the autocrats of the princely states:

> British India . . . can never get responsibility at the Centre unless the Princes come into the scheme. That means that British India has lost the right to claim Responsible Government for itself in its own name and independently of the Princes . . . . Of the two parts of this Federation, British India is the progressive part and the States form the unprogressive part. That the progressive part should be tied up to the chariot of the unprogressive and its path and destiny should be made dependant upon the unprogressive part constitutes the most tragic side of this Federation.[67]

He added bitterly, 'For this tragedy you have to blame your own national leaders'. And, describing the Federation as satisfying the interests of the princes, the Muslims and the Hindu Mahasabha and posing a menance to freedom and the interests of the poor, he concluded with a denunciation of Gandhi:

> What shall I say about the Congress? What was its point of view? I am sure I am not exaggerating or misrepresenting facts when I say that the Congress point of view at the Round Table Conference was that Congress was the only party in India and that nobody else counted and that the British should settle with the Congress only. This was the burden of Mr. Gandhi's song at the Round Table Conference. He was so busy in establishing his own claim to recognition by the British as the dictator of India that he forgot altogether that the important question was not with whom the settlement should be made but what were to be the terms of the settlement . . . . To my mind, there is no doubt

that this Gandhi age is the dark age of India. It is an age in
which people instead of looking for their ideals in the future are
returning to antiquity.[68]

In truth, from 1930 onwards, the Congress and its Gandhian
leadership did little to oppose the appeasement of the princes
embodied in the Government of India Act of 1935. Neither the
leftists in the Congress (Nehru and those who were later to organize
as Congress socialists) nor the communists outside could do much
in this direction. It is true that the leftists took the lead in the
Indian State Peoples' Congress which was formed in 1927, with
people like E.M.S. Namboodiripad (representing Cochin) and
Achutrao Patwardhan (Jamkhed) being on its executive by the
mid-1930s.[69] But the conservatives, with Gandhi's firm backing,
maintained a policy of non-interference with the Indian states,
compromising the burgeoning state people's movement when they
did enter it in 1938–39.[70]

Copland, who has emphasized both the overall policy of non-
interference and the 1938–39 compromise, argues that the latter
was made because the 'High Command' was powerless before the
princes' autocracy and their alliance with the British (in 1939 Lord
Linlithgow had decided to commit troops and police from British
India to stiffen the 'weakened' rulers) but he also notes that they
feared the 'communal element'.[71] This referred partly to the danger
of Hindu–Muslim tensions increasing in states like Hyderabad,
where Hindu subjects faced a Muslim ruler and where the state
peoples' movement was dominated by the Hindu-nationalist Arya
Samajists. But more frequently the situation was like that in Mysore,
where non-Brahman and Dalit subjects faced a Brahman-dominated
administration. Something of this issue was apparently involved in
Rajkot, which Gandhi had made a personal prestige issue and
which was taken charge of by Vallabhbhai Patel: non-Brahman
Girasyars and Bhaiyats and Dalits with Ambedkar's support were
demanding seats on the reforms committee. Efforts of the Congress
Gandhians to deal with this resulted in what Copland calls the
'Rajkot debacle'. While much of this remains an untold story it
seems that here also the compromising position of Gandhi in the
face of Brahman dominance was crippling the anti-imperialist
struggle.[72] Ambedkar's problem in this situation was that he had
no way without a strong party or alliance to put in practice any of

his views about opposing the Federation proposals; at best he could make brief forays to protect dalit interests, as he did in the case of Rajkot.

Besides Federation issues, by 1940–42 Ambedkar was coming into conflict with the British government on a number of issues. The major one was British intransigence on the issue of Mahar *watans*: Ambedkar wanted them made regular landholdings, to be assessed at the normal rate, with Mahar village servants to be paid directly for their labour. The government refused on the grounds that the latter would be too expensive; at the same time it went on raising the 'special' levy on the *watan* lands. When a new bill was brought to increase this levy he reacted with fury. The Mahar *watan* campaign had been building up tempo since 1938–39, with conferences and meetings that drew in Mahars from Marathwada in the Nizam state also. Now in a 'Mahar–Mang–Vethiya' conference attended by 15,000 Dalits at Sinnar in August 1941, Ambedkar stated that while he had previously never joined hands with the Congress, now

> I shall direct attacks a hundredfold more bitter, more virulent, more deadly against the British than I have ever done against the Hindus if my loyalty is going to be exploited for crushing my own people and taking away from them the last dry bone from which they draw their barest sustenance.

He threatened a determined struggle, 'relying on our own strength' and using any means necessary to resist the 'looting' of the British government.[73]

Ambedkar was also angered by the British refusal to include any Depressed Classes representative in the reconstituted Viceroy's Council; a strongly worded protest telegram on this had preceded by a few days the threats of action made at the Sinnar conference.[74] The connection between these events is clear: Ambedkar had met the Bombay governor in early July and he evidently had had expectations of being given a post in the Viceroy's Council. Further the large and militant meeting at Sinnar in August followed an earlier one (also protesting coercion in collecting the levy and threatening a strike, but in somewhat milder terms.)[75] Ambedkar was getting angrier and threatening ever stronger action but at the same time maintaining his government links (for example his place on the Indian Defence Council) and continuing to ask Mahars to volunteer for the army.[76] The climax came on 14 April 1942 on the grand *jayanti* celebration of his fiftieth birthday. Appearing at such an occasion for the first time, Ambedkar warned the British again that the Depressed Classes would fight if not given adequate representation and that their interests were being sacrificed and betrayed in the Cripps Mission. Next time, he told the audience,

> You will have to be ready for action, I don't care what action, constitutional or unconstitutional, violent or nonviolent, peaceful or disturbing . . . . You may be faced with a constituent assembly again. Your place, then, will not be inside the constituent assembly. You will not find any place there. Your legitimate place will be in your own headquarters, manufacturing bombs. Yes, bombs. Make no mistake about it. We can handle hand grenades better than many other people . . . .

And he warned the Congress,

> You are fighting for Swaraj. I am ready to join you. And I may assure you that I can fight better than you. I make only one condition. Tell me what share I am to have in the Swaraj. If you don't want to tell me that and you want to make up with the British behind my back, hell on both of you.[77]

■ THE SCHEDULED CASTE FEDERATION AND THE RETREAT FROM RADICALISM

But the Congress did not formulate any new policy regarding the Dalits, and Ambedkar did not join it. Neither did the Dalits take to making bombs in their headquarters. Nor did the Mahar *watandars* have to carry out any decisive struggle. Instead Ambedkar was appointed 'Labour Member' for the Government of India in early July, thereby joining the Executive Council, and on 18–20 July an All-India Depressed Classes Political Conference, again held at Nagpur, brought the ILP to an end and constituted the Scheduled Caste Federation (known in Marathi as the Dalit Federation) before a mass of 70,000, of which one-third were women, with representatives from Bengal, Bombay, Punjab, UP, Central Provinces-Berar, Madras and Hyderabad.[78]

Following this Ambedkar denounced the proposed Quit India movement, arguing that 'with an aggressive Japan standing at the gate of India' mass civil disobedience would be playing into the hands of the enemy, while resistance to fascist aggression was 'the patriotic duty of all Indians no matter to what political parties they belong.'[79] With communists and Dalits, from different ideological stances but using similar arguments, out of the anti-imperialist struggle, the Quit India movement took place either under the leadership of the Congress socialists or with spontaneous (local, non-Brahman as in the case of the famous Satara 'parallel government') leadership and was, in India as a whole, fairly easily suppressed by the British and hijacked afterwards by the conservative Congress leadership.[80]

The Scheduled Caste Federation was a step backwards from the 1930s radicalism. Its very formation meant giving up the effort to form a broad radical party of Dalit and caste Hindu workers and peasants for the different goal of uniting Dalits on an all-India level. There were two new specific resolutions, one demanding 'separate village settlements' of entirely Scheduled Caste villages 'away from and independent of Hindu villages', and the other renewing the demand for separate electorates on the grounds that in any joint electorate even with reserved seats Dalits would be overwhelmed by caste Hindu voters. These resolutions indicated a reinvigorated distrust of 'caste Hindus' as such and a laying aside of efforts to form a political alliance with them. Aside from this, the Scheduled Caste Federation maintained most of the other specific thrusts of the earlier ILP programme, regarding alliances and peasant and worker demands, and Ambedkar continued as Labour Minister to put a radical programme before the working class. But there was no action linked to these. As Zelliot has put it,

> The actual function of the political party under Ambedkar's leadership from independence until 1956 was to see that the special treatment provisions were properly used, that the discrimination and injustice still practiced was brought to public attention, and that the seats reserved for Scheduled Castes in legislatures were filled by men under obligation to speak for Scheduled Caste interests.[81]

In other words, turning away from the effort to form a broad political party with a vision of revolutionary social transformation built around a class–caste alliance of Dalits and Shudra workers and peasants, the Scheduled Caste Federation and Ambedkar functioned from 1942 to 1956 as the political representative of Dalits, as a special interest group within a statist–capitalist democratic structure.

Ambedkar, again, was clear about this. In a 1943 talk on 'Ranade, Gandhi and Jinnah', clearly preoccupied with the question of leadership and political strategy, he mentioned as the last point in the 'political philosophy of Ranade' that

> In political negotiation the rule must be what is possible. That does not mean that we should be content with what is offered. No. It means that you must not refuse what is offered when you know that your sanctions are inadequate to compel your opponent to concede more.[82]

And in the preface, speaking of those who criticized his scathing attacks on Gandhi and Jinnah, he made an obvious reference to the political process of the time: 'If I am against them it is because I want a settlement. I want a settlement of some sort, and I am not prepared to wait for an ideal settlement.'[83]

Ambedkar's policy of the period was based on the assessment that independence was near and that power was going into the hands of Indians in any case; there was no longer time left for the visions of a socialist future and no organized force to ally with the Dalits in fighting for it. The task for Ambedkar in the existing situation was to ensure that the Dalits got the best possible share in independence that was coming to India; there was really nothing else to be done.

Proposed alliances with non-Brahmans or peasant leaders, which might have provided a mass base for a broad anti-Congress united front which could organize to build a different kind of society, had failed. That with the communists had never even been hoped for. There was no alternative political centre, and any role that Ambedkar could have played in forming one was crippled by the lack of allies. He really had no choice but to use the social force which he commanded, that of the Dalits, to fight as best he could for the interests he had from the beginning taken as his primary commitment. And so came the end of the years of radicalism.

NOTES

1. 'Annihilation of Caste' was first published in 1936 and is reprinted in *Dr Babasaheb Ambedkar: Writings and Speeches*, Volume I (Bombay: Government of Maharashtra Education Department, 1979), pp. 23–90. The second edition contains Ambedkar's account of his conflict with the Jat-Pat Todak Mandal, Gandhi's defense of Hinduism in response to the booklet, and Ambedkar's reply' the gulf between them is stark.

2. Speech at Vinchur, reported in *Times of India*, 21 November 1934, in *Source Material on Dr Babasaheb Ambedkar and the Movement of Untouchables*, Volume I (Bombay: Government of Maharashtra, 1982), p. 123.

3. Eleanor Zelliot, *Dr. Ambedkar and the Mahar Movement* (University of Pennsylvania, Ph.D. dissertation, 1969), p. 243.

4. Sumit Sarkar, *Modern India: 1885–1947* (Delhi: Macmillan India Ltd., 1983), p. 346.

5. Ian Copland, 'Congress Paternalism: The "High Command" and the Struggle for Freedom in Princely India, 1920–1949', in Jim Masselos (ed.), *Struggling and Ruling: The Indian National Congress* (New Delhi: Sterling Publishers Pvt. Ltd., 1987), p. 127.

6. See *Janata*, 6 February 1937 for a full list of candidates, plus four from other parties who were supported. The ILP apparently won all the reserved seats in Marathi-speaking areas and in addition three general seats in the Konkan. The Congress swept Gujarat and North Karnatak, but the showing of the ILP and a few non-Brahmans represented a considerable opposition force in western Maharashtra. The ILP thus became the largest opposition party in the assembly.

7. Sarkar, *Modern India*, p. 349.

8. *Independent Labour Party: Its Foundation and Its Aims* (Reprinted from the *Times of India*, 15 August 1936), ILP Publication No. 1 of 1937, p. 3.

9. *Ibid.*, p. 6–7.

10. *Janata*, 1 May 1937.

11. *Ibid.*, 6 March 1937.

12. *Ibid.*, 18 May 1937.

13. *Ibid.*, 8 April 1937.

14. *Ibid.*, in an article entitled 'The Tyranny of the Khot Landlords of the Konkan', 29 May 1937.

15. *Bahishkrut Bharat*, 16 August 1929, reprinted in Ratnakar Ganvir, ed. '*Bahishkrut Bharatatil Dr Ambedkarance Sphut Lekh* (Jalgaon: Ratnamitra Prakashan, 1981), pp. 210–13.

16. Cited Neil Charlesworth, *Peasants and Imperial Rule: Agriculture and Agrarian Society in the Bombay Presidency, 1850–1935* (Bombay: Orient Longman, 1985), p. 273.

17. *Ibid.*, pp. 273–74.

18. Gail Omvedt, *Cultural Revolt in a Colonial Society: The Non-Brahman Movement in Western India, 1850–1935* (Poona: Scientific Socialist Education Trust, 1976), pp. 194–95.

19. *Bombay Chronicle*, 22 December 1934, in *Sources*, Volume I, pp. 124–26. N.N. Patil appears in later Chari meetings and delegations to the Chief Minister but apparently did not work beyond this area; see *Janata*, 30 October 1937.

20. Ambedkar, in *Writings and Speeches*, Volume II, p. 101, mentions this.

21. *Bahishkrut Bharat*, 16 August 1929.

22. The three caste Hindu ILP winning candidates, Chitre, Parulekar and Chitnis, were all CKPs who had apparently been associated with N.M. Joshi's labour work. Parulekar was later to join the CPI and become famous with his wife, Godutai, for working among tribals in Thane district. Chitnis is referred to as 'Surba Chipnis' and 'Surba Tipnis' in various sources; *cf Janata*, 7 October 1937; 15 January 1938, and *Bombay Chronicle* 12 December 1934 (in *Sources*, Volume I, pp. 124ff).

23. *Janata*, 18 September 1937.

24. *Ibid.*, 19 February 1937.

25. *Ibid.*, 29 October 1937.

26. *Ibid.*, 1 January 1938.

27. *Ibid.*, 8 January 1938.

28. *Ibid.*, 15 January 1938.

29. M.A. Rasul, *A History of the All India Kisan Sabha* (Calcutta: National Book Agency, 1974), pp. 9–11.

30. *Janata*, 15 January 1938.

31. Reported in *Bombay Chronicle*, 6 February 1940, cited in *Sources*, Volume I, p. 211. The activist was the MLA Chitnis/Tipnis. Other agitations reported in *Janata* in 1938 included meetings at Konkanwadi (14 May) and Devarukh (28 May) where a militant crowd of caste Hindus, Dalits and Muslims protested.

32. *Janata*, 27 August 1938.

33. The most detailed coverage is given by Y.D. Phadke, 'The Independent Labour Party and the One-Day General Strike of 7th November, 1938', Paper for the Seminar on the Dalit Movement in Maharashtra, Shivaji University, Kolhapur, 9–11 January 1988.

34. This is documented in Prem Sagar Gupta, *A Short History of the All-India Trade Union Congress (1920–1947)* (New Delhi: AITUC Publ., 1980), pp. 196–316. The Nagpur unity session was also reported in *Janata*, 23 April 1938.

35. Sumit Sarkar, *Modern India, 1885–1947* (Delhi: Macmillan, 1983), pp. 361, 362; Y.D. Phadke, 'The Independent Labour Party and the One-Day General Strike of 7 November 1938', Paper for seminar on 'Dalit Movement in Maharashtra', Shivaji University, 9–11 Feburary 1989.

36. Cited in *Writings and Speeches*, Volume II, pp. 208, 222, 231, 232.

37. Phadke 'One-Day General Strike'.

38. Bhimrao Dhondiba Kardak, *Ambedkari Jalse: Swarup va Karya* (Bombay: Abhinav Prakashan, 1978).

39. Phadke, 'One-Day General Strike', pp. 6–7.

40. Omvedt, *Cultural Revolt*, pp. 264, 361, n. 89.

41. Cited in Phadke, 'One-Day General Strike', p. 8.

42. Dhananjay Keer, *Dr Ambedkar: Life and Mission*, (Bombay: Popular Prakashan, 1962), p. 477; Zelliot, *Ambedkar and the Mahar Movement*, p. 257.

43. *Janata*, 7 May 1938.

44. *Ibid.*

45. Undated letter written from the boat on the way to the Second Round Table Conference, published in Ganjare, *Bhashane*, Volume VI, pp. 14–15. Ambedkar rejected Moonje's efforts to pose the Samta Sainik Dal as a 'Hindu' force ready to combat Muslims.

46. *Janata*, 16 March 1940.

47. *Bombay Chronicle*, 29 April 1942; cited *Sources*, Volume I, 251. 'You have been celebrating my birthday for some 15 years past', said Ambedkar at the time. 'I have never attended them. I have always been opposed to them. You have celebrated my golden jubilee now; let that be the last. Over-regard to leaders saps self-confidence of the masses . . . . One of the great reasons for the downfall of Hindu society and the perpetuation of its degraded position is the injunction of Krishna that whenever in difficulties they should look out for his avatar to redeem them . . . . I don't want you to follow such a ruinous teaching. I don't want you to be dependent on any single personality for your salvation. Your salvation must lie in your own hands, through your own efforts.'

48. See, for instance, *Janata*, 27 March 1937; 16 and 30 March 1940.

49. Many of these are collected in Kardak, *Ambedkari Jalse*.

50. From *Janata*, 27 August 1938.

51. By Kamalsingh Baliram Ramteke, *Janata*, 21 June 1941.

52. *Janata*, 20 October 1937.

53. *Janata*, 23 November 1940; an earlier Bhil conference was held by him in Chilisgaon, *ibid.*, 24 February 1940.

54. *Ibid.*, 23 November 1940; an earlier Bhil conference was held by him at Bhalisgaon, *ibid.*, 24 February 1940.

55. *Janata*, 12 February 1938 and *Times of India*, 14 February 1938; in *Sources*, Volume I, pp. 165.66.

56. In his 1939 talk on 'Federation versus Freedom' he says, 'Fortunately for me I am not one of your national leaders. The utmost rank to which I have risen is that of a leader of the Untouchables. I find even that rank has been denied to me. Thakkar Bapa . . . very recently said that I was only the leader of the Mahars. He would not even allow me the leadership of the Untouchables of the Bombay Presidency' (*Writings and Speeches*, Volume I, p. 346). Caste Hindu prejudice was a real factor for Ambedkar, just as white racism has made it impossible for a Black to be a 'general' leader in the US. There are some reasons to hope that the situation is changing, if we look at the recent roles of Jesse Jackson and Kanshi Ram; but it was certainly not possible for Ambedkar by himself to be a 'national' or a 'class' leader in the 1930s.

57. *Janata*, 9 October 1937.

58. *Ibid.*, 23 January 1949.

59. *Bombay Sentinel*, 14 July 1942, in *Sources*, Volume I pp. 252–53.

60. *Bombay Chronicle*, 9 January 1940, in *Sources*, Volume I, pp. 208–10.

61. *Janata*, 2 April 1938, 28 May 1938.

62. *Ibid.*, 2 July 1938, 23 July 1938; a report of 24 February 1940 described a march of 15,000 peasants at Borsad with the red flag under Yagnik's leadership as a 'golden day' in the Gujarat peasant struggle.

63. *Ibid.*, 10 July 1938.

64. See the letter of Jagjivan Ram to Ambedkar on 8 March 1937 cited in *Sources*, Volume I, pp. 166–67.
65. *Bombay Chronicle*, 27 December 1938 and *Times of India*, 27 December 1938, cited *Sources*, Volume I, pp. 181–84.
66. *Bombay Chronicle*, 19 August 1941, in *Sources*, Volume I, pp. 233–35.
67. 'Federation versus Freedom' in *Writings and Speeches*, Volume I, pp. 345–46.
68. *Ibid.*, pp. 350–52.
69. Copland, 'Congress Paternalism', pp. 126–27.
70. *Ibid.*, pp. 120–28.
71. *Ibid.*, pp. 130–32.
72. See *Sources*, Volume I, pp. 191–97 for newspaper accounts of Ambedkar's involvement with Rajkot.
73. *Bombay Chronicle*, 19 August 1941, in *Sources*, Volume I, p. 234; *Janata*, 23 August 1941.
74. *Bombay Chronicle*, 1 August 1941 and *Free Press Journal*, 1 August, 1941, in *Sources*, Volume I, pp. 232–33.
75. See reports cited in *Sources*, Volume I, pp. 228–33.
76. *Times of India*, 26 September 1938, in *Sources*, Volume I, p. 237. In any case Ambedkar viewed Mahar military service as an important road of advance.
77. *Bombay Sentinel*, 28 April 1942, *Sources*, Volume I, pp. 248–49.
78. Eleanor Zelliot, 'Learning the Use of Political Means: The Mahars of Maharashtra', in Rajni Kothari (ed.), *Caste in Modern Indian Politics* (Poona: Orient Longman, 1970), pp. 52–53.
79. *Bombay Chronicle*, 23 July 1942, in *Sources*, Volume I, pp. 255–56.
80. See Gail Omvedt, 'The Satara Prati Sarkar', and the introduction in Gyan Pandey (ed.), *The Indian Nation in 1942* (Calcutta: Centre for Study in Social Sciences, 1988).
81. Zelliot, *Ambedkar and the Mahar Movement*, p. 55.
82. 'Ranade, Gandhi and Jinnah', in *Writings and Speeches*, Volume I, p. 229.
83. Preface to 'Ranade, Gandhi and Jinnah', p. 208.

CHAPTER 7

'Ambedkarism': The Theory of Dalit Liberation

'Ambedkarism' is today a living force in India, much as Marxism is: it defines the ideology of the Dalit movement and, to a large extent, an even broader anti-caste movement. Yet, just as 'Marxism' as a trend in the working class movement has to be distinguished from the actual theorizing of Karl Marx, so the urge to abolish the social and economic exploitation involved in caste and capitalism (which is the main significance of 'Ambedkarism' as a general movement ideology) must be distinguished from the complex grappling of an individual activist–theoretician with the interpretation of Indian reality.

Ambedkar's thought was not always consistent and it did not (and the same of course can be said for Marx) fully resolve the problems he grappled with. But some themes stand out:

First, *an uncompromising dedication to the needs of his people, the Dalits* (as he said once in response to a legislative council claim that he should think as 'part of a whole'—'I am not a part of a whole; I am a part apart') which required the *total annihilation of the caste system and the Brahmanic superiority it embodied:*

Second, *an almost equally strong dedication to the reality of India—but an India whose historical–cultural interpretation he sought to wrest from the imposition of a 'Hindu' identity* to understand it in its massive, popular reality;

Third, a conviction that *the eradication of caste required a repudiation of 'Hinduism' as a religion, and adoption of an alternative religion, which he found in Buddhism*, a choice which he saw as not only necessary for the masses of Dalits who followed him but for the masses in India generally;

Fourth, a broad *economic radicalism interpreted as 'socialism'* ('state socialism' in some versions; 'democratic socialism' in others) mixed with and growing out of his democratic liberalism and *liberal dedication to individual rights;*

Fifth, a fierce *rationalism* which burned through his attacks on Hindu superstitions to interpret even the Buddhism he came to in rationalistic, 'liberation theology' forms;

And finally, a political orientation which linked a *firmly autonomous Dalit movement with a constantly attempted alliance of the socially and economically exploited (Dalits and Shudras, 'workers' and 'peasants' in class terms) projected as an alternative political front to the Congress party he saw as the unique platform of 'Brahmanism' and 'capitalism'.*

However, Ambedkar, like Marx, did not spend the major part of his active life in research and writing, with political activism as a sideline; rather, the demands of leadership absorbed the major part of his time. The 1930s being a period of intense turmoil there was little space for writing. Though many of his crucial ideas were formed during the 1930s, almost all of his writing came in the 1940s and 1950s, when he was spending most of his time in Delhi, as Labour Minister and the general political spokesman for the untouchables. During the 1930s he not only adopted but sought to give a political embodiment to a general left ideology combined with the theme of caste annihilation. Yet the decade came to an end with the failure of a left alternative to the bourgeois–Brahman Congress, and the 1940s were very different, an era of Congress hegemony was firmly established in the national movement at the same time as the traumatic transition to independence in a period of global upheavals overshadowed everything else. The particular characteristics of this latter epoch have to be understood as a background to Ambedkar's strategy and analysis.

■ THE CONTEXT OF STRATEGY AND THEORY

The 1940s were a period of brutal confrontation with the most reactionary social power known in the world up to that time, fascism; and they ended with the unleashing of atomic energies in the burning of two Japanese cities, forecasting the technological furies that would overshadow human development for decades. For many throughout the world, the peace that followed was a period of hope, with the emergence of newly liberated nations throughout Asia and Africa, and the achievement of socialism by many peoples of the world. That Stalin represented not only 'socialist' development but a brutal tyranny; that socialism came to vast areas not by working class revolt but with the march of the Red Army; that traditional (and sometimes new) elites remained firmly in control of independent Third World nations, all were debatable points that bothered very few in countries like India at the time. The final phases of the independence struggle represented for many an upsurge of hope and a direction towards a popular, socialistic independence.

Yet within India itself the period held a great deal of internal malaise. Several major characteristics defined it, and represented the context in which Ambedkar sought to win some share in liberation for the untouchable masses of India.

1. *The hegemony of Marxism on the left:* in India as in most of the world the liberation of exploited and oppressed groups was to be seen as being realized through socialism, defined in terms of collective ownership of the means of production and working class share in power as exercized through a party acting in its name. Yet this hegemony contrasted with an extreme immaturity and weakness of the communist movement in India, which could not exert any decisive influence on events. As in most other Third World countries, therefore, the hegemony of 'Marxism' evoked a situation in which 'collective ownership' was defined in terms of state ownership; the dominant nationalist party replaced the working

class party with claims to represent the oppressed masses; and 'socialism' came to mean public control and planning of an industrialization conceived on the model of western capitalism.

2. *Hindu–Muslim communalism* was the overriding political reality by the 1940s. The constitution of the 'Muslim community' and the 'Hindu community' as dominant social realities was correlated with the explicit or implict acceptance of 'Hinduism' as the central religious–cultural identity of 'India'. The ideological approach of the Congress progressives was either to argue, with Gandhi, for a reformed Hinduism in which the two communities lived in harmony (i.e., interpreting the 'nation' as a federation of religious communities) or, with Nehru, for a secularism that exalted modernity and defined the 'nation', along with 'class', as transcending what were really feudal and backward religious and cultural identities. The communists essentially followed the Nehru line, with an even stronger emphasis on class. Both accepted the realities of 'Hindu' and 'Muslim' identities, of course—thereby eclipsing issues of caste and linguistic/tribal nationalities. Both gave scope for Hindu nationalism because they did not confront the very basis of the 'Hindu' identity attributed to Indian tradition.

3. The events of independence and partition brought a near-complete *marginalization of Gandhi and Gandhism*. With all the rhetoric of 'panchayat raj' and khadi, it was 'Nehruism' that gained hegemony ideologically. This approach advocated a broad Third World alliance and made 'socialism' and a heavy-industry oriented development—dominated by planning and controlled by the public sector—the themes of power. But with all its reasonableness and 'secular' focus in contrast to Gandhi's 'peasant backwardness', Nehruism, whose main tendency was to override, or at best to ignore, issues of caste and local identities, allowed even more for Brahman dominance. To a very large degree, even while representation in the political sphere broadened, the 'public sector' was to be a high-caste preserve.

In this context, the Dalit movement under Ambedkar's leadership could only be a passive observer of most major events, at best exerting its minor influence to achieve some gains and concessions. The failure of Marxism in India to open itself to fertilization of theory and practice by the anti-caste movements, and the failure of Gandhism to go beyond a spiritualistic and Hinduistic interpretation of a decentralized and village-based development left the anti-caste movement in a vacuum. By the 1940s, it could effectively operate only as a pressure group.

■ CASTE, CLASS AND MECHANICAL MARXISM

Ambedkar had said, in his 1938 speech to the peasants marching to Bombay, that he felt the 'communist philosophy' to be 'closer than any other' (though significantly qualifying this 'in regard to the class struggle of toilers'). It is undeniable that his 'class–caste' paradigm was basically formed during the 1930s in the course of his confrontation with Marxism, *as it was presented to him in India*, thus exerted an important and continuing influence not only over his economic theory but also over his interpretation of caste in society.

We have noted that during the 1920s Ambedkar had dismissed communism by saying that he agreed with the 'ends' of socialism but disagreed with the 'means' of violence. This theme was resurrected towards the end of his life as a major point of defense of Buddhism against Marxism. During the radical years of the 1930s, however, there was no such rejection of Marxism on the grounds of violence. The thrust of Ambedkar's attack was against the religiously-inspired 'non-violence' of Gandhism. In fact the main point of his critique of violence was always that communist-led strikes and actions were often 'adventurous', that they needlessly harmed the weakest sections of the working class (Dalits) and sacrificed people's lives in campaigns that tried to be militant for the sake of militancy. In other words, it upheld non-violence more as a *strategy* than as a principle, and it specifically rejected Gandhian non-violence-as-religious-principle. The critique as such, then, is not a major point separating Ambedkar from 'the communist philosophy', though when it was linked to the denial of the leading role of the proletariat it did become so.

In fact, aside from adding 'caste' to 'class' and 'Brahmanism' to 'capitalism' there were surprising similarities between the basic assumptions of Ambedkar and the leftists. In a situation in which communists and socialists alike took *no* official note of caste in the pre-independence period and simply assumed that radicalism required an explanation of all social problems in terms of their 'class' content, Ambedkar of course strongly insisted on the addition of 'caste' and 'Brahmanism' as crucial social realities. Yet in doing so, he like most of his later followers accepted some crucial assumptions of the 'class' framework.

A serious critical article on Marxism appeared in a 1936 issue of *Janata* and was reprinted in 1938 as a front page article entitled 'The Illusion of the Communists and the Duty of the Untouchable Class'. In taking the relations of production as the basis of the 'economic interpretation of history', the article made a clever twist or reversal in the often-used architectural analogy of 'base and superstructure':

> But the base is not the building. On the basis of the economic relations a building is erected of religious, social and political institutions. This building has just as much truth (reality) as the base. If we want to change the base, then first the building that has been constructed on it has to be knocked down. In the same way, if we want to change the economic relations of society, then first the existing social, political and other institutions will have to be destroyed.[1]

The article went on to make other important reversals. To build the strength of the working class, the mental hold of religious slavery would have to be destroyed; the pre-condition of a united working class struggle was the eradication of caste and untouchability. Similarly, destruction of casteism could be taken as the main task of the 'democratic' stage of a two-stage revolution: it would not be fully anti-capitalist because capitalism would not be opposed to the eradication of caste as such (freeing potential workers from caste restrictions would increase the reserve army of labour) and, at the same time, socialists should welcome the effort at uniting the working class. (Thus there was some unity of interests between workers and the 'radical bourgeoisie' in the 'democratic' stage). The removal of untouchability and caste discrimination is thus the first stage in the struggle for the Indian revolution, and it is impossible for socialists to bypass it. However, expressing great disillusionment with the Congress socialists and Nehru, the article concluded that untouchables would have to pool all their strength into the fight against untouchability, without expecting much socialist help.

The positions taking here represented a reaction to *and a sharing of the assumptions of a* mechanical, economistic form of Marxism. Only 'class' exploitation was seen as having a material base and as being part of the relations or production; caste and all other 'non-class' types of oppression (women's oppression, national oppression, etc.) were seen as primarily socio-religious, in the realm of consciousness and not material life. Ambedkar accepted this framework and simply reversed it to assert the *causal importance* of social–religious–political factors; he took a mechanical architectural analogy and turned it around to give primacy to the 'superstructure'. The logic of the process exemplifies the way in which a mechanical materialism fosters idealism. If caste oppression/exploitation was central (and Ambedkar and all Dalits and low caste activists could not but help understanding it as central) then the basic logic led them to argue that this could only mean that social–religious factors, factors of 'consciousness', were important and even primary. In other words, there was no theoretical trend that sought to analyze a *material base* for caste as Phule had done at a primary level half a century before.

Just as clearly we can see in the argument the results of the often-heard cliche that an anti-caste struggle is a part of the democratic revolution, not of socialist revolution. For communists this could not but mean (at some basic emotional level) that the issue was of secondary importance. Ambedkar of course saw it differently. In effect he was motivated to say: all right, if this is 'only' the democratic revolution this is what *we* have to be concerned about here and now; you far-sighted revolutionary leaders go ahead and worry about the socialist revolution, we have to get on with the immediate task (which you are not helping with in any case); it's all the more urgent to concentrate on this since no one else is around to do it. *we will fight for the democratic revolution.* This logic was what undoubtedly moved Ambedkar, after the 'years of radicalism' won no decisive gains, to put his efforts during the 1940s into building the Scheduled Caste Federation as a strong pressure group within a democratic framework, with an indefinite postponement of a broad revolutionary struggle.

Ambedkar's acceptance of many of the basic assumptions of a mechanical Marxism remained throughout his life and can be seen in his final writings on Buddha and Marx. Its most important aspect is the identification of economic exploitation with private property. Ambedkar's note took it as established that a great many errors in Marx's original analysis (including the concept of the inevitability of socialism, the vanguardship of the working class) made it invalid, but concluded,

> What remains of Karl Marx is a residue of fire, small but very important . . .
> (*i*) the function of philosophy is to reconstruct the world and not to waste its time in explaining the origins of the world,
> (*ii*) there is a conflict of interest between class and class,
> (*iii*) private ownership of property brings power to one class and sorrow to another through exploitation,
> (*iv*) it is necessary for the good of society that the sorrow be removed by the abolition of private property.[2]

Ambedkar went on in this article to argue that Buddhism, in the Sangha, abolished private property more thoroughly and without bloodshed and was therefore superior to Marxism, but that is beside the point. The point is that here he accepted the definition of class and exploitation as being a result of private property. This was the common theme of the Marxism of his time. It led to defining 'socialism' in terms of 'nationalism' in which collective ownership of the means of production (or the abolition of private property) could be achieved through state control; and it continued to accept the idea that modern factory production, i.e., industrialization, constituted the economic basis of socialism. Thus, Ambedkar could term his own version of socialism as 'state socialism' and call for 'nationalization of land', or public control of the 'commanding heights' of the economy much as the Nehru socialists did without much concern for the structures of domination and exploitation embodied in state-owned properties.

Taking standard left economic assumptions for granted had two consequences for Ambedkar and the Dalit movement: First, it led to attempts to formulate a historical theory of caste and social struggle in India that functioned primarily at the 'superstructural' level, stressing factors of political conflict and ideology apart from those of economic development. Second, it effectively suppressed any dialogue with alternative economic models and ignored the degree to which a state-controlled heavy industry would be effectively a Brahman and high caste-controlled economy.

But was there any real alternative before Ambedkar at the time? His 'state socialism' was, after all, part of a very broad consensus that saw development in terms of industrialization and nationhood in terms of a centralized, strong, unitary state; Liberal capitalists shared this as much as socialists, and though they disagreed about whether private or state control would be most effective, all 'developmental economists' by the late 1940s and early 1950s accepted some major role for the state. Today this developmental model has come into question at many levels, from the environmental movement with its rejection of Nehru's big dams as 'modern temples' to the farmers' movement and women's movement, all putting forward calls for some kind of 'alternative development'. But in Ambedkar's time decentralized socialism did not appear as a politically viable alternative. In India, a decentralized, village-based form of development was connected with the Gandhian tradition; to Ambedkar and militant Dalits or non-Brahmans this did not simply promote a village society and development along the lines of Indian tradition, it promoted *Ram-raj*; it was not simply critical of modern science and technology, it was soaked in Hindu religious themes, including the belief in *chatur-varnya*, the moralistic acceptance of *brahmachari* and a claimed principled belief in non-violence. These were not acceptable to Ambedkar nor could they meet the needs of low castes aspiring to liberation. The fact that no other tradition of an alternative decentralized socialism existed in India helped to push Ambedkar towards a bureaucratized state socialism, with all the dilemmas of Brahmanic statism that this involved.

■ THE ECONOMICS OF A FLEXIBLE SOCIALISM

Ambedkar's two major writings on economic issues appeared in the early 1920s, and while they bear the mark of a generally neoclassic economic theory, they also show both his general identification with the working classes and a harsh critique of imperialism.

'The Problem of the Rupee', though dealing with the general history of the state and currency in British India, was published in 1923 in the very specific context of a struggle between nationalists and the British government over the exchange rate. Following the war, the government had maintained a high official exchange rate of 2 shillings (2s.) to the rupee, which was opposed fiercely by Indian businessmen with the backing of the Congress. They attacked it as overvalued, an 'enormous wrong and legalized plunder of Indian resources' which aided the British bureaucracy (whose salaries and pensions became more valuable in terms of the sterling) and British exporters to India at the expense of Indian producers and exporters. They agitated for a low exchange rate of 1s.4d. The government appointed a royal commission; Ambedkar testified before it, broadly supporting devaluation but at a compromise ratio (1s.6d.) which he argued would maintain the interests of the 'business classes' as well as the 'earning classes' who would suffer from the price rise brought about by devaluation.[3]

The book itself was a scathingly critical analysis of British currency policy over the years. Read in the context of current debates on economic policy,[4] it shows Ambedkar as a moderate supporter of devaluation and an economist who assumed that within an open economy India could well compete at the global level (he notes that Indian exports and manufactures gained at the expense of the British during the period of the low rupee).[5] Yet there are qualifications: the concern for balancing capitalist and labour interests, the argument that Indian growth and exports were actually at the cost of falling real wages of the working class, and a tone of hostility both to businessmen and commodity-producing peasants. His conclusion perhaps gives his perspective: with a high ratio, 'the burden . . . imposed upon the active and working element of a society would be intolerable' but a too-low ratio would put the burden on wage earners.

I myself would choose 1s.6d. as the ratio at which we should stabilize . . . (1) it will conserve the position of the investing and earning classes; (2) it does not jeopardize our trade and prosperity by putting any extra burden on the business class; and (3) being the most recent in point of time it is likely to give greater justice to the greater number of monetary contracts most of which must be recent in time.[6]

And in fact it was the 1s.6d. ratio which the British government accepted.

The Evolution of Provincial Finance in British India, published in 1925, also condemns British imperialism in its description of the way in which British fiscal politics had impoverished India. Ambedkar attacked the irrationality of British taxation methods, charging that 'While the land tax prevented the prosperity of agricultural industry the customs taxes hampered the manufactures of the country. There were internal customs and external customs, and both were equally injurious to trade and industry'[7] and that basic taxes like the salt tax and the form of the land tax itself lay most heavily on the poor. It was clear, he noted, that the British government was running India in the interest of British manufacturers.

Both this critique and the discussion in *The Problem of the Rupee* were well within the framework of standard economics: that is, Ambedkar did not see the 'development' of a backward ex-colony as a problem, once the artificial barriers imposed by the colonial state were removed; many aspects of colonial rule were described as progressive (primarily those having to do with establishing the infrastructure for growth) and the primary barriers to progress were seen as more social than economic. The British government, Ambedkar noted, not only exploited economically but it could not act against social evils:

> It could not sympathize with the living forces operating in the Indian society, was not charged with its wants, its pains, its cravings and its desires, was inimical to its aspirations, did not advance Education, disfavoured Swadeshi and snapped at anything that smacked of nationalism . . . the Government of India dared not abolish the caste system, prescribe monogamy, alter the laws of succession, legalize intermarriage or venture to tax the tea planters. Progress involves interference with the existing code of social life and interference is likely to cause resistance . . . .[8]

Ambedkar went on to aruge that it would be social more than economic causes that led to nationalist revolt:

> It is foolish to suppose that a people will indefinitely favour a bureaucracy because it has improved their roads, constructed canals on more scientific principles, effected their transportation by rail, carried their letters by penny post, flashed their messages

by lightning, improved their currency, regulated their weights and measures, corrected their notions of geography, astronomy and medicine and stopped their internal quarrels. Any people, however patient, will sooner or later demand a government that will be more than a mere engine of efficiency.[9]

This period, in other words, sees Ambedkar as a general supporter of a capitalist organization of the economy, assuming its inevitability and capability of providing growth and being amenable to a balancing of interests. In this model, the role of the state was to provide infrastructure and generally handle currency and exchange so as not to discriminate against any of the major business or agricultural classes of the country. Though he referred to Keynes, the period is clearly as much pre-Keynes and pre-'development' as pre-Marx. That capitalist economies could come into major crisis; that specific state-guided development and even state enterprise was necessary to lift Third World countries out of their poverty was not part of economic discourse at this time.

Then came the late 1920s and the 1930s, the depression, the new momentous force for change represented by the Russian revolution, the upsurge of the working class in India itself and Ambedkar's own theoretical and practical confrontation with Marxism. Not only did socialism, defined in terms of state ownership of the means of production, begin to appear as a viable reality for working class emancipation; it also began to seem to be the best route to development for an economically backward ex-colony. Even standard 'developmental economics' by the post-war period began to assume the necessity of a major role of the state. In the context of all of these developments, Ambedkar became a socialist, but not a socialist who had time to work out his economic theory. There were, in fact, no economic writings after the 1920s.

By the middle of the 1930s, he swung into an economic radicalism that included the main themes of his time: the exploitation of capitalists and landlords, the need for state control. His economic thrust underwent a major change. This could be seen especially in regard to agriculture. His early writings had expressed support for small peasant property as the alternative to landlordism (in fact arguing that in terms of available capital equipment, farms were if anything too large); by the time of the Scheduled Caste Federation election manifestos he was arguing that for enhanced production agriculture had to be mechanised. This meant that large farms would replace small ones, and this could be most effectively done through cooperative or collective farms.[10] The notion of state-guided development, oriented to industrialization, was taking precedence.

The climatic statement of this economic radicalism came in *States and Minorities*, written as a submission to the Constituent Assembly in 1948, and expressed in the form of proposed constitutional clauses. As a statement of a general economic and social programme, this is a somewhat eccentric form. In fact, only two years before Ambedkar had rejected the idea of a constituent assembly, in language that made it clear he did not see the constitution as a means for either establishing socialism or liberating the scheduled castes. He had said,

> I must state that I am wholly opposed to the proposals of a Constituent Assembly. It is absolutely superfluous . . . there are hardly any big and purely constitutional questions about which there can be said to be much dispute among Indians. It is agreed that the future Indian Constitution should be federal. It is also more or less settled what subjects should go to the Centre and what to the Provinces. There is no quarrel over the division of Revenues between the Centre and the Provinces, none on Franchise, and none on the relation of the Judiciary to the Legislative and the Executive . . . . The only function which could be left to a Constituent Assembly is to find a solution of the Communal Problem.[11]

Yet, two years later he was submitting a memorandum that sought to make the constitution a means for the establishment of socialism!

The economic section of *States and Minorities* calls for 'state socialism', including for the nationalization not only of basic industries but also of land and its working in collective farms, with peasants treated as tenants of the state. Arguing in terms of both developmental needs and protection of working class rights, Ambedkar wrote, 'State Socialism is essential for the rapid industrialization of India. Private enterprise cannot do it, and if it did it it would produce those inequalities of wealth which private capitalism has produced in Europe.'[12] He described pithily the effects of poverty as making 'Fundamental Rights' meaningless, and talks of capitalist tyranny:

> Constitutional Lawyers . . . argue that where the State refrains from intervention in private affairs—economic and social—the residue is liberty. What is necessary is to make the residue as large as possible and State intervention as small as possible . . . . [But] to whom and for whom is the liberty? Obviously this liberty is liberty to the landlords to increase rents, for capitalists to increase hours of work and reduce rates of wages. It must be so. It cannot be otherwise. For in an economic system employing armies of workers, producing goods en masse at regular intervals some one must make rules so that workers will work and the wheels of industry run on. If the State does not do so the private employers will . . . . In other words, what is called liberty from the control of the State is another name for the dictatorship of the private employer.[13]

Clearly Ambedkar, like all socialists and nationalists of his time, was conceiving 'socialism' as a regimented industrialized economy.

Thus the basic proposals of 'state socialism' called for state ownership and management of 'key' industries and state ownership of 'basic' industries; a monopoly of insurance; and agriculture declared as a state industry, with the state to acquire (with compensation) rights in land, divide the land into farms of 'standard size' and let them out for cultivation to the residents of the village 'as tenants' to cultivate as a collective farm, in accordance with rules and directives issued by Government, with the produce to be distributed in shares among the tenants. It was added,

(ii) The land shall be let out to villagers without distinction of caste or creed and in such manner that there will be no landlord, no tenant, and no landless labourer;

(iii) It shall be the obligation of the state to finance the cultivation of the collective farm by the supply of water, draft animals, implements, manure, seeds, etc.

The state would then levy charges for land revenue, to pay the compensation charges, and pay for the capital goods supplied.[14]

Clause (iii) could be interpreted to argue that the state would provide the necessary inputs according to the wishes of the farming community, or simply provide financing for inputs that may be procured locally; but still there seems to be an assumption (as with private 'industrial–chemical agriculture') that inputs for state agriculture would come primarily from outside the village. Here is an assumption, not only that the state is benign but that agricultural production (like industrial production) can very well be managed and directed from above. The fervor to abolish the inequalities of social relations of ownership is clear (though even here, in allowing compensation, Ambedkar is not going as far as the left radicals), but neither the problems of economic exploitation involved in state management nor those of the process of production in agriculture have been given any thought.

Following this, a completely separate section on the protection of scheduled castes as minorities describes their oppression by caste Hindus and argues strongly not only for a series of safeguards but also for separate electorates and separate village settlements, which the state is to set up by giving Dalits forest lands or wastelands. In regard to this, Ambedkar argues that the roots of discrimination lie in the village system itself:

> So long as the present arrangement continues it is impossible for the Untouchables either to free themselves from the yoke of the Hindus or to get rid of their Untouchability. It is the close knit association of the Untouchables with the Hindus living in the same village which mark them out as Untouchables . . . . It is the system of the village plus the Ghetto which perpetuates Untouchability and the Untouchables therefore demand that the nexus should be broken and the Untouchables who are as a matter of fact socially separate should be made separate geographically and territorially also and be settled into separate villages exclusively of Untouchables.[15]

While this passage is followed by a description of the dependence of Dalit labourers on caste Hindu peasants for wages, it makes no reference to a solution in terms of giving Dalits a share in the land in the same village (in fact the first paragraph rules this out by describing untouchability as a reality even beyond economic oppression), while the section on the 'nationalization of land' makes no mention of whether the nationalized villages of untouch-ables are to be separate. It is as if these are two parallel solutions to the problems of Dalits, one economic, one social, lines which never meet.

States and Minorities is in many ways a puzzling though remark-able book. At one level it shows the heights of radicalism Ambed-kar reached in terms of both economic and caste issues, with his calls for 'state socialism' on one hand and the path of protective measures, separate electorates and separate villages for Dalits on the other. Yet it also shows the disjuncture between these—as if the programme for liberation was itself paralleling the mechanical Marxist posture of 'class' and 'caste' as separate phenomena oper-ating on different levels of social reality.

Not only is there no linkage between the economic section and the scheduled castes-as-minorities section of the book, there is also no linkage to strategy. Ambedkar discussed the fallacies of leaving the construction of socialism to 'the whims of a parliamentary majority', giving this as the justification for the necessity of writing the clauses into the constitution itself. But both in regard to state socialism and to the strong concessions to scheduled castes, was there any possible basis for thinking that the tremendous influence of landlords, capitalists and upper caste Hindus would admit such a constitution?

Ambedkar was after all a political realist. *States and Minorities* was, it must be concluded, not intended as a serious political document outlining a programme but as a manifesto designed to be extreme and provocative, not so much to achieve the implementation of the points it set forth as to draw attention to its author. Its focus was social equality, not a plan for organizing the economic produc-tion of a society. Whether or not he thought it was 'superfluous', a constituent assembly was being called; Ambedkar had not been included though he wanted to be, if only to ensure the continued provision of safeguards for the Dalits. *States and Minorities* was designed to achieve this goal mainly, and secondarily to throw some ideas for the future of India before the public. It was a radical, idealistic manifesto aimed at some very partial but highly political goals.

In the end, what is striking about Ambedkar's economic radical-ism is the extent to which it was interpreted in terms of the rationalistic 'modernism' of his time: it included a belief in the necessity of industrialization, and the guiding role of the state as inherently progressive if it could be shielded from the vagaries of often manipulated political majorities. By the time *States and Minorities* was written, Ambedkar was intensely pessimistic about these 'political majorities'; there was no organizing on general economic issues, and the non-Brahman or Shudra worker–peasant masses seemed ready to identify as 'Hindus' in opposition to the Muslims and sometimes to the Dalits. State protection for Dalits had always been seen as essential, even in his periods of greater faith in the majority; and now in an atmosphere in which India under Nehru appeared set to adopt planning and a 'socialist pattern of society' Ambedkar's main thrust was to look to this state-guided development as a solution.

On the whole, his socialism had grown out of his interpretation of democracy rather than, as with Marxism a belief in the revolutionary destiny and world-creating powers of the proletariat. Thus, while he shared the belief of both liberals and Marxists of his time in the progressive forces of industrialism, science and 'modernity', he distinguished his views from communism both in terms of the means necessary to achieve them and in terms of stressing demo-cracy over the 'dictatorship of the proletariat'. In a sense, 'state socialism' was aptly named in contrast to 'proletarian socialism'; it retained the belief in the state as a necessary phenomenon in even a socialist society and sought a share in power of workers and Dalits without seeing this as creating any unique kind of state. From an orthodox Marxist point of view, this could justify a rejection of Ambedkar as essentially 'petty bourgeois', identifying the idealism (return to religion) and reformism presumed to be implicit in his theory with a kind of backward 'peasantist' conscious-ness; this has invariably been the response of even the most favourable left assessments.[17] But this is not a very helpful classi-fication and implies assumptions about the meaning of 'proletarian', 'peasant', etc., which do not stand the test of time very well.

In fact, the development of 'Ambedkarism' in India can be seen as the particular expression of a world-wide 'democratic revolution',[19] indeed perhaps the most consistent one possible in Indian condi-tions (certainly more consistent than a 'proletarian socialism' which ignored cultural–caste issues and accepted identities such as 'Hari-jan' and 'Hindu), one which had grown out of the experiences and situations of the most oppressed sections of the people. 'Democratic revolution' in this sense almost invariably leads towards some kind of socialism, and this in fact was how Ambedkar saw it. As he wrote towards the end of *States and Minorities*,

> The soul of Democracy is the doctrine of one man, one value. Unfortunately, Democracy has attempted to give effect to this doctrine only so far as the political structure is concerned by adopting the rule of one man, one vote . . . . It has left the economic structure to take the shape given by those who are in a position to mould it. This has happened because Constitutional Lawyers . . . never realized that it was equally essential to prescribe the shape and form of the economic structure of society, if Democracy is to live up to its principle of one man, one value. Time has come to take a bold step and define both the economic structure as well as the political structure of society by the Law of the Constitution . . . . [18]

Ambedkar's specific recommendations for 'prescribing the economic structure of society' was state ownership of basic industries and collective farms; this would be questioned by many today along with his faith in a centralized, industrial factory-based economy. But that the market by itself cannot guarantee equality, that the state must play a defining and guiding role—or rather that the members of society must act collectively through the state to regulate, limit and at points supercede the market—is a thesis that few (at least in the Third World) would question. This flexible 'socialism', coupled with political democracy and non-violent mass struggle, makes Ambedkar's economics still relevant today.

■ THE CULTURAL REVOLUTIONARY THEORY OF INDIAN HISTORY

Issues of interpretation of India's culture and history preoccupied Ambedkar's research and non-political writing. The fact is that all through the 1940s, in the face of political–economic tumult and frustrations, Ambedkar focused his intellectual effort not into the economic problems of India's future but into the political questions of its present (such as Pakistan and partition) and into the cultural interpretation of its past. The great questions of identity concerned him, questions that arose immediately on the Dalits' assertion of autonomy from 'Hinduism' and the dominant cultural–national framework of his time. For the rejection of the Hindu nationalism, which was beginning to acquire a cultural hegemony in India, led to the necessity of answering the following questions:

Who were Dalits if they were not 'Hindus'?
What was their place in Indian society and history?
Who were the other caste groups, Shudras and Brahmans in particular?
What were the driving forces of Indian history?
What would be the driving forces to constitute a future Indian society in a democratic and equalitarian fashion?

These were the questions that drove Ambedkar to the reconstruction of India's caste and religious history. He was not doing this in a vacuum, for in his time, besides the incorporative Hinduistic tendency, there were existing answers within the Dalit movement itself, deriving partially from Phule and expressed most vociferously in the 1920s by E.V. Ramasami (Periyar) of Tamil Nadu.

Phule, during the nineteenth century, influenced on the one hand by the European-originated 'Aryan theory of race' and on the other by the theistic doctrines of the 'Rights of Man', had formulated some very strong answers: Dalits, along with the Shudras, were part of an original 'non-Aryan' community conquered by invading Aryans from whom derived the Brahmans; their unique feature was that they had been the bravest warriors in defense of the subjugated peasant community and so were the ones most discriminated against by the arrogant conquerors. Violence and ideology were the driving forces of history; 'Hinduism' was nothing but the religious deception of Bhats to maintain their hold on the masses; peasants were exploited by Brahmans through the state machinery (consolidation of violence) and religious trickery. A future Indian society would be constructed not from the false 'nationalism' of a Brahmanic elite but from the energy of the Shudra–Atishudra masses, and its construction should begin from the villages (Phule's writings also included important sections on the development of agriculture and what environmentalists today would call 'watershed development').[19] A necessary feature was

the replacement of Hindu superstition by a universalistic, equalitarian (including the important stress on women's rights) and
rationalistic religion which Phule called the 'sarvajanik satya
dharma' or 'true religion of the community'.

By Ambedkar's time, with the impact of socialism and the
limitations of the new framework of 'class–caste', these themes
were expressed mainly in the 'adi' ideologies which continued to
stress Dalits as original inhabitants and Brahmans as Aryan conquerors, continued to insist on religious reform and a radical
rejection of 'Hinduism', but left aside most of the economic element, the overall interweaving of violence/conquest and exploitation—and thus very often came down to general racial themes
which either posed 'caste' against 'class' or simply left 'class' issues
aside.

Ambedkar himself took up some of these themes, rejected
others, and wove a new whole in his interpretation of Indian
history, directed to a large degree to the association of Dalits with
Buddhism.

But Ambedkar was also a man of his time, influenced by the
general assumptions of liberalism, socialism and industrialism. In
many ways, the assumptions of mechanical materialism handicapped
his efforts at giving a historical interpretation of caste. In his early
period he had dealt with economic theory only (though in his very
rational way) in terms of issues of financial and monetary policy,
leaving aside the analysis of exploitation, capital accumulation and
changing forms of production. Later, though influenced by economic radicalism and the belief in the necessity of the state for
development, the impact of mechanical Marxism meant that economic exploitation was interpreted in a way divorced from the
social (caste) structure. For Ambedkar (as for Marx and for Phule)
social processes involved contradiction, violence and exploitation;
but Ambedkar saw these almost entirely in terms of political and
group conflict, without looking at changing economic structures
that underlay or influenced these. This left his interpretation of
ancient Indian history incomplete in crucial ways.

Above and beyond this was his overriding rationalism. This was
clearly a crucial part of his very identity, ranging from the hopes he
placed in industrialism to his insistence on wearing modern dress,
with the greatest critique of Gandhi expressed in his condemnation
of his backwardness: 'the Gandhian age is a dark age'. Here there

were important shades of difference with Phule at many levels: where Phule had excorciated Hinduism primarily for its exploitation and oppressiveness (while also seeing it as irrational), Ambedkar attacked it even more strongly for its irrationality and superstition; where Phule (and other low caste reformers of the nineteenth and twentieth centuries, such as Narayana Guru of Kerala) had still felt the need to incorporate a god in his 'religion', Ambedkar could feel comfortable only with a religion that effectively side-lined god and was itself reinterpreted in a rationalized way. Both stressed the need for religion as a code of morality for an equalitarian society; both attacked Hinduism as a systematization of superstition, hierarchy and exploitation, but Ambedkar used, throughout his works, the discourse of 'reason', of rationality/irrationality, whereas Phule was likely to stress benevolence and compassion as the most important moral value.

In their historical interpretations, similarly, Phule was likely to stress the sheer violence and brutality of conquest, while Ambedkar wrote in terms of calculations and conspiracies. In a sense, their historical interpretations themselves worked at different levels: Phule's was more in the nature of a re-mythologizing, building on and creating new symbols important to the Shudra–peasant community and using the Brahmanic myths and historical figures such as Shivaji from this point of view. Ambedkar, in contrast, was defining himself as a scholar, arguing history, contesting historical interpretations, concerned for the logic and proof of his arguments. In spite of obvious empirical gaps, for instance not dealing with the Indus Valley civilization, his work remains a more enduring part of historical discourse in India, able to contest the Hindu nationalist interpretation on the grounds of historical validity as well as ideological morality.

■ 'HINDU INDIA' AND 'BUDDHIST INDIA'

With Phule and then Ambedkar's writings on Indian history begins the construction of an 'Indian nation' or 'Indian people' not dominated by elite reinterpretations. One of the most recent influential analyses of nationalism, Benedict Anderson's *The Imagined Community*[20] focuses on the degree to which in modern nationalism, the nation as community itself is a constructed phenomenon. In truth, throughout the nineteenth and twentieth centuries the high-caste elites of India had been constructing or 'imagining' it as a Hindu community, incorporating some of the language of democracy but most often using a Romantic imagery stressing a community of blood and race, 'Hindus' as a 'people' inhabiting the subcontinent, assaulted by outside forces defined as 'Muslim', British or whatever, dominated their discourse.[21] While the Congress and left secularists wanted to assert another 'unity of India' inclusive of Muslim and other religious traditions, and Gandhians wanted to reinterpret 'Hinduism' to allow for a significant reformism, both accepted the elements of the framework. In particular they took for granted the identification of the majority of people as 'Hindus' and the identification of the ancient Indian tradition as basically a Hindu one. This was expressed in the common framework of both British and nationalist historical writing, which spoke of 'ancient, medieval, and modern' India essentially as 'Hindu, Muslim and British' (for the nationalists, then, modern) India.

The Phule/Ambedkar/Periyar tradition represents the effort to construct an alternative identity of the people, based on non-north Indian and low-caste perspectives, critical not only of the oppressiveness of the dominant Hindu caste society but also of its claims to antiquity and to being the major Indian tradition. Much more than the 'Hinduistic' perspective it took its stand from a firm rationalism and equalitarianism; the freedom from the needs of the elite to justify, in part if not *in toto*, the dominant caste framework of pre-capitalist society, allowed a much greater expression of democratic values. Thus the tradition appears—with its concern for abolition of caste, for the equality of women, for the economic welfare of peasants and workers, for a rational and scientific society—as the most consistent expression of its time of a broad democratic revolution. The fact that Ambedkar focused his intellectual energies on the task of developing this tradition rather than, say, on the problems of economic liberation of the Dalits might lead to charges of 'idealism'—were it not for the fact that the failure of any other major social–political force to really confront the underpinnings of Hindu nationalism (today expressed so forcefully in the rise of the Bharatiya Janata Party (BJP) and all its kin) made this an urgent need for Dalits and other oppressed.

Ambedkar's basic perspective begins with a firm rejection of the degenerate 'racial' form which Phule's 'non-Aryan theory' had taken by his time:

> As a matter of fact the Caste system came into being long after the different races of India had co-mingled in blood and culture. To hold that distinctions of Caste are really distinctions of race and to treat different Castes as though they were so many different races is a gross perversion of facts. What racial affinity is there between the Brahman of the Punjab and the Brahman of Madras? What racial affinity is there between the untouchables of Bengal and the untouchables of Madras? What racial difference is there between the Brahman of the Punjab and the Chamar of the Punjab? . . . . The Brahman of the Punjab is racially the same stock as the Chamar of the Punjab, and the Brahman of Madras is the same race as the Pariah of Madras. Caste system does not demarcate racial division. Caste system is a social division of people of the same race.[22]

This statement in *The Annihilation of Caste* is as clear as could be made and should stand against all attempts today to use Ambedkar's name as a justification for a racial theory of caste differences.[23] With this, also, though less drastically, Ambedkar's emphasis shifted from Phule's emphasis on conquest, war and violence as factors in history to one in which the main historical development was interpreted in terms of conflict between social systems representing different religious–cultural values, a conflict carried on in terms of both force and violence as well as political manoeuvring and creations of systems of ideological deception.

Ambedkar's extensive writing was published only partially during his lifetime with *The Untouchables* (1948) and *Who were the Shudras?* (1955). Both were books with a fairly limited purpose, with a broader, comprehensive theory being formulated in the background, to be published only as incomplete manuscripts after his death. *Who were the Shudras?* Is in part a refutation of a racial interpretation; it argues that the 'Shudras' were originally a section of Aryans in competition with Brahmans and downgraded in the course of intense factional and political struggle; only later (and it is added as almost an afterthought) were masses of non-Aryans absorbed into the now inferior 'Shudra' category. It is in the introduction that Ambedkar identifies himself as a 'non-Brahman scholar'. *The Untouchables* does not even bother to discuss the racial theory; it argues for a late origin of untouchability, after the major structures of the caste system were formed, when conquered tribals or 'Broken Men' were forced to settle in villages; it also, strikingly, associates the untouchables with Buddhism and their strong degradation with the competition of Brahmanism and Buddhism.

These books were tips of an iceberg that embodied a much more comprehensive theory that Ambedkar was working on up to the time of his death, which he outlined as 'Revolution and Counter-Revolution in Indian History'. In this work, the particular interpretations of the social origins of Shudras and the untouchables was put in a much broader, more fundamentally conceived historical context in which the conflict between Buddhism and Brahmanism is represented as a civilizational clash in the process of social evolution in India.

Ambedkar's thesis is posed most sharply (though without identifying its proponents by name) to the 'nationalist' school which was in reality a Hindu nationalist school. His argument was essentially that no united ancient 'Hindu India' had ever existed; instead there were 'three Indias' preceding the Muslim period. These were:

1. 'Brahmanism', describing the Aryan society of the Vedic period and in reality a barbarian phase;
2. 'Buddhism', with the Magadha–Mauryan empires embodying a 'Buddhist revolution', the rise of civilization and the assertion of basic forms of human equality;
3. 'Hinduism', or a 'Hindu counter-revolution' marked with Pushyamitra Sunga's rise to power in north India and associated with Manu, the triumph of caste, and the subordination of women and Shudras.[24]

Ambedkar's phases represent vastly different social systems, with fundamentally different principles of organizing human life; their conflict was both at the level of a clash of values and of armies. As he argues, 'it is clear that the Muslim invasions are not the only invasions . . . . If Hindu India was invaded by the Muslim invaders, so was Buddhist India invaded by Brahmanic invaders.'[25] There was a racial–ethnic element in all of this in which Ambedkar identifies his heroes to some extent with non-Aryans, for instance arguing that the Mauryan empire was that of the Nagas,[26] but it is underplayed. As he was always concerned to argue, the clash was not a racial one but rather 'social', involving the efforts of a particularly defined social group, the Brahmans, to establish and maintain their superiority.

This is a fundamentally different perspective on ancient India not only from the theorizing of established 'nationalist' historians and political leaders but also from the rather mechanical arguments of leftists, all of which tended to see Indian civilization as a basically 'Hindu' one originating in the Vedic period and preceeding in an unfolding fashion after that. S.A. Dange's crude application of the 'five-stage theory of history' to India begins with an idealization of Vedic Aryan society as 'primitive communism'; even the southern communist leader E.M.S. Namboodiripad treats caste and the village defined by it as a stable structure inherent in Indian society.[27] In contrast, Ambedkar's theory stresses the contradictions and exploitation inherent in caste and the revolutionary 'breaks' in the formation of the system. It denies the ancient character of the 'Hindu' religion; and it also denies, in effect, the inevitably of its hegemony, the irrevocable and essential character of its association with 'India'. In 'Revolution and Counter-Revolution', the victory of 'Hinduism' was not, in contrast to Phule and other 'non-Aryan interpretations', a once-and-for-all result of an Aryan conquest; it came after a period of social developments and group clashes and after an important 'break', even breakthrough into civilization, represented by Buddhism, culminating in the Mauryan empire. In spite of its incompleteness, this approach is methodologically helpful for an on-going analysis of the development of Indian society. It also strikes a theme radically different from his political writings of the 1940s which accepted a 'Hindu' identity.

■ A RATIONAL AND SOCIAL RELIGION

In very many ways, the mass conversion to Buddhism in 1956 was the logical result of this historical–social interpretation: it was Ambedkar's effort to put into practice the assertion of a unique identity of Dalits, and to project it as a possibility for all of India. If his cultural interpretation had seemed at odds with his political writings which accepted the reality of the division of India into 'Hindu' and 'Muslim', now with the conversion to Buddhism he attempted to put his contestation of Hinduism on a material or real footing. Buddhism itself was given a 'liberation theology' interpretation, as *dhamma* or social morality and not *dharma* or religious ethics. Ambedkar's constant comparisons of Buddhism and communism were not simply ways of being 'anti-communist'; the assertion of a socialist content to Buddhism was a kind of insistence on the transformation of existing Buddhism also.

The conversion was the major, massive event of the last stage of Ambedkar's life, overshadowing the transformation of the Scheduled Caste Federation into the Republican Party, overshadowing the alliance of the Samyukta Maharashtra movement as part of a broad left anti-Congress front. These were political and economic thrusts due to which the Dalits were uniting in a broad left movement towards economic emancipation; but the conversion to Buddhism was seen, by Ambedkar and by large numbers of those who took part, as a social rebirth, a gaining of a new identity, a way in which the Dalits were leading, not simply joining, a movement for the recreation of India.

An editorial in his weekly announced its change of name to *Prabuddha Bharat* and interpreted the process of development of the Dalit movement through the names of its organs; from *Mook Nayak* ('Voice of the Silent') to *Bahishkrut Bharat* ('Boycotted India')—both stressing helplessness and suppression—to *Samata* ('Equality') to *Janata* ('The People'), the main journal throughout the 1930s and 1940s, finally to a name that in part identified it with Buddhism but on the other hand simply meant 'Enlightened India'.[28]

Conversion was not an individual act; hundreds of thousands of Dalits joined him in massive open grounds at Nagpur, and as the conversion swept the Mahar community throughout Maharashtra it included the practical consequence of social rebellion, refusing to 'do the work of a Hindu', that is, to carry away dead cattle or perform any of the other of their ordained caste duties. Such refusals, in individual villages, had brought reprisals and atrocities from the 1930s onwards, and they were to be a continuing source of tension in villages throughout the state. Yet the implementation in practice of a non-Hindu identity, socially conceived, was a massive achievement and in many areas it did get the support of caste Hindu peasants, influenced by radical movements and the Satyashodhak tradition.

The inherent problems in simply a 'religious' solution remained; Dalits embracing Buddhism could get caught up in other forms of superstition; very often Ambedkar's very rationalism (in contrast to Phule, the disdain for the idea of reinterpreting existing mass religious traditions) seem simply to have left ground for re-entry of superstitions centred around Ambedkar himself, 'the king of Dalits'. Nevertheless it produced powerful and positive results. With the conversion to Buddhism Ambedkar achieved what Phule and Periyar, for all their resistance to Hinduism, had failed to achieve: making a conscious non-Hindu identity a collective material and radicalizing force in India.

■ THE STRATEGY OF FIGHTING BRAHMANISM AND CAPITALISM

More than any of the other 'social movements' in India, arguably more even than the working class movement (to the extent we can distinguish that from its communist self-claimed vanguard), the Dalit movement has had a political thrust: insistence on a share in power as a precondition for Dalit liberation, interpretation of reservations in terms not simply of economic gain but of access to power, rejection of the politics of patronage all have been major themes up to today and we can see their full expression in Ambedkar: 'we must become a ruling community', was only one of his never-to-be-forgotten slogans.

The political level is one of state power and of the parties that contest for state power; this, not scholarly research even of a radical type, was the milieu in which Ambedkar moved and lived. He was above all a man of strategy, of practical politics, even with his most radical public statements. Thus, even more than the economic goals he placed before the Dalit movement, taking precedence for much of the time over his long-term concerns with cultural–historical reinterpretation, the questions of the strategy and political forms in which Dalits might mobilize for change was central to him and to the legacy he left for the movement.

The core of Ambedkar's political strategy remained constant: 'Brahmanism' and 'capitalism' were the main enemies (and 'Brahmanism' was basically a synonym for 'Hinduism', as nearly all his writings made clear). Dalits, as the super-oppressed and exploited, must maintain their autonomy, but they also needed an alliance with Shudras or 'non-Brahmans' as a group, and a broad worker–peasant mobilization that would be the basis for a political alternative to the Congress, which Ambedkar–like Phule, Periyar, all the social revolutionaries of India—saw as inevitably dominated by upper castes and exploiting classes.

All of these points remain controversial today, of course, and we can only briefly deal with them here. The acceptance and analysis of 'Brahmanism' as linked with 'capitalism' in defining the nature of the Indian state and social system, for instance, is a question of the basic theorization of caste and economic exploitation. The assertion of the need for and possibility of an alliance between the Dalits and Shudras (and not simply as a Dalit–worker alliance, a concept which would assume that the working class had left its caste identities behind), also remains controversial. It is related to the analysis of caste and capitalism, since the possibility of the alliance rests in the identification of 'Shudras' as a caste-exploited toiling section. In spite of their controversial theoretical character, however, an increasingly large section of progressive forces in India have accepted, at least to some degree, these points—in part because a vigorous Dalit movement continues to insist on them.

Just as controversial, however, is the assessment of the Congress Party. In fact, while Ambedkar's characterization of it as 'bourgeois–Brahman' was very close to that of the communists in their early period, it is at odds with the mainstream of left analysis (expressed most eloquently today in the writings of historians Bipan Chandra and Shashi Joshi[29]) which has depicted the Congress as an 'anti-imperialist united front'. This was, for example, the argument used by Swami Sahajanand in his meeting with Ambedkar in 1938.

Ambedkar's rejection of this position was not based on any 'proletarian essentialism' which felt that a non-communist or non-working class nationalism had to be inevitably 'bourgeois'. He argued in terms of the caste character and actions of the Congress leadership (asserting that if it were to be genuinely anti-imperialist he would join it), and there were certainly solid reasons in his time to see its high-caste leadership as much too solidly entrenched and organized to be open to change by the forces he represented. Further, every 'radical' force working with this 'united front' appeared to get absorbed by its more reactionary, and 'Hinduistic' logic; social reformers were enticed by the Gandhian setting of caste-reformism in the language of *Ram-raj*, communists adopted the expedient habit of leaving aside all discussion on the issue of caste/cultural change and simply accepting identities such as 'Harijan' and 'Hindu'. There was every reason to think that only within the framework of *an alternative political centre* could working class and anti-caste forces be unified into being a broad force for cultural as well as economic change.

There was also no reason to assume that the Congress itself as a party should monopolize the essence of an 'anti-imperialist united front': from the beginning the Congress had included very moderate and compromising 'anti-imperialists' while many militant and radical fighters against the British operated outside of it. By Ambedkar's day also, though the Congress was absorbing more of these political forces in practice, stigmatizing its opponents as 'pro-British' and borrowing the language of the left to characterize both itself and its opponents, there continued to be important political forces outside it which were by no means in the hands of the British. A genuine 'anti-imperialist united front' would have to comprise, through some form or another, as many of these forces as possible, and not just remain limited to one party. The problem with the most forceful argument today for the 'anti-imperialist united front' character of the Congress, that of the Chandra–Joshi school, is a logical inconsistency: its basic argument is that rather than building a separate and thus inherently sectarian/diversionary Communist Party fighting against the Congress, the communists should have worked as part of a 'left bloc' along with Nehru and others within the Congress itself. But if activists could be 'communists' without being identified with a particular party, surely they could also be 'anti-imperialists' without being part of the Congress or any other political party. They could also, from outside, have as crucial a chance to influence its politics as from inside. A 'left bloc' could operate to comprise both groups within and without the Congress fold, according to the needs of the time. This was the question not of the effect of having different political formations, but of the effect of their modes of relationship with one another.

Ambedkar rejected the 'left bloc' forming within Congress during the 1930s under Nehru's leadership just as strongly as he rejected Gandhism. He accused Indian socialists of being unfaithful to their ideals due to their upper caste base, and he warned that no socialist movement in India could ignore this issue. The fact was that the Nehruvite left was even more reluctant to give attention to caste than Gandhi was, the masses of youth who thronged Congress campaigns at the time were still very largely high caste, and the notion of Dalit or low caste empowerment, which was so central to their movements for liberation, did not even have a hearing. The neglect of caste issues for the overriding commitment to 'class' was the crucial point in which Ambedkar distinguished himself from the socialist political trend. In other respects, he saw the socialists, and particularly the Lohiaite socialists who took the issue of caste seriously as his firmest allies.

To characterize the Congress as 'Brahman' and 'bourgeois' did not mean that it was incapable of undergoing any change or admitting any low caste people to leadership positions; but rather that its structures of dominance, both organizationally and ideologically, were such as to draw its members into a Brahmanic–Hindu framework of interpreting the 'Indian' nation and into incorporation within a capitalist system. It may be argued that Ambedkar's understanding of this—particularly of the 'bourgeois' character of the Congress, rather of the statist 'Nehru model' of development which it came to accept—was inadequate. The characterization itself, however, and Ambedkar's argument for an alternative political force can be said to have stood the test of time.

▪ DILEMMAS OF THE ALLIANCE

Thus Ambedkar's political career was devoted to finding forms through which Dalits could exert themselves in an autonomous fashion and at the same time build an enduring alliance with non-Brahmans, Shudras, workers and peasants. The problem was that by the 1940s and 1950s, this strategy was becoming more and more difficult to implement.

The alliance attempts went through major phases. The Independent Labour Party, his first political party, put this directly into practice during the radical 1930s, as a worker and peasant party with a red flag and Dalit leadership. But, while it won some major successes (both electorally and in terms of leadership in mass movements) in the Marathi-speaking districts, it could not make an impact at the all-India level. And while different forms of 'peasant–worker' or peasant-based parties were coming up in parts of India, usually with specific ethnic identities, the failure of any national (left) political force to promote an alternative to the Congress, the fact that both socialist and communist trends were working within the Congress, left these attempts isolated.

Under the pressure of events, Ambedkar wound up the Independent Labour Party and formed the Scheduled Caste Federation in 1942. This sought to represent Dalits only but on an all-India scale, and had programmes which focused on Dalit autonomy in the absence of alliances, i.e., separate village settlements and separate electorates. It expressed a general disillusionment with the ability of even poor Shudra peasants to shake themselves out of the 'Hindu fold' and the discrimination against untouchables that this embodied; the long period during which even radical peasant organizing had not touched on caste issues, the failed dialogue with peasant leaders and the non-Brahman parties, was apparently having its effect. Ambedkar continued to see Shudras as oppressed by the caste system, but he was discouraged by their apparent unwillingness to shake off Hindu illusions: as he wrote in one of his unpublished manuscripts,

> It is obvious that these three classes [untouchables, Shudras and tribals] are naturally allies. There is every ground for them to combine for the destruction of the Hindu social order. But they have not . . . the result is that there is nobody to join the untouchable in his struggle. He is completely isolated. Not only is he isolated, he is opposed by the very classes who ought to be his natural allies.[30]

Behind this was also the reality of the overriding political importance of the 'Hindu–Muslim' question, which meant seeing the large body of non-Brahmans as essentially 'Hindus'. Along with leaders and activists throughout the country, Ambedkar was being forced to take the major identities of 'Hindu community' and the 'Muslim community' as the overriding reality beyond either class or regional identities.

A pessimism about a 'peasant' alliance accompanied that about the 'Shudra' alliance. The turn to a traditional left type of economic radicalism, in fact, was also making the prospects of forming a peasant alliance more difficult. As we have seen, Ambedkar had never hesitated to support peasant movements (in spite of the tensions and contradictions between mainly labourer Dalits and caste Hindu peasants) and in his early days he had argued for an economy of peasant small property, expressing fears about the upper caste control that large centralized properties would bring. Thus he supported not only anti-rent campaigns against landlords, but also anti-revenue, i.e., anti-state campaigns. So did the early communist movement; in fact the earliest statements of programmes saw anti-revenue as the central form of peasant struggles in ryotwari areas, comparable to anti-rent struggles in zamindari areas.

After this, however, the communists switched to discussing only anti-money-lender struggles, leaving out the question of the state as a direct exploiter, an extractor of economic surplus; and Ambedkar more or less followed them. Collective farms, i.e., state management, which he proposed as 'nationalization of land', came to be the main radical programme for agriculture. The earlier support for small peasant holdings was gone. Both proposals for collective farms and 'separate village settlements' assumed that within a primarily small holding *if inequalitarian* peasant community it would be impossible for the Dalits and other sections of the landless could fight for and win access to land and other resources. In effect they assumed that there was no overriding common interest that could unite the Dalits (primarily labourers but also small peasants) with a large section of Shudra caste peasants.

But collectives could not be a solution that laid a basis for such an alliance. Peasants with small holdings tend to resist collectivization and top-down cooperative farms; whether one sees this as a 'petty-bourgeois' holding on to small property or as a toiling people's resistance to an oppressive statism. Today, decades of experience of collectivization and nationalism, as well as some of the oppressive aspects of even 'cooperatives' when they are accompanied by pressures on peasants, the promotion of mechanized and high-energy using chemical agriculture, and the forced purchases of peasant products at low prices, are all leading to a search for different kinds of rural restructuring. Decentralization and community control of natural resources, the combination of small individual holdings and collectively-managed 'common property resources', the balance of needs for equity within the village and that of a strengthening of village autonomy and access to resources against the central state, are all becoming major themes of 'alternative development' models. But none of this thinking and experience was available during Ambedkar's time. It was quite natural for him, representing the most 'proletarianized' section of the villages, to place his hopes in collective (or statist) forms in agriculture as well as industry. But, in a long transition in which traditional feudal landlords were gradually being overridden and peasant farmers were coming to confront the 'developmentalist' state, in which landlords extracting rent were being replaced by the state extracting grain levies and money-lenders were being replaced by state agencies as the main source of peasant debt, this meant that it was increasingly difficult to have an alliance with the peasantry.

A 'Dalit–Muslim' alliance has been another theme of movements claiming to fight Brahmanism and capitalism. As will be seen in Chapters 9 and 10, it was strongly supported by sections of the Indian Dalits, particularly in Hyderabad and Bengal. In contrast to the issues of 'Shudras' and 'peasants', however, it has to be stressed that Ambedkar never took this up as a *strategic* alliance. He had his periods of discussion with Jinnah, and even joined him in 1939 in celebrating Congress resignations from the provincial ministries. He wrote in detail on the question of Pakistan as well as on linguistic states, setting out the justifications first for forms of federal autonomy that would have given Muslims sufficiently controlled territories to maintain a broadly united India, then for the existence of a Muslim state itself. But this did not mean, like some Dalit spokesmen today, that he had any great personal attraction for Islam and its presumed militancy, or that he saw a Dalit–Muslim alliance as a core of his strategy.

Nor did he see 'oppressed nationalities' as potential allies; the concept was not even within his framework of thinking. His writings on the issue of linguistic states and on Maharashtra as a linguistic state reveal a strong emotional resistance to 'linguistic nationalism'; they endorse the often-expressed fears that linguistic states would generally mean an increased dominance of large 'peasant jatis', and they argue for the formation of smaller states but more on grounds of administrative rationalism, calling for the break-up of large states into smaller common-language states, i.e., four Maharashtras, three states in each Madhya Pradesh and Uttar Pradesh and so on. Ambedkar's conviction of the overriding caste reality of India was so strong that he did not see separate linguistically-based cultures as a major reality, and he (perhaps understandably) lacked the particular Marxist linkage of language and nationality.

Thus, in a period during which the major social and political forces that might have made a broad liberatory movement possible were becoming separated from one another, with some of their dynamic elements simply absorbed into the Congress; when Gandhians and the leftists alike were being marginalized, when neither 'Shudras' nor 'peasants' nor 'minorities' nor 'oppressed nationalities' appeared as viable allies for building a united movement or coalition with the Dalits, much of the Scheduled Caste Federation organizing was on a pressure group basis. The significant period of the 1940s and 1950s thus appears as a basic defeat of Ambedkar's major project, that of creating a revolutionary and equalitarian mass political platform.

■ THE REBIRTH OF THE RADICAL UNITED FRONT

However both Ambedkar's practical political enthusiasm and the enduring character of his efforts for a non-Congress Dalit–worker–peasant alliance went into another phase at the end of his life, a rebirth that came with the movement for a united Maharashtra state (the Samyukta Maharashtra movement). Strikingly here the issues of nationality or 'sub-nationality' (linguistic nationality), caste and economic exploitation were combined.

Ambedkar had been, as noted, extremely ambivalent on the issue of states reorganization, generally opposing language as a basis for state formation, calling for smaller states. His theorizing on 'nation-formation' did not give scope for seeing language as uniquely a national feature; he generally shared the centralizing tendencies of industrially-oriented modernists and with the majority of India's political elite he accepted partition as a necessity for disengaging from a Muslim minority whose demands for autonomy would have made a strong central state impossible.[31]

Once the call of politics came, though, he was unambiguous: the demand for a united Maharashtra was to be supported, in spite of fears of Maratha caste domination. Part of this was perhaps a

strong Marathi identity; his criticisms of the Maharashtrian Brahman Congress leaders that they wanted a 'rajya of bhats' was
accompanied by the charge that a bilingual Bombay state would
mean a subordination of Marathi-speakers:

> Just as bhatjis built Maharwadas to provide village workers for
> free in India, so our Gujarati shetjis have in an aggressive way
> established a bilingual state that would be useful for them and
> turned all of Maharashtra into a Maharwada for Gujarat.[32]

Even more, he was enthusiastic about the movement because of
its potential for a powerful anti-Congress front. Spokesmen of the
Scheduled Caste Federation took the lead in arguing for a massive
oppositional unity, this time including the communists, and for
militant struggle to achieve a united Maharashtra.[33] It was the
period during which the Federation was being transformed into a
new party, the Republican Party of India, which was now aimed at
becoming a party of all the exploited and oppressed and not
merely of Dalits. The Federation's executive resolution to establish
the party was put in the specific context that the time had now
come to establish one united front to oppose the Congress in the
forthcoming general elections.[34] Y.D. Phadke's study of the
Samyukta Maharashtra movement also argues that Ambedkar
made three conditions for the Republican Party's alliance with the
Samyukta Maharashtra Samiti, that the Samiti would take up the
issues of the rural poor and that it would not just be a one-time ad-
hoc alliance but would be made permanent as a broad, left movement.[35]

In fact this very brief period saw a return to the radical politics
of the 1930s. The Samyukta Maharashtra Samiti represented a
coming together of socialists, communists, Dalits, a new upsurge
of a left–Dalit struggle and the first united left political front in
Maharashtra after independence. It brought forward leaders and
themes, including those rooted in satyashodhak traditions, that
had been part of the broad democratic movement throughout the
colonial period in Maharashtra; at the popular level the upsurge of
'communist tamashas' such as the one led by the Dalit communist
poet Annabhau Sathe could unite themes of caste and class oppression.

Furthermore, it was relatively successful. What could not be achieved prior to independence, a decisive defeat of the Congress in Maharashtra, was done by the Samiti, with many Dalits elected on its tickets. The samiti itself disappeared and Congress dominance returned, but some alliance campaigns remained, focused on the rural poor; most notably Dadasaheb Gaikwad of the Republican Party and radical left peasant leaders such as Nana Patil (hero of the 'parallel government' in Satara and a new member of the Communist Party) joined to lead large satyagrahas for Dalit, tribal and other landless to get forest land for cultivation, first in 1956 and then in 1965, the most massive struggles in India on land and peasant issues before the re-emergence of radicalism during the 1960s. Thus, the formation of a party in which Dalits would lead all exploited sections, and the formation of a united left front were, along with the conversion to Buddhism, major events just before Ambedkar's death.

NOTES

1. *Janata*, 25 June 1938. This may have been written by Ambedkar himself or by A.V. Chitre (information from Y.D. Phadke); at any rate it can be taken as representing Ambedkar's views.
2. *Dr. Babasaheb Ambedkar: Writings and Speeches*, Volume III (Bombay: Government of Maharashtra Education Department, 1987), p. 444.
3. B.R. Ambedkar, 'The Problem of the Rupee', in *Dr. Babasaheb Ambedkar: Writings and Speeches*, Volume VI (Bombay; Government of Maharashtra, 1989), pp. 680–81; see also Rajat K. Ray, *Industrialization in India* (Delhi: Oxford University Press, 1979), pp. 245–47 for a description of the controversy.
4. See Narendra Jadhav, *Dr. Ambedkar: Economic Thought and Philosophy*, (Pune: Sugawa Prakashan, 1993).
5. See B.R. Ambedkar 'The Evolution of Provincial Finance in British India', in *Writings and Speeches*, Volume 6, pp. 425–30.
6. Ambedkar, 'The Problem of the Rupee', p. 681.
7. Ambedkar, 'The Evolution of Provincial Finance', p. 75.
8. *Ibid.*, p. 233.
9. *Ibid.*, p. 234.
10. Election Manifesto of the Scheduled Caste Federation (n.d., probably 1951), Vasant Moon's Collection.
11. B.R. Ambedkar, 'The Communal Deadlock', in *Dr Babasaheb Ambedkar: Writings and Speeches*, Volume I (Bombay: Government of Maharashtra Education Department, 1979), pp. 355–80.
12. B.R. Ambedkar, 'States and Minorities: What are Their Rights and How to Secure Them in the Constitution of Free India', (first published 1947) in *Writings and Speeches*, Volume I, p. 408.

13. *Ibid.,* p. 410.

14. *Ibid.,* pp. 396–97.

15. *Ibid.,* p. 425.

16. For the most recent leftist interpretation see Thomas Mathew, *Ambedkar: Reform or Revolution* (New Delhi: Segment Books, 1991), esp. pp. 134–43. Mathew very cautiously refrains from making his critique of Ambedkar directly.

17. For the main contemporary analysis, see Ernesto Laclau and Chantal Mouffe, *Hegemony and Socialist Strategy* (London: Verso, 1989); for a discussion that is used for analysis of India see the writings of Thomas Blum Hansen, especially *Politics and Ideology in Developing Societies: An Exploratory Essay* (Copenhagen, 1991).

18. Ambedkar, 'States and Minorities', p. 412.

19. See Bharat Patankar, *Jotiba Phule ani Sanskrutik Sangarsh* (in Marathi) (Bombay: Lokwangmay, 1991).

20. Benedict Anderson, *The Imagined Community: Reflections on the Origins and Spread of Nationalism.* London: Verso, 1983).

21. See Hansen, *Politics and Ideology.*

22. 'Annihilation of Caste', in *Writings and Speeches,* Volume I, p. 49.

23. For example, *Dalit Voice* which takes the 'racial' line of interpretation has never dealt with these writings.

24. *Writings and Speeches,* Volume III, pp. 419–20.

25. *Ibid.,* Buddhists today, in response to Ayodhya claims, are seeking the Buddhist stupas and caves underlying 'Hindu' ones in India. The 'Pandava caves' near Nasik in Maharashtra could be cited as an example: their main figures are Buddhist ones from the Satavahana period. The current struggle (1992) over 'liberating' the Bodh Gaya centre for Hindu control also exemplifies the issue.

26. *Ibid.,* p. 273.

27. S.A. Dange, *India: From Primitive Communism to Slavery* (New Delhi: Peoples Publishing House, 1972). This is savagely critiqued by D.D. Kosambi, 'Marxism and Ancient Indian Culture', in A.J. Syed (ed.), *D.D. Kosambi on History and Society* (University of Bombay, Department of History Publications, 1985); and E.M.S. Namboodiripad, *Kerala:Yesterday, Today and Tomorrow* (Calcutta: National Book Agency, 1968).

28. *Prabuddha Bharat,* 4 February 1956.

29. Shashi Joshi, *The Struggle for Hegemony in India, 1920–1948: The Colonial State, the Left and the National Movement, Volume I: 1920–1934* (New Delhi: Sage, 1992). Bipan Chandra, Mridula Mukherjee, Aditya Mukherjee, K.N. Panikkar and Sucheta Mahajan, *India's Struggle for Independence, 1857–1947* (New Delhi: Penguin Books, 1989).

30. 'The Untouchables: Children of India's Ghetto,' in *Writings and Speeches,* Volume V (Bombay: Government of Maharashtra, 1989), pp. 115–16.

31. See *Pakistan or the Problem of Partition* and Asim Roy, 'The High Politics of India's Partition'.

32. *Janata,* 15 October 1956; also 5 November 1956.

33. *Janata,* 17 December 1955.

34. *Janata,* 6 October 1956.

35. Y.D. Phadke, *Politics and Language* (Bombay: Himalaya Publishing House, 1979), pp. 60–61, 241–42.

CHAPTER 8

Mysore, 1930–56: The Politics of Ram-Raj

In contrast to the dramatic events in the Marathi and Telugu-speaking areas, Mysore state (indeed all the Kannada-speaking districts), represented a kind of backwater in the last decades of colonial rule. There was neither an Ambedkarite (as in Maharashtra) nor a Marxist (as in Andhra) challenge to Congress hegemony among the Dalits, or among the masses in general. Nevertheless, perhaps even because of this lack of a clear political challenge, the Mysore case allows us to discern some major themes of the bourgeois–Brahman incorporation of Dalits in modern India.

Gandhi, as has been noted, described Mysore state as a model of *'Ram-Raj'* and indeed the Kannada-speaking districts provided fertile ground for 'Harijan' activity after 1930. Nevertheless, 'Gandhism' was only one of the ideological components that guided state politics, another being state-directed modernization: Although Gandhi himself had condemned industrial civilization as 'satanic', the state was in the forefront of efforts to sponsor industrialization. Economic planning and other versions of 'state capitalism' were taken up quite early, and an application of the 'Bombay Plan' to Mysore in the 1940s summed up this experience: 'In fact, the era of experimentation is past; the principle of State ownership and management had been firmly established and is bound to play a decisive role in the post-war industrialization of the state'.[1]

A third component was non-Brahmanism, which in its Mysore incarnation lacked the revolutionary social ideology of pioneers such as Phule and Periyar and took instead the shape of a caste movement, with the politics of reservation as a focus and with the ultimate result of constituting various sections of non-Brahmans as interest groups fighting for their share of the pie. It was easy enough for Dalits to be inserted in this process as a very unprivileged interest group but one that was still given access to some meager share of wealth and status, enough to keep it quiet and enough, also, to arouse resentment among other poor sections. In this way Mysore did become a model *'Ram-Raj'* but one with a modern Ram, a flourish of technology, and an effort to assimilate and ignore Shambuk rather than openly punish him for demanding equality.

The patterns of politics in Mysore were set from the decade of the 1930s, and they lasted until the late 1970s. It is sometimes argued that the regime of Devraj Urs (1972–80) represented a break with the patterns of Kannada politics because of his populism and building of a kind of alliance with minority small castes (including Dalits and 'other backward castes' against the peasant-based Vokkaligas and Lingayats who had dominated politics till then.[2] However, Congress politics in Karnataka had some element of populism from the beginning, and a building of a base among the scheduled castes, minorities and high castes to confront a political 'opposition' basing itself among the middle peasant castes was a strategy which began during the 1930s and solidified with Indira Gandhi's leadership during the late 1960s. Urs represented only the specific Karnataka version of this.

The real break with this incorporative model in Karnataka came, we would argue, not with Urs nor any ruling party politics, but with the emergence of a new Dalit movement during the 1970s represented mainly by the Dalit Sangarsh Samiti, a new opposition farmers' movement, the Rayat Sangh and a women's movement. By the end of the 1970s a tentative alliance had emerged. These movements based themselves not on Gandhism, caste competition 'non-Brahmanism' or statist modernization, but on ideological trends which were weak though still evident during the period of this study. These were Marxism, which had only a limited spread in the Bangalore working class and a small presence in the Bombay Karnataka and coastal districts during the 1950s; Ambedkarism, which had been centred mainly in the Kolar gold mines; and Lohiaite socialism, which emerged during the 1950s as a distinctive effort to take up the problem of caste from within the socialist tradition, making its impact in Karnataka with a peasant movement in Shimoga district.

This chapter, therefore, will focus on the role of Gandhism during the 1930s and then examine the process of non-Brahman politics to see how these came together to set the dominant pattern of incorporation of Dalits in Karnataka state. A final section will look at the significance of 'Lohiaism' as a new ideological trend in anti-caste politics.

■ GANDHISM IN KARNATAKA: MORAL UPLIFT AND LEGAL REFORM

'Originally they were called Holeyas and Madigas. That name was changed and they were styled as Panchamas and then as Depressed Classes. Only a few years back they were called Adikarnatakas, and now they are known as Harijans'. So remarked one Mutta-swamy Gowda in a debate in the Mysore legislative council in 1935, and the remark aptly captures the way in which the Gandhian 'Harijan' identity rapidly gained hegemony.

The 'Harijan movement' took shape immediately after the Poona Pact, and became a major national campaign from 1932 to 1936.[3] The movement had basically three strands. The first was 'moral and spiritual uplift' (including some attention to educational and minimal material living conditions) through the Harijan Sevak Sangh. The second was legal reform, which, during the mid–1930s, focused on efforts at legislation, undertaken in alliance not only with liberals but also some prominent conservatives and Hindu Mahasabhites, aimed at opening up at least some temples to the untouchables. The third strand, less noted in the literature, was the encouragement of 'nationalist' anti-Ambedkarite Dalit organizations, most notably the All-India Depressed Classes League (or

Akhil-Bharatiya Dalit Jati Sangh) founded in Kanpur on 16–17 March 1935, and the Bihar Khet Mazdoor Sabha, founded in 1937, both under the leadership of Jagjivan Ram and aimed, respectively, against Ambedkar on the one hand and the Kisan Sabha on the other.[4] Strikingly, these latter organizations did not come to Karnataka, obviously because here the Gandhian–Congress leadership had no radical Ambedkarite or kisan movement with which to contend.

The Harijan Sevak Sangh emerged directly out of the Poona Pact. A quickly called meeting of caste Hindu representatives in Bombay on 25 September 1932 presided over by Madan Mohan Malaviya called on caste Hindus to 'secure by legitimate and peaceful means an early removal of the social disabilities of untouchability, including temple entry'. On 30 September a public meeting resolved to set up an 'All-India Untouchability League' charged with opening public wells, dharmshalas, roads, schools, crematoriams and burning ghats as well as 'public temples'. The League was set up with a constitution adopted at Delhi on 26 October. Then after one of his flashes of inspiration, Gandhi resolved to change the name to 'Harijan Sevak Sangh'.[5]

Ambedkar opposed the League/Sangh on two points: first, he insisted that the goal of any organization working on the problems of the Dalits should not simply be the 'removal of untouchability' but the eradication of *chaturvarnya*, the caste system itself. Second, leadership should be in the hands of untouchables. These demands were unacceptable to Gandhi, for whom the primary purpose of the Sangh was not to be an organization of Dalits for emancipation but a body for the reform of Hinduism. With these differences the split between Ambedkar and Gandhi crystallized, and the Gandhians in the Congress went ahead with their 'Harijan programme'.[6]

Gandhi's nation-wide 'Harijan tour' (7 November 1933–2 August 1934)[7] gave birth to widespread activity in the Kannada-speaking district. According to one account

Karnataka was in the forefront of the Harijan movement. Branches of this Sangh were soon started in Bijapur, Belgaum, Karwar, Mangalore, Coorg and Bellary, with Hubli as the headquarters. When Gandhiji toured Karnataka in connection with the movement, he met a great enthusiasm everywhere.[8]

The British had a somewhat more jaundiced viewpoint and reported that when Gandhi visited Mysore in 1934 crowds gathered only out of curiosity: 'there is very little enthusiasm over the Harijan movement'.⁹ Nevertheless, numerous branches were founded in the state also. There it came under the lead of Gopalaswamy Iyer and another prominent Gandhian, Tagadur Ramachandra Rao.

A 'Mysore Report' given by T. Ramachandra in Gandhi's weekly *Harijan* gives a picture of its typical activities:

Religious: 123 Harijan bhajans were conducted by the workers of the League. In the village of Kengeri Harijan bhajans were also attended by the local caste Hindu youth who partook in prayer and prasad. After the bhajans, talks were given on moral and spiritual uplift.

Temperance and Sanitation: With the kind cooperation of the Bangalore Temperance Federation and the Mysore State Red Cross society, who supplied us with charts, lantern slides and literature, 49 lectures were delivered to the Harijan slum quarters in Bangalore city, five in Mysore city and 43 in rural parts.

In the village of Tagadur, the workers of the Khadi Centre and the Satyagraha Ashram organized the sweeping of the village and Harijan quarters, in which work the Sannyasis of Ramakrishna Math, Mysore, took part. The workers are daily visiting the Harijan quarters and educating children in the Ashram school.

General: On the motion of Mr. P. Subbarama Chetty, MLC, the chairman of the Provincial Board Working Committee, the Bangalore City Municipal Council have promised Rs 2000 in this year's budget to give lighting and sanitary conveniences in the city slums inhabited by the Harijans. Similar appeals have been made to other municipalities in the state.

A largely attended meeting of Harijans and caste Hindus was held in Chintamani during the month. It was addressed by the presidents of the Kolar and Bangalore districts and important office-bearers of the League. A local centre was formed for intensive Harijan work.

Mr. G. Gopalaswamy Iyer has been provided with one second class pass over the Mysore State railways for doing Harijan work . . . .

Notice of resolutions and interpellations have been sent by the members of the Representative Assembly requesting the government to introduce legislation throwing open public tanks, wells, roads and resthouses to all castes and communities, with a penalty clause for anyone obstructing the use thereof. Another resolution asks the government to appoint a whole-time officer and a separate staff and allotment of funds to look after the interests of the Harijans.

A Harijan Sevak Sangh has been formed in Bangalore Cantonment. In Davanagere a Harijan Sahaja Sangh has been formed and they are conducting a school for the Harijan children.

Medical Relief: 950 Harijans were treated during the month in the Deena Seva Ayurvedic dispensary, which is given a grant of Rs. 30 per month by the League. The Assistant to the doctor pays regular evening visits to the Harijan quarters throughout the city, addressing people on health and sanitation . . . (*Harijan*, 9 September 1993).

The thrust is clear. On one hand, bhajans, *harikathas* and exhortations against drinking alcohol, meat-eating, animal sacrifice, extravagant expenditure, the whole realm of a Sanskritizing moral uplift. An important part of this was the adoption of the campaign against the Basavi form of 'prostitution', as 'caste Hindu ladies' visited Harijan quarters in Bangalore and Mysore to lecture on the issue and two big village conferences were held in April–June 1936 in which the 'Harijans' resolved to give up the custom and appealed to the government to make it a penal offence.[10] In such activities Gandhian dedication joined hands with other middle-class 'moral uplift' efforts (the Temperance League, the Red Cross). On the other hand, there was lobbying with the state to provide some minimal social services. Education was an important focus, and by 1940, 14 day schools and 17 night schools, with a total strength of 666 pupils, were conducted by the Harijan Sevak Sangh.[11]

Legal reform was also an important effort. The Poona Pact provoked a vigorous attempt at the national level to do something about temple-entry, at a time when militants such as Ambedkar were losing interest in it. The model was provided by a bill proposed by C.S. Ranga Iyer in the Central Legislative Council, backed by prominent liberals and Mahasabhaites. In Mysore the Anti-Untouchability League under the leadership of T. Ramachandra drafted a bill in March 1933, arguing for the respectable antecedents of the legislation, providing for temples to be thrown open on a non-compulsory basis to Dalits.[12]

Appeals for this legislation included pious sentiments about the uplift of the Depressed Classes, the exhortations of Swami Vivekananda to the Mysore ruler, and the Maharaja's own exhortation that 'sincere workers should act to link the government to the people' and 'interpret the one to the other' and that 'the long silence of the Depressed and the humble will be broken and the full responsibilities for their well-being shouldered by the educated and well-to-do. classes.'[13] Murugesaram Pillai, the most radical Dalit spokesman of the time, injected a warning note: if temples were not thrown open, 'the Hindus in Mysore will be totally alienating the sympathies of 10 lakhs of people who might have to break away from the Hindu fold and get converted to another religion.'[14]

All of this was to no avail. The government simply declared that it could not take any action regarding temple entry. No legislation was passed. In 1936 the Dalits were invited for the first time by the maharaja to take part in the Dussera darbar; in 1938 an order was given for the entry of untouchables to the Jain temple of Shravanabellagola at Bellur, and withdrawn after vigorous protest by the Jains. And this was the sum total of administrative action by the state on religious rights of the Dalits during the 1930s.

Very little was done by the Gandhians, also, for the land rights which were emphasized in the Dalits' own initiatives and in their appeals in the assembly. The only exception was a 'conference of workers in the Harijan cause' organized on 16 June 1935 in Mysore and presided over by Jawaharlal Nehru: resolutions appealed to the government to give land for agricultural colonies in the Irwin Canal area, sites for houses, provision of drinking water facilities, increased grants for hostels, scholarships and other school fees, and preferential appointments in government service.[15] But there was little else besides appeal to the government. A similar stress on welfare services could be seen in the Deena Seva Sangh, led by L.N. Gutil Sundaresam, which emphasized in non-caste terms the 'moral and material uplift of the masses', working among slum dwellers, cotton mill workers and scavengers, starting morning and evening schools, providing medical services and employing four full-time workers to toil the state.[16]

The dominant Gandhian–Brahmanic reform effort was thus focused on religiously-defined moral upliftment coupled with appeals to a paternalistic state. Gandhians never targeted the system as 'exploitative' and never spoke against caste as a system or campaigned against traditional caste duties within the *jajmani* system; the entire mobilizing effort of the Harijan Sevak Sangh and similar bodies was from the top down, mobilizing the middle classes and upper castes to act 'for' the downtrodden and conspicuously avoiding scope for the Dalits to organize themselves.

In spite of these limitations, the Gandhian efforts were, until perhaps the 1970s, practically the only forum where some kind of philosophy of equalitarianism and social mobility could reach any significant number of rural Dalits. Thus, for example, Edward Harper reports for the Malnad area of Shimoga district in the late 1960s,

> Discontent among Holerus is sometimes fostered by Government officials or Congress party workers who hold 'Harijan uplift' meetings in which speakers promulgate a philosophy of equalitarianism, exhorting untouchables to assert their newly acquired legal rights, to improve themselves by acquiring land, to refuse to become indentured, to hold their heads high, and to bathe more frequently.[17]

Harper also reports the negative response to these appeals by many Dalits, who were sceptical about the possibility of acquiring land and the difficulties of breaking with bonded labour. He thus describes a minimal improvement in the position of the Dalits, coupled with a strong underlying 'hostility' towards the entire system which (at the time he was writing) had little scope for open expression.[18]

Thus the 'alienation' threatened by Murugesaram Pillai could never really be organized, and Mysore Gandhism did in many ways function to hold the Dalits within the statist economic system and within the Hindu religion, primarily by making it almost impossible for a radical Dalit leadership to emerge. But that alienation was there, that considerable bitterness existed even during the 1930s, can be seen in a report by a Maharashtrian Mahar who visited Bangalore with a group of engineering students in 1937. He described impressive educational and employment achievements, including four hostels for untouchable students, two special colonies, two medical clinics, free education for untouchables from primary school to the time of gaining employment, and a good number of Dalits in high-level employment. After seeing this he was reluctant to ask students of the Harijan Sevak Sangh hostels what their views were on Ambedkar, assuming their expressed 'love for the Maharaja' would be carried over to a warmth for the Hindu religion itself. But the militancy of the response surprised him:

> When Ambedkar said two years ago that we can't get any rights in Hinduism and got support from all parts of India, what was the reaction of your people and other Hindus in the state? 'We not only agreed with conversion, but at that time we all decided to become Muslims. Though other Hindus fear Untouchables' conversion, still they don't have the strength to prevent it. Mysore officials themselves don't agree that temples should be open to untouchables. Then what need do we have for a religion that has no humanity? Humanity is more important than wealth or authority. So it seems that not only in Maharashtra but in the most progressive Hindu state in India, you can find Ambedkar's followers![19]

■ DALITS, NON-BRAHMANS AND THE POLITICS OF RESERVATIONS

While in Mysore Gandhism provided both an incorporate ideology and an institutional mechanism whereby reformist Brahmans could build a kind of alliance with Dalits, the non-Brahman movement, centred not on radicalism but on the all-pervasive politics of reservations, provided an equally important context for assimilation.

Though the reservations policy in Karnataka has one of the longest histories in India,[20] at its inception and for a long time afterward it was oriented to general 'non-Brahman' (or 'backward caste') concessions without special provision for the Dalits. The Miller Committee of 1919 had recommended only general provisions for non-Brahmans (within 7 years they were to get 50 per cent of higher level appointments and two-thirds of lower level ones) and this became the basis for a subsequent government order. There were no special provisions for the Dalits and would not be until they were given political reservations in 1940. This contrasted with the rapidity with which the Dalits made and won special claims in other parts of India, and reflected their politically weak position. But the general reservation policy during the 1920s and 1930s led to a situation in which the 'non-Brahmans' became a loose and contenious alliance of different caste groups and communities, engaged in political opposition to the dominant Brahmans but quarreling about each other's share of the general allotment. Tensions developed between Hindu non-Brahmans and Muslims; there were continual murmurings that Lingayats and Vokkaligas were getting the dominant share; and there were even gloomy predictions from higher non-Brahman spokesmen that 'if special preference were given to the Depressed Classes then there would be only two dominant groups in the civil services—the Brahmans and the DCs!'[21]

Natraj calls this 'the first public admission on the part of caste Hindus of a fear of Harijan domination—a cry that is heard all too frequently today'.[22] The whole situation existing during the 1930s suggests to him a kind of '*deja vu* in reverse' in which most politics becomes focused on maneuvering for a share of the pie with the argument that one's own caste/community is really the most backward and oppressed while others are using the general policy of reverse discrimination to move ahead. This saw the stamping of the Dalit as a kind of 'sarkari brahman' even while they were in the worst position:

> The most pathetic and distressing was the position of the Depressed Classes. They had few spokesmen. Few, if any among them, made it to the top in the civil services. I cannot think of a single Harijan member of the council. Naturally their solitary spokesman, Murugesan Pillai, expressed the fear that by being clubbed with the non-Brahman group all smaller communities would be swamped. On many occasions we see him debating whether to continue as part of the uneasy non-Brahman alliance.[23]

But the 'pathetic and depressing' aspect of the position of the Dalits during the 1930s was not so much in being at the bottom of the social-economic ladder; that was true throughout India and in many material ways their condition in Mysore was better (it certainly impressed Dalits from Maharashtra). Rather it was the general fearfulness, passivity and patronage orientation of their leadership.

Here there was some contrast with developments among non-Brahmans during the 1930s, especially the major Vokkaliga and Lingayat groups. The rural links that were being developed from 1930 onwards by elite urban non-Brahmans gave them the self-confidence to allow space for a more general nationalist participation—and this moved the rural masses more than patronage and reservation benefits. The Praja Paksh and the Praja Mitra Mandal had merged in 1935 to form the People's Federation; the series of conferences on peasant issues planned by the Federation was given up under pressure from the authoritarian state, but the direction was evident. The Federation won most of the seats in the 1937 election, but it was clear both that the future lay with the rising tide of nationalism and that the large non-Brahman peasant communities no longer needed the crutch of support from a princely state.

An upsurge in state people's movements was going on at the time, unleashed by the Haripura Congress resolution in February 1938 and generally coinciding with an all-India worker and peasant radicalism.[24] The Mysore Congress, now dominated by non-Brahmans, held its first session as an independent body on 11 April 1938. This was followed by the 'Vidurasurathan incident' in which 32 people, mainly peasants, were killed in police firing over a flag-raising dispute. Though the Gandhians sought a compromise, a militant second session of the Mysore Congress attended by 30,000 people at Viduras resolved to hold a 1938 'September satyagraha'.[25]

Gandhi sought a compromise in Mysore on the grounds that it was one of the cases where the state peoples' movements was taking on a 'communal' complexion. Thus his secretary Mahadev Desai, who came to Mysore, charged in his report that the Mysore Congress was 'not representative' because of little Brahman involvement and Muslim opposition.[26] In fact there was a general process in many states in which a majority community on joining the Congress was taking the national movement in hand and using it to challenge the role of outsiders/high castes/religious minorities who had dominated the states' administrations. The situation in Mysore was actually far more benign than in places like Hyderabad where the dominance of the Arya Samaj bad severe Hindu–Muslim ten--sion, and one may wonder whether in fact the Gandhians feared most the potential anti-caste, anti-Brahman aspect of radical movements. In any event, the Mysore non-Brahman leaders let themselves be argued into a compromise, and politics in the state settled back into its placid processes of negotiation.

Dalits, however, remained aloof from even this much struggle. The testimony of the Adi-Karnatak Abhirridhi Sangham and the Adi-Jambara Abhiriddhi Sangam of Bangalore (basically Murugesaram Pillai's organizations) before the Srinivasa Iyengar committee on constitutional reforms in 1938 was that

> When Responsible Government is introduced, it will naturally lead to the predominance of certain communities not sympathetically disposed towards the aspirations of the Adi-Karnatakas, and therefore there is every likelihood of their position not being in any way improved under a scheme of Responsible Government—with power in the hands of communities by whom they had been kept down in the past.[27]

This represented a clinging to a beneficent autocracy that contrasted with Ambedkar's militant nationalist opposition to the princely states. It also represented a tendency to accept an alliance with Brahmans and other 'minority' castes out of fear of domination by the large peasant-based non-Brahman castes; this was also in contrast to Ambedkar's continuing efforts to build a Dalit–Shudra alliance against Brahmanism.

The Dalit position taken here was an outcome of a situation in which sections of a Brahman elite had worked for over a decade to build up some base in a 'Harijan' constituency, while non-Brahmans had mainly focused on reservation-oriented interest group politics. Dalits were partly rewarded for their loyalty when the Government of Mysore Act of 1940 reserved 67 of 310 seats for minorities and of these 30 for the Depressed Classes; the position was thus set for the post-independence situation in which Dalits would be constitutionally and legally guaranteed a share as 'scheduled castes'. But the failure to evolve a political vision of liberation, or to organize an autonomous Dalit movement, or become participants in any vigorous movement against the system is stark. There was no Dalit liberation movement in Mysore state, only processes of incorporation accompanied by unresolved problems of social and economic exploitation and the underlying hostility that continued to be generated by them.

■ LOHIAITE SOCIALISM: PEASANTS AND ANTI-CASTE MOVEMENTS

Marxism and Ambedkarism, as we have seen, never had much force in Karnataka before the recent decades. During the 1950s, though, we see the entry of another ideological trend, that of Lohiaite socialism, which in crucial ways was a break both with Gandhian reformism and the mechanical Marxist focus on 'class' which until then had affected all sections of socialists in India.

Member of the Uttar Pradesh Congress Socialist Party, Dr. Ram Manohar Lohia had resigned from the CSP in 1939 along with others in protest over communist domination, and had been one of the militant underground leaders in the 1942 movement. After independence he broke with the Congress to help form the Socialist Party (SP). In 1952 the SP merged with the Kisan Mazdur Praja Paksh (a party with its biggest base in Andhra, drawing on the Ranga non-communist rural organizing tradition, though Acharya Kripalani was its nationally known leader). This culminated in the Praja Socialist Party (PSP), and in 1955 Lohia and other 'left wing militants' broke from the PSP to revive the Socialist Party, which had its greatest national base in the south. Although the Socialist Party (later the Samyukta Socialist Party) remained small and electorally unsuccessful, it is credited by political scientist Rajni Kothari with being 'the most dynamic among the non-Congress parties'.[28] This was partly due to its strategy, initiated by Lohia, of an anti-Congress 'Grand Alliance', and partly due to its innovative policy on caste, class and gender issues.

Lohia saw caste as a crucial aspect of domination and exploitation in India, and projected an alliance of 'Shudras, Harijans, Muslims, Adivasis and women' as central to a revolutionary movement. He stressed the need to build up the leadership of these sections:

> With faith in the great crucible of the human race and equal faith in the vigour of all the Indian people, let the high-caste choose to mingle tradition with mass. Simultaneously a great burden rests on the youth of the low castes. Not the aping of the high-caste in all its traditions and manners, not dislike of manual labour, not individual self-advancement, not bitter jealousy, but the staffing of the nation's leadership as though it were

some sacral work should now be the supreme concern of women, Sudras, Harijans, Muslims and Adivasis.[29]

The caste system was blamed for excluding 80 per cent of the country's population from public life, causing the enslavement of the country, and maintaining low productivity in both agriculture and industry: Its destruction was the 'supreme need of public life'. And the programme of the Socialist Party and related organizations included demands for 60 per cent reservations (preference in politics, government service, military, trade and industry); purifying religion of the taints of caste; promotion of inter-marriage as a long-term solution and common dining as an immediate programme of integration; and a consciousness-raising call for studies, debates and seminars on the issue of caste.[30]

Much of this was drawn from the decades-long struggle of Dalits and non-Brahmans. But Lohia's attention to women's oppression went beyond that of Ambedkar (and in this he is perhaps comparable to Phule) and included an open attitude on sexuality that represented a break with Hindu *pativrata* puritanism. In a 1953 essay on 'the two segregations of caste and sex' as the primary factor in the degeneration of India, he argued,

India is perverted today; with all their talk of sex purity, the people are by and large dirty in their ideas of marriage and sex . . . . Celibacy is generally a prison-house . . . . It is time that young men and women revolted against such puerilities. They should remember that there are only two unpardonable crimes in the code of sex conduct: rape and the telling of lies or breach of promise. There is also a third offense of causing pain or hurt to another, which they should avoid as far as possible.[31]

Lohia insisted that a women's movement should focus on the needs of the 80 per cent low-caste toiling women—needs in which such minimal facilities as drinking water were more important than legal reform: This attitude on issues of sexuality and marriage, which are central to the right to live a life not subordinated to that of husband/father/son, gave Lohia a unique position in the India of his time.[32]

Lohia is criticized by the Marxist left for neglecting 'class struggle', for not linking his anti-caste programme to one of ending economic exploitation, and for having a generally 'reformist' perspective: 'He does not advocate a revolution—peaceful or otherwise—involving the overthrow and destruction of the existing order. He aims at its reform . . . without endangering its foundation', writes one critic.[33] Later, in the 'Marxist-Lohiaite' debates that were to take place in the context of Karnataka's Dalit Sangarsh Samiti, Marxists accused the Lohiaites of ignoring the immediate exploiters of Dalit agricultural labourers in their policy of trying to have a 'Dalit–Sudra alliance' that included the dominant castes. It was also argued that the Lohiaites tended to fall into reformist illusions regarding electoral politics when those close to them came into power in Karnataka.[34]

To a large degree these accusations seem unfair. Lohia was redressing the Marxist neglect of caste by attempting to give a specific programme on caste issues, and by seeing the caste system (and gender relations) as a specific structure of oppression in Indian society. Lohia himself was perfectly aware that sections of 'shudras' were often the most brutal direct oppressors of the Dalits. At times he argued that such castes as the Nairs, Mudaliars (Vellalas), Reddis, Marathas, Lingayats and Vokkaligas were not actually 'shudras' but 'for all practical purposes equal to the Kshatriya–Vaishya of the North'.[35] He also argued for dealing with local exploiters even when they were part of a broader alliance of the oppressed:

The inequalities of exploitation are grossest in those lands where poverty is great . . . . There is little clamour or organization against the massive exploitation in local communities, against oppressive tyrannies of a local order arising out of mutual relationships among the local powerful and locally depressed. Such relationship as exists between the rack-renter and the shop-keeper, the moneylender and the artisan, the landowner and the agricultural labourer, the consumers and the government together with the stockists, the police must be fully and publicly exposed. Organizations must be formed and campaigns conducted with a view to reforming these relationships. More often than not, the exploited and exploiter in such relationships constitute the depressed part of humanity: they are both poor in the background of international or Euro-American living standards. Some have mistakenly thought that they should not raise local disputes for fear that these might divide the masses. The way to raise these vast masses consisting also of the petty exploiter to decent living standards is to bring local relationships into the open and to campaign and organize vigorously against local tyrannies and exploitation.[35]

This was a clear enough position and not so different from the classical Marxist argument for a 'united front' against a main enemy or Ambedkar's arguments for unity of workers, peasants, Dalits and Shudras against a 'Brahman–bourgeois' Congress. More to the point, the main thrust of Lohia's economic orientation was different in crucial ways from the traditional Marxist (and Ambedkarite!) position, drawing more on Gandhi, oriented to political decentralization, rejecting large-scale production and heavy industry, perceiving state bureaucracies as well as private capital as exploitative[36] Lohia argued, for perhaps the first time in India, that the conflict between the private sector and the public sector coincided with that between the 'bureaucratic high-caste' and the 'trading high-caste', i.e., between Brahmans and Vaishyas, and was thus only illusory and superficial; instead, a 'total rebellion is the only way out'.[37]

At certain points Lohia urged that the anti-caste cause be taken up through 'class organizations', with the Kisan Panchayat in particular playing a major role, arguing that the subordination of the peasant mass organization to the upper-caste party leadership blocked this.[38] In fact the major entry of 'Lohiaism' into Karnataka socio-political life seems to have taken place in the context of what some have called one of the few real peasant movements in recent decades, the 'Kadoga satyagraha' in Shimoga district.[39]

Shimoga, next to north and south Kanara, had one of the highest concentrations of big landholdings in Karnataka, and with leadership from socialists and some Congressmen a tenants' organization had been formed in the Malnad area in 1946 with a demand for 'two-thirds' share to the tenant. In 1948 a separate and somewhat more radical association was formed in Sagar taluk based on the backward caste Dewar tenants, and its struggle reached a climax in 1950–51 centring on Kadogu village. The movement won no dramatic victories (and also neglected the Scheduled Castes and agricultural wage issues), but the provision of *vethbegar* by backward caste tenants was halted, landlord–tenant relations were formalized, and by 1974 with the populist measures of Devraj Urs tenants did gain some access to land.[40] This struggle took place under the leadership of the Socialist Party; Lohia himself visited the district in 1950 and later wrote praising the courage and common sense of the poor peasant men and women in the struggle.[41]

'Lohiaism' did, then, have militancy. Nevertheless there were some clear ways in which his theoretical and practical positions could be called 'reformist'. In crucial ways he lacked the sharpness and revolutionary attitudes of both the Ambedkarites and the Marxists. With regard to caste and Hindu religion, his liberal attitude towards Hinduism reflected the 'Sanskritizing' north Indian traditions of protest rather than the militant anti-Hindu stance of such southern leaders as Phule, Periyar and Ambedkar. Symbolic was his call for temple-entry long after militant Dalits had rejected it. Lohia's eloquence on cultural issues often simply sought the liberal strand within Brahmanic–Hindu tradition, for instance in contrasting the orthodox 'Vaisishtha' tendency with the liberal 'Valmiki' tendency, in playing up Draupadi in contrast to Sita as the ideal Hindu woman but without dealing with the oppression suffered by either. Lohia's approach was based on the faith that 'Hinduism' could be purged of caste hierarchy and Brahmanism. In remaining within this framework, without a sharp critique of the limits of religious reform and in the context of focusing on reservations as a general anti-caste programme, it can be argued that the result was a general preservation of the caste equation, only in the more 'modern' form in which castes are transformed into interest groups and vote banks.

Similarly, Lohia lacked the Marxist sharpness on the issue of economic exploitation, the analysis of capital accumulation and the relations of production. He never stressed the linkage of caste and exploitation as such; he wrote instead of 'spiritual and moral decline', 'repression' and 'segregation'. This meant visualizing caste at an idealistic level, as a superstructural feature—which is how most Lohiaites in India continue to argue the issue. Similarly, whatever his innovative economic programme, the vision of decentralized village-oriented development was never translated into a path of struggle to achieve this; Lohia remained limited to parliamentary politics. And at this level, his antagonism to the Nehru model of heavy industrialization and planning got translated into a blanket 'anti-Congressism' centred around bringing all the opposition together in a 'Grand Alliance'. This theme has remained in the opposition to this day and by including such communal and Brahmanic forces as the Jan Sangh/Rashtriya Swayam Sevak Sangh/ Bharatiya Janata Party tradition it simply substitutes an unprincipled unity that makes more difficult the building of a true opposition growing on the basis of an alternative vision.

Lohiaism, then, did not come into Karnataka as an ideology of full-scale Dalit liberation but rather as a reformist trend which was in some ways compatible with the liberal co-optation patterns that had been established in the '*Ram-raj*' atmosphere of the state. Nevertheless, Ambedkar considered the socialist tradition that Lohia represented closer than almost any other political force, and it is arguable that many of Lohia's limitations were those of his time, when an anti-statist decentralized political economy had little material base to build itself as a force.

NOTES

1. Bjorne Hettne, *The Political Economy of Indirect Rule: Mysore, 1881–1947* (New Delhi: Ambika Publications, 1978), p. 302.
2. See M.N. Srinivas and M.N. Panini, 'Politics and Society in Karnataka', *Economic and Political Weekly*, 14 January 1984; Lalitha Nataraj and V.K. Nataraj, 'Limits of Populism: Devraj Urs and Karnataka Politics', *Economic and Political Weekly*, 11 September 1982; and James Manor, 'Pragmatic Progressives in Regional Politics: The Case of Devraj Urs', *Economic and Political Weekly*, Annual Number, February 1980.
3. A.C. Pradhan, *The Emergence of the Depressed Classes* (Delhi: Bookland International, 1986), p. 250.
4. On Jagjivan Ram's life see Prabhakar Maxwe, *Shri Jagjivanram: Vyakti and Vichar* ('Jagjivan Ram: Person and Thought') (Mumbai: Somayya Publications, n.d.).
5. Pradhan, *Emergence*, p. 240.
6. *Ibid.*, see also *Source Material on Dr. Babasaheb Ambedkar and the Movement of Untouchables*, Volume I (Bombay: Government of Maharashtra, 1982), pp. 101–08, 120–23.
7. Pradhan, *Emergence*, p. 243.
8. G.S. Malappa, *History of the Freedom Movement in Karnataka*, Volume II (Mysore: Government of Mysore, 1966).
9. Cited in Hettne, *Political Economy*, p. 187.
10. *Harijan*, 6 July 1936.

11. *Ibid.*, 4 January 1936.
12. See reports in *Harijan*, 13 May 1933 and *Proceedings of the Mysore Representative Assembly*, June 1933.
13. *Ibid.*
14. *Ibid.*, October 1933, p. 261.
15. *Harijan*, 6 July 1935.
16. *Ibid.*, 16 November 1935.
17. Edward Harper, 'Social Consequences of an Unsuccessful Low Caste Movement', in James Silverberg (ed.), *Social Mobility in the Caste System in India* (The Hague: Mouton, 1968), p. 56.
18. *Ibid.*, pp. 50, 57.
19. T.B. Bhosle, 'Ambedkar's Disciples in Mysore State', *Janata*, 11 December 1937.
20. See the papers given at the Seminar on Reservations, Karnataka Study Forum, 1982.
21. Cited in V.K. Nataraj, 'The Politics of Reservations', paper presented at Seminar on Reservations, Karnataka Study Forum, Mysore, 8–9 August 1982, pp. 4–5.
22. *Ibid.*, p. 5.
23. *Ibid.*, p. 9.
24. Ian Copland, 'Congress Paternalism: The "High Command" and the Struggle for Freedom in Princely India 1920–1949', in Jim Masselos (ed.), *Struggling and Ruling: The Indian National Congress* (New Delhi: Sterling Publishers Pvt. Ltd., 1987), pp. 121–40.
25. Hettne, *Political Economy*, pp. 196–98.
26. Copland, 'Congress Paternalism', pp. 130–31; Hettne, *Politial Economy*, p. 198.
27. Cited in Hettne, p. 110.
28. Rajni Kothari, *Politics in India* (New Delhi: Orient Longman, 1970), pp. 187, 318.
29. Ram Manohar Lohia, *The Caste System* (Hyderabad: Ram Manohar Lohia Samata Vidyalaya Nyas, 1979), p. 105.
30. *Ibid.*, pp. 113–14, 122–23.
31. *Ibid.*, pp. 7–8.
32. It would be interesting to investigate if there was any influence on Lohia of the Oudh Kisan Sabha led by Baba Ramachandra, which had by the mid-1930s (under the leadership of Ramachandra and his wife Jaggi) developed some fairly radical positions on women's issues, including calls for equality in the family and assertion of the legitimacy of all unions between men and women (which among the lower castes were frequently formed in violation of Brahmanic norms). See Kumar Kapil in Kum Kum Sangaria and Sudesh Vaid (eds.), *Recasting Women* (New Delhi: Kali for Women Press, 1988).
33. Ajit Roy, 'Caste and Class: An Interlinked View', *Economic and Political Weekly*, Annual Number, February 1979, p. 306.
34. Discussions with V. Laxminarayana, K. Shrikant and Dalit Sangarsh Samiti activists; any reading of the Marxist literature on the Kannada struggles during this period will make the point obvious.
35. Lohia, *Caste System*, p. 143.

36. *Ibid.*, pp. 24–25.
37. *Ibid.*, p. 112.
38. *Ibid.*, pp. 10–16.
39. Srinivas and Panini, 'Politics and Society in Karnataka,' p. 69.
40. M.V. Nadkarni, *Farmers' Movements in India* (Ahmedabad: Allied Publishers, 1987), pp. 19–22.
41. Lohia, *Caste System*, p. 12.

CHAPTER 9

Andhra and Hyderabad, 1930–46: Foundations of Turmoil

By the 1930s and 1940s, in spite of internal regional peculiarities, the Telugu-speaking areas can be analyzed as a unit. Developments in one region had their impact on another and many leaders exerted influence at the level of the linguistic region. A dynamism was driving the whole area forward.

Some all-India developments were finding a centre here. In the background of a strong peasant movement and developing resistance to the Nizam's autocracy, the radicalization of politics throughout the country took on a revolutionary thrust in Andhra. A Communist Party unit was set up here and it acquired a strong base among all sections of exploited rural toilers and went on to lead the largest peasant revolt in Indian history. At the same time, the communalization of Indian politics was seen in the hegemony of Hindu fundamentalism within the Congress-led nationalist movement in Hyderabad, polarized against Muslim fundamentalism which was providing the main base for the regime. Both the Telengana peasant revolt and Hyderabad Hindu–Muslim tension climaxed in the tumultuous events of the transition to independence. Finally, in spite of all this, the establishment of Congress hegemony became nearly complete: what is remarkable in its triumph over the communists is not the brutal suppression of the Telengana revolt but the fact that subsequently it was able to erode the party's greatest mass base in India,[1] while the ruthless takeover of 'Azad Hyderabad' coupled with a policy of some concessions to Muslims within the framework of a 'Hinduistic' Congress effectively kept Hindu–Muslim tension in the region at a low level after independence.

What role did the Dalits and the caste issue play in all of this? As we have seen, a vigorous autonomous Dalit movement had emerged in both coastal Andhra and Hyderabad during the 1920s. Dalits constituted an economically and socially radical and anti-fundamentalist force which resisted absorption into either a strong 'Hindu' or a strong 'Muslim' identification, agitating for rights to land and fair wages and, as such, feudalism and for combining the fight against social and economic oppression. Yet during the 1930s and 1940s we find them being pulled in various directions by the major forces in Telugu politics, either into the communist movement or into a pro-Hindu Congress or pro-Muslim politics of patronage, without being able to affect events very much. By the 1940s the 'Adi-Andhra' movement in the coastal districts had disappeared, its leading activists absorbed as either Congress or communist 'Harijans'. In Hyderabad, crucial sections of the factionalized, vociferous Dalit petty-bourgeoisie were pulled into pro-Hindu or pro-Muslim/pro-Nizam positions, overwhelmed by the promises of patronage on the one hand or the tides of nationalism on the other, each representing a social power base and accompanied with convincing ideological rhetoric. The sections who aligned themselves with Ambedkar tried to constitute a 'third force' but were unable to do so effectively; in Hyderabad during the 1940s both the rationalistic thrust and organizational incapacity of Ambedkar's all-India leadership becomes clear.

In the end, an Ambedkarite 'Dalit movement' had little impact. The common erosion of both Dalit and left politics in post-independence Andhra remains a crucial puzzle in the analysis of contemporary India, while the events of the last decade of colonial rule—the rising peasant movement of the 1930s, Telugu nationalism, the joining of the two in the Hyderabad armed revolt and its subsequent suppression—are central events of the transition to independence. This chapter will examine the background of these events from the perspective of the Dalit movement.

■ Coastal Andhra: Peasants and Communists

During the late 1920s a strong peasant movement arose in the coastal Andhra districts which by the 1930s became the centre of the region's politics. This region of Madras Presidency saw a tumultuous combination of a strong market-oriented peasant cultivation and the highest prevalence of the zamindari system in the face of the buffetings of the Depression and the apparent prosperity of the war years.[2] In caste terms the peasant movement was based primarily on the Kammas, who found themselves politically confronting a Brahman-controlled Congress and the landlords (often Velamas and Reddys) dominating the Justice Party. Some of the Kammas associated themselves with N.G. Ranga and later struggled for dominance in the Congress, while the more radical youth led in the formation of a Communist Party unit. Both sections fought it out in the late 1930s for control of the peasant movement, and competed to win over and organize agricultural labourers and Dalits.

The organized peasant movement dated from 1923 when Ranga, a Kamma of Guntur district, returned from England and formed a local Ryots Association after the 1920–21 upsurge in the region. The organization marked time during the dull decade of the 1920s, but in 1928—the same year as Bardoli put the cause of anti-revenue movements on the political map—the Andhra Provincial Ryots Association was founded at Guntur. It had a moderate programme of rural reconstruction, scientific agriculture, cooperation and organization on immediate economic issues.[3] But within a year a vigorous agitation against the government's proposed increase in revenue rates gave it a radical impetus, and by the second conference at Vijayawada, Ranga was putting forward the slogan of 'kisan raj' or 'ryot raj' ('peasant rule'). From 1930 demands were made for moratoriums on debt and rent arrears. About the same time a Zamindari Ryots Association (of tenants) formed in 1926 was taken over by new leadership associated with Ranga, and took a radical turn including a big struggle against the huge Venkatagiri Zamindari in Nellore district in 1931. The demand for abolition of zamindari began to be voiced.[4]

Ranga was jailed during these agitations, and after his release in 1934–35 began to move into the Congress, with the organizing of both peasants and Dalits. He founded the Peasants' Institute for training cadres at Nidubrolur in his home district of Guntur and began to tour the district with the slogan of 'kisan raj'.[5] During the same period a 'Harijan Seva Dal' was formed with the active support of his wife and both toured in Guntur and Krishna districts, launching a temple entry campaign in the village of Govada. Associated in this 'Harijan' work were other notable social reformers such as Unnava Lakshminarayan, author of *Mallepalle* and Guduru Ramchandra Rao, the Krishna district reformer who had inaugurated the first Adi-Andhra conference in 1917. The general secretary of the Andhra branch of the Harijan Sevak Sangh, M. Bapineedu, was also a colleague of Ranga.[6]

Along with this Ranga began pushing for an all-India peasant organization. This was at first opposed by the Bihar movement,[7] but it gained the support of the Congress Socialist Party, which was formed in January 1936 at Meerut by a group of young Congress leftists who, like Ranga, were concerned to carve out for themselves a unique identity and base within the Congress fold. Thus, an 'All-India Kisan Congress', with Ranga and Jayaprakash Narayan as joint convenors, and Swami Sahajanand presiding, was formed during the 1936 Lucknow session of the Indian National Congress. It had two main points of action: a demand for abolition of all systems of landlordism, and a demand for abolition of land revenue (to be placed by a graded income tax). A process of distancing from the Congress began with a change of name to 'All-India Kisan Sabha' and though the second session in Maharashtra in December 1936, with Ranga presiding, again coincided with the INC session, it was the last one to do so.[8]

When CPI organizing was initiated in Andhra in 1934 a struggle for dominance began in the Kisan Sabha and the Congress Socialist Party. The period between 1938 and 1942 saw intense factionalism among communists and non-communists in the Kisan Sabha. Ranga, a leader of the anti-communist faction, was a focus of this and in the fourth session of the Sabha at Gyay in 1939 his presidential address was not accepted, while a strong political resolution 're-flected the left ideology of the time' in stressing agrarian revolution

284 / Dalits and the Democratic Revolution

as central, the worker–peasant alliance, and the unity of the people against imperialism through the Congress.[9] Ranga describes fighting communist opposition to get the goal of fighting imperialist domination declared to be 'a democratic state of the Indian people leading ultimately to the realization of Kisan-Mazdur Raj'.[10] Intense factional struggles were going on in the Andhra Ryots Association also, and the communists succeeded in winning over a large percentage of the cadre coming out of Ranga's Peasant Institute.[11]

Yet, until Hitler's invasion of the Soviet Union in June 1941 led the Indian communists to offer support to the British regime in 'people's war' against fascism, there was little programmatic difference between the communists and their 'Ranga-ite' or socialist rivals. Much of what went on seems a war of slogans: Ranga initially talked of 'kisan raj', the communists pushed 'mazdur raj' and in response Ranga adopted 'kisan–mazdur raj'. But if the communists were making this a point of difference it was a bit puzzling, since Lenin himself had declared the Russian revolution to be the 'democratic dictatorship of the proletariat and the peasantry'. While claiming to possess a 'scientific' ideology, the CPI appeared to suffer from good deal of ideological confusion as it stubbornly resisted bringing the peasantry into the slogan.

What 'mazdur raj' or the 'dictatorship of the proletariat' in fact signified was a communist determination to keep control of mass organizations. The consequences of this were decisive when in 1942 a Central Kisan Council meeting attacked the biggest mass independence struggle, the Quit India movement, as 'acts of mob violence . . . sabotage, destruction etc.' which 'create conditions of anarchy and disruption which are being taken advantage of by the fifth column agents for their nefarious ends' and appealed to kisans and the people to turn aside from 'the path of sabotage and terrorist and destructive activities'.[12] Within a year not only had Ranga quit the Kisan Sabha but such other major independent peasant leaders as Indulal Yagnik and Swami Sahajanand had also become inactive. Hard mass organizing work won the communists control of the Sabha in Andhra and many other areas nationally, and in coastal Andhra they used the opportunity provided by the lifting of the British repressive machinery from 1943–44 to broaden their base impressively.

The Andhra communists were unique in India in being drawn from the main non-Brahman castes. Of their regional leadership,

P. Sundarayya, Ravi Narayan Reddy and Badam Yella Reddy were all Reddis (the latter two from Hyderabad state), while B. Basavapunniah, C. Rajeshwar Rao, C. Vasudev Rao and N. Prasad Rao were Kammas. (This Kamma–Reddi dominance lasted well into the post-independence period and included D.V. Rao, T. Nagi Reddy, Chandra Pully Reddy and Kondapalli Sitaramayya.) This origin has been criticized as leading to a '*kulak*'-oriented party with a tendency to compromise with rich peasant interests. A typical characterization is that by Dhanagare:

> The rich Kamma kulaks formed the class base of the Andhra Communist Party and provided the party with funds and workers . . . . The leading Communists of the Andhra delta and Telegana were well-to-do peasants and came either from the Kamma or the Reddy caste of peasant proprietors. It was therefore to the interests of the rich peasants who dominated the party that all other subordinate agrarian classes, such as the small holders (middle peasants) and tenants and sharecroppers (poor peasants), quite as much as the landless labourers, formed an alliance and launched a combined offensive against the handful of rich absentee landlords . . . .[13]

Although Dhanagare goes on to note that 'the power and dominance (of the big landlords) could not be threatened otherwise', this criticism is an example of an analysis whose most extreme form can be seen in the left critics of the Telengana movement such as Barry Pavier and Jacques Pouchedass who see the entire pre-independence peasant movement, with all its communist leadership, as sacrificing the interests of the rural poor to those of 'dominant caste rich peasants'.[14]

The approach raises many questions. First, it is unclear whether 'agrarian classes' can be so clearly demarcated; doing so has been most often a matter of dogma rather than empirical analysis. Second, characterizing caste-groups such as the Kammas and Reddis as 'peasant proprietors' also reflects a questionable absorption of caste into class; both groups included a large range, from poor peasants (and even labourers in the case of some of the coastal Kammas)[15] to landlords; most of the communist leaders did in fact come technically from landlord and not even 'rich peasant' families. If this class/caste origin conditioned their approach (which it undoubtedly did), even more severe questions could be raised about the Brahman origins of Indian communists in other states—and it leaves the question of how they could, if they did, continue to dominate a movement even when it recruited so many of a lower class/caste origin.[16]

More important is the question of whose interests were object-ively served at the time. While it was certainly in the interests of the rich peasants to form an 'alliance of all agrarian classes', *it was equally in the interests of the landless and poor peasants*. In fact, the '*kulak*'-dominated leadership of the Andhra peasant movement did more to organize agricultural labourers than anywhere else in the country. With the foundation of the Agricultural Labour Union in coastal Andhra it grew to a membership of 60,000 in 1945–46 compared to figures of 5,000 to 15,000 in other regions.[17] Local wage struggles began to be organized and many of these were quite militant. A study focusing on the east Godavari area shows a very militant line in the 1938–39 period, climaxing in a 15-day strike of 10,000 labourers in 13 villages, met by heavy state repress-ion and the jailing and killing of leaders. It was partly because of this that after the revival of the union in 1943 a strike for wages focused against the single biggest landlord in the village.[18] Hargopal, reporting on the study, considers this a retreat from militancy, but it is equally arguable that the more moderate movement of the later period was more effective in meeting the interests of the labourers.[19] There certainly were limitations in agricultural labourer organizing and perhaps even more in confronting the problems they faced as members of 'untouchable' castes, but it is hard to argue that these were due mainly to an alliance strategy.

There was also no clear difference between the communists (whether from '*kulaks*' or of other castes) and the non-communists on this issue. While Ranga is characterized as a typical 'rich peasant' leader (and later in life he turned to the pro-capitalist Swatantra party), still his efforts to draw agricultural labourers and Dalits into an alliance during the 1930s and 1940s were not so different from those of the communists. As he wrote,

The Peasants' Institute has been advocating, from its very in-ception, a harmonious comradeship between the peasants and workers on the land, based upon a mutually settled relationship between the prices of agricultural products and wages, both to be made dependent on decent and rising living standards of both peasants and workers. The Andhra Kisans have long ago realised the need for a common front to be put up by both the landed and landless kisans.[20]

Even stronger language about the need for an alliance was used by the Bihar leader Swami Sahajanand in 1938:

Of late, some people have begun a tirade against the Kisan Sabha in the name of agricultural labourers. According to them, kisans are exploiters. Their object is not so much to serve them as to flirt with zamindars who are the common enemy of both kisans and khet mazdurs. They should realize that the service of the khet mazdurs and friendship with the zamindars are contradictory . . . . The khet mazdurs are after all landless kisans. Those who had lands yesterday have none today, and those who have them today will lose them tomorrow, and thus, while possessed of lands, they are kisans, and deprived of them we call them khet mazdurs. But this process is progressively going on and there can be no strict line of demarcation between these two sections of kisans. Those who seek to draw one are the common enemies of both.[21]

This hard-hitting speech referred not to Trotskyites or other 'left' critics but to the Congress-sponsored activities of Jagjivan Ram. During the 1930s Ranga, Sahajanand, the communists—and Ambedkar—all called for an alliance between peasants and agricultural labourers. Arguments that this was mistaken or represent simply 'rich peasant' interests have the flavour of the academy about them.

Yet there is an interesting difference between the way Ranga and Sahajanand articulated the issue: while Sahajanand insisted on 'no strict line of demarcation' and distinguished his groups solely in terms of landholding, Ranga spoke of two clearly distinct sections which had common interests in the framework of a commercialized economy. The 'Bihar tradition' of rural organizing, up to the present, has been for radicals to include agricultural labourers along with the peasants in 'kisan sabhas' or 'kisan samitis' and speak of them as 'landless peasants'; while the 'Andhra tradition' was either to form separate agricultural labourer organizations or to speak clearly of 'kisan–mazdur' and 'ryot–coolie sangams'. This difference, it can be argued, reflected differences in commercialization and differing caste links with agrarian structure in the two regions. In Bihar there seems to have been more caste overlap, whereas in coastal Andhra the line between 'peasant' and 'agricultural labourer' coincided with the caste difference between the Kammas and the Madigas and Malas. Dalit militancy was intensifying the militancy of agricultural labourers, including the resistance to any form of bondage; Ranga, for instance, noted in one of his studies that

> In spite of such abnormal rise in their wages fewer and fewer Panchamas are anxious to become annual servants because their standard of comfort and their idea of self-respect have changed for the better in the last 50 years . . . . It is curious how these Panchamas prefer to live an independent day-labourer's life to that of an annual servant.[22]

However, none of the main 'peasant organizers', including the communists, *theoretically recognized* this role of caste. The issues of demands for wasteland (forest lands, government-owned lands, *perambok* lands in Andhra) were never given a special place in Kisan Sabha programmes, nor did the communists recognize the way in which *vethbegar* was articulated in terms of caste and represented the traditional feudal form of caste exploitation of labour. Yet both issues were coming up everywhere in the Dalit movement, and both issues were to become central in the Telengana revolt. The problem was that, regardless of how much they recognized the importance of or took up issues of 'social oppression', the left failed to deal with the economic articulation of caste.

■ DALITS IN COASTAL ANDHRA

Following two conferences in 1930, 'Adi-Andhra' organizing had come to a standstill for five years. The next initiative was that of the Gandhians: Congress 'Harijan' organizing began with the formation of the Andhra branch of the Harijan Seva Sangh at Vijayawada in November 1932. Two caste Hindu reformers,

K. Nageswara Rao of Krishna district and M. Bapineedu, were its president and general secretary respectively. Two Dalits, Vemula Kurmayya (Krishna district) and Narlachetty Devendrudu (West Godavari) were joint secretaries. Both had been active during the 1920s; Devendrudu had been chairman of the reception committee of the third Adi-Andhra conference and was later nominated to the Madras legislative council, while Kurmayya was chairman of the reception committee for the eighth conference at Vijayawada.[23]

Then Ambedkar's announcement of conversion from Hinduism in 1935 sparked another round of activity. Younger Dalits became energized, such as Eali Vedappalli (1911–71) of East Godavari, who organized a round of Adi-Andhra conferences in that district, and Geddada Brahmaiah (1912–50) who became secretary of an Adi-Andhra Sangham in 1935, organized a number of district conferences between 1938–1940 and edited an *Adi-Andhra Patrika*.[24] Another publication, *Jayabheri*, was started by the well-known writer Kusumu Dharmanna (1898–1948) of Rajamundry. This became a sort of mouthpiece for the Ambedkarite group. Dharmanna also presided over many Adi-Andhra conferences in his district, and had made use of the Dalit overseas connections, travelling to Rangoon to collect money for his weekly. He later became inclined towards Islam and established connections with B.S. Venkatrao in Hyderabad. He was known as a powerful poet, writer and speaker, with one of his poems, 'Nalladorathanamu' ('brown bureaucracy') becoming famous as a Dalit reply to a popular song, 'We don't want to be ruled by white people'; Dharmanna asserted, 'We don't want a country ruled by black lords'.[25]

State level 'Adi-Andhra' organizing was resumed. In 1935 the tenth conference was organized at Rajamundry, inaugurated by M.C. Rajah and with one of the older generation leaders, Kusuma Venkatramaiah (who had earlier been associated with the Ramachandra Rao sevashram) presiding. This was evidently anti-Ambedkarite in tone and very little of any consequence came from it. The eleventh conference was held in 1936 and then the twelfth and final conference at Tallaveru in East Godavari in 1938 saw a confrontation between the young radicals and the more established organizers. The organizers, in a period of reformist stress on temple-entry, wanted a resolution for this, but the youth, led by Pamu Ramamurthy of East Godavari district, opposed it as a concession to Hinduism. Bhagyareddy, the invitee president of the conference, supported this opposition in one of his last public acts. The final resolutions included demands for reserved seats for untouchables from the panchayat level to the legislative councils; enforcing sanctions against those opposing the presence of untouchable children in schools; job reservations; formation of labour cooperatives and credit banks, and the demand for forest/wastelands for Dalits. No mention was made of the agricultural wage issues coming up at the time.[26]

But this was the last of the 'Adi-Andhra' conferences. The largest section of Dalit leadership was getting absorbed into the Congress with its 'Harijan' terminology and its reiteration of a Hindu identity. The few who opposed this strongly such as Kusuma Dharmanna were discredited by their pro-Muslim stance. In many ways this reformist 'Hinduization' can be traced to the writings of Boyi Bhimanna, the young Dalit writer of East Godavari district who was described by some of the Congress Dalits as 'our guiding spirit'.[27]

Bhimanna's first published writings, around 1936, described the inhuman conditions of village life, 'highlighting the need for establishing a socialistic pattern of society'. Then *Paaleru* ('A Farm Boy') published in 1940, showed Dalit village struggles and sufferings at the hands of a landlord and unenlightened father; the way out is depicted as town-based education and service in the bureaucracy. *Kooli Raju*, written in 1941 and published in 1947, described the agricultural labourer movement in the villages, but had its resolution when a Dalit woman is elected as government head. Finally, *Raaga Vasishtam* (1940), described the marriage of Vasishta and Arundhati, emphasizing a 'strong casteless Hindu nation' and arguing that 'Harijans are Aryans'.[28] These writings depict the rural base of caste–class conflicts, but they show a Hindu incorporationism and a middle-class reformist solution. This also seems to have been accompanied by an anti-Muslim orientation.[29]

On the other hand, the militancy of lower-class Dalits was increasingly being expressed in communist agricultural labour organizing, in active struggles so patently lacking in the resolutions of the Adi-Andhra conferences. Many young Dalits joined the movement from the early 1940s, including Guntar Bapaiah, Prasad Rao, M. Sriramalu (all of Krishna district), Konar Rangarao, R.A. Kottaya, Kandhi Kaithaya Nagabhushama (of East Godavari),

K. Mohan Rao (East Godavari) and M. Svarnavamanaya.[30] Guntur Bapaiah became general secretary of the Agricultural Labourer Union (ALU) and K. Suryaprakash Rao became its president from 1941 to 1943. Even then the strong anti-Ambedkar stance of the communists aroused tensions. Suryaprakash Rao, for example, reports that his final alienation from the party came in 1944 when a resolution of the ALU described the Muslim League as a 'political party' but called the Scheduled Caste Federation a 'communal organization'. He opposed this and circulated a dissenting note emphasizing the economic and social degradation of Dalits and the need for unity of the toiling masses, arguing finally that social upliftment was even more important than economic upliftment. He finally left the organization.[31]

Although the communists initiated some anti-untouchability measures they provided no ideological alternative to the Congress in terms of absorbing Dalits into a Hinduistic reformism. Their universal acceptance of the term 'Harijan', in the face of the strong opposition to it not only from Ambedkar but also from organized Dalits everywhere, shows this. At an organizational level there was an unwillingness to accept any kind of Dalit autonomy; and at the level of culture and identity there was an inability to provide an alternative to the Brahmanic Hindu interpretation of Indian history.

Both Congress and communist opposition helped to create an anti-Ambedkarite atmosphere in the Andhra coastal districts. Ambedkar's preoccupation with Maharashtra organizing before 1942 and then his involvement in Delhi also meant that little effort was made, in spite of the promise of radicalism shown in Andhra. After a visit to the Krishna district on 30 September 1944, a branch of the Scheduled Caste Federation was formed under one Buldas Swamy, but it did not gain any strength. A local organizer, Ekambaran of Gudivada in Krishna district, recalls that Ambedkar's meetings put a major emphasis on self-respect, but that activities of the Federation were limited to fighting atrocities and celebrating Ambedkar *jayanti*.[32] In that period of turmoil, with an aroused mass of Dalits, this could not compete with the hard organizing and the real economic issues being taken up by the communists or the patronage and co-optation offered by the Congress. The independent Dalit movement of coastal Andhra faded away after the late 1940s.

■ HYDERABAD STATE: YEARS OF GROWING TENSION

The years after 1930 in Hyderabad state saw growing radicalism, partly diverted into Hindu–Muslim tension and partly expressed in a communist domination of the Andhra Mahasabha and intensive rural organizing. These two factors, along with the growing influence of Ambedkar, provided the context for Dalit organizing during the period.

Growing Hindu–Muslim tension was embodied in the dominance of the Arya Samaj over nationalist Hindus, and in the rise of the Majlis-i-Ittehad-ul Mussalman politicizing commoner Muslims against the more integrative but aristocratic 'mulki' Deccani ideology. With state support for full-time paid propagandists, the Majlis began a conversion campaign which focused to a large extent on the vulnerable untouchables. Along with the state's patronage and a mild amount of anti-*vethbegar* legislation, it provided a basis for Dalit attraction to a Muslim alliance.[33] The Arya Samaj responded with attempts to reconvert, and communal clashes began to occur.

In 1938–39 a major satyagraha campaign in Hyderabad was part of the rising national militancy, but took on a dangerous communal character. After 6,000 satyagrahis had been arrested, Gandhi himself called on the Hyderabad State Congress to call off the campaign. But the damage had been done; as Leonard notes, 'the 1938 satyagraha both demonstrated and solidified existing political divisions; it dealt a death blow to an indigenous, all-inclusive mulki movement.'[34] Anti-imperialism in Hyderabad, in other words, was being expressed as anti-Muslim. The Nizam regime announced constitutional reforms in July 1939 but there were no strong group of moderates to respond to a compromise.

While the Arya Samaj was rising within the Congress fold, communists were gaining dominance over the strongest of the linguistic–cultural organizations, the Andhra Mahasabha. Communist organizing in the state had begun only in 1938 when the newly formed unit of the CPI got in touch with members of progressive groups in Hyderabad, ranging from members of the Mahasabha and Maharashtra Parishad to the 'Comrades' Association' among progressive Muslims. In 1939 these groups converged into the Nizam State Communist Committee. The Andhra Mahasabha became the centre of activity, and communists found a base in the rural areas of Telengana where commercial agriculture was beginning to provide scope for a newly assertive peasantry.

Early campaigns focused on *vethbegar*; D.V. Rao, the leader of Nalgonda district (to become the most militant base of the Telengana revolt), noted that there had been spontaneous rebellions against the all-pervasive practice even before the 1930s, while the laws passed against it by the Nizam regime provided a new scope for organizing. The Mahasabha took up the campaign and in 15–20 villages throughout the district *vethbegar* imposed by officials came to a stop.[35] Opposition to land revenue was also taken up; interestingly, while landlords were in the forefront Rao claims that labourers were often the most militant, having an interest in it because they were themselves small landholders.[36] By and large, though, it seems that Dalits remained peripheral to much of Andhra Mahasabha organizing: However, as one study shows for a village in Bhongir taluk (a central area of Nalgonda), in cases where activists deliberately appealed to the Dalits there was relatively more participation.[37]

The growing radicalism was seen when the 1940 session of the Andhra Mahasabha voted to boycott the constitutional reforms and demanded full responsible government as well as the abolition of *vethbegar*, rack-renting, eviction of tenants, jagirdari and the tax on tapping of toddy trees and a reduction of taxes and rent. At the eighth conference in 1941 Ravi Narayan Reddy and Badam Yella Reddy, both active in the communist group, were elected president and vice-president of the Mahasabha. By the 1944 Bhongir session it was claimed that the organization had 100,000 members, and when over 8,000 were mobilized to attend the conference there was little the pro-Congress 'Gandhian' right wing could do but walk out. The communists had the organization as well as the rural districts of Telengana to themselves.

The communists in both Telengana and coastal Andhra have been criticized for their lack of political education, for their 'failure to create an alternative ideological hegemony.'[38] There were in fact popular plays such as *Ma Bhoomi* and a library movement that included translations of Lenin, Stalin and Gorky as well as *Mallepalle*.[39] But the use of *Mallepalle* and the fact that Ravi Narayan Reddy headed the Hyderabad branch of the Harijan Sevak Sangh indicates that communist appeals to Dalits did not transcend a caste Hindu 'progressiveness'. Similarly, the militancy of communists against the feudal autocracy only masked the fact that the

ALITS AND THE DEMOCRATIC REVOLUTION

'bourgeois' Congress was itself ready to move against it; its ability to do so, following independence, was undoubtedly a major factor in sapping communist strength. In other words the communists seemed to embody popular militancy more than direct it. As D.V. Rao's description of the process indicates,

> Ever since we started in 1941 . . . we were in the thick of the movement and had no time for education. Whatever programme we made was based on our experiences. We were operating in a fast-changing situation, running after the people. It was just physically impossible to have a proper educational plan.[40]

Dalits and women,[41] both major participants in the massive mobilizing that took place, were in many ways the major sufferers from this lack of education and creative ideology.

In Hyderabad city itself the communist leadership remained in the hands of progressive Muslims and high caste Hindus from the mixed Deccan cultural tradition of the city. At least a couple of these tried to maintain contacts with Dalits. Raj Bahadur Gaur, the CPI leader, wrote a letter to the *Deccan Chronicle* in 1945 supporting the SCF demand for separate village settlements, though opposing separate electorates.[42] Similarly, Dr. Jaisooriya, a later leader of the Peoples' Democratic Front (formed by the communists during their banned period to fight the 1952 elections) wrote in an article in 1945 that 15 years before he had formulated the economic and political programme for the Depressed Classes which Subbiah, the pro-Ambedkarite Dalit activist, was attempting to follow.[43] But there is no evidence that these initiatives had any support from the overall party group, and Gaur makes no mention of Dalits as a factor in his later recollections on the Telengana period—just as Venkatswamy's Dalit history ignores the communists.[44]

In the meantime, the Ambedkar's impact was being felt. Hyderabad's proximity to Bombay Presidency was a factor here. In a trip to Ellora in December 1934, for instance, Ambedkar and his colleagues found Muslim authorities refusing to give them water at Daulatabad.[45] During the early 1940s conferences on the Mahar *watan* issue were organized in border villages to attract Marathwada Dalits, most notably at Talavade of Sholapur district.[46] In December 1938 an 'Aurangabad District Dalit Conference' was held at Makranpur near Chalisgaon. Speaking at it, Ambedkar unleashed a heavy critique of Hyderabad state and its policies. Resolutions asked for *inam (watan)* lands to be given to Dalits, implementation of the laws abolishing *vethbegar*, and facilities for education.[47] Gradually, then, Hyderabad state Mahars were being drawn into the orbit of Ambedkar's organizing.

■ DALIT ORGANIZING IN HYDERABAD

Dalit activities in Hyderabad began to gain in momentum, if not depth, than before the radical 1930s. A host of young educated Malas, a few Madigas and some Marathi-speaking Mahar and Chambhar youth in Marathwada stood behind new leaders.

Most prominent among these, dominating the scene for two decades and sometimes known as the 'Hyderabadi Ambedkar', was B.S. Venkatrao (ca. 1890–1953), originally Bathula Ashaiah. Returning to Hyderabad in 1922 after working in the engineering department in Poona, he managed to parley a position as overseer in the public works department into a small personal fortune. He was described as a powerful and magnetic speaker, dominating the movement through his personality as well as financial sponsorship. Venkatswamy gives him a more favourable verdict than any other leader of the period:

> He sacrificed his all in the cause of the community and died a pauper. He was generous without calculations. He had a lovable individuality and a dynamic personality . . . . Who ever dreamt that Ashaiah, a bonny boy of Bangaru Basthi, would be the future 'Hope' of the community and that his juvenile corpulent body would be the dynamic personality to capture the hearts of the downtrodden, who spontaneously conferred on him the popular title of 'Rao Saheb'[48]

Slightly younger than Venkatrao was J. Subbiah who was to head the SCF and become 'Ambedkar's man' in Hyderabad. But Subbiah was the most unpopular of the group, described by Venkatswamy as dictatorial and opportunistic, wining and dining people like P.N. Rajbhoj (a 'whiskey and ice-cream' culture) to maintain his position as head of the SCF: 'By his deadly smiles, cruel kindness, obsequious courtesy and self-seeking and odious activities, through his faked-up organization, he earned the malediction of his community'.[49] Shyam Sunder (1908–73), on the other hand, the most openly pro-Muslim of the group, was praised by Venkatswamy: born in Aurangabad, he evidently sought to exemplify the syncretic aristocratic Hyderabadi culture, and though 'considered a nightmare by his Hindu opponents, he truly carved a soft corner in the hearts of the Depressed Classes by his organizing ability, lofty thoughts, magnificent courage, inexorable strength, polished manners and delicious humor'.[50]

Ambedkar's Depressed Classes Conference of 1930 and the events surrounding the Poona Pact made little impact on Dalits in Hyderabad; the Congress initiative with the Harijan Sevak Sangh was also of little consequence, though Thakkar Bapu visited Hyderabad in January 1933 to launch the state branch. Then came Ambedkar's decision to convert, described as a 'veritable bombshell' in stimulating massive discussions on conversion throughout the country. In the already conversion-tense atmosphere of Hyderabad it galvanized the Dalit community. Venkatrao, Arigay Ramaswamy and the entire youth group attended a Maharashtra Untouchable Youth Conference in January 1936 in Poona. Impressed by the 'fire-eating speeches of the Maharashtra leaders', they organized a Youth League of Ambedkarites with Venkatrao as president and Venkatswami, one of the educated youth, as secretary. Its aims were to organize youth; to support Ambedkar in leading untouchables out of the Hindu fold; to enlighten people on the evils of Hinduism; to oppose conversion at present but search for a new democratic religion; and to organize a vigorous campaign on socioeconomic disabilities. Bhagyareddy Varma supported the effort but without active participation.[51]

Now disputes focused on pro-Muslim versus 'Ambedkarite' responses to the declaration of leaving Hinduism. Quite expectedly Muslims used Ambedkar's announcement to step up pressure for conversion to Islam. Several Dalits became active, including Kusuma Dharmanna in the coastal regions and Peesari Veerani, a Hyderabad Mala who had confronted Gandhi himself in a 1935 visit and now became a propagandist for Islam under the name of P.V. Sardar Ali.[52] After the intensified Hindu–Muslim conflicts of the 1938–39 satyagraha, Venkatrao himself began to lean in a pro-Muslim direction. In 1938 he took the initiative of forming a

Hyderabad State Depressed Classes Association (DCA), known in Urdu as 'Pashta Qaum'. In contrast to the Youth League this was politically oriented to the Nizam's regime, and in May 1939 sent a memorandum to the Nizam's Executive Council demanding separate electorates.[53]

Then the announcement of constitutional reforms in July polarized Dalit opinion. Initially most of the young radicals were associated with the DCA, including Subbiah, Venkatswamy and others. But resistance to Venkatrao's line developed and an open fight between Subbiah and Venkatrao in January 1940, in which Subbiah slapped Venkatrao, split the organization. Charging that Venkatrao was aiding Kusuma Dharmanna in propagating Islam, the youth group then joined Arigay Ramaswamy in reviving the Hyderabad State Adi-Hindu Mahasabha. Only Shyam Sunder, then president of a DCA-linked Student's Union, stayed with Venkatrao.

The split lasted until 1942 when all factions went to Nagpur to attend the founding meeting of the Scheduled Caste Federation on 18–20 July 1942. They appealed to Ambedkar, who counselled compromise. When Venkatrao, who up to that time had been described in glowing terms in *Janata*,[54] refused to come around, Ambedkar advised the others to organize as the Scheduled Caste Federation but without official affiliation to the all-India body. On their return, a general body meeting of the Adi-Hindu Mahasabha voted the change of name to the Scheduled Caste Federation, denounced the conversion to Islam, and adopted the Nagpur resolutions. Subbiah was chosen as president, Venkatswamy as general secretary.[55] Now the DCA and SCF were contesting for hegemony in the Dalit community of Hyderabad state.

Some rural influence of both sections is discernible from the beginning, though documentation remains incomplete. For example, Sukam Achalu in Nalgonda and Butti Rajaram in Karimnagar apparently did some rural organizing for the SCF, to the point that when Achalu was denied an SCF ticket for the 1952 elections and stood instead on behalf of the People's Democratic Front, he was elected with the highest majority in India.[56] Butti Rajaram was said to be a cousin of a member of the Hyderabad group, Prem Kumar, and was a constable who became a fruit contractor and built a good base for the SCF in Karimnagar district.[57]

The leaders in Hyderabad were Mala, but it is striking that

Venkatrao's DCA, rather than the pro-Ambedkarite SCF, seemed to be more influential in the Marathwada region. Most educated, young Marathi-speaking Dalits were with the DCA, including Sopanrao Dhanve (of Latur), Ganpatrao Waghmare (a Chambhar of Parbhani), Govindrao Gaikwad (of Aurangabad), Hanmanthrao More (Nanded) and Madhavrao Nirlikar (Parbhani).[58] Both the DCA and SCF were using Ambedkar's name in the Marathwada region, but the DCA's pro-Muslim orientation and propaganda gained sustenance from the fact that the Nizam was actually implementing some reforms, including granting wastelands to Dalits, while the communists were absent from the area and the Congressites (organized in the Maharashtra Parishad) were doing nothing to take up the economic or social issues of rural Dalits but were instead emerging as a 'Hinduistic' organization based almost exclusively among the middle-caste peasantry and upper castes. The land given to Dalits by the Nizam, in fact, became a major source of conflict in Marathwada after the Congress takeover, when caste Hindu 'Congress leaders' sought to snatch it back and Dalits who resisted were made objects of attack.

Hyderabad Dalits now became a bit vocal on economic issues. The various organizations all included the issue of *vethbegar* in their programmes; Tamil 'Adi-Dravidians' in Hyderabad city began to organize on the issue of employment; while at least one Mala, Pittela Laxminarayana, a mechanic in the Lallaguda Railway workshop, became an activist in the labour union.[59] A 1945 booklet by P. Venkatswamy, *The Voice of the Downtrodden*, expressed the mood in its conclusion:

Our vital interests are one with the downtrodden masses of India, irrespective of caste and creed . . . . In the countries where political democracy is established it has not enabled the masses to free themselves from exploitation, unemployment, hunger and slavery. Political democracy is incomplete without economic democracy . . . . Just as the British Indian masses will never escape from the indigenous system of exploitation we also have to remain as the bondslaves of the capitalists and landlords of the State . . . . Formal changes in political institutions will do no good to the starving masses unless far-reaching and collosal changes are incorporated in the economic structure of society.[60]

NOTES

1. In terms of popular votes for assembly seats in Andhra, the communists won 22.0 per cent of the vote in 1951–52, 29.6 per cent in 1954–57, and then there was a steady decline to 19.53 per cent in 1962, 15.30 per cent for the two parties in 1967 (CPI, 7.52 per cent and CPM 7.78 per cent), 9.16 per cent in 1972 (CPI, 5.98 per cent, and CPM 3.18 per cent) and 4.8 per cent in 1978 (CPI, 2.4 per cent and CPM 2.4 per cent). The various socialist parties sank even more, from 18.32 per cent in 1951–52 to 0.43 per cent in 1972. The decline of the communist electoral hold in Andhra contrasts with its steady growth in the states of West Bengal and Kerala. See Tables I and II in G. Ram Reddy and B.A.V. Sharma (eds.), *State Government and Politics: Andhra Pradesh* (New Delhi: Sterling Publishers, 1979). Of course, the rise of a lower caste and Dalit-based Naxalite movement in Andhra during the 1980s contrasts with this previous electoral decline.

2. For an overview see Christopher John Baker, *The Politics of South India, 1920–1937* (New Delhi: Vikas, 1976); and Carolyn M. Elliot, 'Caste and Faction among the Dominant Caste: The Reddis and Kammas of Andhra', in Rajni Kothari (ed.), *Caste in Indian Politics* (New Delhi: Orient Longman Ltd., 1970). It can be noted that Elliot's analysis includes 'Kapus' along with 'Reddis'; recently they have sharply begun to differentiate themselves as a 'backward' caste, engaging in protest and rioting against the 'dominant' Kammas.

3. N.G. Ranga, *Revolutionary Peasants* (New Delhi: Amrit Book Co., 1949), p. 61.

4. Baker, *South India*, pp. 131–37, 200–11; Ranga, *Revolutionary Peasants*, p. 63.

5. Baker, *South India*, pp. 261–65; Ranga, *Revolutionary Peasants*, p. 75.

6. N.G. Ranga, 'Reminiscences on Harijan Welfare', *Andhra Pradesh State Harijan Conference Souvenir* (Hyderabad, 1976, pp. 23–26.

7. Ranga, *Revolutionary Peasants*, p. 69; Ranga also claims that the communists and socialists were opposing it but he could convince the CSP to cooperate.

8. M.A. Rasul, *A History of the All-India Kisan Sabha* (Calcutta: National Book Agency, 1974), pp. 3–11.

9. Rasul, *Kisan Sabha*, p. 51.

10. *Ibid.*, p. 55; Ranga, *Revolutionary Peasants*, p. 71.

11. Ranga, *Revolutionary Peasants*, p. 76, estimating that 'nearly 30 per cent of our own graduates and 90 per cent of the erstwhile CSP Andhra youth' were won over by the Communists.'

12. Rasul, *Kisan Sabha*, p. 89.

13. D.N. Dhanagare, 'Social Origins of the Telengana Insurrection (1946–1951)', *Contributions to Indian Sociology*, 8, 1974, pp. 117, 127.

14. Barry Pavier, 'The Telengana Armed Struggle', *Economic and Political Weekly*, August 1974 and *The Telengana Movement, 1944–51* (Delhi: Vikas, 1981), reviewed by D.N. Dhanagare, *Economic and Political Weekly*, 18 December 1982, and reply by Pavier, 'Once More on Telengana', *Economic and Political*

Weekly, 5 March 1983; and Jacques Pouchedass, 'Peasant Classes in Twentieth Century Agrarian Movements in India', in Eric Hobsbawm (ed.), *Peasants
in History: Essays in Honour of Daniel Thorner* (Delhi: Oxford University
Press, 1980).

15. N.G. Ranga, *Economic Organisation of Indian Villages*, Volume II (Bombay:
Taraporevala and Sons, 1929) gives a survey of three villages in the dry areas of
Guntur district which showed 200 Kammas (both men and women) supplementing their livelihood by working as day labourers, and 60 Kammas employed as
annual servants.

16. Akhil Gupta, 'Revolution in Telengana, 1946–1951 (Part One and Two)',
South Asia Bulletin, 4, 1–2, spring-fall 1984.

17. P. Sundarayya, *Telengana People's Struggle and Its Lessons* (Calcutta, Dessay
Chabha for the CPM, 1972), p. 145, gives a figure of 175,000 members of the
Andhra Provincial Kisan Sabha for the same year.

18. G. Hargopal, Caste–Class Dimensions of Dalit Consciousness: The Case of
Delta Andhra', Paper presented at the TDSS Seminar on State-Specific Caste-
Class Situation, Lonavala, 27–29 December 1987; citing a study by G. Partha-
sarathy and K.V. Ramana, 'Peasant Organisations in Razole', pp. 5–7.

19. *Ibid.*, Many social scientists today argue for an association of 'militancy' and
'violence' with a poor-peasant low-caste base and moderation with a middle
caste-middle peasant base. (See for instance David Hardiman, 'Politicization
and Agitation Among Dominant Peasants in Early Twentieth Century India',
Economic and Political Weekly, 28 Febraury 1976). There are some at least
methodological questions about this assumption. It often confuses 'violence'
with 'militancy' and classifies under 'violence' everything from physical attacks
on 'class enemies' to looting of grain and destruction of property. More
important, it begs the question of strategy—as if the rural poor do not also
need strategic thinking and very often act in terms of it (i.e., on those occasions
when the rural poor refrain from violence or militancy, they tend to be seen as
caught in the grip of 'tradition' and not as taking 'strategic' action).

20. Ranga, *Revolutionary Peasants*, p. 89.

21. In Rasul, *Kisan Sabha*, p. 29. The CPI-led Kisan Sabha position, as articulated
in 1953, was 'While thus intensifying the organizational work of the Kisan
Sabha itself, the Sabha has to pay its utmost attention to help in the formation
of independent agricultural labourer organizations wherever these organizations are necessary for the protection and safeguarding of the interests of
agricultural labourers and other rural labourers. In those places where these
organizations do not exist, the agricultural and rural labourers should be drawn
into the Kisan Sabha itself . . . . Whether the agricultural labourers are drawn
into the Kisan Sabha itself, or helped to form their own independent organization, the Kisan Sabha has to make it one of its foremost tasks to take upon
itself the defence of the interests of these sections of the rural poor. For, it is
only by uniting the entire rural populace in a strong, well-knit united front that
the Kisan Sabha can secure its basic objects of abolition of landlordism without
compensation and the free distribution of landlord's land among agricultural
labourers and poor peasants' (*Ibid.*, p. 318).

22. Ranga, *Economic Organization of Indian Villages*, p. 170. In contrast it seems
that Kammas were willing to become annual servants for other Kamma households; here the 'patronage' quality of the relationship was clearly different.

23. M.B. Gautam, 'The Untouchables' Movement in Andhra Pradesh', *Harijan Conference Souvenir* (Hyderabad, 10–12 April 1976), pp. 71–72; Boyi Bhimanna, interview, 23 June 1988.
24. Gautam, 'The Untouchables' Movement', pp. 70–71; B.J. Raju, 'The Champions of the Downtrodden in Andhra Pradesh', *Ibid.*, pp. 99–101.
25. *Ibid.*, pp. 99–100; Boyi Bhimanna, interview, P.R. Venkatswamy, *Our Struggle for Emancipation* (Secunderabad: Universal Art Printers, 1955), Volume I, pp. 178, 200.
26. Gautam, 'The Untouchables' Movement', p. 71.
27. Jagambar Jaganathan, interview, 24 June 1988; Boyi Bhimanna, interview.
28. Report on the Published Works of Boyi Bhimanna (pamphlet, n.d.), pp. 2–6.
29. Boyi Bhimanna, interview.
30. Ekambaran and K. Suryaprakash Rao, interviews taken by Surendra Jondhale, 16 June 1989.
31. *Ibid.*
32. Interview by Surendra Jondhale with Ekambaran, 3 August 1990.
33. Gupta, 'Revolution in Telengana', Part I, p. 10; see also Karen Leonard, 'Aspects of the Nationalist Movement in the Princely States of India', *The Quarterly Review of Historical Studies*, XXI, 1981–82 and 'Hyderabad: The Mulki–non-Mulki Conflict', in Robin Jeffry (ed.), *People, Princes and Paramount Power: Society and Politics in the Indian Princely States* (Delhi: Oxford University Press, 1978).
34. Leonard, 'The Mulki–non-Mulki Conflict', p. 95.
35. D.V. Rao, interview with Peter Custers.
36. *Ibid.*
37. K. Srinivasalu, 'Telengana Peasant Movement and Changes in the Agrarian Structure: A Case Study of Nalgonda District', Ph.D. dissertation, Jawaharlal Nehru University, School of Social Sciences, 1988, p. 105.
38. Gupta, 'Revolution in Telengana', Part I, pp. 13–15.
39. This is stressed by Srinivasalu, 'Telengana Peasant Movement', p. 287ff.; on Andhra see Hargopal, 'Caste–Class Dimensions of Dalit Consciousness', pp. 6–7.
40. D.V. Rao, interview.
41. For an important study of women's involvement stressing their own perception of the experience see Stree Shakti Sanghatana, *'We Were Making History': Women in the Telengana Movement* (New Delhi: Kali for Women Press, 1989).
42. Venkatswamy, *Our Struggle for Emancipation* Volume I, p. 286.
43. *Ibid.*, Volume II, p. 551.
44. Raj Bahadur Gour, 'Hyderabad People's Revolt Against Nizam's Autocracy', in Gour, *et al.*, *Glorious Telengana Armed Struggle* (New Delhi: New Age Printing Press, 1973) mentions Subbiah only once and then in passing, p. 86.
45. See reports in *Janata*, 1 March 1941 and 8 March 1941.
46. S.S. Narvade, *Dr. Babasaheb Ambedkar ani Hyderabad Sansthan* (Marathi) (Pune: Sugawa Prakashan, 1988), p. 23.
47. Reported in Bombay Secret Abstract for 14 January 1939, in *Sources*, Volume I, p. 185.
48. Venkatswamy, *Our Struggle for Emancipation*, Volume II, p. 658; see also interview, J. Jaganathan, 24 June 1988.
49. Venkatswamy, *Our Struggle for Emancipation*, Volume II, p. 661.

50. *Ibid.*, Volume II, p. 654.
51. *Ibid.*, Volume I, pp. 80–101.
52. *Ibid.*, Volume I, p. 64, 130.
53. *Ibid.*, Volume I, pp. 184–97.
54. *Janata*, 24 April 1937.
55. Venkatswamy, *Our Struggle for Emancipation*, Volume I, p. 250.
56. *Ibid.*, II, p. 644.
57. *Ibid.*, II, p. 522; Venkatswamy's work generally has an anti-Ambedkar and anti-SCF tone and so may not cover its activities fully.
58. *Ibid.*, I, p. 263.
59. *Ibid.*, II, p. 450.
60. *Ibid.*, II, pp. 336–37.

CHAPTER 10

Hyderabad and Andhra, 1946–56: Revolution, Repression and Recuperation

■ DALIT AND COMMUNIST LEADERS, 1946–52

The feudal autocracy of Hyderabad faced the imminent prospect of British withdrawal with the unrealistic hope of proclaiming itself an independent nation. It sought to lay the ground for this by declaring elections for December 1946 under a system that gave 50 per cent Hindu/Muslim representation based on 'interest groups' rather than territorial constituencies. There was increasing polarization and at points near-chaos in the state, with the growing fundamentalist power of the Razakars coming to replace the state itself and the communists taking advantage of this to build up rural centres of near-autonomous power, particularly in Nalgonda and Warangal districts. In this uncertain context, Dalits themselves were hopelessly divided and confused.

There were by this time six identifiable Dalit organizations. The biggest groups were still the SCF led by Subbiah and the DCA led by Venkatrao. The DCA accepted the reforms, the SCF along with the Congress and the communists rejected them. Besides these, objecting to the 'domineering' tendencies of both Subbiah and Venkatrao, P. Venkatswamy and Shyam Sunder came together in an Independent Scheduled Caste Federation which proposed a 'conditional acceptance' of the reform. In addition, the Adi-Hindu Social Service League, a pale remnant of Bhagyareddy's organization run by his son Gautam, also rejected the reforms, as did the Dalits grouped around Arigay Ramaswamy and working in the Congress, while an Arundatiya Matunga Mahasabha, based on the Madigas, pushed for separate electorates and a conditional acceptance.[1] In the actual elections Venkataro and Shyam Sunder were both elected, while five people from a list submitted by Venkatrao were later made nominated members.

More confusion followed. In February 1947 the British announced the transfer of power, with the princely states given the option of joining the newly independent states of India or Pakistan or remaining independent. On 11 June 1947, Hyderabad issued a declaration of independence. This set off increased factionalism and ferment among both Dalits and communists, at the local as well as national scale.

Ambedkar's reaction was immediate: he denounced the Hyderabad declaration and a concurrent announcement by Travancore state as creating 'a new problem which may turn out to be worse than the Hindu–Muslim problem as it is sure to result in the further Balkanisation of India.'[2] But there was divided opinion on this issue within the SCF leadership in the country.

Ambedkar himself, throughout the 1940s, had been concerned about finding a solution to the 'communal' problem by assuring Muslims of sufficient representation through separate electorates.[3] At points a political alliance was made, for example in joining Jinnah and the Muslim League to celebrate 1 October 1940 as 'Deliverance Day' because Congress ministries resigned.[4] But the final declaration of independence and partition led him to decisively throw his lot with the Congress. This was based on his preference for a strong and centralized state and conviction that the extreme 'federation' required to keep the Muslims within the same country would be harmful for Independent India.[5] By 1947 he was reportedly making a decision to negotiate with the Congress.[6] The opposite line was taken by other national leaders, in particular J.N. Mandal of Bengal and Shivraj of Madras. Shivraj perhaps was influenced by the Tamil tradition of a claim to autonomy (in a period during which the Dravidian movement was emerging to demand 'Dravidastan' along with 'Hindustan' and 'Pakistan' and the Muslims were showing signs of recognizing this claim).[7] Mandal was working in the context of West Bengal where a Dalit–Muslim alliance offered a base for a non-Congress political force. The fact that in October 1946 the Muslim League had given one of their allotted quota of seats to Mandal was taken as a proof of goodwill and used by the pro-Muslim Dalits of Hyderabad to show the advantages of such an alliance.[8]

Thus in Hyderabad Venkatrao and Shyam Sunder crystallized their pro-Muslim position. At a June conference in Salour, Aurangabad, they called on Dalits to 'declare an open revolt against caste Hindus' and to 'strengthen the hands of the Muslims of Hyderabad for maintaining political power.'[9] Subbiah himself showed tendencies to compromise with a pro-independence position but after Ambedkar's strong statement of June, he kept silent.[10]

The stance of the DCA leaders was bringing them closer not simply to the regime but to the militant and semi-fascistic power represented by the Razakars, the private armed force organized by the Nanded lawyer, Qasim Razvi. When Hyderabad independence day celebrations were held, these included a public meeting near the residence of Venkatrao in which Razvi and other Muslim leaders were speakers along with Shyam Sunder, while Razakars in white uniforms and armed with spears guarded the crowd. Few Dalits were present at the meeting, according to Venkatswamy, and many of those that were, especially the women, were sullen and abusive.[11] However, lack of mass support did not prevent the two leaders from making strong statements. Speaking from the platform of the Ittehad and appealing to the 'Deccani' tradition, Shyam Sunder claimed,

> Here in Hyderabad we are all living under a benign ruler who is not a foreigner but is one among us. We have our own culture, heritage and tradition. We have been living in this land of Deccan . . . and as the political consciousness increased and as our community reacted to the increasing economic standard it began to assert itself in the body politic . . . . We would rather

fight with the Government and gain our concessions and legitimate rights than to play into the hands of the caste Hindus to be
a pawn in the political chess . . . . It is a well-known fact that
the Muslims do not treat the Depressed Classes in the way in
which the Hindus are doing. As they believe in equality and
justice both by religion and faith, naturally the Depressed Classes
feel more at home with them than with the chauvinistic, class
conscious and highly individualistic Hindus.[12]

And Venkatrao:

I am certain that the Depressed Classes, Muslims, Christians
and the vast bulk of Hindus . . . will rally around the throne of
Hyderabad and prove before the world that Hyderabadis are
prepared to lay down even their lives to maintain their independence and their own cosmopolitan Hyderabad culture and
expression of lasting harmony between the different races and
creeds who have flourished here happily for ages together.[13]

In contrast in Ambedkar's denunciation of the tyranny of the
Nizam, of Razakar atrocities and of forcible conversions to Islam
was a clarion call for freedom:

The Scheduled Castes of Hyderabad should under no circumstances side with the Nizam and the Ittehad-ul-Muslimeen.
Whatever the tyranny and oppression which the Hindus practice
upon us, it must not warp our vision and swerve us from our
duty. The Scheduled Castes need freedom, and their whole
movement has been one of freedom. That being so, they cannot
support the Nizam.[14]

He then called on Dalits both in Hyderabad and Pakistan to
migrate to India.

However, Ambedkarites in Hyderabad state were too weak
organizationally and politically to articulate their position, let alone
implement it. Venkatrao and Shyam Sunder were using the opportunities facing them to make mass contacts, often provocative: on
6 June 1948, for instance, Shyam Sunder organized a 'separate
electorate day' in which activists sent to the rural districts told the
landless Dalits that land would be distributed to them by state

officials.[15] Venkatrao in turn was accused of touring Bidar district and inciting Dalits there to 'loot, kill and forcibly occupy the lands of Brahmans, Lingayats and Banias.[16] During the same period Venkatrao, who had been given a position as minister of education in the regime of 'Azad Hyderabad', was using it to maximize his base and the government cooperated with him to the extent of approving his amendment to a proposed education bill for Dalits to create a 'one-crore fund'.[17] All this time the Ambedkarites and the pro-Congress Dalits in Hyderabad city were barred to their homes by fear of Razakar tyranny on the streets.

But if the Dalit leadership was divided and confused, this was equally true of the local and national communist leadership, whatever their claims to a 'scientific' Marxism–Leninism. The Andhra CPI compromised with pro-Muslim elements by declaring the Ittehad to be a 'people's organization' and offering it 50 per cent of the seats in a proposed constituent assembly.[18] The Hyderabad city committee even supported the demand for 'Azad Hyderabad' and while they were overruled by the Andhra state committee, they succeeded in having the ban on communists temporarily removed in May 1948.[19] This of course was after a period during which the all-India communist leaders had been treating the Muslim League and the Congress on par as representing anti-imperialist forces among Muslims and Hindus respectively.

The twists and turns in the all-India leadership must have been extremely misleading to the Andhra communists. There was a tendency to assess the transition to independence in terms of abstractions and a kind of revolutionary romanticism. If Ambedkar showed a negative pragmatic realism in treating independence as inevitable and focusing his political efforts on making concrete gains for Dalits within the bourgeois regime-to-come, communists took to the opposite extreme. In the 1948 second party congress, P.C. Joshi's 'reformist' leadership was replaced by B.T. Ranadive, who gave a call for an all-out insurrection on the thesis that there was now an 'intertwining of the two stages of revolution' with the national bourgeoisie and rich peasants going over to the side of the ruling class. Turmoil on an international scale and the rising tempo of liberation movements in China and southeast Asia may have fostered this mood of revolutionary optimism, but the forced uprisings ordered throughout India by Ranadive had disastrous results, with innumerable communists jailed or killed and with complete chaos overtaking the party and its organizations. From May 1948 the Andhra communist leadership began putting forward a 'Maoist' line of united front, two-stage revolution and national liberation struggle, but this also took on rather fantastic overtones when Telengana was characterized as the 'Yenan of India', a base for launching an assault on power in the entire country, and it was held that

> Armed guerrilla resistance had to be developed in several parts of the country and these areas were to be converted into liberated areas with their own armed forces and state apparatus; later, towns were to be liberated by the armed forces from the liberated areas.[20]

Telengana was already a myth-in-the-making; its prestige made C. Rajeshwar Rao the party secretary-general in May-June 1950. He continued as such only till May 1951 as the 'right' party group of S.A. Dange, Ajoy Ghosh and S.V. Ghate began organizing against him and by May 1951 Ajoy Ghosh had replaced him and the central committee had decided to officially call off the Telengana struggle.[21] In the four climatic years of the transition to independence there were thus three changes of CPI leadership and accompanying reversals of political line, and it was only a visit to Moscow and the intervention of Stalin himself that could create a consensus in the party that the path of the Indian revolution would be 'neither the Russian path nor the Chinese path'. Even this document, however, still did not recognize that conditions in India during the 1940s were radically different from those existing either in Russia in 1917 or in China during the 1920s and 1930s.

In a sense, then, as far as a politically and organizationally effective all–India guidance was concerned, both the Dalits and the communists in Andhra were on their own.

■ THE TELENGANA PEASANT REVOLT

While confusion in the all-India leadership may have left the Andhra communists at sea, local administrative confusion made the Telengana revolt possible. In a situation described as that of 'political instability and near anarchy',[22] Hyderabad in 1948 saw the Razakars gaining 100,000 members by August and the Nizam regime left without the will or capacity to control them. Venkatswamy wrote,

> Day by day the normal life of the State was deteriorating. The Razakars were playing havoc everywhere: loot, plunder, arson and maltreatment of women was the order of the day. The tales of their ravages and cruelties were pouring into the city from hundreds of villages all over the state. People were fleeing in every direction, shelterless and helpless.[23]

But this signalled the final crisis of the regime, and the 'near anarchy' gave the communists opportunity to seize power in the Telugu-speaking rural areas. There was a semi-spontaneous party-led insurrection in most parts of Nalgonda, Warangal and Khammam districts; a parallel administration (described as a 'gram raj' in the vernacular and as 'village soviets' by the communists) was set up in nearly 4,000 villages. This was backed up by a thin line of armed forces: by April 1948 the party could organize six 'area squads' of 20 fighters each and 50–60 'village squads'; by the end of August it was claimed that about 10,000 peasants, students and party workers were actively participating in village squads and some 2,000 in mobile guerrilla units. Acquiring arms remained a major problem.[24]

In the 'agrarian revolution' that was central to this, the thrust was directed against the biggest landlords, while the party sought also to represent the interests of the poor and landless. One million acres of land were said to have been seized and redistributed. The first land to be taken, and nearly one-tenth the total, was government-held forest and wasteland. After this, surplus lands were seized, in a process in which the ceiling allowed by the party was first fixed at 500 acres dry land and 50 acres wet land; a lower ceiling was enforced against pro-Nizam landlords.[25] Later, though mainly in Nalgonda district, the land ceiling was lowered to 200 dry and 20 wet, and then to 100 dry and 10 wet.[26]

Such relatively high land ceilings and the continual process of compromise evoked the left criticism that the party was representing a 'rich peasant' interest. But, given the strategic needs of seizing power, in a situation in which the party had been working in most of the villages for only around five years, it is hard to know how some such broad alliance could have been avoided. There is no evidence to show that a firm 'poor peasant' policy could have won enough mass and militant support to sustain a movement that attacked not only landlords and the Nizam regime but village leaders as well, and would have to defend itself against an well armed and trained professional army.

Some of the dilemmas inherent in rousing the poor and landless, especially Dalits, for land struggles in the period of the Telengana revolt are brought out in a recent dissertation by K. Srinivasalu. This examines the actual process of land control and struggle in three villages in various taluks of Nalgonda district, the strongest centre of revolt, in an effort to provide 'documentation from below' of the struggle and to analyze the 'interface of caste and class'.[27] As the only study investigating actual socio-economic conditions and processes of organizing at the ground level, it is an important mirror to the proliferating macro studies and contentious generalizations about the Telengana revolt.

Srinivasalu discusses several important points. While there was enthusiastic response everywhere to the call to occupy common lands and wastelands, the response to the challenge of occupying surplus land of landlords was 'lackadaisical', in spite of the notoriety of these landlords.[28] Srinivasalu explains this by noting that because the common lands were considered to belong 'to all' they were open to redistribution, while Dalits and other landless were reluctant to challenge the 'ownership' claims of the rich. An additional factor may well have been that, as in so many other cases of efforts to give 'land to the landless', the surplus lands of big landlords are rarely vacant but given out to tenants who in many cases are middle-caste peasants; for the Dalit landless to claim such lands would provoke a larger-scale conflict. Confronting a numerically tiny landlord minority or a distant state is a different matter from confronting a large peasant caste-community itself rooted in the land and including many poor.[29] Dalits were understandably apprehensive about the situation. All admit that after the revolt the only distributed lands that could actually be kept were the government forest and wastelands, though in some cases landlords sold much of their surplus acreage, mostly to non-Brahman communist sympathizers, though in a few cases to Dalits.[30]

Interpreting the 'anti-feudal' character of the Telengana revolt purely in terms of land, its seizure and occupation, would be a mistake, though a natural one if property ownership is considered the sole basis of exploitation. Instead Srinivasalu's analysis (and much of the description of the struggles that actually went on in Telengana supports it) focuses on two other factors, which he calls *gadi* (the political power of the landlords) and *vethi* (*vethbegar*). Describing the latter as a 'universal and all-pervasive mode of exploitation' in the region, Srinivasalu calls it a deformed version of the *jajmani* system and notes that it symbolized feudal subordination for all groups. The opposition to it could thus unite peasant cultivators, artisans and other village servants and Dalits.[31]

Another important issue was agricultural wages. Wage increases were demanded from fairly early, but no struggles were reported on the issue. Communist-dominated village committees, however, fixed higher wages, and following the Indian army repression (apparently when the landlords attempted to reimpose the older, lower wages) there was a wave of agricultural labourers' strikes in 1949, including workers in 150 villages in Warangal district; in some cases women led these strikes.[32]

But the actual role of Dalits in the struggle appears to have been a subordinate one. Claims that 'most of the recruits in the *dalams* came from the untouchable castes (Malas and Madigas) and from among the tribals'[33] are unsubstantiated, except for the obvious fact that once the communists were driven into the forests the tribals were the main group they worked among. Leaders such as D.V. Rao and Sundarayya depict the participation of Dalits as much more passive, arguing mainly that the Nizam's agents and landlords failed to split the people on the caste question and 'win over the Harijans'; in nearly all the villages the Dalits were on the side of the communists.[34] There is also, notably, no depiction of a Dalit woman (while there are other poor and low-caste women) in the searching account of women in the Telengana revolt carried out by the Stree Shakti Sanghatana of Hyderabad.[35] In fact it seems that the communists very rarely took up the social issues of untouchability. D.V. Rao's statement, 'When we were working in the villages caste tensions did not arise. Caste differences were limited to the house, except for untouchables'[36] is typical. The communists aimed at 'unity' (which they thought could be achieved with the acceptance of the social constraints of the old order) and within this framework sought to deal only with some of the economic problems of the poorest sections of the society.

Thus claims of Marxist academics that Dalits constituted the 'main force' of the *dalams* or of the revolt in general (Dhanagare) of that 'the party was being continuously driven to the Left by poor peasants and agricultural labourers' (Pavier)[37] seem more examples of romanticism. It may be possible that if the party had from the very beginning vigorously pushed agricultural labourer issues or taken up anti-untouchability with fervor, it could have won a sustained and militant response. But even this is questionable given the objective conditions of the Telengana region. In coastal Andhra, with a background of a half-century of commercial agriculture, spontaneous resistance by Malas and Madigas had wiped out much of traditional caste-forms of bondage and replaced 'bonded labour' by wage-paid daily labour even before the communists entered. In the much more backward areas of Telengana, dominated by an unrelieved feudal aristocracy, there is little evidence of such a strong resistance. It would have been difficult for the CPI to leap over decades of history in the course of a few years of revolt.

In any event, the unity created and the fervor of large sections of the population was not enough to withstand the entry of the Indian army. On 13 September 1948 the army swept in. There was little effective resistance to the often brutal repression that followed. According to Sundarayya's account, in over 2,000 villages of Nalgonda, Warangal, Karimnagar, Khammam and Hyderabad, 300,000 were tortured and 50,000 were arrested and kept in detention camps. Some 10,000 were said to be in camps even till July 1950. About 2,000 were killed and 5,000 imprisoned for years.[38]

The Telengana revolt unleashed a debate within the communist leadership about whether to call off the struggle or not. Although the 'Andhra thesis' seems to have presented it as the beginning of a 'liberation war', Sundarayya, arguing the CPI(M) line, claims that it should have been carried on as simply a 'peasants' partisan struggle' to defend gains won. But by the time these arguments were being made, the communists had simply been forced into the forests and hills by the overwhelming military strength, leaving the majority of peasants defenceless. Gupta's comment is telling:

The dominant reason why the movement 'failed' was that it was successfully suppressed. We have seen how the peasant army managed only limited success against the Nizam's troops. In front of the Indian forces they were pathetically overmatched. Faced with almost certain extermination in the plains, the Communist cadres ran into the forests. But they were even less prepared to fight a secret, guerrilla war than a conventional one.[39]

It was not only a question of the Indian regime's military strength; it was also that a discredited feudal regime was now replaced by one that could claim to be the democratic 'anti-imperialist front' of the Indian people. This had been the communist line for over a decade. Now that the Congress whom they had depicted as an essential ally at the national level was taking over, they could not easily convince people who were not experiencing direct repression that it had suddenly become an enemy force, particularly when it was displacing feudal gangsters and looters. In most of Hyderabad state the army was greeted as a liberator, certainly in Marathwada, also in parts of Telengana.[40] That its takeover included direct army atrocities against many of the poor and support for return of the worst landlord oppressors, as well as direct Hindu reprisals in many areas against Muslims and Dalits who were presumed to be 'pro-Razakar' did not immediately change the power equation. Communists, unable to fight any longer on an armed level, did have to fight in some way to defend the gains made. But large sections of the exploited, including Dalits, who may well have had reservations about the democratic role of the Indian state, were in no position to express them and faced a situation of repression.

■ DALIT REORGANIZING, 1948–56

While the communists were attempting to survive repression in Telengana and Dalits in Marathwada were confronting reprisals from caste Hindu Congressmen, the factionalised Dalit leadership of Hyderabad city went through a period of intense reorganization. Following the 'Police Action', in fact, many ran for shelter to the Congress or its associated organizations.

Venkatrao was arrested. Shyam Sunder, the most militant and fiery of the pro-Nizam spokesmen, was out of the scene for some years, sent on a mission to Europe to represent Hyderabad's right to independence before the U.N. When he returned, at the time of the 1952 elections, with his usual verve he put up the board of the old Depressed·Classes Association and announced his candidacy.[41] But by that time the DCA had gone out of existence. A large section of its membership simply fled into the Congress fold, joining a newly formed Dalit Jatiya Sangh, allied with one Dharam Prakash who was the leader of a group that had split from Jagjivan Ram's Depressed Classes League ('Dalit Jatiya Sangh' was the normal Hindi translation for the league) and was under the patronage of the Hyderabad Congress. M.B. Gautam was its general secretary and Mudiguna Laxmaiah, a rich Madiga shoe factory owner who had previously led the Arundatiya Matunga Mahasabha, was its president. Some of their political opponents later protested against the 'ex-Razakars' in this group.[42]

Others, including Arigay Ramaswamy, formed a Hyderabad State Depressed Classes League. This picked up some of the old activists, such as K.R. Veeraswamy, a post-graduate from Madras University and a Mala who had been in the SCF, and Sampath Babiah, a Mala who had been president of the DCA for some time and was said to have been a Razakar chief. J. Sarvesh, a Tamil Dalit who had been general secretary of a 'state unemployed union' went on to become the organizing secretary of the League.[43] By the time of the 1952 elections, both of these sections had joined the Congress itself.

The SCF did not fare too well. There was a split in protest against Subbiah's 'dictatorial methods', with young activists such as P.V. Manohar and Vemula Yadgir Rao leaving to form a 'United Scheduled Caste Federation' (USCF).

During the 1952 elections the USCF allied with the socialists, apparently without much success, and the SCF established an alliance with the front organization of the banned communists, the Progressive Democratic Front (PDF). This was in spite of the Ambedkar's expressed policy at that time of *not* allying with communists; it proved to be beneficial. In fact the election results clearly showed that, whatever their mistakes and vacillations, their militant struggles had won the communists a popular base. They contested a total of 108 seats in the assembly elections, winning 36 of 51 in coastal Andhra, 36 of 45 in Telengana (all of these in the central districts of the revolt and 5 of 12 in Rayalseema. At least two of the winners were second-rank Dalit activists who had formerly been with the SCF. In addition 10 socialists allied with the PDF won seats, while the SCF itself won five assembly seats (two in Marathwada and three in Telengana) and one Lok Sabha seat with the help of the PDF.

But the leadership crisis in the Hyderabad SCF erupted after the elections. Complaints against Subbiah's arrogance, corruption and ineffectiveness had simmered for long, and in January 1951 a delegation of his opponents presented a memorandum to Ambedkar during the latter's visit to Hyderabad as a state guest. Following the mediocre performance of the SCF in the 1952 elections and concrete evidence that Subbiah was acting against directives, the all-India SCF finally took action and a 26 March 1953 meeting at Delhi, presided over by Ambedkar, dissolved the Hyderabad unit.[44] However, while the crisis showed itself in the Hyderabad organization, in many ways its roots were in the national-level failure to organizationally build SCF units, inherent in SCF from the beginning.

> The general complaint against Dr. Ambedkar was that since he got into the cabinet, he completely lost contact with the Depressed Classes masses. Whatever information he got about their deplorable plight was only through prejudiced channels. Moreover, he was so busy with his portfolio that he practically found no time to think of the amelioration of the condition of our brethren.[45]

So Venkatswamy expressed the complaints of the people of Hyderabad. Similarly, from coastal Andhra, Suryaprakash Rao argues that 'Ambedkar got the wrong contacts in Andhra Pradesh . . . he visited there very late; he had no information about the ideas/ideology prevalent there.'[46]

Ambedkar himself, in building up the SCF during the late 1940s, had frequently argued that 'I have only to give a call and people will mobilize.' But such organizational methods proved inadequate outside of Maharashtra. The SCF functioned in practice as a federation of organizations already built up, and in most cases Ambedkar could only choose local lieutenants and put complete trust in them to build up the organization; when these proved incompetent or corrupt, the organization suffered.

Though the SCF was organizationally weak in Hyderabad, there was tremendous pressure to take some kind of action after 1948–50.

After the Police Action, a severe repression had been unleashed on Dalits and Muslims by the victorious 'Congressites' caste Hindus. Venkatswamy reports,

> The political bungling of the power-intoxicated Razakar leaders resulted in the massacre of hundreds of Muslims and Depressed Classes. The districts of Parbhani, Nanded, Aurangabad and Bidar were the worst affected where much innocent blood was shed.[47]

Janata, which up to the point of the Police Action and been describing 'Razakar atrocities', now began to focus on the retribution by the 'state Congress goondas', the pulling down of Dalit houses, violence against men, women and children. A report by B.S. More claimed that only the rich had fled, and on returning looked for scapegoats, picking on the poor Mahars, Mangs and Chambhars rather than the well-off who had actually given money to the Razakars. In this sensitive situation, with the majority of people in Marathwada 'uneducated and under the tyranny of tradition', Congress 'Harijan' propagandists were urging Dalits to engage in temple entry programmes, with the result that they were only getting beaten up by caste Hindus 'and then the State Congress says this is only because of their previous Razakar connections!'[48] Tarring all with the Razakar brush was a useful tactic in a low-key rural class–caste warfare.

A key element in this was land—land promised to the Dalits by the Nizam government, apparently seized by them in many cases in the chaos of the period, taken back by the victorious returning Congress caste Hindus. And in this context the new Congress government made its politics clear when it started snatching back some of the common lands given to Dalits, on the excuse that they were cultivating it instead of planting trees on it as they were supposed to.

Following the 1952 elections, the SCF, led by the two MLAs from Marathwada, Shamrao Jadhav and Madhavrao Nirlekar, organized resistance to these evictions. While directed against the Congress-ruled Hyderabad state, this was also an assertion of organizational strength vis-a-vis the caste Hindus. Nearly 1,500 satyagrahis were arrested in the struggle, 'the first of its kind in Hyderabad state', according to Venkatswamy.[49] With the leadership of P.N. Rajbhoj and the local Marathwada activists, it was carried on until 16 November 1953 when the Hyderabad government agreed to restore the lands.[50]

▪ DALITS AND COMMUNISTS IN ANDHRA

In spite of being the centre of communist rural revolt and a fairly significant Dalit movement, the turbulent 1940s ended in Andhra with the establishment of hegemony by the 'bourgeois–Brahman' Congress. How do we assess this period?

The failure of the Dalit movement to go forward was inherent in the transition from the ILP to the SCF. During the 1930s Ambedkar had been on the leading edge of an all-India left wave, taking the initiative not only in regard to the problems of untouchables but in creating a worker–peasant based political alternative to the Congress, carrying a red flag and organizing militant struggles on social and economic issues. The failure of this effort, to a large degree due to the lack of response by broader left forces, led to a step backward represented by the SCF. This meant focusing on winning concessions for Dalits while independence was taken for granted; going to the 'national' level and thereby relying on a series of local 'lieutenants' rather than trying to build an ideologically unified organization; substituting the organizing of Scheduled Castes as such for efforts to form a broad alliance of Dalits and non-Brahmans, workers and peasants; and substituting a programme of the resettlement of Dalits away from villages dominated by caste Hindus (the 'separate village settlements' demand) for a strategy of changing the rural socio-economic structure.

Thus, at a time when Dalits in Hyderabad were going through their greatest political traumas and were being pulled to the left, there was little national direction. The separate village settlement programme had little real meaning in Andhra, where the major practical economic issues were opposing *vethbegar*, obtaining government forest and wastelands, and winning higher wages as agricultural labourers or workers. These were issues taken up by Ambedkar and the ILP in Maharashtra; in Andhra and Hyderabad they appeared in most Dalit programmes, but by the 1940s it was the communists who were spearheading whatever organizing occurred on these issues.

Conversely, communist inadequacies on caste issues, described in chapter 5, also existed in Andhra. Communists did get involved in 'anti-untouchability' campaigns; they did take up the interwoven socio-economic exploitation of Dalits; Hyderabad party leaders did attempt to build bridges with the Dalit leadership in the city. But none of this was done as a part of party policy or theorized as a crucial aspect of the Indian revolution. As far as an understanding of 'social issues' was concerned, D.V. Rao's statement that caste issues were not important *except* in the household, *except* for untouchables' must surely stand with the recent comment by Namboodiripad as a revelation of communist blindness to the problem: that the 'Harijan issue' was a 'mundane' diversion from nationalist organization.

However, all said and done, achievements of the communists in Telengana in a very short period of less than a decade have to be recognized. These achievements stand out most clearly when a comparison is made between Telengana and Marathwada. The communists may not have done much about getting 'surplus lands' for Dalits, but if the estimate of winning 100,000 acres of forest and common lands for cultivation by Dalits and the landless is correct, it was a very impressive gain.

Equally important is the fact that this was done in the context of building and maintaining unity between Dalits and the caste Hindu rural poor. In Marathwada the opposite happened. Dalits had long demanded land, but this was given by the Nizam regime at a time when the Gandhian and Arya Samajist Maharashtra Parishad was doing little to organize rural economic struggles. The result was that Dalits responded to pro-Muslim leaders like Shyam Sunder and Venkatrao. This, then, identified them with the hated Razakars, an identification heightened by the fact that some of them apparently did grab the land of caste Hindus who had fled repression. After the Police Action, caste Hindus unleashed reprisals against the Dalits and the state used the occasion to reappropriate much of the land that the Nizam's regime had given, something it did not dare to do in Telengana regarding government land. The SCF-organized satyagraha got much of this restored, but the result of the whole process was a widening gap between caste Hindus and Dalits, in which caste Hindu power-holders could legitimize their repression by depicting Dalits as anti-national. This 'Dalit–*bahujan*' split and the intensification of a fundamentalist Hindu cultural identification among the caste Hindus made Marathwada different not simply from Telengana but from western Maharashtra and Vidarbha, where the Satyashodhak movement had rooted a more democratic leadership among the non-Brahman masses. The consequences lasted well into the post-independence decades in Maharashtra where Marathwada became a scene for anti-Dalit rioting and, in the context of the Dalit struggle for common lands, provided the main rural base for caste tension and a growing Shiv Sena influence in the late 1980s.[51]

At the same time, ironically, Dalits and communists both failed at the level of cultural interpretation and identity formation, a crucial part of creating an 'alternative political hegemony'. The communists had a very intensive cultural programme as part of the Telengana movement, including using traditional forms such as *burra katha* and low-caste and Dalit performers, but it seems that the content of these remained the preoccupation of traditional Marxism, with little effort to engage even Telugu history and culture. In their turn the radical Dalits in Hyderabad spent their time emphasizing a 'non-Hindu, non-Aryan' identity on an abstract level; and while Ambedkar's conversion to Buddhism was accompanied by his own prolific reading and writing on ancient Indian history, this also used a rationalistic and abstract interpretation that contrasted with the way Phule had earlier used such important peasant symbols and myths as Bali Raja in his interpretation of history. Buddhism, in other words, held an appeal for educated Dalit radicals, but little resonance among the Dalit masses. And this 'non-government' of communists and Dalits with the vernacular tradition was happening at a time when Hindu fundamentalists, represented in Andhra primarily by the Arya Samaj, were reinterpreting tradition from a Brahman, absorptive point of view, using Dalit writers and Dalit 'pandits' to instill a sense of participation in a Hindu identity through such figures as Vasishtha and Arundatiya.

The co-optive power of the Congress could win some impressive victories. This worked at many levels: in the extension of influence through the machinery created by the 'Harijan Sevak Sangh' and 'Depressed Classes League', including the absorption of their key personnel into the ministries; in limited anti-feudal reforms such as the Jagir Abolition Act of 1949 and the Hyderabad Tenancy and Lands Act of 1950; in the continuation of the various programmes for untouchable education begun under the British regime; in acceding to (under pressure of the peasant struggle in Telengana and the SCF satyagraha in Marathwada) the granting of forestlands/ wastelands to Dalits; in the fact that Andhra had the first ex-untouchable chief minister in independent India, chosen after a stand-off between the two powerful contestants.[52]

Writing about a later period, Hargopal described the particular effectiveness of the Congress policy towards Dalits:

> As a part of the new strategy in the late sixties and early seventies Mrs. Gandhi resorted to target group approach. The 'harijans' were identified as a specific group . . . . The strategy not only envisaged new specific schemes for the harijans but the entire mass media was pressed into service for the purpose of propaganda. The land reforms, distribution of pattas and house sites, S.C. component programme with subsidy and so on 'trickled down' to some harijan families here and there. It is not that their conditions [were] qualitatively altered nor their social relations transformed. The electoral rhetoric and massive propaganda resulted in two significant consequences: one, harijans became conscious of their conditions and their identification with Mrs. Gandhi gave them a new sense of social consciousness resulting in greater assertion for dignity and self-respect; two, the special focus on a particular section annoyed a large section of non-harijan agricultural labourers coming from the other backward groups and alienated them from the Congress party and their harijan brethren.[53]

In reality, the whole strategy had its roots in the pre-independence Dalit movement and the Gandhian-influenced process of developing a response to it. The movement identified Dalits as a specially oppressed and exploited section and succeeded in establishing the legitimacy of their claims to justice; Gandhi transformed them into 'harijans' and the bureaucratic process of dependency-creating patronage made them into a 'target group'. In the absence of an equivalently powerful strategy from the revolutionaries, this was sufficient for their political incorporation.

Dalits within the Congress found they could do little: 'we were almost slaves of Congress',[54] says one ex-MLA and nationalist activist; they recognized that it was only the SCF that was organizing struggles for the Dalits. But the main movements fighting against mass enslavement in Andhra had remained so isolated from one another that their mutual historical accounts (whether communist assessments of the Telengana struggle and early peasant organizing, or Dalit reports of Hyderabad state organizing) do not even recognize the existence of the other struggle as a part of an overall fight. This helped to make it possible for the slavery imposed on Dalits and other exploited classes and castes to be reconstructed rather than abolished after the end of colonial rule.

NOTES

1. Venkatswamy, *Our Struggle for Emancipation* Volume II, (Secunderabad: Universal Art Printers, 1965), pp. 359–60; Jaganathan, interview.
2. *Bombay Chronicle*, 18 June 1947, in *Sources*, Volume I, p. 341.
3. See for example B.R. Ambedkar, 'Communal Deadlock and a Way to Solve It', Address delivered at the session of the All-India Scheduled Caste Federation, Bombay, 6 May 1945, reproduced in *Dr. Babasaheb Ambedkar: Writings and Speeches*, Volume I (Bombay: Government of Maharashtra Education Department, 1979).
4. See *Times of India*, 6 January 1940 and Bombay Chronicle, 11 January 1940, both in *Sources*, Volume I, 207–10, and Venkatswamy, *Our Struggle for Emancipation*, Volume II, pp. 175–80.
5. *Pakistan and Partition of India*, reprinted in *Dr. Babasaheb Ambedkar: Writings and Speeches*, Volume 8 (Bombay: Government of Maharashtra, 1990).
6. *Free Press Journal*, 10 April 1947 in *Sources*, Volume I, p. 336.
7. See, e.g., Anita Diehl, *Periyar E.V. Ramaswami* (Bombay: B.I. Publications, 1978), pp. 26–65.
8. Venkatswamy, *Our Struggle for Emancipation*, Volume II, pp. 350–51.
9. *Ibid.*, pp. 386–87.
10. *Ibid.*, pp. 391ff.
11. *Ibid.*, pp. 406–7.
12. *Ibid.*, pp. 420–21.
13. *Ibid.*, p. 422.
14. *Ibid.*, p. 427; see also *The National Standard*, 28 November 1947; in *Sources*, Volume I, pp. 348–50.
15. Venkatswamy, *Our Struggle for Emancipation*, Volume II, pp. 488–92.
16. *Ibid.*, p. 455.
17. *Ibid.*, pp. 378–82. Ambedkarites later fought to get the use of much of the actual funding for Milind College, the first college of the People's Education Society in Aurangabad, which brought them into conflict with Telugu speakers.
18. See Sundarayya, *Telengana People's Struggle and its Lessons* (Calcutta: 1972), p. 27.
19. D.N. Dhanagare, 'Social Origins of the Telengana Insurrection (1946–1951)', *Contributions to Indian Sociology*, 8, 1974, p. 124; D.V. Rao, interview.

20. Cited in Mohan Ram, 'The Telengana Peasant Armed Struggle', *Economic and Political Weekly*, 9 June 1973, p. 1026.
21. Akhil Gupta 'Revolution in Telengana, 1946–51', *South Asia Bulletin*, 4 (1–2), Spring-fall 1948, part I, p. 21.
22. Dhanagare, 'Social Origins', pp. 122–23.
23. Venkatswamy, *Our Struggle for Emancipation*, Volume II, p. 454. For *Janata* reports of atrocities against Dalits in Marathwada by Razakars see issues of 24 January and 22 May 1948.
24. Gupta, 'Revolution in Telengana', part I, p. 16; Dhanagare, 'Social Origins', pp. 123–24; Sundarayya, *Telengana People's Struggle*, pp. 60, 65, 91–93.
25. D.V. Rao, interview.
26. Gupta, Revolution in Telengana, part I, p. 17, part II, p. 22; Sundarayya, *Telengana People's Struggle* and Dhanagare, 'Social Origins'.
27. K. Srinivasalu, 'Telengana Peasant Movement and Changes in the Agrarian Structure: A Case Study of Nalgonda District', Ph. D. dissertation, Jawaharlal Nehru University, School of Social Sciences, 1988, pp. 36–37, 39–40.
28. *Ibid.*, pp. 247, 249.
29. *Ibid.*. Such conflicts are not infrequent in land struggles.
30. *Ibid.*, pp. 247ff.
31. *Ibid.*, pp. 39, 95, 101. See also I. Thirumali, 'Dora and Gadi: Manifestation of Landlord Domination in Telengana', *Economic and Political Weekly*, 29 February 1992.
32. Sundarayya, *Telengana People's Struggle*, pp. 243, 259.
33. Dhanagare, 'Social Origins', p. 128.
34. Interviews, D.V.Rao, Chandra Pulla Reddy.
35. Stree Shakti Sanghatana, '*We Were Making History*': *Women in the Telengana Struggle* (New Delhi: Kali for Women Press, 1989).
36. D.V. Rao, interview.
37. Pavier, 'The Telengana Armed Struggle', *Economic and Political Weekly*, 1974, August, p. 1418.
38. Dhanagare, 'Social Origins', pp. 125–26.
39. Gupta, 'Revolution in Telengana', Part II.
40. Venkatswamy, *Our Struggle for Emancipation*, Volume II, p. 363.
41. *Ibid.*, p. 557ff.
42. *Ibid.*, p. 583.
43. *Ibid.*, p. 596.
44. *Ibid.*, pp. 621–24.
45. *Ibid.*, p. 625.
46. Suryaprakash Rao, Interview, 16 June 1989.
47. Venkatswamy, *Our Struggle for Emancipation*, Volume II, p. 518. Interviews, J. Jaganathan, B.S. More.
48. B.S. More, Report in *Janata*, 11 December 1948; see also *Janata* 9 and 23 October 1948.
49. Venkatswamy, *Our Struggle for Emancipation*, Volume II, pp. 654–55; B.S. More, interview.
50. *National Standard*, 17 November 1953; in *Sources*, Volume I, pp. 415–16.
51. On the riots over the 'renaming' of Marathwada University see the Atyacar Virodhi Samiti, 'The Marathwada Riots: A Report', *Economic and Political*

Weekly, 12 May 1979; Gail Omvedt, 'Class Struggle or Caste War?' *Frontier*, 30 September 1978; S.P. Punalekar, *Caste, Class and Reaction: An Overview of the Marathwada Riots* (Surat: Centre for Social Studies, 1979), though none of these accounts bring out the pre-independence background.

52. See Pothakuchi Sama Sivarao, 'Sanjivayya, a New Light of the Modern Age', Andhra Pradesh Harijan *Souvenir* (Hyderabad, 10–12 April 1976), pp. 58–60.

53. Hargopal, 'Caste-Class Dimensions of Dalit Consciousness: The Case of Delta Andhra, Paper presented to the TDSS Seminar on Caste–class, Lonavala, December 1987, p. 12.

54. Interview, Jagambar Jaganathan, 24 June 1988.

NOTES

Conclusion

■ DALITS IN INDEPENDENT INDIA

And so came independence, proclaimed in hope but enforced by the Indian army in Telengana, 'Congress goondas' in Marathwada.

Though he called for Dalits to associate themselves with an independent India, though he himself drafted its Constitution and was a minister in its first government, Ambedkar looked towards the gaining of independence with a fair amount of foreboding. In the background of the bloody partition riots, the assassination of Gandhi, the trauma of the takeover of native states in which Dalits in Hyderabad had suffered atrocities under vengeful returning Congressmen after those of the Razakars, he warned the Constituent Assembly in 1949,

> On 26 January 1950, we are going to enter into a life of contradictions. In politics we will have equality and in social and economic life we will have inequality . . . . We must remove this contradiction at the earliest possible moment or else those who suffer from inequality will blow up the structure of political democracy which we have so laboriously built up.[1]

This itself was a dramatic contrast to Nehru's more famous 'tryst with destiny'. But within a few years, even more disillusionment had set in, with Ambedkar himself saying, in a moment of rage regarding atrocities in 1949, 'I myself will burn the Constitution!'[2]

Dalit perception of the achievements of independent India thus varied dramatically from that of the elite, and by the time of the revival of the movement in the 1970s, his followers were repeating Ambedkar's threats, claiming the need to desecrate the national flag, burn the Constitution as well as the *Manusmriti*. Their powerful poetry attacked with equal fervor ancient traditions and 'modern' accomplishments; they claimed that they 'had no country', that there was no room for the 'new sun' that their movement had brought:

> From pitchblack tunnels
> they gather ashes
> floating on jet-black water
> and reconstruct the skeletons
> of their ancestors,
> singing hymns
> of their thoughts
> worn of shreds.
> There is no entry here
> for the new sun.
> This is the empire
> of ancestor-worship,
> of blackened castoffs,
> of darkness.[3]

What provoked this black vision—a pessimism contrasting to the hopes of the majority, in a country which had won independence as a result of a long drawn-out struggle and a powerful movement with a significant base among the worker–peasant masses, led by a government which not only associated itself with the progressive states of the third World but also declared itself, first, committed to a 'socialistic pattern of society' and then (in its greatest phase of dictatorial government, to be sure) to be a 'secular, socialist republic'? What was it that led Ambedkar himself in the end to be disillusioned with the promises of progressiveness, declaring Nehru to be 'just another Brahman'?

The political situation of the Dalit movement has to be clearly underlined: at the time of independence and after, Dalits had not become, as their leaders had hoped, powerholders themselves; the movement was not controlling events, it was suffering a process of co-optation and incorporation. Repression continued, open and brutal in the villages, suave and vicious in the institutions where men and women of low castes inched their way forward, but it was overlaid with co-optation, the winning over of individuals with a few crumbs and the erosion of movement organizations, accompanied by the overflowing paternalistic and benign rhetoric of the party which Ambedkar had described as the 'party of Brahmans and the bourgeoisie'.

In fact the most sophisticated traditional ruling class in Asia had modernized itself sufficiently to beat back all major challenges, whether from workers, peasants, non-Brahmans, Dalits or peripheral 'nationalities'. It had managed to evolve a sophisticated strategy to rule, which included an ability to characterize the middle-caste peasants as 'exploiters' and 'affluent' while appealing to the 'rural poor', Dalits and the 'weaker sections.' In effect, the political strategies of the Congress, sharpened by Indira Gandhi in the face of rising mass protest, sought to unite the low castes with the Brahmans against the Shudra middle castes, and agricultural labourers with industrialists and the bureaucracy against the mass of the peasantry. And in this it was successful enough to remain the main powerholder, able to marginalize a left challenge even when its majorities sank dangerously low.

What was the nature of the economic strategies and structures of the system? It described itself as 'socialistic'; its Marxist opponents debated its characterization as 'capitalist' on 'semi-feudal'. In fact, India's developmental path (known more generally as the 'Nehru model') had elements of all three.

The society as a whole swung into decades of planning, focusing on the creation of a strong heavy industrial base under the public sector, largely in the direction of what Ambedkar himself had seen as the desired path of development. There was no 'nationalization of land' or formation of agricultural collectives, but there was clearly public control of the 'commanding heights' of the economy. The Nehru–Mahanalobis planning model has been compared to that of the Bolsheviks; in fact it was a very pronounced version of the concern for rapid industrialization and the reliance on the state that was pervading almost all Third World countries at the time, after the clear experience of Depression and the achievements of Keynesianism on one hand and the early successes of the erstwhile Soviet Union on the other hand had given a good deal of prestige to various forms of statism. It was no wonder that India swung towards a statist model or that the Congress could see itself as embodying a 'peasant revolution': in the words of a village Congress activist and former freedom fighter, 'what is the difference between you (the Communists) and us? You're twelve annas, we're four annas.' 'Four-anna socialism' suggested the moderation of India's public sector-planning effort, which unlike the Bolshevik version managed to maintain a parliamentary democracy, but the 'secular and socialist' aspect was not simply rhetoric. A strong public sector (two-thirds of organized sector employment was in the public sector) underlying the considerable progress of many industries especially in the early decades helped India claim leadership of the 'nonaligned' Third World, while the injection of a veneer of Gandhism with 'panchayat raj' and a khadi-village industries programme laid the basis for claiming a unique Indian version of the model.

Yet economic exploitation, impoverishment and misery continued, while political democracy did not end the domination of an elite. Within three decades it was clear that a still-surviving caste system was continuing to structure these. Further, it seemed these structures, of economic exploitation, social oppression and political subordination, were being furthered by the very 'Nehru model' which had promised to bring development, prosperity and a more equalitarian society.

'Land reforms', argued the left and Dalit radicals, had never taken place in a thoroughgoing way. In fact land reforms fairly thoroughly ended much 'feudal' landlordism in most of the country, but this type of bourgeois land reform was far different from a radical 'land to the tiller' programme. At most the top Brahman and upper-caste landlords had lost their position; land had not been given in a massive way to the landless and by and large caste continued to be heavily correlated with agrarian position, as Table 11.1 indicates. Not all Dalits were landless labourers, but they were more likely to be poor peasants and landless labourers than

TABLE 11.1
Caste and Agricultural Occupation

	Upper caste	Middle caste	Lower caste	Scheduled caste	Total
Agriculture					
Farmer	24.38	7.57	6.95	1.54	7.35
Cultivator	43.91	53.30	41.79	27.05	41.35
Share-croppers	3.91	6.18	6.17	8.50	6.50
Agricultural labourers	1.09	11.91	16.85	36.19	18.70
Forestry, Fishing and Livestock	0.62	1.39	3.31	2.30	2.42
Total in Agriculture	73.91	80.35	75.07	75.66	76.32
Others	26.09	19.65	24.93	24.33	23.47
Total	100.00	100.00	100.00	100.00	100.00

Source: A late 1960s table cited by P.C. Joshi, 'Perspectives on Poverty and Social Change', *Economic and Political Weekly*, Annual Number, February 1979, p. 363.
Definition of categories: 'The *upper castes* were defined as those who according to custom used the sacred thread; the *middle castes* as those from whom Brahmans take water by tradition; and the *lower castes* as the other castes who were not scheduled.' *Farmers* were those who 'cultivate their own land mainly by hired labour'; *cultivators* 'who cultivate . . . with the help of other household members and partly by hired labour'; *share-croppers* 'who take up the cultivation of others' land on a crop-sharing basis and cultivate without hired labour'; and *agricultural labourers* as those 'who work on other's land on the basis of wage payment'.

non-Dalits. While many Dalits and Adivasis were small peasants, they had been so even in the caste-feudal society of the pre-colonial period; there is no evidence that the reforms of the independent Indian state significantly changed their position.

Statistics on agrarian class relations and land concentration show that while there was a growing proportion of agricultural labourers in the workforce, concentration of landholdings and overall landlessness of rural families remained about the same (Tables 11.2a and 11.2b). Broadly speaking, while many peasant families were being marginalized and some were giving up increasingly 'uneconomic' small parcels of land, there was also a process whereby the landless and land-poor were claiming land for cultivation, most often 'forest' or 'waste' lands. This in fact was the form land struggles took throughout the decades of independence,

TABLE 11.2a
Distribution of Rural Households by Landholding

	Percentage of households		Percentage area operated	
	1953–54	1970–71	1953–54	1970–71
Not operating land	28.2	27.5	—	—
Small holding (0–2.49 acres)	28.0	32.9	5.4	9.2
Medium holding (2.5–9.99 acres)	28.2	29.4	28.6	37.5
Large holdings (10 acres & above)	14.6	10.4	65.9	53.2

TABLE 11.2b
Estimated Operational Farm Holdings and Area Operated

	1970–71	1980–81	1985–86
Percentage of Operational Holdings			
Marginal (0–1 hectare)	50.9	56.4	58.1
Small (1–2 hectares)	18.9	18.1	18.3
Semi-medium (2–4 hectares)	15.0	14.0	13.5
Medium (4–10 hectares)	11.2	9.1	8.1
Large (over 10 hectares)	3.9	2.4	2.0
Percentage of Area Operated			
Marginal	9.0	12.1	13.2
Small	11.9	14.1	15.6
Semi-medium	18.5	21.1	22.3
Medium	29.7	29.7	28.7
Large	30.2	23.0	20.2

Source: The basic source for Table 11.2a is National Sample Survey data; and for Table 11.2b is the Agricultural Census, cited in Centre for Monitoring the Indian Economy, *Basic Statistics Related to the Indian Economy, 1985* and *Basic Statistics, 1989*, both cited in Gail Omvedt, 'The "New Peasant Movement" in India', *Bulletin of Concerned Asian Scholars*, 20, 2, 1988, p. 20.

and it did win some results. Yet, while the agrarian hierarchy may not have intensified overall, it was a highly stratified one to begin with and the Dalits were at the bottom of it.

More than that, the agrarian sector as a whole was getting depressed and marginalized as a result of the processes of economic development. This was not accidental; developmental planning in the decades of the 1950s and 1960s assumed the necessity of what economists called the 'transfer of resources' from agriculture, of what one of the most important Indian planners described as 'incremental primitive socialist accumulation.'[4] This was done through various mechanisms, including financial policies which set high exchange rates that discriminated against the primary sector in favour of industry, restrictions on farmers selling their produce, government monopoly purchases and occasionally levies, import of cheap foodgrains from abroad, all designed to ensure cheap and abundant food for the cities and a growing industrial working class.[5]

The overall result was an unbalanced industrialization which left most of the rural areas impoverished and created an increasing gap between the organized sector (approximately 10 per cent of the workforce, according to government statistics) and the unorganized sector, defined as including agricultural labourers, cultivators, non-agricultural self-employed and unorganized wage labourers. In 1968 this small organized sector represented 23 per cent of GDP; by 1987 its share had risen to a whopping 37.8 per cent.[6] Statistics also show that incomes of not only agricultural labourers but also peasants were significantly below those of organized sector employees (in 1981 peasants earned, on an average, one-third of that earned by the organized sector workers, agricultural labourers one-fifth); they were even lower than those of unorganized sector wage workers (Table 11.3). Further, whereas nearly all economists (including Ambedkar in his early economic writings) assumed that 'wage earners' were the most impoverished sector of the economy, by the 1980s it was clear that the 'self-employed' as a group were poorer than the wage-earners as a group, even when the latter included the most impoverished section of agricultural labourers, and in spite of the vast undercounting of working women, particularly in agriculture and other 'self-employed' categories. (A more accurate accounting of the number of workers would have seen the relatively smaller shares of GDP held by 'self-employed' workers spread over an even larger number of workers.) The depression of the entire agricultural sector is also seen in the fact that in India, as in almost all Third World countries, agriculture and the primary sector in general claimed an increasingly smaller share of the GDP while continuing to be the home of a large and sometimes stagnant share of the workforce (Table 11.4).

The significance of these economic patterns for the Dalits is that

TABLE 11.3
Income of Organized and Unorganized Sector Workers, 1981

	Workforce (thousands)	Average annual income per worker (Rs.)
1. Wage and Salary Earners	965	4,468
A. Organized Sector	229	10,851
(Public)	155	10,643
(Private)	74	11,289
B. Unorganized Sector	736	2,482
(Agricultural Workers)	555	1,703
(Non-agricultural Workers)	181	4,871
2. Self-employed	1,260	3,549
A. Cultivators	925	3,000
B. Non-cultivators	335	5,066

Source: Centre for Monitoring the Indian Economy, *Basic Statistics, 1985, Volume 1* (Bombay 1985), Table 10.1.

TABLE 11.4
Distribution of GDP and Labour Force by Sector

	1965		1980	
	% GDP	% Labour Force	% GDP	% Labour Force
Low-income Countries				
Agriculture	44	78	32	70
Industry	28	9	37	15
Services	28	13	31	15
Middle-income Countries				
Agriculture	20	57	12	44
Industry	33	17	38	22
Services	46	26	50	34
Industrial Market Economies				
Agriculture	14	14	3	7
Industry	30	38	37	35
Services	56	48	60	58
India				
Agriculture	44	73	38	70
Industry	22	12	26	13
Services	34	15	36	17

Source: *World Development Report, 1986 and 1990.*

they had a disproportionate share in the most impoverished agricultural sector. As Table 11.5 makes clear, 76.4 per cent of Dalits (and 87.1 per cent of Adivasis) were in the agricultural sector in contrast to 61.4 per cent 'others'. As small peasants and other petty producers they suffered directly from the general discrimination against the primary sector, and as wage-earners they suffered indirectly.[7]

In the non-agricultural sector, the Dalit foothold in an industrial workforce and their ability to gain some benefits from reservations gave them a better share. Reservations did help Dalits move ahead in government jobs, and were crucial to the fact that a small middle class section could pull itself up and with this, provide some resources and hope to a wider mass. But they did not seem to significantly shake upper caste control of the public sector: by the time of the Mandal Commission report, in 1979–80, the estimated 25 per cent 'upper castes' still controlled nearly 70 per cent of all government jobs and 90 per cent of the most powerful bureaucratic 'Class I' positions (Table 11.6).

In the cities, caste continued to be a channel to many industrial jobs (the traditional discrimination against Dalits in the weaving section of mills was never fought against nor did it vanish automatically; rather it became irrelevant as automation became more important), while outside the factor the social sphere continued to be nearly totally defined in terms of caste relations. Within the villages, many of the most severe practices of untouchability were fought or abolished; interdining began to be more widely practised, and many villages began to allow Dalits to draw water from the common wells. Yet even where this was true, villages were still structured in terms of caste-based wards, and even where new villages were set up (for instance to resettle people displaced by dam or other projects) the old wards, including the 'Maharwadas', were simply duplicated. And the more severe forms of untouchability retained a wide hold, as a survey of the Harijan Sevak Sangh in the early 1980s (see Table 11.7) suggests. This also showed regional variation; it is striking that Andhra, followed by Maharashtra, shows significantly less prohibition on the use of wells, hotels and temples. In the one case a strong left movement (though it also has to be admitted that Kerala, with an even stronger communist presence, shows a high incidence of caste barriers), in the other the powerful Ambedkar-led Dalit movement

TABLE 11.5
Scheduled Caste and Scheduled Tribe Occupations, 1981

	SC		ST		Others		Total	
	Lakhs	%	Lakhs	%	Lakhs	%	Lakhs	%
1. *Agricultural Sector* (a + b)	289 (19.5)	76.4	192 (13.0)	87.2	999 (67.5)	61.4	1,480 (100.0)	66.5
a. Cultivators	107 (11.6)	28.3	120 (13.0)	54.4	698 (75.4)	42.9	925 (100.0)	41.6
b. Agricultural labourers	182 (33.87)	48.1	72 (13.0)	32.7	301 (53.2)	18.5	555 (100.0)	24.9
2. *Non-agricultural Sector*	89 (12.0)	23.5	28 (3.8)	12.9	628 (84.2)	38.6	745 (100.0)	33.5
Total (1 + 2)	378	100.0	200	100.0	1,627	100.0	2,225	100.0

Source: CMIE, *Basic Statistics*, 1985, Table 1.8C.

TABLE 11.6
Representation of Caste Groups in Central Government Services

	Scheduled castes and tribes	Backward castes	Forward castes	Total
Class I	9,891 (5.68%)	8,169 (4.69%)	155,966 (89.63%)	174,026 (100%)
Class II	165,982 (18.18%)	97,063 (10.63%)	649,880 (71.19%)	912,925 (100%)
Class III and IV	118,282 (24.40%)	91,975 (18.98%)	274,430 (56.62%)	484,687 (100%)
All Classes	294,155 (18.72%)	197,207 (12.55%)	1,080,276 (68.73%)	1,571,638 (100%)

Source: Government of India, *Report of the Backward Classes Commission (Mandal Commission)* (New Delhi, 1981), Volume 2, page 92. 'Central Government Services' includes ministries and departments; autonomous bodies and public sector undertakings; the percentages were very similar in all, with forward castes more highly represented in the ministries and departments (78.34 per cent of all classes, and 90.23 per cent of Class I positions)—i.e., in the more politically powerful positions.
As defined by Mandal Commission, Scheduled Castes and Scheduled Tribes represented 22.5 per cent of the population, Backward Castes 52 per cent and Forward Castes 25.5 per cent.

and radical democratic heritage of the non-Brahman movement, perhaps made some difference. Overall, however, it seems clear that both stark forms of caste discrimination, particularly against Dalits, as well as remnants of the *balutedari* system as a channel to occupational entry remained potent in rural India.

Nor were their implications always recognized. In 1992 there were pervasive starvation deaths among weavers in Andhra, the economic cause being the increasing inability to make a living from their occupation. Yet few of the left comments on this bothered to question why it was that weavers, as a community, had managed to have so little recourse to any work other than the traditional caste occupation, even 46 years after independence.[8] The starvation deaths of a particular caste community in an environment where other castes were eating adequately were stark evidence of the walls of the caste system.

TABLE 11.7
Indicators of Untouchability

States	Total villages surveyed	Village wells prohibited	Temple entry prohibited	Hotel entry prohibited
Andhra	60	17	16	14
Gujarat	141	89	130	126
Karnataka	100	100	100	100
Kerala	68	68	68	68
Maharashtra	61	29	26	4
Madhya Pradesh	199	92	95	95
Orissa	50	50	50	50
Haryana	47	7	23	—
Rajasthan	75	61	63	—
Tamilnadu	148	115	136	36
Madurai district	72	72	72	72
Uttar Pradesh	170	55	78	113
Himachal	51	—	51	51

Source: Harijan Sevak Sangh survey cited in Sharad Patil, 'Should "Class" Be the Basis for Recognizing Indian Backwardness?', *Economic and Political Weekly*, 15 December 1990, Table 2.

Specific structures of economic exploitation and social discrimination thus seemed to have remained intact, if adjusted and transformed, while politically, from caste-based 'vote banks' to Brahman dominance in the administration, caste seems to have remained a major determinant of power. Much of the political history of independent India can be 'read' in caste terms: Brahmanic power at the centre, upper caste non-Brahmans in state governments; bourgeois–Brahman appeals to low castes (the 'KHAM' alliance) when challenged by a middle caste peasant-based political force. Evaluating this, intellectuals in the Nehru tradition saw the central power as progressive, regionalism and middle castes, peasants as 'backward'; Dalits often saw it in the opposite way but were embittered by the barriers they came up against on all sides. By the late 1960s as economic disparities and tensions increased, these new expressions of revolt were bursting out.

■ THE UNFINISHED REVOLUTION

The year 1968 seemed one of transition. Economic tensions in the post-independence years were at their height with slowdowns of growth, famines, growing rural tensions and rising strikes and mass protests. Into the conflagration, with the world itself seemingly caught in Maoist and new left fervor, the Naxalbari revolt in north Bengal threw its spark. Then came a massacre of 42 Dalit agricultural labourers in Kilvenmani village of the major Brahman-dominated, highly inequalitarian Thanjavur district of Tamil Nadu, where mainly women and children were barricaded into a blazing hut. 'Will the Green Revolution turn into a Red one?' now became a common query, followed up by 'will the caste war turn into a class war?' as similar rural and some urban massacres and rioting of low-caste challenges spread throughout India in the following years.

The first Dalit response came from Karnataka, where Shyam Sunder, the fiery pro-Muslim leader of Hyderabad who had settled in Gulbarga after independence, organized the Bheem Sena. A book written later threw out the challenge:

> They burn . . . the hundreds of millions of Untouchables (Mool Bharatis) in India. They burn physically when the caste Hindus burn them, their families, their homes, their harvests, their honours to perpetuate their centuries-old stronghold on them. They burn mentally when they think about their untouchable existence, even today in this enlightened decade of seventies and in the 'largest' democracy in the world.[9]

Shyam Sunder spread his Bheem Sena throughout many of the cities of India, fostering a tradition of militancy and a proclamation of a 'Dalit–Muslim alliance'.

But it was the coming of the revolt to Bombay, the centre of India's capitalism, and its sweeping of the state which had been the strongest centre of the early Dalit movement and still had the most powerful institutions of incorporation in the Republican Party factions, which proclaimed it for all of India. Growing out of the bitterness of Bombay working class life and the power of its mass mobilization and media access, the Dalit Panthers, formed in 1972, utilized Naxalite imagery:

the entire state machinery is dominated by feudal interests, the same hands who for thousands of years under religious sanctions controlled all the wealth and power, today own most of the agricultural land, industry, economic resources and all other instruments of power.

So proclaimed their manifesto. Their poetry attacked the illusions of democracy, proclaimed their oneness with the raw world of streets and slums, mocked at the traditions of Brahmanism, and called for revolt. Again, in the words of the manifesto,

> We want a complete and total revolutionary change . . . we do not want a little place in the Brahman Alley. We want the rule of the whole land . . . . Change of heart, liberal education etc. will not end our state of exploitation. When we gather a revolutionary mass, rouse the people, out of the struggle of this giant mass will come the tidal wave of revolution.[10]

After Maharashtra, there were unfolding waves of struggle, as it became clear that a new movement upsurge was taking place. In Karnataka, while the Bheem Sena had not survived, a Dalit Sangarsh Samiti, born out of an eruption in 1973 of rioting after a Dalit minister described conventional Kannada literature as *bhoosa* or cattlefeed, went on to become the organizationally strongest and longlasting Dalit movement in the country. In Gujarat, Dalit Panthers were formed after rioting over extending reservations to 'backward castes' focused attacks on Dalits. In many regions Dalit militancy fed directly into the Naxalite movement, especially in Bihar and Andhra, where they formed the base of organizations such as the Indian Peoples' Front (IPF) and the more underground, armed struggle-oriented Peoples' War Group (PWG). But the militancy of a caste-oppressed section was also not so easily contained even in revolutionary parties; in Andhra a separate Andhra Dalit Mahasabha was formed in 1984 after a series of village atrocities, and by the late 1980s a number of leading Dalit cadre had left the PWG and other parties, claiming Brahman domination and a second-class status for the low castes existed even there.

These organizational events, as well as the continuing village tensions and 'atrocities' were the result of a grassroots upsurge and self-assertion among young men and women now gaining some education, becoming aware of the democratic promises of the late twentieth century as well as their own tradition, no longer willing to accept a subordinated status. They made the Dalit movement in the 1970s and 1980s one of the most powerful of India's 'new social movements', and so compelling was its ideological appeal that the Jharkhand leader of a worker–tribal alliance in central India (the 'Jharkhand movement') used its imagery to describe the very nature of revolution:

> The communists have prepared various blueprints of revolution like National Democratic Revolution, Peoples' Democratic Revolution, New Democratic Revolution and many other forms using mysterious terms hardly understood or even remembered by their own followers, not to speak of the toiling millions at large, while India needs a simple New Dalit Revolution, a policy of red and green flag combining the struggle for social emancipation with that against economic exploitation to storm the citadel of internal colonialism in the country.[11]

■ WHAT PATH TO LIBERATION?

But what exactly was a 'Dalit revolution'? Ambedkar had argued, in one of his tracts, *Mukti Kon Pathe?* (What Path to Liberation?), that a necessary condition was the overthrow of 'Hindu' religious–ideological hegemony. He had tended to see economic and social oppression as separate structures, taking up 'cultural' (religious, ideological) change as the way to challenge Hinduism, socialism as the way to overcome economic exploitation. But always Ambedkar, and all the militant Dalit activists of India, had seen the necessity of combined struggle, dealing with both social and economic issues. At times it seemed as if a mechanical stress on economic solutions was met with an equally mechanical insistence on cultural–religious ones; indeed the most militant organization of the new movement, the Dalit Panthers, split on this issue in 1974–75 with one faction associated with 'Buddhism' and the other with 'Marxism'. Yet this was a temporary break; nearly all came to agree on the need for combining 'class–caste struggle', whatever the interpretations of it, and it became practically enforced upon the Indian left as a necessary feature by the end of the 1980s. In this sense, the idea of the

Indian revolution as a 'new Dalit revolution' or 'Dalit democratic revolution' was becoming a hegemonic one.

This was not the main problem. It was not the combination of economic and social radicalism that was problematic but, by the end of the 1980s, the meaning of both. Strikingly, in the crisis of the 1980s, so different from that of the late 1960s and the 1970s which had seen the Naxalbari revolt and the raising of the flag of economic radicalism which culminated in the Emergency, Dalit social radicalism seemed to make more and more sense, but the economic radicalism which it had adopted from the left had become increasingly problematic.

The Dalit movement had had its organizational flowering in the era of Marxism: the 1920s and 1930s not only saw the disillusionment with capitalism fostered by the depression and the rise of fascism, but a new hope, represented (whatever its flaws) in concrete form by the erstwhile Soviet Union. This was not simply that planning and state-led development were coming to seem (to even more traditional economists) as a prerequisite for economic progress; even more than this was the powerful promise of the end of exploitation, emancipation for all, the dream of a society in which equality could be achieved. These dreams, this goal of both a totalistic and scientific understanding of oppression as well as the actual achievement of the social reality of a 'classless' society, were concretely embodied in a particular theory with a particular interpretation of economic exploitation in terms of 'class' and private property and of the road to overcome this through 'collective ownership' institutionalized through the state, guiding the 'forces of production' to a fossil-fuel based steel-centred industrialization.

I have argued that the overall effect of this on the Dalit movement was, in the end, rather negative. No Dalit leader, aside from Ambedkar, did his own thinking on economic issues; and Ambedkar himself had no time for independent research or support for going against the tide on economic issues after his plunge into the movement. It meant the overall acceptance of 'industrialization' as the way out of the presumed backwardness of agrarian life; it meant the identification of 'socialism' with statism and overlooking the degree to which state institutions were the major basis of upper-caste power in India. It meant also a mechanical separation of 'economic' and 'social' factors, so that caste, equated with social, came to be treated in a way removed from the economic sphere and seen as resulting either from ideological/religious domination (as with Ambedkar's theory) or from simple racial conquest (as with many other Dalit leaders).

By the 1980s, the clear crisis of traditional socialist ideology meant not the 'end of history' for all efforts to create an equalitarian society, but the opening up of the way for alternatives.

In the pre-colonial period, the only significant alternative to Marxism of one brand or another as a total social ideology was Gandhism. Indeed, it was the inadequacies of Gandhism that in many ways pushed Dalit and anti-cast activists into the framework of a mechanical Marxism. Gandhi's 'Harijan programme' offered a challenge to high-caste Hindus wishing to re-legitimize their tradition, but it could only appear as hypocritical and repressive to anti-caste militants. Gandhi's path sought to combine a village-oriented decentralized vision of development with a reformed Hindu spirituality. For all its attractiveness, in the 1930s and 1940s there seemed little technological base to challenge a statist/industrial focus, and Gandhism did too often devolve into a spiritualism that refused to really challenge caste domination; this was particularly evident with most of his major disciples who were high-caste Indians, who inevitably looked at tradition in a Brahmanic way and behaved with their followers in very paternalist if not patriarchal ways. Ambedkar's verdict, that 'villages are cesspools' and 'the Gandhi age is a dark age', was not at all unreasonable in its period.

In this context, Ambedkar's full scale rejection of Hinduism and assertion of an alternative identity was explosive and revolutionary. Marxists have tended to see Ambedkar's Buddhism as the most 'reformist' part of his entire philosophy,[12] but it was the conversion announcement of 1936 that galvanized Dalits throughout India and it was the choice of Buddhism that lay down the challenge for an alternative *Indian* identity. Ambedkar attempted, in his writings and research, such as that of 'Revolution and Counter-Revolution', to provide a framework for this. But too little was done in the colonial period. Phule (and in Ambedkar's time a few other Dalit ideologues) had taken significant steps towards the reinterpretation of mythologies and the recreation of identities at a mass level; but there were still too few educated Dalits to take on the task, and too few interested activists of higher castes, particularly when those adopting left ideologies ignored tradition totally, accepting large parts of·it (such as basic 'harijan' and ·Hindu' identities) while claiming to reject it.

By the 1980s there was a clear crisis of all traditional ideologies. The general crisis of Marxism and the failures of statist versions of socialism brought about an entirely new era for democratic and liberatory movements, one in which ecological and decentralist themes as well as issues of 'non-class' exploitation, revolving around patriarchy, race, ethnicity, caste, had to be admitted as central. These gave a·renewed life to 'Gandhian' themes in India, but the fact was that ecologists were slow to learn the lessons of caste and tended to uncritically praise pre-colonial Brahmanic traditions and Hindu 'spiritualism' as contrasted with western materialism and dominating behaviour with nature. Here the Dalit reinterpretation of tradition coupled with Ambedkarite rationalism, had major themes to offer, and indeed by the 1980s the unraveling of Nehruvian secularism as well as socialism meant that an engagement with the more rabid upper caste Hindu 'fundamentalist' forces had to revolve around the creation of an alternative cultural tradition.

Thus by the 1990s, in a period in which 'Ambedkarism' and Dalit themes were gaining ground everywhere as an alternative ideological framework, in a period in which the necessity for 'combining' economic and social themes could no longer be denied, the scope for dialogue was growing. The need was greater than ever. The Dalit movement, nurtured out of centuries of exploitation and oppression, given a basis in the new forms of surplus accumulation and new ideological openings of the colonial period, taking off in the 1920s in a period of intense economic and social change, was only beginning to enter its maturity. 'Now, now', proclaimed the poet who had unabashedly entitled his first book after Bombay's redlight district, *'now we must, like sunflowers, turn our faces to the sun.'*.

NOTES

1. Cited in Dhananjay Keer, Dr. Ambedkar: Life and Mission (Bombay: Popular Prakashan, 1962).
2. 'MIC Bharatiya Ghatna Jalin!' in Bhashane, Volume 6, p. 87.
3. Vilas Rashinekar, 'No Entry for the New Sun', in Daugle (ed.), *Poisoned Bread: Translated from Modern Marathi Dalit Literature*.

342 / Dalits and the Democratic Revolution

4. See Sukhomoy Chakravarti, *Developmental Planning: The Indian Experience* (New Delhi: Oxford University Press, 1989) and also the general critique (and admission) of third world states' policies of 'primitive accumulation' in *Challenge to the South: Report of the South Commission* (New Delhi: Oxford University Press, 1992).

5. The most elaborate discussions of pricing and financial policies involving the 'transfer of resources from agriculture' are by neo-liberal economists; cf. D. Gale Johnson, 'Agriculture and the Liberalization Process' in Authur Krause and Kim Kihwan (eds.), *Liberalization in the Process of Economic Development* (Berkely: University of California Press, 1991)..

6. Centre for Monitoring the Indian Economy, *Basic Statistics on the Indian Economy, 1990, Volume I: All-India* (Bombay, 1990), Table 8.7B.

7. The dependence of agricultural labourers' wages on the general prosperity/ profitability of the agrarian economy is controversial only to a section of the left; generally trade unionists accept the fact that wages can be fought for only to the level an 'industry' can afford to pay; while in agriculture there was an additional factor that the wage-dependent labour force was pushed up (and thus the bargaining power of workers was pushed down) by the very fact that people could not survive on small holdings.

8. 'Starvation Deaths in Andhra Pradesh', *Frontline*, 6 December 1991.

9. Shyam Sunder, *They Burn* (Bangalore, Dalit Sahitya Academy, 1987), pp. 13–14.

10. In Barbara B. Joshi (ed.), *Untouchable! Voices of the Dalit Liberation Movement* (London: Zed Books, 1986).

11. A.K. Roy, *New Dalit Revolution* (Patna, 1980).

12. See, for instance, W.N. Kuber, *Ambedkar: A Critical Study* (New Delhi: People's Publishing House, 1991), esp. p. 304.

Index

16148 Bajy 7230/9-11-90